www.wadsworth.com

wadsworth.com is the World Wide Web site for Wadsworth and is your direct source to dozens of online resources.

At *wadsworth.com* you can find out about supplements, demonstration software, and student resources. You can also send email to many of our authors and preview new publications and exciting new technologies.

wadsworth.com
Changing the way the world learns®

UNSPOKEN WORLDS

Women's Religious Lives

Third Edition

NANCY AUER FALK
Western Michigan University

RITA M. GROSS
University of Wisconsin—Eau Claire [Emerita]

Wadsworth
Thomson Learning™

Australia • Canada • Mexico • Singapore • Spain • United Kingdom • United States

Cover: A farm wife from the state of Orissa in eastern India decorates the walls of her home with rice-flour paintings dedicated to Lakshmi, goddess of prosperity and a special protectress of Hindu housewives. When invoked by chanted prayers and beautiful paintings, Lakshmi will protect the household and fill it with abundance. Creation of graceful temporary designs and paintings is a religious practice special to women in many regions and sectarian traditions of India. Throughout the world, as this photograph and book shows, women's religion is often a matter of doing and creating, with extensive involvement of the body and senses as well as of the intellect.

Philosphy Editor: Peter Adams
Editorial Assistant: Mark Andrews
Marketing Manager: Dave Garrison
Print Buyer: Robert King
Permissions Editor: Joohee Lee
Production Service: Shepherd Incorporated
Text Designer: Christy Butterfield
Copy Editor: Julie Kennedy
Cover Designer: Janet Wood
Cover Image: Stephen P. Huyler
Compositor: Shepherd Incorporated
Cover and Text Printer: Webcom, Limited

Printed in Canada
1 2 3 4 5 6 7 04 03 02 01

For permission to use material from this text, contact us:
Web: http://www.thomsonrights.com
Fax: 1-800-730-2215
Phone: 1-800-730-2214

Library of Congress Cataloging-in-Publication Data

Unspoken worlds : women's religious lives / [edited by] Nancy Auer Falk, Rita M. Gross.—[4th ed.].
p. cm.
ISBN 0-534-51570-3
1. Women—Religious life. I. Falk, Nancy Auer. II. Gross, Rita M.
BL458 .U57 2000
200'.82—dc21

00-033410

Wadsworth/Thomson Learning
10 Davis Drive
Belmont, CA 94002-3098
USA

For more information about our products, contact us:
Thomson Learning Academic Resource Center
1-800-423-0563
http://www.wadsworth.com

International Headquarters
Thomson Learning
International Division
290 Harbor Drive, 2nd Floor
Stamford, CT 06902-7477
USA

UK/Europe/Middle East/South Africa
Thomson Learning
Berkshire House
168-173 High Holborn
London WC1V 7AA
United Kingdom

Asia
Thomson Learning
60 Albert Street, #15-01
Albert Complex
Singapore 189969

Canada
Nelson Thomson Learning
1120 Birchmount Road
Toronto, Ontario M1K 5G4
Canada

In memory of our teachers, Mircea Eliade and Joseph M. Kitagawa, and in gratitude also to our teacher Charles H. Long. They may not have always agreed with what we said, but they gave us the training and, at crucial times, the latitude to say it.

Contents

Preface

HISTORY OF *UNSPOKEN WORLDS*

In 1974, two young women scholars sat down at a national meeting to discuss a concern that was mutual for them. Many scholars were beginning to insist that the study of women's religious lives, roles, and thought should become an important area of inquiry in religious studies. Rita had already made several important proposals about how such study should be done in our own cross-cultural sector of the discipline. Meanwhile, Nancy was teaching a course on women in religion and wanted to incorporate Rita's suggestions. But she had a problem. She had found no reading materials suitable for students that could do this. In fact, barely any materials suitable for use in such a course existed at all. Rita, who had also tried to teach a course on women and religion, had similar problems. In the summer of 1975 Nancy and Rita spent a week working together to begin a project that would address that problem.

Out of those conversations, with the help of fifteen other scholars, came a collection of case studies called *Unspoken Worlds: Women's Religious Lives in Non-Western Cultures*, published by Harper and Row in 1980. We had no idea at that time that this book would one day go into a second and then a third edition—that it would still be in demand at the start of the twenty-first century, more than a quarter of a century after we began our work together. The success of this book has contributed to the development of gender studies in religion, and we are happy to know that it has been used by so many students, teachers, and scholars over the years. Moreover, the enormous growth of gender studies in religion demonstrates the accuracy of our insights long ago when so little material was available on women and religion that a common reaction to the attempt to teach such a course was, "How are you going to get a whole course out of that!" Now teachers of courses on women in religion have an opposite problem: "What should I select for my course from among the voluminous materials available on women and religion in virtually all cultural contexts? What methodological perspectives shall I take up from the wide variety that is now available?"

We were delighted when Wadsworth Publishing Company offered us the opportunity to re-issue an expanded version of *Unspoken Worlds* after the Harper edition went out of print during the late 1980s. In that new edition, we retained all the articles that had been in the original volume and made several important changes. The most important change is that, having been offered more pages by our publisher, we seized upon the opportunity to drop our initial volume's artificial distinction between "non-Western" and "Western" religions. We expanded the book with seven new articles, four treating aspects of Christian and Jewish women's experience. We also added "A User's Preface: Editor's Guidelines," which is now incorporated into this preface. We have found that the six-part organizational structure that we developed for the first edition has continued to serve us well. We want to continue to explain to our readers why we chose to organize the book as we did.

In the second edition, we also appended to each article lists of "Further Readings," intended to help students who wished to pursue a subject further, and we also included an extensive bibliography at the book's end.

The third edition brings further changes, although we have retained the original introduction, which follows this preface. In this edition, for the first time, we invited authors who had contributed to the previous editions to update their articles if they so desired. They were also requested to update their biographical information and their lists of suggested readings. But we dropped the extensive bibliography at the end for two reasons. It is now simply beyond the scope of a book such as this to include a comprehensive bibliography on women and religion. There are now so many other bibliographic resources that ours would have been redundant. Moreover, by now many of our readers will have access to computer data bases that should help them to find sources on the areas of greatest interest to them. We hope that at least some of these wonderful new sources have drawn part of their inspiration and challenge from earlier editions of *Unspoken Worlds.* For this third edition we also added five new articles on topics that we had wanted to include earlier to achieve better balance in the examples provided. Unfortunately, adding these new materials has required us also to drop, for the first time, articles that had previously been included. Four articles from the first or second edition no longer grace our pages.

A USER'S PREFACE: EDITORS' GUIDELINES

Although this book is written by many authors, it is not an anthology. It has been painstakingly forged into a coherent whole, which evolves from simple vivid portraits of individual women to analyses of complex systems. It contains a single, unified discussion of the manifold possibilities of women's religious lives in the world's varied religious traditions. This book is best read from beginning to end, rather than randomly. Furthermore, the various introductions—both to the book as a whole and to its various sections—are integral parts of the text, essential to a full understanding of the book's contents.

Our approach is conscious and deliberate: we illustrate cross-cultural patterns in women's religious lives. Because few scholars have a broad enough range of expertise to document such patterns through individual research, we have assembled a kind of collage, drawing on the fieldwork or historical research of numerous scholars. Our desire to keep our materials vivid and sharply focused—to draw readers into women's worlds—has led us to prefer case studies as our medium of illustration. Our desire to illumine patterns that cross cultural and religious boundaries—to stress commonalities in women's experience rather than differences—has also led us to reject several simpler methods of organizing our materials. We have chosen not to cluster materials by tradition, or region, or historical period, because such an approach would blur and scatter patterns, rather than drawing them out and emphasizing them. However, the teacher who prefers to work with such more conventional groupings can readily do so while using this book. We have identified the time and tradition or place of each study in each of our chapter titles in order to facilitate such regroupings. Teachers who prefer to use this book in this way may wish to use it as a "reader" for one of the more general, survey-style texts now on the market.

Our own classifications and the patterns that we seek to illumine are discussed in detail in our introductions, to the first and third editions, which will follow this preface. Introductions to the book's several sections further specify these patterns and point out each separate chapter's relationship to them. Also important to the organization of the book is the increasing complexity of each pattern, as well as the increasing complexity of each section's level of analysis. The book begins with simple but arresting portraits of strong women who have served as religious leaders. It continues by describing examples from two cultures of an ancient type of role in which women have exercised religious leadership. Next it turns to the household and family-based concerns of women who combine religious practice with more "ordinary" lives. The book's last three sections explore more complex patterns as women's concerns and movements are set into a variety of religious and cultural contexts. To understand these latter chapters, it is helpful first to understand the more basic patterns discussed earlier in the book. Therefore, if teachers rearrange our readings into a "world religions" or historical format, they should first read the book from beginning to end themselves so that they can fill in this basic understanding for their students.

No teacher or student could possibly have enough background to cover all the cultures and historical epochs cited in this book. We have therefore taken several steps to aid those who use our book, whether as students or as teachers. Most importantly, this book is designed to be self-sufficient; that is, each chapter offers enough information about its setting to make it understandable without forcing the reader to seek information outside the volume. Realizing that many of our readers will be students with little previous knowledge of our authors' various fields of study, we have also minimized the use of technical jargon. We have further eliminated most foreign terms, keeping only the original names of very central practices and concepts. Each foreign term is used in simplified form; it is also defined and explained at the time of its first occurrence in the text. For readers who wish to explore further, each of our writers has listed additional readings that will help readers probe more deeply the issues raised in the initial article.

ACKNOWLEGDMENTS

Several sources of support have been crucial to the appearance of this book. First of all, as in earlier editions, we must thank each other for encouragement and critical thinking. Each of us has, once again, spent many, many hours editing and checking both the other's work and the work of new contributors to our volume. The final product is, as before, a blend of the thinking and literary styles of each of us, so closely woven that they cannot be disentangled. Next, we want to thank both our old and new contributors for both their careful work and their patience with us. Many of the former, no longer green young scholars, have taken time from very busy schedules to check and update articles and reading lists. A few have even emerged from retirement to help *Unspoken Worlds* reach a new generation. As for our new contributors, we are very grateful indeed for their wonderful new essays and their patience with the sometimes extensive editorial meddling that we have indulged in with some of their manuscripts. We especially thank author Robert Baum, whom we discovered very late during our search for a West African article, and who produced his very fine essay for us in just a little over one month's time.

We are also grateful to Nancy's Department of Comparative Religions at Western Michigan University for providing much of the back-up support needed to assemble the final version of our manuscript. Nancy's secretary Gwen West has very patiently done much typing and retyping of prefaces, introductions, reading lists, author's biographies, and sometimes even author's manuscripts. Gwen has also by now become highly skilled at the fine art of catching and dispatching emailed manuscripts, for our own busy schedules this time around have prevented us from meeting in the same space to edit new manuscripts as we did previously, and we have hence been forced to enter the computer revolution. We owe continuing thanks to Nancy's colleague Byron Earhart for entries he supplied to our second edition lists of Further Readings for chapters by Kyoko Nakamura and the late Youngsook Kim Harvey, as well as much early commentary and advice on our volume. We also owe thanks to Mary Hegland, who helped with an early version of Erika Friedl's list while Dr. Friedl was away in Iran. We must thank friends Nikki Bado and Kay Jordan as well for prodding us into thinking that a new edition was a real and viable possibility.

We also would like to thank the following academic reviewers for their comments on the manuscript for this edition: Norma Baumel Joseph, Concordia University; Judith Martin, University of Dayton; Vivian-Lee Nyitray, University of California, Riverside; Sharon Welsh, University of Missouri.

Finally, we wish to thank our households, who lived with us while we lived with our book. Nancy especially thanks her husband, Arthur, for his patience while enduring many nights of foraging from the refrigerator while she worked late, many days of not seeing her at all, and several episodes of shortened temper during times when computers were in rebellion and nothing seemed to go right the first time.

Introductions

INTRODUCTION TO THE FIRST EDITION: PATTERNS IN WOMEN'S RELIGIOUS LIVES

As graduate students in the same program (not at the same time) in the cross-cultural, comparative study of religion, we were taught that we were seeking to understand *homo religiosus,* "religious man." Intended as a parallel to "political man," "economic man," and so on, the phrase "religious man" asserted that religion is as basic and spontaneous a form of human expression as working in communities, pursuing wealth, or any of the other aspects of human activity that had been accorded the distinction of their own academic disciplines. We were preparing for a life work that would be studying "religious man's" various and fascinating practices and statements and that would be trying to capture the patterns of human experience and intent that had given rise to them.

We were supposed to infer (the issue was never directly discussed) that, of course, "religious man" was used generically to include all humans. In practice, however (although the realization came to us slowly), it was clear that our discipline focused quite literally on religious *man*—that is, on the males of the religious community. In our field whole volumes and courses were devoted to minute analyses of men's interpretations and practices; when women entered the descriptions at all, they entered them peripherally, as bearers of children or as singers on the sidelines. Rita, while still a graduate student, became extremely unhappy with the prospect of spending her life studying essentially the religious male. While working at the doctoral level during the late sixties, she began to call for a study of "religious woman" as well as religious man and to suggest that the failure to take into account women's religious expressions indicated a serious flaw in our discipline's approach.

This volume is, in large part, an outgrowth of that insight and that call. Despite an initial and, to some extent, continuing resistance, Rita's critique has proved accurate time and again in every facet of religious studies. More specifically, the book grows out of conversations between the two of us that started at professional meetings some years later, when we had developed some expertise in the roles of women in particular religious traditions and we both were trying to teach courses that compared women's roles in various religious traditions of the world. The lack of adequate sources made such courses a frustrating enterprise; there were no books surveying women's religious roles cross-culturally and precious few detailed studies of any aspect of women's religious lives in any culture. So we asked ourselves, "Why not search for people who are also trying to understand religious woman and pool our findings to create a volume that our students and theirs can use?"

Assembling such a book involved three tasks. The first, carried out largely outside this volume and prerequisite to it, essentially involved fleshing out the critique of our field by trying to discover just why our discipline had left us such a skewed and incomplete picture of women's religious lives and roles. More conservative scholars in religion tend to say that the discipline's inattention to women is an inevitable consequence of women's lesser degree of involvement—especially as priests or theologians—in the world's religions. In other words, they seem to be claiming that religion actually *is* a predominantly male enterprise and that the neglect of women only reflects the fact that women are genuinely less important. There are two problems with this argument. In the first place, women have always been conspicuous in some arenas of religious life, such as the shamanic practices described in several places in this volume, in domestic rituals such as the ones that we have grouped in Part III, and in many varieties of "new" religious movements. Yet, even in the arenas in which women are conspicuous, their activities still receive scant attention. In the second place, although many religious systems are quite male-dominated, very few have had only male membership. Thus women inevitably have some kind of religious lives, even if these consist only in responding to male-defined ideals and expectations (see Part IV). If we are making a genuine effort to recall the whole human experience in religion, it stands to reason that women's experiences must still be a significant part of the picture.

The attempt to justify our discipline's neglect of women's experience and practice on the basis of women's lesser prominence in religion is, however, largely a hasty rationalization. Most scholars who would make such an argument have spent little time in trying to determine whether or not women's roles are actually significant. The source of distortion is far more subtle, and is found in the habitual assumptions of scholarship itself. These are more readily traced through a second excuse that is commonly offered for our discipline's scant attention to women. As some of Rita's own mentors told her when she first voiced her critique, the generic masculine is said to "cover" and "include" the feminine; that is to say, when we have understood religious man, we will *de facto* understand religious woman as well. Thus the charge that our discipline ignores women is called irrelevant and the challenge to study women separately is said to be superfluous. This argument is made despite the fact that there are few, if any, religious systems in which men's and women's religious lives are indistinguishable. What such assertions in fact reveal is that, like practically every other discipline focusing on "human studies," the study of religions has unconsciously operated with an "androcentric," or male-centered, model of humanity. That is to say, it has assumed that central and significant humans are male and has investigated the world from the male point of view. When such a perspective is taken, women, like any other segment of religious life, will be seen only as they appear to men. All too often this has meant that we don't really see women as human beings at all, but as objects, symbols, appendages to someone else's enterprise, as problematic others to be assigned a neat "place."

Clearly our volume had to find a very different kind of vision. It could not be a book about how religions view women. Too many times in our experience people had written about various religions' views of women without the slightest awareness that they had failed to tell us anything about women as human beings. We were not told about the texture of their lives, and we had no way of knowing for sure whether the views portrayed corresponded in any way to women's self-concepts. Since most religions' views of women have been recorded and shaped by men, the study of these views all too easily becomes an extension of androcentrism.

To offer a new vision, our volume had to take up women's lives; it had to place women in center stage—as men had been placed so often in the past—and to meet them as subjects, not objects, with their own experiences and aspirations. We had to create an understanding of women's own enterprises, whether the world around them defined these as "in" or "out," respectable or shocking. We had to show that women have their own perspectives and claims on religion, even in systems in which men have traditionally done most of the acting and talking. If our authors did discuss men's ideas about women, they needed to show how such ideas actually affected women's efforts and religious options. Most importantly, our readers needed to come to see women of other traditions as real human beings, who know pain and release, frustration and fulfillment, just as other humans do. In short, like our teachers and many respected colleagues, we proposed to help our readers discover new and meaningful religious worlds. But we would explore the so-far unspoken religious worlds of women rather than the much more familiar religious worlds of men.

Once we had a clear idea of what kind of book we wanted to achieve, we could begin our second task, that of "recovering the data" that would let religious woman appear. The study of religion has so persistently ignored women that we were overwhelmed by the task's enormity. What kinds of examples should we search for and how? First, we opted for an anthology, because at this point in the study of religious woman no two people had enough expertise to recover the variety of activities and cultural and religious contexts that we hoped to bring together. Second, we chose to search for case studies rather than survey articles, because case studies would allow the closer view of the human experience that we hoped to capture. We wanted new rather than old materials; since resources of any kind on women's religious lives were hard to find, it seemed inappropriate to duplicate what was already available. Following much the same reasoning, we limited our scope to those traditions customarily defined as "non-Western," because excellent studies have appeared elsewhere on women in Judaism and Christianity. Within this boundary, we tried to provide at least one sample from every major non-Western religious tradition and/or cultural region of the world.

As we began our search for contributors, we swiftly learned that our fellow historians of religion could not command materials on women's religious lives in enough different areas of specialization to give us a volume with the range that we had hoped to achieve. So we turned to cultural anthropologists and area specialists who had gathered such materials through their own field research. Inevitably this meant that a large part of our volume would focus on contemporary forms. But, since we thought it important to show that religious woman has a history, we included several studies on women of the more distant past.

Originally we had intended simply to reveal the rich variety of women's religious lives. Here we succeeded beyond our best hopes. The papers that came to us showed women in their own religious arenas and in the religious worlds of men. We met young women and old, urban and rural, in public and in private, as leaders and as followers. But, as we worked through the separate studies, we discovered that our authors had also revealed significant unities. This allowed us to complete our third major task, that of trying to put in order the materials that we had gathered.

Two interlocking themes predominate in all the sections of the book. The more important theme is the contrast between extraordinary callings and everyday concerns in women's religious lives. The ordinary calling of women in traditional societies around the world has been that of mother and housewife. Women's religion can either call women away from that ordinary venture to enterprises that are usual for both women and men, or it can validate and support women in their ordinary roles as mothers and housewives. Religious systems vary quite dramatically in their accommodation of or hostility to both extraordinary women and women called to fulfill ordinary roles. Thus a second theme—running through the entire book and especially noticeable in its latter half—explores the level of support women find, whether they are called to extraordinary ventures or bound up in everyday concerns.

The book's first section explores the discontinuity, as well as continuity, between everyday concerns and extraordinary callings. By far the more dramatic pattern is that of discontinuity, in which women who follow an extraordinary calling break out of, or somehow transform, the usual role. Some leave it behind altogether, as does Jnanananda, the Hindu guru described in the first section of our volume; others continue to be wives and mothers but effect reversals in former and often oppressive family structures. Good examples are Julia, the first woman we encounter in the book (Chapter 1) and the Korean shamans of our fifth chapter, whose lives we explore in the second section of our book.

But the religious impulse does not have to bring so explosive a rupture; thus we find also a pattern of continuity, where women's religious life supports and validates women's everyday concerns. This pattern is best seen in our section on housewives' rituals (Part III), which explores a variety of ways in which women have integrated religious practice into their own domestic worlds. Here they preside over life and death and continue on a religious level the modest but essential work for the well-being of their families that has always been a hallmark of women's everyday life.

The distinction between ordinary concerns and extraordinary callings remains an important motif of our book's second half as well. Most of its chapters either take a longer historical view of the extraordinary venture or describe situations in which the interplay between the two types of careers can be seen more clearly. But the second half of the book emphasizes more explicitly the other significant theme that runs through our volume—the greatly varying degree of support that women's religious enterprises receive within differing types of religious and cultural systems.

In one way or another, whether or not they operate within a religious context that is overtly male dominated (as do the Hindu and Muslim women of section three), the women studied in the first half of the book seem to find or make for themselves sufficient accommodation to their needs and aspirations. But in some situations in which men dominate religious institutions and ideologies, women's options can be far more limited. Our fourth section explores two variants of this pattern: first, the relatively rare cases, such as that of the Muslim tribal women, in which women are confined to the ordinary domestic round and their ordinary callings are not supported by religion and ritual; second, those cases of extraordinary women who may be successful in making a new kind of place for themselves only to find their efforts eventually undercut and frustrated by the system. Examples of this pattern include the Buddhist nuns of ancient India and Sayo Kitamura of contemporary Japan.

Students in the West who know only the great male-dominated "world religions" are less accustomed to religious systems in which women and men share a balanced measure of opportunity and power. Our authors have explored women's roles and activities in three such systems in Part V. The balance is achieved quite differently, however. In one pattern, such as that of the ancient Kallawaya tradition of the Bolivian Andes, women and men have separate spheres that are essentially equal. Another kind of pattern of balance and equality is found in the Tantric Buddhist tradition of India and Tibet. In this case, gender is irrelevant to attaining the tradition's highest goal.

The final section does double duty: it returns to the opening critique concerning our discipline's failure to study religious woman in her own right, and it also explores a complex pattern in which—despite a seeming male dominance in religion—women's bodies, which menstruate and give birth, become a major focus of both women's and men's religious lives. A male-dominated religion focused on a female function may be confusing, but only if one holds to an androcentric view. Who's really in charge here anyway? The answer may be neither men nor women, or perhaps both women and men. One conclusion to be drawn is that the data on women's religious lives and, consequently, the interaction of women and men in religious systems as well are much richer and far more complex than anyone imagined when people were content to study "religious man" alone. In fact, it seems clear that, to study religion properly, we must also begin attending to the women who have constituted and do constitute at least one-half of almost all of the world's religious communities.

INTRODUCTION TO THE THIRD EDITION

As we have noted in our preface, for both the second and third editions we have retained our first edition's organization, with its six major themes. We have, however, added quite a bit of new material. Our first section, "Encounter: Extraordinary Women," now includes four vivid portraits of extraordinary women to introduce readers to the world's wide variety of achievements by women of deep religious commitment. African diviner Julia and Hindu guru Jnanananda of our first edition and Catholic activist Dorothy Day of the second edition have been joined by a second activist, Victoria Way DeLee of the American Protestant holiness tradition and the U.S. civil rights movement. Our second section, "Women Called by Spirits: Shamans and Savants," addresses more directly the problem of "calling" by deities or spirits and the shamans' or mediums' roles that develop out of such callings—possibly the oldest of all religious specialists' roles held extensively by women. Here we have added a series of sketches of Chinese roles based on such callings to our first edition's article on women shamans of Korea.

Our third edition's third section, "In the Wings: Rituals for Wives and Mothers," remains essentially the same as that of our second edition, with some revisions and updating. Here six studies of ordinary women's rituals of India, Central America, and the Middle East describe religious activities that women carry out among themselves and sometimes within their own special spaces. When we published this volume's first edition, this realm of religious practices special to women was relatively unrecorded. By now, it has become far more carefully documented and studied.

This volume's Part IV, "Out of the Shadows: Women in Male-Dominated Systems," includes two new articles. The story of an African indigenous prophet who challenged her nation's colonial rulers—and lost—joins that of the somewhat more successful woman founder of a Japanese "new religion," repeated from our first edition. A new, upbeat, account of enclosed Catholic nuns outwitting their bishop in Counter-Reformation Europe contrasts with our older and somewhat more somber analysis of the disappearance of Buddhist nuns from India. We have also republished in this section our second edition's account of how Jewish women of a rather special congregation found their way into ritual spaces once reserved for men.

Part V, "Success Stories: Women and Men in Balance or Equality," retains our first edition's studies of Tibetan Buddhism's "accomplished women," celebrated as models and teachers, as well as the redoubtable Rosinta who banishes bad luck in the Bolivian Andes. From our second edition, this section has also retained its analysis of the Shakers, who understood their founder, "Mother" Ann Lee, to be the second coming of Christ, come to redeem women. But our current edition pairs with Rosinta's story an account of Mexican women healers that also takes its start from the balanced-gender worldviews once common in both Central and Andean America.

Our final section, "Women's Power: Mythical Models and Sacred Sources," is largely unchanged from our second edition. A Vodou priestess of Brooklyn, by way of Haiti, an Apache female deity and the rites of girls who temporarily become her, and the women—and men—of aboriginal Australia introduce readers to a kind of women's power rarely encountered by most Westerners.

On Transliteration

Of necessity, our volume includes a number of names and terms from the languages and dialects of the regions that our authors have studied. For the sake of consistency, and because most of our readers will not be familiar with scholarly systems of transliteration for these areas, we have romanized these terms in the simplest way possible, omitting diacritical marks whenever this is feasible.

Rita M. Gross
University of Wisconsin—Eau Claire

Nancy Auer Falk
Western Michigan University

I

ENCOUNTER

Extraordinary Women

Encounters with four women of extraordinary courage, callings, and personality initate us into the complex fabric of women's religious lives.

All four of these women transcend the norms of their cultures in significant ways. Two of them, Julia, a village woman of Mozambique, East Africa, and Satguru Jnanananda Saraswati of Chennai (Madras), South India, are from cultures unfamiliar to most North Americans. Consequently, readers may not immediately appreciate how far they go in breaking with standard patterns for women's lives. The second two, Victoria Way DeLee, an African American civil rights activist from South Carolina, and the late Dorothy Day, founder of the Catholic Worker movement, may not initially seem unusual to us. But when we reflect on their lives of activism and social protest, we readily see that they, too, differ significantly from norms set for women in North American culture. We also come to realize how much they have departed from and criticized the usual social and economic rules of North America.

Once Julia was a respectable Christian laywoman in Africa, and a wife and mother like most other women of this volume. Now she has become a traditional medium and diviner, embracing an older option for leadership in African life. On many nights she seeks possession by African gods, and through those gods, for messages and aid for her people. Julia has not broken completely from her old domestic life; she continues to run her homestead and to work in the fields. But her new role has greatly changed her relationships to her family and community.

Dorothy Day's path may at first glance seem also to move her towards a traditional religious role, as she leaves her radical intellectual's life in Greenwich Village to make a place for herself within the Roman Catholic Church. But the place she made was unique, breaking with all the roles most commonly assumed by Catholic women. As founder and leader of the independent lay Catholic Worker

Movement, Day was neither a nun, nor a sister, nor a conventional wife and mother. Nonetheless, in her new role she nurtured and sheltered the helpless and poor—activities so typically "female" that the author has labelled her a "Catholic earth mother."

Like Day, Victoria Way DeLee is a Christian laywoman and social activist whose energies are fueled by deep religious commitment. Her church, however, is of the American Protestant holiness tradition, and her energies are expressed through work on behalf of the U.S. Civil Rights Movement. One prominent theme in the essay on DeLee, as in the two that come before it, is the power of religion to transform a life that initially seems fractured and disjointed—and in DeLee's case also steeped in rage—and to bring that life focus, presence, and courage. Noteworthy in this essay is the fact that DeLee's husband works with her, and their efforts to benefit all people of color are also efforts on behalf of their children's future.

Satguru Jnanananda Saraswati is perhaps the most radical of the women of this section, because her religious commitments have carried her altogether outside of the normal social pale. Once a wife and mother, she is now a religious renouncer, whose relationships with her former family continue only insofar as some of them have become her disciples. Even her relationship to gender is transformed; thinking in gender distinctions, she claims, is something that a "realized" person goes beyond. "In fact," she says, "I sometimes refer to myself with the masculine pronoun." Her role as *guru*, spiritual guide to disciples, was also more common to men than to women in traditional India, although women *gurus* now are appearing more often. Yet still the Satguru Jnanananda approaches those disciples like a mother chiding and encouraging her children. And they in turn all address her as "Ma," or Mother.

1

Julia: An East African Diviner

MARTHA B. BINFORD

I met Julia by accident. Lamanga, a friend from a Rjonga village in Mozambique, East Africa, where I was doing my fieldwork, dropped by my hut and announced that we were going for a walk. After an hour on the narrow paths, tripping over vines and roots, I stopped lamenting the fact that I had left my notebook at home. Lamanga was giving me nonstop information of the sort dear to an anthropologist's heart, but I couldn't have written it down anyway, since every inanimate object seemed bent on attacking me. I appreciated Lamanga's visits and the whirlwind tours he took me on, but I never knew what to expect next. Suddenly, we emerged from deep bush into a clearing with two paths leading into a rather large, well-kept homestead of several huts. Three of the huts faced east, as was customary, but the fourth, set apart from the rest, faced west. Lamanga hesitated a moment, then took the public, or eastern, path and walked slowly toward the homestead. I looked curiously at Lamanga; he was usually quite uninhibited and barged right into people's homes at any time of the day or night. This time he stayed on the front walk and called out a greeting, asking permission to enter.

A woman walked slowly out of one of the huts and stood looking at us, her hands on her

---

MARTHA B. BINFORD received her Ph.D. in Anthropology from Michigan State University in 1971 after two years of fieldwork in Mozambique. She was formerly Associate Professor of Anthropology at the University of Michigan–Dearborn. Her major research interests are the study of religion, symbolism, and cultural dynamics.

Author's Note The research on which this paper is based was made possible by a National Institute of Mental Health Research and Training Grant, 1968–1971.

hips. I was immediately struck by her poise and dignity and the feeling of power that exuded from her. She was in complete control of the situation. Here was none of the obsequious eagerness to greet me that I had already learned to distrust, since it seemed to hide fear and suspicion of me, the only white person in this village of almost two thousand tribal people. She was looking us over very carefully.

"My gods don't hate whites. Come in." Laughing, she moved slowly forward to greet us. Her husband came out of one of the huts and stood slightly behind her while she initiated the ritual exchange of news. This, too, was most unusual, since it was typically the men who exchanged the news while their womenfolk stood respectfully behind them listening. She asked how I was. I responded, "I am well, mother, thank you." She nodded and began her part of the ritual exchange.

"I am well, my husband is well"—this with a flick of her hand to indicate whom she meant. "And my children are well." She paused to study my face. "My goats are well, my chickens are well, my pigs are well, and my oxen are well." She was looking intently at me, and when I began to smile she laughed with delight. I had understood what she was saying and knew that it was peculiar to detail the health of one's livestock. She was testing me.

"I had heard that this one is different. She is not a mission woman. All they know how to say is 'good morning' and 'good evening.' They don't know our language." She had used bad grammar and pitched her voice in a high falsetto to mimic a missionary, venom in her tone. The other villagers had seemed anxious to convince me that they were good Christians, and those who were pagans had been avoiding me. Since I had begun to despair of convincing the villagers that I wanted to learn about all their customs, not just those they had adopted from the whites, I found Julia's attitude a refreshing change. I was also most thankful for the tortuous hours spent studying the Rjonga language with my assistant, Valente.

After being introduced to Rolando, Julia's husband, Lamanga asked if we could return later when Julia played her drums and her gods "came out" (possessed her). I finally realized who she was. This was Julia, the famous diviner and healer whose drums I had heard beating in the bush almost every evening since my arrival in the village. I looked more closely at her, understanding why I had felt power in her. For a Rjonga woman, she had a fantastic self-assurance, standing with her head slightly thrown back, looking down her nose at us. One foot was forward of the other so that one hip jutted out, and her hands were crossed over her breast. No other Rjonga woman stood like that, in such a deliberately arrogant pose. I was quite taken by her. She was dressed like other village women—a short-sleeved blouse, a long cloth wrapped around the waist dropping to her ankles, and a dark scarf tied around her head so that no hair showed. But her jewelry was uncommon. She wore a bracelet of red and black beads on her left wrist and, on the second and third fingers of her left hand, rings an inch thick, made of the same red and black beads that were on her wrist.

Julia responded, "This is a good night, a special night, because my gods have asked me to play the drums. I played the drums yesterday a little, out of habit, to keep in practice. I must play even if they don't want to come, but tonight they will." She gestured toward the hut behind us, whose doorway faced west. "I go to the gods' house every morning, where I keep my medicines and bones. I throw the bones to know if it is a special night for the gods or not."

Lamanga stuttered a little with excitement. "What should Marta bring as a gift to the gods?" Julia looked at him somewhat scornfully. Lamanga was a nominal Christian who had stopped attending church years before, but she enjoyed needling him about it still.

"You have walked in the church too long. You should not need to ask, you should know. How can I tell what the gods want? But it must be metallic—coins, pins, needles."

She told Rolando to escort us out of the homestead on the western path. He stayed with us, but behind us, until we reached the main path. He was an attractive middle-aged man, not without his own dignity, but he paid deference to Julia because of the power of her gods. We shook hands at the fork in the path, and, as we walked back to my hut, Lamanga told me a little of Julia's story and explained the meaning of the eastern and western paths and of the red and black beads.

Everyone in the village was surprised when Julia became a diviner, because she had been a staunch member of the Swiss Mission church. Her daughters were married, her husband and two grown sons had good jobs in Lourenço Marques (as the capital was called in 1968), and the family was upwardly mobile. Lamanga hinted that it had annoyed Rolando considerably that his wife had reverted to pagan ways just when the family was doing so well. Nonetheless, about three years ago, Julia had suddenly gone as an apprentice to a diviner and less than a year later had returned to Mitini and "sealed" many of the paths into her homestead. Christian households typically have many paths leading into them, but Julia had blocked all but the traditional eastern and western paths to protect her homestead from the witchcraft or sorcery of people envious of her newly acquired power. Lamanga explained that the east is associated with the living; paths into homesteads are from the east and must be used by all visitors, especially nonrelatives. The west is associated with the dead. Corpses are carried out of homesteads on the western path, which is regularly used only by members of the family or by non-kin who have permission from the family. Anyone using the western path without permission would be accused of witchcraft or sorcery.

Lamanga went on to explain the three major categories of gods in the Rjonga pantheon. Ancestor gods are particular to each family. They may visit an occasional illness on their living relatives if they feel neglected or if they think that their relatives have been misbehaving. The color white is associated with the ancestors and only white cloths, livestock or wine are offered to them. The Rjonga are quite emphatic that their "own" gods never kill people as do the other two kinds of gods. These other two kinds are "foreign" gods believed to belong to the Nguni (Zulu) and Ndjao tribes. The "foreign" gods possess people, so that they are forced to become diviners or be killed by the rejected gods. I knew that these two tribes had actually conquered the Rjonga in battle in the past. Now, it seemed, their gods continued to conquer them in the present. The color black is associated with the Nguni gods, who are male, while red is associated with the Ndjao gods, who are female and less powerful. This explained the meaning of Julia's red and black beads. Most diviners have two possessing gods. The colors of her jewelry let villagers know who her gods are.

People consult diviners for different reasons. Some may want to know the future—for example, if a certain plan or journey is a good idea. The majority, however, have been visited by some sort of misfortune and want to know its cause and remedy. Most people who went to Julia were ill. Her gods would possess her and speak through her in an arcane language, divining the cause of the illness. Sometimes the god would also prescribe a cure; other times it would send the patient to another healer for a cure.

THE GODS SPEAK

I could not return that evening because of a crisis in my homestead, but I made arrangements to go another time. About ten days later a messenger summoned me. Lamanga, who was visiting again, my servant, Carlos, and another guest went with me through the night to Julia's homestead. When we arrived, the small circular hut was very crowded, and the light was so dim that it was difficult to see. Chairs were brought in for us, and we sat down just inside the door. An oilcan was upended in the entrance with a kerosene lantern set on it, the wick turned very low. The still red coals of a dying fire could be seen behind the central beam, which served as an upright.

A woman, one of Julia's apprentices, was seated in front of the beam in a trance. Another apprentice, a man, was seated to her right. They both lived with Julia. Lamanga whispered that they were in trance tonight so that they might be purified. Angelica—the female apprentice—had four strings of shells around her otherwise bare head. Around her naked torso a string of beads crossed under her breasts and over her back. Over her shoulders, tied loosely under her chin, was a white cloth. She was sitting cross-legged, knees high, her hands on her knees, with a red cloth draped over her legs. A third cloth, wrapped around her waist, appeared to be her normal clothing. During her possession, Shanda—the male apprentice—often retied the white cloth or wiped Angelica's brow with a corner of it. I noticed a miniature mattock on the ground by Angelica's right hand. She was shivering and trembling; occasionally she jerked and twitched convulsively. The drums were beating loudly. The people chanted with the drums while Angelica continued to shiver; sometimes she stretched her hands out rigidly at her sides, just beside her knees, and shook all over. She made horrible groaning sounds like a person being punched in the stomach. Her head twisted spasmodically, jerking high over one shoulder, held there tautly while the rest of her body shivered and trembled, caught by her god. I could see Julia beating the large drum while other people shook metal carraca-like instruments that rattled. Angelica picked up the little mattock and began shaking it in rhythm with the drum, a smile on her face. When she put it down again, the music and singing immediately ceased, and she began to talk in a small, baby-like voice. The people laughed as someone told me that her god was afraid of whites and would not stay. The drums began beating again, and this time she picked up a knife, which she flourished as if in a fight. When she put it down, all was quiet, and Julia leaned forward, asking her questions.

During her trance Angelica had divined the cause of a person's illness and specified certain measures to be taken. She groaned and grunted as she came out of the trance, and people greeted her by telling her which god had possessed her, since diviners can remember nothing of what happened during the trance. Julia helped her out of her ceremonial regalia, and Angelica dressed in her normal clothes. The people relaxed and exchanged greetings with me and my friends; there was much laughter and talking while Angelica was told what happened when she was in trance. Hardly had she settled back against the upright, apparently exhausted, when Shanda, the male apprentice, began to jerk and twitch and be torn by those awful guttural groans. He was possessed but came out of trance relatively quickly.

Then, within minutes, Julia's god seized her. She began to grunt and tremble, as the other two had, while a young boy helped her take off her clothes and put on the ceremonial attire. Lamanga whispered that her "spirit helper," who is chosen by the god, must be pure, someone who has never had sexual relations. While Julia was dressing and grunting, the rest of the people chatted and laughed as if nothing unusual were happening.

I watched the young boy dress Julia. She wore a band around her head to which was attached a brush made of ostrich feathers. The Zulu used to wear these devices in battle to confuse the enemy. Julia was dressing as a warrior because her god had been one in life. A gazelle skin fit over her head and extended down over her chest and back, worn like an armor. On her right wrist was a ring made of hyena hide. Beads crossed over her breast and back, and a small trumpet made of ivory or bone hung on her chest. Also on her chest was a pouch with medicines; Lamanga speculated that they probably included the nose of a hyena and maybe part of an elephant's trunk. A black cloth was tied around her shoulders, and shells were strung around her head. The boy handed her a small shield made of cowhide, which she put on her arm. In one hand she held a *tchoba*, a sort of whisk used to brush the head and shoulders, and in the other a long root from which the shield was slung. She continued to wear her ordinary bronze bracelets—circles whose ends didn't meet so as not to "tie up the power of the god." A small knife was laid on the ground near her.

When she was fully dressed, Julia placed the various objects on the ground and began to dance toward the back of the hut. I craned my head to see. A huge forked limb was planted in the back of the hut, with a red and a black cloth draped over it; Lamanga said that the limb was like an altar. Julia stayed on her knees there for about ten minutes. Then she came forward and picked up the knife, shield, and root and began to mimic a warrior in battle. She thrust and feinted with the knife in what seemed an expert manner, then began to come toward me on her knees, the knife flickering and darting in front of her. She came closer and closer, sometimes throwing the shield up in front of her face as if to protect herself. She arrived in front of me, still on her knees, and we stared each other in the eye. I felt that she was very much "there" and was testing me again, as she had done the day we met for the first time. The drums were beating loudly, the people near me drawing away. My guest gripped my arm in obvious fear, but I shook him off and smiled at Julia, who smiled faintly in return. I was amazed by her enormous power and by the force of her personality. She danced at my feet, always on her knees, the knife weaving in front of her. Then, suddenly, she placed the knife, shield, and root on the ground at my feet. I could feel the knife blade across the toe of one of my shoes. She danced back a little, looking at me, then picked up her paraphernalia and retreated to the front of the hut, where she did a long pantomime of a warrior in battle. She subsided momentarily, then began to tremble and make horrible grunting sounds. Her throat was wracked by the cries torn from her and by occasional fits of coughing. The others were talking to each other, watching Julia from time to time. Obviously all of this was preliminary, and no one would pay serious attention until the god arrived. The grunting, groaning, and trembling continued for some time. Suddenly Julia spoke in a deep, guttural voice totally unlike her own: "I will see all of you, tell everything, destroy all of your secrets." The people fell quiet.

"Kakulu, kakulu, kakulu. Kakulu, white woman." The others replied "kakulu." Then she began to chant. She sang a phrase, and the people repeated part of it.

"What house is this which is preferred by men?"

"It is preferred by men," the people chorused.

"What village is this in which I am so adored by boys?"

"You are adored by boys."

The chanting continued until the drums stopped playing. Julia settled down in a corner by the drums and signaled her young helper to start playing again.

Then her god began to speak in earnest, and the people present sang a refrain after each utterance.

"I want to get out. I want to speak with the gods. I want to speak with my wife. I want you to play the drums. My father showed me everything. I want to come out. I want to tell you everything. I want to come out and meet the white. I want to come out with my woman. Let me play the drums. With my gods. My father made me see with my eyes. I want to get out to cooperate with the white. I want to tell you everything. In the middle of this land I want to make myself happy with my own spirit. To be happy with the white grandparents. To tell secrets of your grandsons. To cooperate. I want to tell all of you, the whites also. Good, good, good, good, good."

Julia grunted and coughed, then began to sing again. The drumming and singing continued for some time, then she spoke again, addressing Lamanga directly.

"I want to speak to my grandson only" [that is, "to the young man"].

"Yes," Lamanga replied.

"And he will tell his white friend."

"I am here."

"I don't want to leave him. He arrived with his white friend. I come to speak to my grandson only. I want to speak to him only, I want to please him—and his white friend who came here to my homestead. I want to cooperate with the white grandparents. What is it that the white woman wants in my house? Play the drums so that I can come out boiling! I want to live well in the midst of my family. We will visit each other every day. I speak only with the white woman. I will speak with my grandchildren only. Sit down and play the drums; I want to hear them with my ears."

She spoke in this vein for some time, her utterances constantly punctuated by a chorus from the people. When the session was over, Rolando translated the entire episode for us. He also told me that for several nights Julia's god had been visited by my own ancestors, who had "come across the seas" with me to take care of me in the village. My grandfather had gone to Julia's homestead in the night to visit with her god and to learn about his "work." Julia's god had explained that Julia had not wanted to "have the materials of the gods" but that she had inherited her gods from her family and had no choice. My ancestor and Julia's god spoke for a long time. The former Zulu warrior told my grandfather how he had come many years ago, when there was a war, and how he was killed in battle. His spirit, wanting to be hidden, sought refuge and found it in Julia, in whom he was now sheltered. Occasionally he would "come out" to treat someone who was sick or to help someone about to die. He also helped people who had problems with their family or neighbors. Sometimes he helped good people who came from far away. My ancestor had assured Julia's god that I was a good person with no evil intent. Julia's god was curious about my purpose in the village, so my grandfather had explained that I simply wanted to learn about the people's life and customs. The god was satisfied that I was to be trusted. I was stunned by my good fortune in acquiring unsolicited endorsement by one of the most powerful diviners in the kingdom. I would not fully comprehend the reasons for it until some time later.

Several days later Julia requested to hear the tape I had made of her possession. My assistant Valente and I went to her house in the early afternoon, and Julia, with her two apprentices and her spirit helper, gathered around to listen. There were many exclamations of wonder from the listeners—especially Julia, who reacted to herself grunting and groaning with loud "ohs!" After listening, we chatted and I asked permission to come another day to learn about Julia's conversion, her medicines, and everything else she could tell me. She agreed readily and began a long explanation of what had led up to the god's revelations during her possession. It was essentially what Rolando had already told me but richer in texture and details.

After my first visit to Julia, she wanted to sleep in the spirit house. Her husband was afraid to sleep alone in the other hut, so he went with Julia. Rolando fell asleep immediately, but Julia lay awake for a long time. Then she fell asleep, and one of her gods, the Zulu warrior, came to her. When he arrived, he shook Julia awake and asked her if she could see the two white spirits, my grandparents, who were just coming into her homestead.

Julia couldn't see them. The white spirits arrived at the doorway and asked permission to come in. Julia's god asked the white spirits, "What do you want in Julia's homestead?" They said they had come to visit and to see all the materials (meaning the bones, clothes, medicines, etc.) of the gods. The god said that they couldn't enter because, once in, they might not want to leave again: He didn't want white spirits in his house because "the races don't understand each other." The whites answered, "We haven't come to do harm," but Julia's god wouldn't let them come in. He said, "Perhaps you want to take these materials outside and burn them or throw them away." Then the white spirits asked for a place to rest outside. They stayed on the verandah, where they sat down on their own chairs, which they had brought with them. They also had some papers in their hands. They stayed there a long time, resting. Finally they got up, said goodby, and went to the homestead where I lived. After they left, Julia woke up and began to think about what had happened. She looked at the door and saw that it was closed. Then she understood that she had not been dreaming and that the spirits had really come, because when she had gone to sleep the door had been open. She woke Rolando and told him what had happened. He demurred saying, "Perhaps you dreamed all this because Marta was here in the afternoon." Julia insisted, "No, they really came."

Two nights later the same thing happened again, except that Rolando wasn't there. When the white spirits returned, Julia's god asked again, "What do you want here?" They replied, "Nothing; we came only to see." Then the white spirits explained that they had come to Africa because they knew that their granddaughter had been sent there and they wanted to take care of her. They were now living in my homestead. Julia's god still wouldn't allow them to enter the spirit house, and this time they didn't stay to rest but returned instead to my hut. On other nights Julia's god went to my homestead to visit with my grandparents, and long conversations ensued. As before, Julia told Rolando what had happened.

I was enchanted by this story and assured Julia that, if my ancestors were indeed with me, it was as they had said. All of us were interested only in learning and meant no harm. She said she knew that. She also said that her god had told her people that I was good and should be helped. I was also quite interested in her husband's reaction, so "Western" in nature. He apparently did not believe in Julia's spirits, and I remembered Lamanga's telling me that Rolando and his sons wanted to become *assimilados*, Portuguese citizens. *Assimilados* were "civilized" people, and I could clearly see that having a "witchdoctor" in the family might be an embarrassment to his ambitions.

Different members of the family came on several occasions to hear the tape of Julia's possession. Her elder daughter told me that she had never believed in her mother's gods until she heard my tape. It was clear to her now that her mother truly "had gods," because she spoke ancient Zulu and in a man's voice. She knew that Julia could not speak or understand Zulu. The daughter also said that she was pleased that her mother was a diviner; she had been very lonely, with her husband, sons, and daughters living in the capital city while she stayed in the bush. Now, said the daughter, her mother had company. This was an intriguing comment. I wanted to hear more about the events that led up to Julia's becoming a diviner, so I made arrangements to speak with her again.

My assistant Valente and I arrived in Julia's homestead around five in the afternoon and found no one at home. Valente, a Christian, showed none of the nervousness that had beset Lamanga. He led me into the homestead, and we waited for Julia, who finally appeared. She left us soon afterward to go clean up after a day of working in the fields. Being a diviner was a part-time job, and she, like all the other villagers, had to tend her crops in order to eat. A few minutes later she joined us, and we exchanged news and pleasantries. Finally I asked whether she could tell me how the gods had come to her. She gave me a sharp look.

"What will you do when you have that knowledge?"

"I will learn." She laughed and said that it was all right. As she started speaking, her apprentice Angelica joined us.

JULIA'S STORY

"Before I was born, my mother was often sick. She went to the hospital many times, but they could do nothing that helped her. Finally her family consulted a diviner who threw the bones, which directed that she go to the family altar and stay here. She would become pregnant, and she should give the child the name of the god who sent the sickness. So my mother bought the 'clothes of the gods'—cloth of various colors—and went to pray at the family altar. Then she became pregnant. The time came when I was born, and my parents went again to the diviner, who said to call me Musengele because that was the name of the god who had sent my mother's sickness.

"When I grew up, I became sick, and they sent me to the hospital, but they couldn't cure me there. So they went to the bones, and the bones said to send me to my mother's mother's home to live. When I arrived at the entrance of my grandmother's homestead, even before I had a chance to speak, I was cured.

"I have two kinds of gods. The female comes from my mother's house. The male comes from my father's. The god tells me his name is Mahlabazimuke. He is the chief one. The female is called Nyankwabe."

While listening, I watched Angelica, who was obviously taking vicarious pride in this tale. Occasionally she would look contemptuously at Valente, as if to remind him of the traditional power he, a Christian, had forsaken.

Julia continued her story, saying that she had not begun her apprenticeship until many years after she married and after her parents and grandparents had died. Since I knew that possessing gods become hereditary once they are established in a family, this reference to the death of her parents and grandparents was very meaningful. Julia became the heir to the family gods who, in native belief, sought among the living the descendants of their dead hosts until they found a new host. Refusal to become a living host for the gods could lead to the death of the person the gods sought. The "chosen" person could not automatically become a diviner, however, just by being sought out by the gods. He or she then has to enter into an apprenticeship with an established diviner that might last anywhere from a few months to several years.

Julia went on to say that, after her children were born, she became sick and went to the hospital. She had a pain in her lower right side, but they couldn't cure her. She spent a long time seeking a cure from the European doctors and from native healers, without success. She went to the hospital several times, and finally the doctors at the Swiss Mission hospital decided to operate on her. When Julia arrived at the hospital for her operation, she was told to lie down so that blood could be drawn from the vein in her arm. Her vein collapsed, and she interpreted this event as a sign that the gods didn't like her being there. She indicated that she didn't want to go through with the operation. The European doctor, apparently in disgust at her native "superstitious" belief, told her to go home and seek a cure. By this time Julia was becoming desperately ill, and, though her husband preferred to continue trying European medicine, he finally consented to consult the bones. The bones said that the gods were causing her illness, so the unhappy couple sought a diviner. The diviner gave Julia three kinds of medicines. As soon as she started taking them, the gods "came out" because they had been so long repressed. They possessed her and spoke through her mouth: "We want you to go far away to be treated, so we can work." It is believed that the possessing gods have themselves been diviners and healers in life and that they seek hosts so that they can continue their work after death. Julia didn't like the first diviner she had consulted and insisted that she go far north to a diviner there.

Her husband and sons took her north to this diviner so that she could begin her apprenticeship and learn the "things of the gods." When she arrived, her god asked to be treated as fast as possible so that they could return home quickly. All this was three years ago, Julia told me. She observed that the god was strange in that he liked everything to be done in a hurry. Since he had been well fed and well treated in the north country, Julia was never seriously sick now. Occasionally she might feel unwell, and, if her husband was home, he still tried to get her to go to the European hospital. But her god would immediately come out and say, "I don't like hospitals," and within a few days she would be well again.

I reflected on what her daughter had told me about the loneliness of Julia's life before she became a diviner. Her two sons were unmarried, so she had no daughters-in-law to live with her; her sons and her husband lived in the city where they worked. They came home to the village only occasionally for holidays or weekends. Julia had lived completely alone in her homestead, tending the family fields unaided. Her only companionship came from the other members of the Swiss Mission church in the village, which she attended regularly. Sometimes she would go to the city to visit her family, but she could rarely stay long because of the necessity of caring for the crops. She was an attractive middle-aged woman, perhaps in her forties, quite intelligent and intense, and it must have been difficult for her to accept a life of drudgery and boredom. Now, instead, her home was full of people. She had two apprentices who lived with her and helped her in the fields. She had the young boy who was her spirit helper and who tended her cattle. The cattle themselves were a sign of her success. Diviners charge their patients fees, and apprentices pay princely sums for their tutelage. She had converted this wealth into cattle, still the most prestigious symbol of affluence to the Rjonga. People sought her out continuously. Her life was now full, and she had achieved an importance rare for a man and almost unheard of for a Rjonga woman.

I asked if I could come back sometime and ask her more questions. After thinking a while, she agreed: "I can't refuse to help you, since you came to learn the life of the people. The country has received you, and I have no right to refuse my help. But the story of the gods is very difficult." Suddenly she began to speak again, telling me in much greater detail how her husband had been convinced to let her become a diviner.

She had gone to the capital city to visit her family and had just finished making dinner when her gods saw that it was almost time for her daughters to return from school. I started, since I had been unaware that her young daughters had also lived in the city. Yes, she assured me impatiently, they had lived in the city when they were children; now they were married and still remained there. It was most unusual for unmarried daughters not to live with their mothers in the village, helping with the daily chores. This put Rolando's upward mobility in a new light. He had been determined, indeed, to surpass the limitations of village traditional life, and Julia had borne the brunt of his ambition, being forced to live alone without the comfort of her daughters.

Village women had told me often that one of the few consolations of married life was having daughters who shared one's burdens and eased the loneliness of a woman's lot somewhat.

Julia continued her story by telling how her gods came out and paralyzed her hands. Her ankles were also paralyzed, so that she was forced to lie down on the bed. When her family came home, she could hardly breathe, nor could she speak. When they touched her, she felt like a corpse, as if the blood had stopped running. After a while her gods began to speak through her: "We want you to send Julia far away so we can be treated. If you don't do it, someday you will find her dead. And we want you to arrange now for all the money for the diviner who will treat us. We don't want to spend a lot of time there in our apprenticeship."

Then the gods disappeared. Julia's husband and daughters were frightened for a while and encouraged her to follow her gods' demands, but, when after a few days she started feeling better, Rolando changed his mind. She became sick several more times with paralysis and convulsions, but again her husband did nothing, although she felt that her life was threatened. Finally a son, Rafael, came home from the north where he was working. He said that his mother should leave the church and seek relief from the diviners. And so, finally, the family planned for the trip to the north. Rolando and Rafael got together the prepayment that would guarantee a speedy treatment. Rafael went ahead and arranged for a diviner to take Julia as an apprentice.

After Julia's arrival, the diviner began to treat her with the special medicines demanded by her gods. After three months Julia became sick for three days, vomiting bile and having difficulty breathing. On the fourth day her gods came out and said, "Why are you making Julia delay? We have already paid the fees, and we said we wanted to go home quickly. But you still send her to do your work in the fields and around the homestead. If you continue, we will kill her and you will be to blame." The next day Julia was all right again and could sit up. The diviner, convinced of the power of Julia's gods, began treating her with the last of the medicines, then arranged for a big feast. At this feast the power of Julia's gods would be tested to see if they were authentic. People from all over the area would attend this feast and examination, and Julia's family would come north to see if she "graduated."

On the day of the final rituals, many people came to the diviner's homestead bringing drums to play for the gods. This public validation of a diviner's power was very important. Without it, a diviner would be accused of being a quack and would have no patients. Before beginning the tests, Julia was taken out of the homestead into the bush so that she could not see what tests were being prepared. The people in the homestead took the "gods' clothes"—the cloths of special colors in which diviners dressed—and wrapped them in a bundle. They took Julia's gold ring and gave it to a man to hide; he put it in his pocket. The ring symbolized Julia's marriage to the gods and was called "money." Julia removed her head scarf to show me the gold ring tied to a lock of hair over her forehead, which was normally hidden from view. A goat had been killed for the feast; its gallbladder was removed and given to another person to hide. All these hidden objects were tests for Julia's gods. If the gods were "authentic," she would have no trouble finding the hidden objects. One of the primary duties of a diviner is to discover hidden things, be they material items or secrets or knowledge of the future.

Julia was brought back from her seclusion in the bush and given medicines so that her gods would come out. Quickly they possessed her, and she fell to the ground. Then she got up and began to sing and dance. The people called out: "If you are a real god, find the house where your clothes are hidden." Still possessed, she began to search and found the house and the clothes wrapped in a bundle. She came out of the house dressed as a diviner, her breasts bare and covered with beads, a black cloth wrapped around her waist. She carried the small shield in one hand, a knife in the other. Again the gods began to dance through her body. The people called: "Now find your money," referring to the gold ring. Julia danced and sang a new song. Then her gods told the people to be quiet, and she sat down on the ground to think. The gods began to sing again, and the drums picked up the song and beat out a rhythm that lifted Julia off the ground into another dance. She danced directly to the person who had the ring and sat down in front of him. "You have the money. Put it here," she said, holding both hands cupped in front of him. The man asked where he had put the ring, and her gods pointed to his pocket. He took it out and gave it to her while the people laughed and clapped. Then her gods were told to find the goat's gallbladder; they found the person who had it right away. The people clapped more, the gods danced a while longer, then left. Julia was herself again. This ended her tests; she had passed with flying colors, and the people ate and drank, feasting far into the night. Julia stayed in the north for three more days, finishing the medicines for her gods, then came back to Mitini and started curing. By the time I arrived, she was a famous and powerful diviner.

CONCLUSION

After hearing this story I finally understood why Julia had so unexpectedly endorsed me through her god. She had lived a life of loneliness in the village while her family lived in the city. Other women had a similar lot, but Julia was clearly more intense, vibrant, and intelligent than the majority of village women. She chafed against living out her life as the family drudge, tending the fields alone day after day. Furthermore, she had a history of spirits in her family. This provided the mechanism by which her life could be changed. After the original hosts of the family spirits—her parents and grandparents—had died, it was natural that the family spirits should seek her out. She had originally been named by a spirit; this in itself would attract the spirits to her. The only obstacle in her way was her husband's ambition, which had led to her lonely state in the first place. Despite Julia's repeated illnesses, convulsions, and paralysis, her husband refused to believe that she "had gods." I have no doubt that she was truly on the verge of death, since she was fighting for her own social survival. The intervention of their son had convinced Rolando to let her go as an apprentice and set up practice.

But it was clear that her family was still quite ambivalent about her power and authenticity. Her daughters said that they had not believed in her spirits until they heard my tape, and Rolando believed that she had dreamed about my ancestors simply because she had met me. Although Rolando was traditional enough to be afraid of her gods and to defer to her power, which was clearly accepted by others as real, he still did not accord her full belief. My journey to their homestead to meet Julia, my attendance at her possession, the questions I asked, and my sincere admiration of her had finally impressed her family to a degree that she had been unable to achieve herself. Being white, I validated her power and eased her family's anxiety about their being accepted as "civilized" people. Each of us was marginal to village life, each was suspected by others of unknown schemes. But Julia had been quick to see what I had not. I had inadvertently helped her gain respect in her own family; her public endorsement of me through her god made villagers relax and be less afraid to speak to me about their lives. Julia had responded to my interest by utilizing a very important principle in Rjonga life: reciprocity. Thus each of us had helped the other find acceptance and tolerance in the social spheres important to us. I had made a good and powerful friend.

Further Readings

Junod, Henri Alexandre. *The Life of a South African Tribe*. 2 vols. New Hyde Park, N.Y.: University Books, 1962.

*Morris, Martha B. "A Rjonga Curing Ritual: A Functional and Motivational Analysis." *The Realm of the Extra-Human: Ideas and Actions*, edited by Agehananda Bharati. Vol. 3, *World Anthropology*. The Hague: Mouton, 1976.

——. "Rjonga Settlement Patterns: Meanings and Implications." *Anthropological Quarterly* 45, no. 4 (October 1972).

Turner, Victor Witter. *The Drums of Affliction: A Study of Religious Processes among the Ndembu of Zambia*. Oxford, England: Clarendon Press, 1968.

——. *Forest of Symbols: Aspects of Ndembu Ritual*. Ithaca, N.Y.: Cornell University Press, 1967.

*Former name of Martha B. Binford.

2

The Catholic Earth Mother: Dorothy Day and Women's Power in the Church

DEBRA CAMPBELL

Roman Catholic Women's struggle for equal access to the ordained priesthood is a relatively recent development.[1] The hierarchical power structure of the Catholic Church, a closed system in which decisions trickle down from the pope through the ranks of the (male) bishops and priests to "the people" below, has precluded the possibility of women's full participation in the church's ministry, not to mention women's power within the institutional church. As the twentieth century draws to a close, the Catholic Church remains polarized on the question of women's ordination, with substantial grassroots support on both sides.[2] Pope John Paul II has spoken unequivocally in "Ordinatio Sacerdotalis" (30 May 1994), stating that the church has no authority to alter its traditional stand excluding women from the priesthood.[3]

Both the stalemate on women's ordination and the growing involvement of laywomen and sisters in the unordained ministries of the church raise important questions concerning the kind of power women can and should have in the church. To ask whether women should be able to join the existing ecclesiastical power structure almost inevitably raises related questions. Might women point the way to an alternative vision of power and leadership within the America Catholic Church? What form might Catholic women's power or leadership assume? Can women improve upon the male patterns of authority and find ways to function efficiently without falling into the all too familiar power trap?

DEBRA CAMPBELL is Associate Professor and Chair of the Department of Religious Studies at Colby College in Waterville, Maine, where she has also served as Director of Women's Studies. She has published articles on Catholic women and modern women's religious history in *Signs*, *Commonweal*, *Crosscurrents*, and *The Christian Century*. She is working on a book on twentieth-century Catholic women's departure narratives.

Most feminists agree that it would be a serious mistake to emulate male hierarchical power structures, but we have few models of specifically female alternative forms of power at our disposal. This is especially true in the ecclesiastical realm. Traditional works in American religious history contain few exemplars of women's power or leadership. Nevertheless, upon closer inspection, we find some instances in which women have wielded a *kind of power*.

This essay explores one such instance and focuses upon the contribution of Dorothy Day to the debate on how women's power has actually functioned in the recent past in the American Catholic Church. It does not recommend Day as a "role model" for today's women. Instead it suggests that we examine Dorothy Day's experience as an illuminating example of how one twentieth-century Catholic woman achieved a unique kind of authority which paradoxically both challenged and acknowledged the male hierarchical authority structure of the Roman Catholic Church. Day was a laywoman, a convert, who developed her own personal model of a Christian life involving total commitment in the world, a model that allowed her to sidestep traditional constraints and to exercise an alternative form of leadership within the American Catholic Church. In the process Day became a celebrity. Long before her death in December 1980, Day's name and story graced the pages of secular and religious presses with surprising frequency. Articles in *The New Yorker* and *The New Republic* as well as in *Commonweal* and *America* examined Day's lifestyle and her unique Christian witness.[4] Day's vision and power were not derivative; they sprang from her own personal experiences. Therefore in order to understand the nature of Day's power we must first turn to her life.[5]

The daughter of a sportswriter, Dorothy Day moved during her childhood from Brooklyn to Oakland to Chicago as her father went from newspaper to newspaper. The San Francisco earthquake of 1906 had a profound effect upon young Dorothy Day. She relived it in a recurring childhood dream:

> As soon as I closed my eyes at night the blackness of death surrounded me. I believed and yet was afraid of nothingness. What would it be like to sink into that immensity? If I fell asleep God became in my ears a great noise that became louder and louder, and approached nearer and nearer to me until I woke up sweating with fear and shrieking for my mother. I fell asleep with her hand in mine, her warm presence by my bed.[6]

Even as a child Dorothy Day grappled with the supernatural. It is poignant to note that only her mother could save her from the menacing God she apparently connected with the natural calamity of the earthquake. Day's memories of the earthquake are intermingled with those of another disturbing event which had transpired only a few days before; she had seen her mother faint suddenly and crash to the bedroom floor. Both events combined to give young Dorothy a sense of overarching natural tragedy and to impress upon her the fragility of her mother and of the earth itself. The aftermath of the earthquake also taught her a lesson which she would teach others in later life, "the joy of doing good, of sharing whatever we had with others."[7]

Meanwhile the Day family suffered another loss. After the paper plant in San Francisco was destroyed in the earthquake, Dorothy's father had to move the family to Chicago. The contrast between their California home, "a bungalow surrounded by trees and flowers," and their six-room flat on the South Side of Chicago, which overlooked a "cement paved yard with neither tree nor blade of grass," deeply moved young Dorothy.[8] She began to identify closely with the poor. Even after another move to a house in a nicer neighborhood, she continued to haunt the poorer sections on the West Side, pushing her baby brother in a carriage "through interminable gray streets, fascinating in their dreary sameness, past tavern after tavern." Even in these grim surroundings, young Dorothy found signs of hope in the tiny gardens tucked into odd corners of the ghetto and in the homey odors wafting by. In her autobiography she recalled it all in delicious detail:

> The odor of geranium leaves, tomato plants, marigolds; the smell of lumber, of tar, of roasting coffee; the smell of good bread and rolls and coffee cake coming from the small German bakeries. Here was enough beauty to satisfy me.[9]

In this adolescent attraction to the poverty of Chicago's West Side and to its multifarious smells we see Dorothy Day's social conscience and her nascent sensuality awakening simultaneously. Both came to fruition during the next decade. At sixteen Day entered the University of Illinois at Urbana. She read Dostoyevsky, Gorky, and Tolstoy. She mingled with the literary crowd and began to write. She joined the Socialist Party. Then in 1916 she moved with her family to New York City.

Soon Dorothy Day was a "radical" journalist writing for *The Masses* and *Call* and living among the bohemians in Greenwhich Village on the eve of the First World War.[10] Malcolm Cowley writes about Day's legendary drinking abilities in *The Exile's Return*.[11] Day gained this reputation in a Village bar called the Hell Hole where she had sat "in a sort of trance" while her good friend Eugene O'Neill recited Francis Thompson's "Hound of Heaven" from memory.[12] There were other even more intimate scenes with O'Neill in the Village during the winter of 1917–1918. Often, after the Hell Hole closed at three or four in the morning, Day and O'Neill

> would venture out into the cold, making their way down to the East Side, stopping off frequently at taverns on the way. . . Dorothy had a room on the East Side, and when they got there, she would put the shaking and exhausted O'Neill to bed and then lie beside him under the covers and hold him close to her trying to keep him warm. During such moments, Dorothy said, O'Neill would ask her, "Dorothy, do you want to surrender your virginity?" In O'Neill's usual sodden condition, this question would have been pointless. Even so, said Dorothy, she always turned the question aside. Early in the afternoon, when O'Neill awakened, he would call Dorothy, wherever she happened to be working then, and have her meet him at the Hell Hole to begin the cycle again.[13]

During the decade between 1917 and 1927 Day worked as a freelance journalist in New York, Chicago, and New Orleans and remained politically active. She went to prison twice, first in 1917 with other participants in the Washington march for women's suffrage,[14] and later in 1923 when she was caught in a raid on the Wobblies headquarters in Chicago. In 1924, when a Hollywood studio paid her five thousand dollars for the movie rights to her autobiographical novel, *The Eleventh Virgin*,[15] Day seized the opportunity to retreat from the fray and write. She used the money to buy a cottage on Staten Island that she shared with Forster Batterham, a biologist with anarchist sympathies. In 1927 Day gave birth to Batterham's child, a daughter named Tamar. In December of the same year, Day was baptized a Roman Catholic, a step that alienated Batterham and ended their relationship.

Day had long been engaged in a protracted spiritual quest. Even in her Greenwich Village days she had puzzled her friends by her intermittent visits to Catholic churches.[16] Day's deepening relationship with Batterham and the love of nature they both shared intensified her religious feelings. "How can there be no God and all these beautiful things?" she continued to ask.[17]

Finally, after the birth of her daughter, Day entered the Catholic Church. She explained her reasons in her autobiography.

> I knew that I was going to have my child baptized, cost what it may. I knew that I was not going to have her floundering through many years as I had done, doubting and hesitating, undisciplined and amoral. I felt that it was the greatest thing I could do for my child.[18]

Then, in order to be able to raise her child properly, Dorothy overcame her own hesitation and followed her infant daughter into the Catholic Church.

The rest of the story has become a familiar chapter in American religious history. For several years Day sought a way to combine her new religious commitments with her old political convictions. She dutifully submitted to the Roman Catholic Church's official condemnation of socialism and thus found herself sitting on the sidelines, watching her former comrades engage in actions that, in her heart, she still considered right. In December 1932, when she covered a communist hunger march in Washington, D.C., for a Catholic journal, Day felt herself torn apart by conflicting loyalties and conflicting emotions. As she later recalled:

> I stood on the curb and watched them, joy and pride in the courage of this band of men and women mounting in my heart, and with it a bitterness too that since I was now a Catholic, with fundamental philosophical differences, I could not be out there with them. I could write, I could protest, to arouse the conscience, but where was the Catholic leadership in the gathering of the bands of men and women together, for the actual works of mercy that the comrades had always made a part of their technique in reaching the workers?
>
> How little, how puny my work has been since becoming a Catholic, I thought. How self-centered, how ingrown, how lacking in a sense of community.[19]

Shortly after this difficult episode, Day returned from Washington to New York and met Peter Maurin, once aptly described as "a cross between a bum and a twentieth-century Isaias."[20] Together Day and Maurin founded the Catholic Worker movement, launched in May 1933, with its threefold plan to spread Catholic social teachings in a penny paper called *The Catholic Worker*, to settle in urban outposts called Houses of Hospitality where volunteers would live lives of poverty and service to the poor, and to establish experimental farming communes, models of noncapitalist Christian communal living.

The Catholic Worker movement has become synonymous with the name Dorothy Day. It has had its ups and down, but has remained dedicated to the original ideals of voluntary poverty, social justice, peace, and solidarity with workers and the poor. It has also expanded geographically and in the size of its membership. Judged by the standards of longevity and growth, the movement is a success. In 1980, the year Dorothy Day died, *The Catholic Worker* had between 85,000 and 100,000 subscribers.[21]

The Catholic Workers, an organic, decentralized movement in a hierarchical church, remains a monument to Dorothy Day's vision and her leadership. Clearly it was Day and not Maurin who kept the movement together and mobilized its members when the occasion demanded it. Maurin played a crucial role in the founding of the movement when he introduced Day to a whole body of European Catholic social thought, which widened her vision of the church as a vehicle of social reform. Nevertheless, as historian Mel Piehl maintains, Maurin's importance was "more personal and symbolic than programmatic or intellectual."[22] In a pinch, it was Day who coped with concrete problems and made pressing decisions. As John Cogley, a Chicago

Catholic Worker who had ample opportunity to watch the interaction between Maurin and Day, observed: "[Maurin] was obviously uncomfortable in the feigned role of leadership. Unless the questions were abstractly philosophical or sweepingly historical he would turn helplessly to Dorothy Day for an answer."[23] Moreover, Piehl reminds us, Maurin was also "strategically useful," a "symbolic helpmate" in a church that implicitly rejected the notion of female leadership.[24]

Ironically, Dorothy Day herself paid lip service to the same sexual stereotypes she refuted in her day-to-day life. She once wrote that "Men are the single-minded, the pure of heart in these movements. . . Women by their very nature are more materialistic, thinking of the home, the children, and all things needful to them."[25] It is significant to our discussion to note that this was written by Day, a single parent, who devoted almost half a century to one movement. Elsewhere, however, Day argued in favor of women's unique qualifications for the job that the Catholic Workers were doing. "Perhaps it is easier for a woman to understand than a man," she affirmed, "because no matter what has occurred or hangs overhead, she has to go on with the business of living. She does the physical things and so keeps a balance."[26] From her own experience as a woman and as a mother, Dorothy could see that women's ineradicable link to "the physical things" was not a spiritual liability but a responsibility and a gift.

In a church with clearly delineated lines of authority, Day openly urged others to pursue alternative channels, to bypass established authorities in the interests of justice and peace. "When I started *The Catholic Worker,*" she affirmed, "I asked no permissions, expected no recognitions."[27] In 1963 she urged Catholic activists in Los Angeles:

> We must follow where the spirit leads. So go ahead, . . . don't look for support or approval. And don't always be looking for blame either, or see opposition where perhaps there is none. . . I beg you to save your energies to fight the giant injustices of our time, and not the Church in the shape of its Cardinal Archbishop.[28]

During the New York City gravediggers' strike in 1949 Day had chosen the same approach and supported the strikers while Cardinal Spellman had openly opposed them. Nevertheless, Day could still maintain that "if the Chancery ordered me to stop publishing *The Catholic Worker* tomorrow, I would."[29]

For all of her ideological independence, Dorothy Day was a traditional Catholic who staunchly upheld the authority of the church amidst the turbulence of the 1960s. Daniel Berrigan recalls how she supported the church's position on sexual ethics to the letter and ". . . broke friendships, tossed free-loving hippies out on their ears, forbade Catholic deviants access to her paper." Only later did she mellow and renew her old friendships with married priests like Berrigan's brother Philip.[30] Dorothy Day also remained aloof from the drive for democracy and lay rights in the church in the 1960s and the Catholic women's movement, which gained momentum in the following decade. Doris Grumbach, an observer at a conference on women in the church held in Westchester, New York in November 1970, noted that seventy-two-year-old Dorothy Day appeared out of place among "the smartly suited nuns and laywomen and men. . . and nattily dressed priests." Nonetheless, Grumbach maintained that Day was "in action and practice the most liberated [woman]" in a room which included such figures as Sidney Callahan and Betty Friedan. All Day had to do was reiterate what she had said all along:

> Yes, we have lived with the poor, with the workers. . . the unemployed, the sick. . . We have all known the long loneliness and we have learned that the only solution is love and that love comes with community.[31]

Here we reach the heart of Dorothy Day's approach to the leadership of her movement, her emphasis upon community grounded in love and compassion. Looking back upon her experiences in the late 1920s when she was a freelance writer taking care of an infant daughter, she recalled the profound loneliness she had experienced and she reflected:

> I was to find out then, as I found out so many times, over and over again, that women especially are social beings, who are not content with just husband and family, but must have a community, a group, an exchange with others. A child is not enough. A husband and children, no matter how busy one may be kept by them, are not enough. Young and old, even in the busiest year of our lives, we women especially are victims of the long loneliness.[32]

When Day referred to the long loneliness, she meant not only her own situation, but the human condition in general. And yet, for Day, there was a special female dimension to the long loneliness as the above quotation indicates. Day originally encountered the phrase in the writings of the English nun, Mary Ward (1585–1645). Ward had written: "We women especially are victims of the long loneliness."[33]

The underlying goal, to fight against the long loneliness, explains much about why Dorothy Day's movement is an anomaly in the institutional church and why Day's style of leadership contrasts with that exercised by bishops and cardinals. Granted, Day could occasionally take control and wield power *as if* she were at the helm of a hierarchy. When John Cogley and some Chicago Catholic Workers disagreed with Day's absolute pacifism during the Second World War, Dorothy Day issued an ultimatum to the dissenters: either distribute *The Catholic Worker* (which propagated Day's position) or split with the movement.[34] John Cort, a convert who joined the Catholic Workers in the 1930s after his graduation from Harvard, has called the movement "an extraordinary combination of anarchy and dictatorship."[35] On the issue of pacifism Day appears to have inclined in the direction of dictatorship. This is part of what Daniel Berrigan had called her "absolutely stunning consistency."[36] Day categorically rejected all forms of violence, war, and bloodshed. And yet, this very position which she maintained so intensely, even dogmatically, is, upon closer examination, deeply rooted in her larger vision of the Catholic Worker movement as a community intended to stave off the long loneliness.

As Abigail McCarthy, a close follower of the movement since her college days in the 1930s, has observed, a salient trait of the Catholic Worker houses and farms has been their separate, autonomous, family-like structure. The Houses of Hospitality were homes in which Dorothy Day played the role of mother and sister.[37] Because her goal was community and peace and justice Day eschewed all formal structures and institutionalized means of control. As Mel Piehl puts it:

> For Dorothy Day, a social revolution would be worthwhile only if it was also homelike. By making the themes of community and domesticity that had always been important to her parts of the fabric of Catholic Worker life, she made its radical Christian idealism seem homey as well.[38]

If life with the Catholic Workers was homey, it was also rigorous and physically uncomfortable. Writing in 1952 Day reported that many Houses of Hospitality still lacked central heating and indoor toilets. The Philadelphia House still used oil lamps and shared its water faucet, located in the alley, with several other residences.[39]

Notwithstanding, Catholic Worker houses attracted a variety of volunteers during the forty-seven years in which Day stood at the center of the movement. Julia Porcelli, who joined the Catholic Workers in New York in the 1930s, did so because she "didn't see many people living by faith" and was "very hungry for things of the spirit." Porcelli confessed: the Catholic Workers were "the people I wanted to be with. There was brotherhood, there was unity, there was family."[40] The movement also attracted a growing minority of Catholic college students, male and female, who were full of idealism but without an outlet for their energies during the Depression.[41] The Catholic Workers represented a way to be involved in the struggle for social justice and still avoid the more radical movements condemned by the church. Ex-seminarians rethinking their vocational plans found homes in the Houses of Hospitality as did working-class Catholics like Margaret, a young Lithuanian woman from a mining town in Pennsylvania who came with her infant daughter Barbara and tended the stove when she was not hawking *The Catholic Worker* on the New York City streets during the early years of the movement.[42]

Then, especially in the years following the Second World War, there were college-educated, upper-middle-class Catholics like Michael Harrington who came to the Catholic Worker fresh from Holy Cross and sought to recover in the movement a Catholic social justice tradition that was slipping out of the sight in a church increasingly enamored with militarism and bourgeois culture. Ultimately Harrington chose to follow Day's example in reverse; he moved from the Catholic Church to socialism. But he never forgot Dorothy Day and he readily acknowledged his debt to her and to the movement.[43]

Dorothy Day had an uncanny ability to persuade people to confront themselves and thereby find their own vision and power. Wilfrid Sheed relates how, during the Vietnam War, Day persuaded several young men to go to jail rather than face induction into the army. While they were in jail, the men lost their faith. Sheed underlines the irony: "the fact that those young men had lost their faith was heartbreaking to [Day]. And she had urged them into it!"[44] Day's pacifism and her pivotal role in the Catholic Worker movement were both rooted in her boundless maternal instinct. When, during the Korean War, a reader of *The Catholic Worker* castigated her for her lack of compassion for "the poor kids in Korea," she responded trenchantly: "If it refers to our soliders, the phrase is maudlin, and I don't think it means the children being killed by our bombs."[45]

The volunteers came to the Catholic Workers not merely to give but also to receive. Like Julia Porcelli they came for the family. Wilfrid Sheed recalls that "every possible blueprint for a Catholic left was hammered out in the back room while Dorothy doled out soup in the front. . . Yet the talk *was* the movement as much as the soup."[46] Day certainly did not confine herself to the task of ladling soup, but there was a touch of domesticity to every aspect of life in the Houses of Hospitality. When the seamen went on strike in New York City in 1936–1937 Day housed as many strikers as she could and set up a store-front commissary near the waterfront especially for the strikers. She raised four thousand dollars to feed them for several months. When strikebreakers threw a paving stone through the commissary window Day informed readers of *The Catholic Worker:* "half the stone is used to bolster up the stove and the other half is used to keep the bread-knife sharp, as we are slicing up 150 loaves of bread a day."[47]

Typically, Dorothy Day sought to bring her readers into the kitchen with her, to share her work and her community and to help them to stave off the long loneliness. Strictly speaking, Day did not administer or lead the Catholic Worker Movement; she mothered it in the best, most profound sense of the term. In collaboration with Peter Maurin she conceived it and brought it to term. From 1933 until her death in 1980 she remained the center of the movement, its constant source of life and strength. Volunteers came, attracted by Day, her vision, and her community. Even if they disagreed with Day they left enriched, with a new sense of their own identities and their own power.

In an expanded footnote in *Bare Ruined Choirs* Garry Wills describes Dorothy Day as a "Catholic earth mother" who "mothered her principal charge [Peter Maurin] and then mothered a whole succession of others through the years."[48] Wills calls the Catholic Worker houses "way stations" for "troubled young men" in transition. As Julia Porcelli reminds us, the houses were more than remedial units; they were homes. Nevertheless, Wills correctly calls attention to the transient character of the Catholic Worker population. Dorothy Day was the only constant; the other members were in transit.

Will's choice of the earth mother archetype focuses our attention upon other important aspects of Day's function within the community. Day brings to mind the earth mother at the center of the ancient religions that preceded the rise of Yahwism, "a powerful female figure who was at once virgin and mother, wife and sister, and who rescued the dying God from the power of the underworld." Like Day and the Catholic Workers the ancient earth mother religions celebrated "the release of captives, justice for the poor and security against invasion, as well as the new rain, the new grain, the new lamb and the new child."[49] Although the image may not be a perfect fit, it is an apt metaphor for Day's pervasive maternal presence at the center of the Catholic Worker movement for so many years. It also calls to mind other important moments earlier in Day's life: her childhood dreams of a raging God soothed only by the warm presence of her mother by her bed, her adolescent walks with her baby brother through Chicago's West Side when she began to empathize with the poor while she marveled at the beauty of their tiny gardens, and finally her ambivalent relationship with the cold, shivering, dependent Eugene O'Neill during the winter of 1917. Motherhood was a revelation to Dorothy Day. When she became a mother she realized her own special need for a community beyond her daughter and discovered her special ability to help others through the long loneliness.

Dorothy Day was not a Catholic earth mother simply because of her selfless service to others; the earth mother archetype is far richer than that. Dorothy Day was not Mother Teresa, an unquestioning daughter of the church content to bathe the wounds inflicted by the present system without asking how we might shut off the source of the pain. Daniel Berrigan calls attention to Day's profound inner strength and to the penetrating critique of the status quo, which she came to symbolize simply by being utterly consistent in her refusal to accept war, injustice, and poverty. He compares Day to Christ and Buddha and explains: "At length, all was said and done. So she stood there, or sat down, like Christ, like Buddha." Dorothy Day stayed put; her movement revolved around her. And yet, as Berrigan insists, staying put can be a revolutionary act. He thanks Day for paving the way for the destruction of the nuclear reactors at King of Prussia, Pennsylvania, in September 1980. "The best tribute that we could offer Dorothy is that we too would stand somewhere, or sit down."[50]

What can Dorothy Day's life teach us about women's power in the Roman Catholic Church? It shows that it is possible for a woman to form and lead a decentralized movement for peace and justice, even disagree with her bishop on occasion, and still remain a faithful, devout Roman Catholic. It confirms the fact that the hierarchical model of authority does not exhaust the possibilities open to the church; the extended family model might be more compatible with a strong stand on peace and social justice. Implicitly, Day's experience illustrates the wisdom and practicality of confronting the issue rather than the authorities whenever possible. Granted, Dorothy Day had no trouble making this clear-cut distinction; for her, the church's authority structure was not one of the issues.

The power Dorothy Day wielded as earth mother bears little resemblance to the type of power required to run a tight ship or a competitive corporation. From Day's maternal style of leadership we learn that movements are best served by leaders who, like the best mothers, train others to move beyond them to claim their own power and vision. When Dorothy Day died, many wondered whether the Catholic Workers could survive without her. Clearly they have, and subsequent editors of *The Catholic Worker* have self-consciously set out to move beyond Day and Maurin in order to remain within the spirit of the original movement. From Dorothy Day the Catholic Workers (and others inspired by her example) have learned to seek the source of renewal and growth within their own communities and within themselves rather than asking for direction from above or without. The power epitomized by Dorothy Day, the Catholic earth mother, is the kind that empowers others rather than entrenching itself. Ultimately it is the only kind of power that can be passed on with confidence to future generations of women (and men).

Notes

1. The earliest organized drive for Roman Catholic women's ordination began with St. Joan's Alliance, an English Catholic women's suffrage society established in 1911 and rededicated in 1959, to promoting women's rights within the church. In 1963 the Alliance formally petitioned the Second Vatican Council to discuss women's ordination.

2. Jim Naughton's *Catholics in Crisis: The Rift Between American Catholics and Their Church* (New York: Penguin Books, 1996) examines the pain and fragmentation that this polarization can cause on the local parish level.

3. See translation in *Commonweal* 121 (17 June 1994): pp. 4–5.

4. *Commonweal* has been especially attentive to Dorothy Day over the years. Some important articles on Day which have appeared elsewhere include: a symposium on Day and the Catholic Worker movement in *America* 127 (11 November 1972); Dwight MacDonald, "Profiles: The Foolish Things of the World," *The New Yorker* (4 October 1952): pp. 37–56 and (11 October 1952), pp. 37–52; Colman McCarthy, "On Dorothy Day," *The New Republic* 168 (24 February 1973): pp. 30–33; several articles in *Cross Currents* 39 (Fall 1984): pp. 257–310.

5. Biographical information on Day's life is drawn from William D. Miller, *Dorothy Day: A Biography* (San Francisco: Harper and Row, 1982); Mel Piehl, *Breaking Bread: The Catholic Worker and the Origin of Catholic Radicalism in America* (Philadelphia: Temple University Press, 1982); Dorothy Day, *The Long Loneliness: An Autobiography* (San Francisco: Harper and Row, 1952; rpt., 1981).

6. Day, *Long Loneliness*, p. 20.

7. Ibid., p. 21.

8. Ibid., p. 23.

9. Ibid., p. 37.

10. For a discussion of the context in which Dorothy Day found herself see Leslie Fishbein, "The Failure of Feminism in Greenwich Village before World War I," *Women's Studies* 9 (1982): pp. 227–89.

11. New York: Viking Press, 1951, p. 69.

12. Miller, p. 110.

13. Ibid. Day revealed this to a companion in February 1974. Miller (p. 111) maintains that Day recognized some of herself in O'Neill's character, Josie Hogan, in *Moon for the Misbegotten*.

14. See Day's account of the prison experience in *The Long Loneliness*, pp. 72–83.

15. New York: Albert and Charles Boni, 1924.

16. Miller, pp. 112–13.

17. Day, *Long Loneliness*, p. 134.

18. Ibid., p. 136.

19. Ibid., p. 165.

20. Leo R. Ward, *Catholic Life U.S.A.* (St. Louis: B. Herder, 1959), p. 189.

21. Nancy L. Roberts, "Building a New Earth: Dorothy Day and 'The Catholic Worker'," *The Christian Century* 97 (10 December 1980): p. 1217; *The New York Times* (1 December 1980, D12) estimated 85,000 subscribers while *Newsweek* (15 December 1980), p. 75 supplied another figure: 90,000.

22. Piehl, p. 64.

23. Quoted in Abigail McCarthy, "Confronting Dorothy Day," *Commonweal* 104 (13 May 1977): p. 297.

24. Piehl, p. 65.

25. Ibid.

26. Quoted in McCarthy, p. 318.

27. Quoted in Piehl, p. 91.

28. Quoted in Piehl, p. 92.

29. Quoted by Dwight MacDonald in "Profiles," *The New Yorker* (4 October 1952): p. 39.

30. Daniel Berrigan, "Introduction" to *Long Loneliness*, p. xiv.

31. Doris Grumbach, "Father Church and the Motherhood of God," *Commonweal* 93 (11 December 1970): pp. 268–69.

32. Quoted by Miller, pp. 211–12.

33. Quoted by Piehl, p. 83.

34. See Piehl, pp. 155–56.

35. "My Life at the Catholic Worker," *Commonweal* 107 (20 June 1980), p. 364.

36. Berrigan, "Introduction" to *Long Loneliness*, p. xix.

37. McCarthy, p. 318.

38. Piehl, p. 80.

39. Day, *Long Loneliness*, p. 187.

40. Quoted in Miller, p. 270.

41. Day, *Long Loneliness*, p. 186.

42. Ibid., p. 185.

43. See, for example, *The Boston Globe* (6 October 1983): p. 2. On Harrington's experience with Day and the Catholic Workers see Harrington's *Fragments of the Century* (New York: Saturday Review Press/E.P. Dutton, 1972, 1973), pp. 17–23; Piehl, pp. 172–78.

44. Wilfrid Sheed, "Dorothy Day," *The Nation* 231 (20 December 1980), p. 661.

45. Quoted by Piehl, p. 81.

46. Sheed, p. 661.

47. Quoted by Cort, p. 365.

48. Garry Wills, *Bare Ruined Choirs: Doubt, Prophesy and Radical Religion* (New York: Dell/Delta, 1974; c 1971, 1972), p. 59.

49. Rosemary Radford Ruether, "Motherearth and the Megamachine: A Theology of Liberation in a Feminine, Somatic and Ecological Perspective," in *Womanspirit Rising: A Feminist Reader in Religion*, eds., Carol P. Christ and Judith Plaskow (San Francisco: Harper and Row, 1979), p. 47.

50. Berrigan, "Introduction" to *Long Loneliness*, pp. xxii–xxiii.

Further Readings

Coles, Robert. *Dorothy Day: A Radical Devotion*. Reading, Mass.: Addison-Wesley/Merloid Lawrence Book, 1987.

Ellsberg, Robert, ed. *By Little and By Little: The Selected Writings of Dorothy Day*. New York: Alfred A. Knopf, 1983.

Forest, Jim. *Love Is the Measure: A Biography of Dorothy Day*. New York: Paulist Press, 1986.

Klejment, Anne and Alice Klejment, eds. *Dorothy Day and the Catholic Worker: A Bibliography and Index*. New York: Garland Publishing Company, 1986.

Merriman, Brigid O'Shea. *Searching for Christ: The Spirituality of Dorothy Day*. Notre Dame: University of Notre Dame Press, 1994.

O'Connor, June E. *The Moral Vision of Dorothy Day: A Feminist Perspective*. New York: Crossroad, 1991.

Roberts, Nancy L. *Dorothy Day and the Catholic Worker*. Albany, N.Y.: State University of New York Press, 1984.

Ryan, Cheyney. "The Woman Who Burns Herself for Christ." *Hypatia* 9 (spring 1994): pp. 21–39.

For the history of the discussion of women's power in the American Catholic community, see Mary Jo Weaver, *New Catholic Women: A Contemporary Challenge to Traditional Religious Authority*, 2nd ed. (Bloomington: University of Indiana Press, 1995).

3

Religious Responsibility and Community Service: The Activism of Victoria Way DeLee

ROSETTA E. ROSS

From the period of slavery through modern times, black religious women in the United States have viewed duty to God as the principal impetus to "work" for their communities. In the mid-nineteenth century, Sojourner Truth felt called by God to speak against slavery. Immediately after emancipation of slaves, many educated black women felt "a strong conviction of duty" to go South to teach newly freed persons. Around the turn of the century, Nannie Helen Burroughs and the National Baptist Convention's Women's Convention linked social and spiritual regeneration with racial advancement. During the U.S. civil rights era, religious black women were leaders and followers in various crusades of the movement. Today, Marian Wright Edelman campaigns for children's rights because of values learned from the religious context in which she was reared.[1] All of these women lived out their response to God by working for the African American community and for the larger society.

Although most U.S. citizens direct ordinary attention to making life more comfortable, historically much of the black community has had to think about how its members will survive at all. Commenting on the legacy of racialized slavery in the United States, Audre Lorde observes that, for the majority of their history in the United States, black women were not meant to survive as human

ROSETTA E. ROSS received her Ph.D. in Religious Ethics from Emory University and is currently Associate Professor of Christian Ethics at United Theological Seminary of the Twin Cities in New Brighton, Minnesota. She has published articles on the civil rights movement, public life, and women's lives.

Author's Note: An earlier version of this article was published in *Living Responsibly in Community* (Lanham: University of America, 1997) edited by Frederick E. Glennon, Gary S. Hauk, and Darryl M. Trimiew.

beings.[2] Because their everyday lives included conventional and institutional repression of African Americans, these women's ordinary activities became hard work. This work included anti-slavery agitation, educating and structuring basic survival for freed blacks, orienting and resettling northern migrants, civil rights activism, and various other forms of civic or political activity. Relying on what they believed was God's provision, the women demonstrated fidelity to God through persistent practice, often taking risks to change conventions that hindered their survival and well-being.

Community leader and civil rights activist Victoria Way DeLee is another example of a woman in this tradition. Responding to what she felt was God calling her to "help those who can't help themselves,"[3] DeLee worked to relieve suffering in her local community. She initially led protests, boycotts, and pickets, and later organized voter registration campaigns and school desegregation efforts to improve life for African Americans and other poor people in Dorchester County, South Carolina. Coming of age in the rural South amidst the post-Reconstruction legacy of racial repression and subjugation, DeLee's social activism was derived from her Christian upbringing and fueled by religious fervor. By her early twenties, she saw civil rights work as God's work. This essay explicates the context of DeLee's emerging social consciousness and interprets her voter registration and school desegregation activities as exemplifying a tradition of religious black women who respond to God by working for their communities.

RACIAL OPPRESSION AND BIRTH OF THE CIVIL RIGHTS MOVEMENT

Victoria DeLee registered to vote in 1947 at age twenty-two. By this action, she participated in the work of breaking down barriers to black social and political participation that had been the norm in South Carolina since a formal statute of 1716 restricted voting to "every white man (and no other)." In addition to black people, this statute denied the franchise to "non-Christians, the poor (those either without freehold of at least 50 acres or not liable to pay fifty pounds in taxes), apprentices, covenanted servants, 'any seafaring or other transient man,' and, of course, [white] women."[4] Although general suffrage for adult men had been established in the United States by the U.S. Constitution since 1870, voting rights for African Americans were still obstructed by exclusionary race, class, and gender statutes when DeLee registered.

This was particularly true in the South. Post Civil War barriers to black enfranchisement and full political participation had been initiated along with Reconstruction in South Carolina. By the turn of the century these barriers were consolidated. After the Civil War, South Carolina's provisional governor Benjamin Franklin Perry convened an 1865 Reconstruction Constitutional Convention that "adopted laws limiting voting and office-holding to free white men at least twenty-one years of age." During that same year, the state legislature adopted "an elaborate Black Code" which relegated African Americans to a status similar to that during slavery. The 1866 Voting Rights Act, one means by which the U.S. Congress responded to such politically regressive action, did not long abate growing barriers to black enfranchisement. By 1868 the Ku Klux Klan became active across the state, and political violence or other intimidation was common.[5] This backlash against Reconstruction gains established a political climate that made way for electing "Pitchfork" Ben Tillman as governor in 1890.

Tillman entered office with an agenda of securing white supremacy. He pledged this in his inaugural address: "The whites have absolute control of government, and we intend at any hazard to retain it." With Southern black populations swollen from slavery, the Fifteenth Amendment to the United States Constitution that enfranchised black men had been producing significant political election gains for African Americans. In response, Tillman and the state legislature replaced election of local government officials with gubernatorial or legislative appointments. The legislature also revised the state's constitution, requiring a poll tax, literacy test, and (harking back to the 1716 restriction) property ownership for voter registration. Other laws fashioned to disfranchise African Americans included a statute resulting in loss of voting rights for offenses "that blacks were especially prone to commit,"[6] and a law of 1882 required that votes be thrown out when voters failed to place "special ballots" in special boxes "placed in every polling place for each office on the ballot."[7]

Legal and conventional repression in South Carolina continued well into the 1950s. After the 1944 Supreme Court decision striking down the Texas white primary,[8] South Carolina Governor Olin Johnson called a special session of the state's legislature to enact statutes that would ensure continued disfranchisement of African Americans. Repression especially was directed toward the National Association for the Advancement of Colored People (NAACP), the primary formal means of black advancement against racial repression from 1918 through the late 1950s. In 1956, legislation in South Carolina made "unlawful the employment by the state, school district or any country or municipality . . . any member of the National Association for the Advancement of Colored People, and to provide penalties for violations." That same year, the state's legislature appointed a committee to investigate NAACP activity at historically black South Carolina State College. During its next session the legislature passed a bill requiring each organized NAACP chapter to file with the Secretary of State "a list showing the names and addresses of all its members."[9] Legislative actions against the NAACP were complemented by informal local practices. In 1957, for example, the South Carolina Council on Human Relations reported use of economic pressure in Orangeburg and Clarendon counties to discourage NAACP participation.[10]

As was the case also with general southern repression of the NAACP, South Carolina's anti-NAACP sentiment resulted from judicial victories over racial restraints in the state. In 1946 in two separate NAACP cases Federal District Court Judge J. Waites Waring ruled South Carolina's white primary unconstitutional. This decision and others like it across the South opened the way for nascent civil rights activity. The year after Waring's ruling, the Reverend R. B. Adams, an NAACP member and the young pastor of St. John Baptist Church in Ridgeville, urged his congregants to seek voter registration. On one Sunday of that year, Victoria and her husband S. B. DeLee decided to follow Adams's direction, and on the following Monday they traveled by train to the county seat in St. George where Victoria registered. Although Adams's prompting was the immediate cause of her registering, DeLee's decision also arose from her seeing in enfranchisement a possibility for changing local practices of repression which long had troubled her. The vision and determination to change the way things were had arisen in DeLee already when she was a child.

COMING OF AGE IN RURAL SOUTHERN RACIAL OPPRESSION

Virginia Way was born the daughter of Essie Way on April 8, 1925, in the town of Ridgeville, Dorchester County, South Carolina. During Victoria's childhood, the Way family (including Essie, grandmother Lucretia, Victoria, her two sisters, and a male cousin) lived as tenants of a local white farmer. Essie worked as a maid for her landlord and other local white households to support the family. Lucretia Way reared the children, worked as a field hand, and further supplemented family income by taking in laundry.[11] Victoria was greatly affected by seeing her mother and grandmother labor relentlessly for as little as 25 cents per day. Remembering those times, she says, "Well, really, we were treated like slaves, because when the white people came in and said that you had to go to work, you had to work whether you wanted to or not. . . . [I]t was in my mind from a little girl when my grandmomma and them were being treated like that, I used to say 'well, one day I'm gonna fix it.'"[12]

DeLee's vision to "fix it" went beyond her family to her community. Along with the circumstances of her mother and grandmother, conventional violence against African Americans in Dorchester County influenced her profoundly. "They used to, back there in them days lynch people," she says. "They'd hang 'em. If a black person did something, they would take them in the woods and hang 'em."[13] DeLee recalls standing by as a child when the prospect of violence was used to intimidate her grandmother. She recounts a white landowner named Bub Cummings riding an ox by her grandmother's house specifically to tell Lucretia of his chance to have the first shot at a black man, Mr. Fogle, who was killed in the nearby town of Dorchester for allegedly whistling at a white woman. "I can see it as if it was yesterday," DeLee says.

> We were, my grandmomma had this beautiful flower yard in the front of her house, you know. And she had all these rose bushes and stuff. And we were out there in the rose bushes. I can remember that it was sometime in the year, that she was in, we was in the flower yard. And he call out to my grandmomma. And he say, "Mom Cretia." 'Cause they would call her Mom Cretia or Aunt Cretia. It was Mom Cretia. And, uh, he tell her, "Come here." He say, "I'm in a hurry. I got to go 'cause they done promise me that if I git there they gonna give me the first shot at that niggah. And I'm going to git the first shot!" He was gon' be in the group of the first people to shoot.

After the lynching was over, DeLee says, Cummings returned to further intimidate her grandmother by recounting details of the event:

> And all she could do was just sit there and listen. She wasn't allowed to say nothing back to him. And when he was gone, she just cried, and she just prayed and was crying how awful it was. And they said they [castrated him] and stuffed them in his mouth while they shoot him. And they shoot him piece by piece. . . . That thing stuck in my mind. Here this man being killed, and I overheard. He didn't care. He talked right in front of us. "If you do so and so, we'll have you killed, you niggers this and that. . . ." That's all they would call us back there was niggers, you know, they didn't try to butter it up at all.[14]

This violence and intimidation made a lasting impression on Victoria, as did Victoria's own personal encounters with racial repression and violence.

Although she knew she would have to become an adult before she could take significant action towards change, Victoria began rebelling in small ways at a young age. When children in the Way family were old enough to work, they went to the fields with Lucretia. "[W]henever we would work in the field," she says, "my grandmomma then tell us what to do. Soon as her back would turn, I'd go contrary to it, and let the white man see that I could, I wasn't gonna be doing it the way he wanted it." Seeking to assert her own will in this way caused another event which left an indelible impression on Victoria's mind. She says,

> One particular time, this white man told me that I was nabbing the cotton, leaving it

back there, and I said, "I didn't." And he said, "Yes you is." And he told my grandmomma what I was doing, and he hauled off and slapped me out. That man knocked me in my head 'til I fell out. . . . And my grandmomma had to beat me, had to beat me until this man was satisfied. . . He said, "That's enough. That's enough." I'll never forget it.

Obviously, Lucretia Way's action was an effort to protect Victoria from further violence or even death. Reflecting on the event years later, DeLee says, "My grandmomma just, had to just beat me, 'cause she know if not he could, would have killed me." At that time, however, Victoria was not able to accept her grandmother's actions. "She told me afterwards, when we come home," Victoria says, "but I don't think right then I had ever forgiven her for beatin' me for that white man, 'cause I felt like she didn't had to do it. And I told her so. I said, 'I don't see where you had to beat me to satisfy him. I wouldn't beat one of my children to satisfy him.' She say, 'But you don't know. If I didn't, he would have killed you.'"[15]

Victoria's experiences also parallel those of other black girls growing up in the era. Katie G. Cannon identifies what Lucretia Way sought to do as instilling "functional prudence," the ability to maintain a zeal for life while recognizing the dangers of racism. Describing the lessons that southern African American elders sought to teach children during the early twentieth century, Cannon shows how Zora Neale Hurston and Hurston's fictional character Janie's elders sought to inculcate functional prudence because certain attitudes could pose threats to their physical survival. Both Hurston and her character Janie were reprimanded or punished by grandmothers (and even fathers) for having "too much spirit," a "sassy tongue," a "stiff neck." Maya Angelou tells of a similar experience in one segment of her autobiography. Recounting events following her interaction with two white women in a local Arkansas shop, Angelou records her grandmother's response: "'Mr. Coleman's granddaughter, Miss June, just called from the General Merchandise Store.' [Momma's] voice quaked a little. 'She said you was downtown showing out.' . . . I decided to explain and let her share in the glory. I began, 'It was the principle of the thing, Momma'—I didn't even see the hand rising, and suddenly it had swung down hard against my cheek. . . . 'You think . . . these crazy people won't kill you? You think them lunatic cracker boys won't try to catch you in the road and violate you? You think because of your all-fired principle some of the men won't feel like putting their white sheets on and riding over here to stir up trouble?' . . . Momma's intent to protect me had caused her to hit me in the face, a thing she had never done and to send me away to where she thought I'd be safe."[16]

In spite of Lucretia Way's intent, Victoria understood efforts to curb her will as more oppression. In addition to racial repression, she says, "my grandmomma was so strict on me. She beat me all the time, and try to keep me straight." These circumstances and Victoria's "spirited" perspective led to her early marriage so she could begin to "get what I wanted done." By the time she was fourteen, Victoria had developed a plan to run away from her grandmother's defensive severity in order to strike out violently against whites. "[White] people used to do a lot of fox hunting and coon hunting," she says, "and I was hoping when they ganged up together hunting foxes, somehow or another I would be able to kill a good many of them. That was my plan." Fortunately, this plan was thwarted by Victoria's best friend who convinced her that getting married would provide freedom from her grandmother. Victoria thought this was a good idea, and at age fifteen, on December 21, 1940, she married her suitor, S. B. DeLee.[17] Once she entered civil rights activity, DeLee experienced a refocusing of her energy away from violent retaliation back toward her original goal "to fix it" for black people some day.

RELIGIOUS INFLUENCES IN DELEE'S EARLY LIFE

At Lucretia's insistence, regular church participation became a part of Victoria's early life. Whenever Lucretia went to Bethel Methodist Church, she took her four grandchildren with her. "[M]y grandmomma was a church-goer," DeLee recalls. Perhaps pointing to the origin of her later attraction to her current pentecostal denomination, DeLee also says her grandmother practiced holiness. "[W]hen I was raised in the Methodist church, it was clean," she says. "Really and truly my, my grandmomma and those, they was sanctified people. They was so sanctified."[18] Regular family prayer was also a part of DeLee's childhood; Lucretia prayed every evening. However, as a girl, Victoria questioned the efficacy of entreating God for help. DeLee says:

> That's when I learned to pray. My grandmomma always taught me how to pray, but. . . I didn't believe in God all the time. 'Cause, you see my grandmomma say God would fix it. He knowed how. 'N' she would be just prayin' and cryin' all in the night. 'N' then I went to wonderin' what kind of God is that? If he gon' fix it, why would He let the people do what they was doing to her? Why she had to work so hard? Why she work for 25 cents a day? Why we had to go out there and bring a bag of those white people old clothes and stuff home and things like that? And, then, she think God would, she jus' believe in God. I didn't believe in Him. And she would have me down on my knees, she'd be prayin' in the night, teachin' me the Our Father prayer, you know. I'd quote the Our Father prayer with her. And then after we done say the Our Father prayer, then she would pray. Oh, my Lord, and my grandmomma just cry and pray. And I'd be down there jus' cussin' away in my mind. I was sayin' 'Don't you worry, I'll fix it for my grandmomma. I'm gon' fix it.[19]

By the time she was a pre-teen, Victoria became attracted to the active youth usher board at nearby St. John Baptist Church, where she later became a member. Although DeLee says she attended church as a child only because her grandmother compelled her, she continued regular church attendance after her marriage and throughout her life. Her husband, S. B., also was a regular church member at St. John Baptist where the couple met.

DeLee did not immediately give up her dreams of revenge in favor of social and political action, but events following her marriage disposed her to refocus her energy. Especially important among these were the birth of her first child Sonny B. DeLee in 1942 and a compelling sermon that she heard soon after. Recalling her excitement about their son and the sermon, DeLee says:

> [O]oh when that baby born, I had love that baby! You know how, your first baby, ooh. And I went to church that Sunday with my first new baby. And the preacher preached a sermon. I'll never forget that. . . . I think it was all for me. And he was saying, "You could git by, but you wouldn't git away.". . . And I listen at that message. And every time I look at that baby. . . . And he said that whatever them white people do to you. . . God had they number, and He right way they live. And if they didn't git it, they children children children would git it. . . . and then he brought out that whatever *we* do, we might git by, but our children would reap what we sow. . . . And he just went on. And every time I looked at that baby, and looked up, and that preacher jus' went on. And ooh, my

> God, for the first time I see myself. And I say, "Oh, Lord, way should I turn?" 'Cause I already did some things [to whites]. And I still had. . . planned on killin' 'em. I meant to go about and kill some white people just like they had kill all them black people. . . .and when that preacher preached that sermon that Sunday, I got converted to myself right in that church, right there. . . . And I say, "Ooh, there is another way. Uh huh, I can't do that, 'cause my baby gonna reap it. And I love my baby."[20]

Later that day, DeLee walked approximately three miles to Lucretia Way's home to seek her counsel. She says, "I walk and went to my grandmomma house that evenin' and tote that baby. And I told her, and I went and start tellin' her, and I went to cryin'."[21] Lucretia advised DeLee to seek forgiveness:

> I went to my grandmomma, and she said that before God would convert my soul I would have to love the white people. She said, "You got to *mean* it." And, sure enough, the Lord answered my prayer and I started to love white folks. But I stand up all right. I let 'em know that they wasn't going to run over me.[22]

The minister who preached this sermon challenging DeLee to refocus was the same Reverend R. B. Adams who introduced her to voter registration and the NAACP. The DeLees were members of his St. John Baptist Church for nearly thirteen years after their marriage. During the mid-1950s, however, she says, "[t]hey had a big mixed-up in the church,"[23] and the DeLees left. The family next spent a year at Surprise Baptist Church in the nearby town of Dorchester, where some of S.B.'s relatives were members. During their tenure with Surprise Church, Bishop James Ravenel, of the House of God, a pentecostal denomination,[24] began a radio ministry in the Ridgeville area. His messages particularly appealed to the DeLees because he emphasized "holiness." DeLee recalls that, like others attracted to Ravenel's message,

> We just started one Sunday. Everybody was going out to hear him. After he started revival, we went out there to go hear him. It was going on a good while. And we went out there, and he went to teaching in the scriptures. And he went to, and we went to reading, and. . . then our eyes come open, then about holiness. And that you had to be holy.[25]

During one meeting of the revival, DeLee experienced another conversion, saying, "I got saved that night, and I was the happiest woman." The family continued to attend the revival meetings and eventually became a part of Ravenel's ministry. Consequently, Victoria and S. B. DeLee were founding members of the House of God congregation at Ridgeville. DeLee recalls the beginning of their local congregation:

> Bishop Ravenel run [the revival] for seven weeks. . . . And then, we got busy. We just had meeting right there. So we decided to, that we was going to build a church. . . . We built, first, you know, we built it, I call it a little small sanctified church. 'Cause back yonder all sanctified churches used to be, you could pinpoint them out amongst all the rest, because it was just something put together. But, and then after years, we add on. And then a few years back ago, we tore the church down and built a real church. Now we really got a nice church up there now. But, that's how we got with the holiness. And that, as I say, when we find out it was right, we receive the baptism of the Holy Ghost, and then we built this church.[26]

A significant factor in the intensity with which DeLee carried out her activism seems to have been the combination of her natural assertiveness with the spiritual independence and compulsion she experienced after she entered the House of God holiness denomination.[27] Both of these undergirded her consistently expressed dissent against oppressive local laws and conventions.

DELEE, THE CHURCH, AND VOTER REGISTRATION

DeLee entered the public arena as a local activist, seeking to improve the welfare of African Americans or to maintain traditions integral to their survival. As early as 1948 she expressed concern about education of community children by leading a protest against the county school board to prevent firing a teacher whom DeLee valued as someone who cared for "all the children."

JohnEtta Grant had begun her teaching career at Clay Hill Elementary School in Ridgeville. Grant, a native of Charleston, owned a car and commuted twenty-six miles from Charleston to Ridgeville to teach. That Grant did not board in the town where she taught was unusual. It was even more unusual when other teachers from Charleston stopped boarding to commute with Grant. After this turn of events, the town resident with whom teachers traditionally boarded contacted local authorities, who told Grant that she must move into the county or lose her job. Upon learning of this, DeLee organized parents who together travelled by train to the county school board meeting in St. George.[28] DeLee recalls:

> [T]he trustee board went to try to fire one of our teachers because she wouldn't board out—Every teacher had come into Dorchester County then, we had the little schools out here, they would make them, they had to board in this area where they teach school at. And so this woman. . .she had a car and she would drive from Charleston here. And. . .Mrs. Banister didn't like it because the woman wouldn't board with Mrs. Banister. See she wasn't gon' board with nobody. That's why [she] bought a car. . . .her name was Miss. . .JohnEtta Grant. JohnEtta Grant was that black teacher. And, boy, she was one to stand up. She was the teacher that first started to teaching all my children. My oldest son. . .she taught him. And she taught all the children. . . .So they went to fire this teacher.
>
> And I got all the parents to come together, and we had a meeting one night. And we baffled that school board. And that's the first time blacks ever stand up in this area to white people. And we got on that school board, and then they couldn't fire the woman. So that was the first thing that really, to me we accomplished.[29]

For DeLee, perhaps equally as important as the protest was her experience and memory of this event as the first time African Americans of the area challenged restrictive racial practices. Experiencing the success of African Americans working together in this instance surely influenced her use of cooperative community activity during later years of her work. She saw the event as a success of the community, saying, it was the first thing that "*we* accomplished."

Victoria DeLee's entrance into the civil rights movement resulted in large part from her desire to vent anger she felt about racial repression. Although her faith challenged DeLee to reconsider the meaning of resistance, she maintained her desire "to fix" the oppressive circumstances under which African Americans lived. In view of her early rejection of the idea that God would make a real difference in her grandmother's life, it is perhaps ironic that, after discarding plans for violent reprisals against whites, DeLee later found a powerful outlet for channeling her energy through preaching about voter registration in a rural black church.

DeLee was twenty-two years old when she began civil rights work in 1947 by obtaining her own voter registration certificate. Let us recall that Reverend R. B. Adams, pastor of St. John Baptist Church, had preached about civil rights and had urged his congregation to attempt voter registration. When Adams's promptings caught DeLee's attention, she and her husband traveled fifteen miles by train to St. George, the Dorchester County seat, where registration was held. DeLee recalls that when they arrived there was a room full of blacks who "were given permission to register." An attendant was moving the process along by calling out "Next!" whenever another person was allowed to go to the inner office for registration. The DeLees moved into the room and sat with the crowd. When the attendant said "next," Victoria rose to her feet. Upon seeing her rise, the person who should have been next sat down because he thought he was out of turn. DeLee says, "But I got on up. I went like I was next. When I went in there to register, [The registrar] said, 'who brought you?' I said, 'I brought myself.' I had on a black overcoat because I was pregnant with Vicky. I'll never forget. I had both of my hands in my pockets."

Because she had come without "permission," the registration agent told DeLee he could not register her. She insisted that he would, and the two argued back and forth. Finally, standing in front of the door and keeping one hand in her pocket as if she had a weapon, DeLee told the registrar that he would not leave the room if she were not given her "civil rights." The agent finally complied, telling DeLee not to let others know of her success. DeLee said she would not consent to such a thing, and upon leaving the room she "went right on out there and went to talking right loud to everybody" about the registration.[30]

Empowered and encouraged by her own success, DeLee came to regard voter registration as one vehicle by which she could make a difference. "I'll never forget that day!" she says. "That was a good feeling day. I felt so good that I got, made that man registered me!" She became tenacious in efforts to register other persons. "Then I went out, and I start talking to people," she recalls; "I start tellin' 'em 'bout my registration certificate. I come back to the church, and I get up in the church and tell the preacher how I get my registration certificate. And the preacher went to telling everybody how they must do like I done."

DeLee's memory of her pastor's sanction by telling others to follow her example suggests its importance. Occurring so early in her life, it surely affirmed DeLee's developing sense of her self. Moreover, Reverend Adams clearly felt it significant to encourage DeLee's activism. He introduced DeLee to the South Carolina NAACP Field Secretary, the late Reverend I. DeQuincey Newman. Newman oversaw the NAACP's state registration drive and particularly promoted DeLee's activities. "So when I started working," DeLee says, "then they start to working with me. Oh, I had a lot of help from the outside, you know, to help me work with this."[31] In addition to persuading others to seek registration, DeLee transported persons to registration sites (and to polls), organized applicants for notaries public, and trained and organized other voter registration workers.

DeLee encountered frequent attempts to obstruct her as she registered voters, including various forms of harassment and sometimes physical violence. In 1956, presumably in reaction to NAACP efforts, the White Citizen's Council meeting at Ridgeville Elementary School asked South Carolina Governor George B. Timmerman, Jr., to stop NAACP activity in the state. Over 200 persons attended this meeting.[32] During the next two years the state legislature and county legislative delegations enacted restrictive statutes which significantly inhibited NAACP work.

Throughout the decade, state and local statutes and conventions severely limited voter registration efforts. At one point DeLee became so frustrated with obstacles to black voter registration that "she took two carloads of twenty people" to the Justice Department in Washington to seek federal assistance. She told one reporter:

> We had just enough money to buy gas and have one hamburger and a drink on the way there and back. I came to Washington, and brother, did I raise said [sic]. I wanted them to send some federal men down to help register voters. They said, "go home, Mrs. DeLee and we'll do something" and I said "the only way I'll understand is if you send someone." They didn't come for a week so I went back myself and went from door to door in the Justice Department and told them if they didn't send someone I'd bring everybody up there.[33]

The Justice Department responded by sending several personnel to oversee voter registration activity in three South Carolina counties, including Dorchester, where persons had complained about opposition to black registration. Justice Department activity in the state caused reaction at the highest levels. Responding to the probes in South Carolina, Governor Ernest F. Hollings sought to protect "the state's sovereignty and [said] that the 'harassment' that the people of Clarendon, Dorchester and Williamsburg counties have been put through by the FBI is going to stop."[34]

DeLee persevered against opposition, and when needed, improvised in other ways to achieve success. In 1960, responding to repression of the NAACP, DeLee founded the Dorchester Voter's League. Through the Dorchester Voter's League, she continued coordinating voter registration and other county civil rights activities. After years of persistence, black voter registration increased significantly. By 1958, 412 African Americans of Dorchester County were registered to vote. This was only 7.2 percent of the county's total registered voters.[35] However, in 1968, 4,556 African Americans were registered. This represented an increase to 33.5 percent of total county voters.[36]

DELEE AND SCHOOL DESEGREGATION

As DeLee continued to register voters she encountered varieties of civil rights practice, including school desegregation efforts. The major school desegregation activity in South Carolina began with the Clarendon County suit, one among the several decided in the 1954 Brown ruling. Initially filed in Federal District Court on May 16, 1950, the primary purpose of the Clarendon case was to improve education provided for black children. Originating in 1949 as an attempt to secure bus transportation for black students, the case grew into an effort to desegregate schools:

> Distressed by the evident inferiority of the facilities provided for their children, Negro parents filed a petition with the County board of education in November, 1949, asking for equalization of educational opportunities. . . . As it became increasingly evident that no steps were being taken by the authorities to bring the Negro schools up to the standard of those maintained for white children, the decision was reached to make a frontal attack upon the segregated schools.[37]

Even though the Clarendon case was among those decided in the Brown decision, South Carolina continued to resist integration. It was at least fifteen years later before any semblance of full desegregation occurred across the state. One year after Brown, Governor George Bell Timmerman declared, "South Carolinians 'are determined to resist integration' of the races in the public schools. . . . 'There shall be no compulsory racial mixing in our state.'"[38] Furthermore, South Carolina's delegation to the 1955 White House Conference on Education, arguing that integration would disrupt the state's past progress in education, presented a report from the state saying "public schools will not be operated in South Carolina on a racially integrated basis."[39] In further resistance to the Brown decision the state's legislature appointed a special unit, the State School Committee of Segregation, headed by State Senator L. Martin Gresette, to ensure the continuation of segregation. By 1960, the Committee of Segregation recommended, and the legislature approved, a statute "repealing specific requirements for segregation in South Carolina." The strategy of this legislation was to eliminate "a major point on which school integration suits [had] been brought into Federal Court."[40]

Over the next five years, various legislative actions frustrated desegregation. Even though the state was under fire to submit integration plans for each of its 108 school districts to the U.S. Office of Education, by the 1965 school year only 38 districts had approved compliance plans. Dorchester County Districts One and Three were among four districts which had not filed any compliance plans by 1965. Moreover, Dorchester County Districts One and Three turned away thirteen parents who took their children for the opening day of school that year.[41]

The DeLees initiated desegregation activities in Dorchester District Three in 1964 when they attempted to enroll two of their children at Ridgeville Elementary School. Other parents later joined them. However, school district officials repeatedly resisted these efforts by allowing only a few students to be received at any given time. By March 1966, Dorchester County Three submitted an acceptable voluntary desegregation plan.[42] Dorchester's plan, like that of most other districts in the state, was called freedom of choice. Placing the burden of desegregation on the African Americans, the plan allowed parents to choose which schools their children would attend. Under the burden of full responsibility for initiating and carrying through desegregation efforts, black parents and children were caught between the national requirements and local segregationist sentiment, which caused economic and physical retaliation for desegregation activity. Freedom of choice began for Dorchester County District Three in spring 1966. Fearing severe reprisals, most black parents and children in Dorchester County and others across the state took the physically, financially, and emotionally safer route of leaving things as they were.

In March 1966, DeLee led the list of plaintiffs in a suit seeking to completely desegregate the district's schools, filing in behalf of her sons Van and Elijah.[43] The effort to desegregate county schools took more than five additonal years of court battles, strategizing, and protesting. While none of DeLee's activity had been met with enthusiasm from white county residents, her desegregation work met exceptional resistance.[44] During this period the DeLee home was frequently shot into and at one point was completely destroyed by fire. DeLee says, when

> we went to integrate the schools, that's when the whites really started trying to kill us, [even though] they were trying to kill me for the longest. Before that house burned down, it would look like a polka dot dress where the bullet holes from where they would shoot in the house. . . . One night I was sitting in the chair, and I was rocking the baby. When I rocked back like that, the bullet went right through by my face and went in the wall. . . and just missed me. . . . And the sheriff couldn't find nobody, couldn't catch nobody.[45]

In addition to initiating court action, DeLee led demonstrations, encouraged other parents to oppose segregation, and frequently sought to meet with school district officials.[46] She also engaged organizations which could assist her work. After filing suit on behalf of her sons in March, on April 2 DeLee attended the Conference on Education Desegregation sponsored by the S.C. Advisory Committee to the U.S. Civil Rights Commission. This conference encouraged activists and suggested strategies for achieving desegregation.[47]

As DeLee continued to resist school segregation, the scope of her activity expanded to include Native Americans. She encouraged local Native American parents to join desegregation activity. Until that time Native American children had attended a third county school system geographically located within District Three. Although the district's 1966 approved desegregation plan asserted freedom of choice, when Native American parents sought to exercise choice, "those choices were uniformly denied[,] even though the choices of black children were uniformly granted." When officials refused Native American enrollment by freedom of choice, DeLee organized "demonstrations against [their] having to attend [the] inadequate school." Following several days of protests, the district superintendent agreed to admit fifteen Native American children "on the basis that that number would not overcrowd the white school."[48]

Although the district asserted freedom of choice plan, when the group sought an order requiring the district to admit all Native American children who chose to enter the white schools, Presiding Judge Robert Hemphill prevented full exercise of that choice by Native Americans. Hemphill "announced that he had 'heard' that there had been some demonstrations and that he wanted to make it clear that 'there will be peace in the valley.' He stated several times his willingness to cite these people in contempt and to have a marshall sent down to arrest them." Hemphill enjoined further demonstrations and issued an order upholding the superintendent's decision to admit only fifteen Native American children.[49] In addition to enjoining demonstrations, Hemphill acted to suppress DeLee's participation in further desegregation efforts in other ways. When she went with Native American parents to enroll the fifteen children in Ridgeville Elementary School, marshals arrested her for disobeying the demonstration injunction. Judge Hemphill placed DeLee under a $10,000 bond and ordered her to show why she should not be held in contempt of court.

DeLee and others continued desegregation work, however, and because it progressed so slowly they also demonstrated beyond the state. By 1969, only 10 percent of black students attended white schools, and no white students attended black schools in District Three. That year the U.S. Department of Health, Education, and Welfare (HEW) set the fall as the deadline for full school desegregation. At the same time, White House news reports said HEW could relax desegregation guidelines to give schools with special problems additional time.[50] Responding to these reports, South Carolina and Mississippi field workers for the American Friends Service Committee organized a multi-state grassroots bus caravan to Washington to protest relaxation plans. Dissatisfied with desegregation progress in Dorchester County, DeLee joined the caravan.[51] As a participant in this protest, she expressed her disappointment with the federal government's slowdown first to Jerris Leonard, Assistant Attorney General for Civil Rights, and later to Attorney General John Mitchell. The passionate posture through which DeLee presented herself to Mitchell was captured in a photograph which presented the protest as a reminder to the nation of the problems continuing in the South.[52] When she returned home, DeLee encountered threatening letters, phone calls, and other harassment as a result of her participation.[53] In spite of consistent attempts by

DeLee and others, schools in Dorchester County District Three were not completely desegregated until 1971.

THE COMMUNITY CONTEXT OF DELEE'S DORCHESTER COUNTY WORK

In spite of DeLee's very strong role as leader, her successes would not have been possible apart from the support, cooperation, and complementary vision of many members of the local community. DeLee's work reflected the community's moral perspectives and social aspirations, and much of her story reveals the community's story. DeLee acknowledges the importance of this support and the parallel vision of community members to accomplishments in the county. Successes came about, she asserts, because the community worked together. "I didn't make the change by myself," DeLee says, "'cause if it wasn't for they help, and God in front leadin' all of us, we wouldn't have made this change in Dorchester County."[54] DeLee has observed that black county residents were not unanimous in their feelings about the social system. However, those who felt as she did supported the work. "[J]ust like you got 'em now, you got quite a few different groups of people, types of people," she says, "and one of 'em was at that time the men folks. . . who wanted some freedom and justice. . . . They backed me up 100 percent."[55] Reflecting the interdependence necessary to national civil rights successes, the interplay of DeLee's individual goals with those of her community is apparent through groups' and individuals' willingness to act with her.

Black churches and black church networks were among the most meaningful supporters of protest activity in the country. As was the case throughout the movement, civil rights practice was compatible with the religious belief of many civil rights participants. This affinity yielded the leadership, support, and camaraderie which in turn enhanced the individual, community, regional, and national vitality of the movement. For DeLee, this affinity was evident through her long-term interaction with three ministers, as well as through various relationships with other religious movement workers and leaders. R. B. Adams, the Baptist minister and NAACP member who first planted the seed for DeLee's enfranchisement and encouraged her efforts, inaugurated her interaction with state NAACP leadership. The late I.D. Newman, United Methodist minister and former South Carolina NAACP Field Secretary, encouraged DeLee and coordinated much of her local, regional, and statewide activity with his own efforts to realize state NAACP goals. Bishop A. Ravenel, DeLee's first pastor in the House of God Church, continued support of her activity as did Adams.

DeLee recognized the benefit of this congruity of religious faith and practice. She says that "the faith that I had in God" brought her motivation and energy. "I always stuck to the church. . . because I was brought up in the church, and then after I got married, I still stuck with the church," she says.[56] In addition, DeLee was aware of the positive interaction of her faith and practice with the religious belief and practice of others. She says,

> When I left from the Baptist Church, I went to the House of God Holiness Church. And God fix it so the leadership that I had there. . . Bishop Ravenel was the type of minister. . . believed in standing up and fighting for what you want. He believed in the NAACP. . . . and he never discouraged me.

Furthermore, DeLee saw the significance of having a religious community to support her work.

> And then, another thing, because if you know yourself, and . . . if you're going to a

church, and you are doing something and the people approve of what you are doing and every once in a while they praise you, it makes you feel good at, you know, and you go on doing it. And Bishop Ravenel was good at that. He would always say, "Sister DeLee is, we got to respect her for her leadership because [of] what she is doing to help her people . . ." and this and that and the other. And it always was something to encourage me. He never talked anything negligent about me. . . .[57]

At the local level DeLee relied significantly on ministers and local churches to carry on her activity. She organized the Dorchester County Voters' League through cooperation with ministers who allowed her to address their congregations. Later she held meetings in churches and worked with ministers in various ways to communicate to congregations.

In addition to the support she received from black churches, groups of black community members also supported DeLee's work through the Dorchester County Voters' League. This included looking to her for leadership and adjusting to some of the specific contingencies which caused her to take the lead. One of these was DeLee's gender. DeLee says

the reason [black men] was willing to follow me, men folks would not get as far as I've gotten doing what I was doing. Because they was killing them men folks, see. They would kill black men. They'd throw black mens in jail. They'd beat 'em up, and all this sort of thing. Well, with me, they wouldn't come out, you know, that bold and just do me like that.[58]

Those community members who were sympathetic to her activity saw the possibilities in cooperation, and related to DeLee and each other by undertaking tasks and roles as needed to benefit the group. One quiet supporter was local black mortician Benjamin Waymer. Waymer, who did not participate on the front lines, frequently raised bail for the activists. "Nobody knows all the great things 'bout Benjamin Waymer," DeLee says.

Mr. Waymer played a big part. . . . [W]hen they would throw us in jail. . . wasn't for Benjamin Waymer, I don't know what we would have done. We would have never been able to made the progress that we did. We had no money! And the most of us had no property and whatnot. Benjamin Waymer had his own. . . . And he would bail us out!. . . The blacks in Dorchester County owes Benjamin Waymer a part of they life, because he was in the background. He didn't demonstrate. But. . . whenever we needed money, Benjamin Waymer contributed to us.[59]

Many black women in the community also supported DeLee's efforts and the community's goals. Reflecting both her religious concern about personal holiness and the significance of community solidarity, DeLee reports that local black women followers of the civil rights movement were solidly behind her. "[T]he black women, they supported me so much, because of all my getting around. . . I wouldn't be with women, the most time I would be with men folks. But the women had so much faith and confidence in me," she says, "I've never been accused of nobody's husband, man or nothing. Never has!"[60] However, a few women like Cora DeLee and Anna Williams often were able to support DeLee more closely than some others. They regularly traveled with DeLee around the country to transport persons for registration and voting, encouraged others to support movement activity, attended various meetings, and stood with DeLee in various confrontations with local authorities, often suffering repercussions as she did.

Perhaps the most important personal support DeLee received was from her spouse. S. B. DeLee supported his wife's efforts emotionally, financially, and physically, providing security and camaraderie which undergirded her work. Financially, Mr. DeLee's acceptance and support of his spouse's work is a key factor which literally made it possible for DeLee to participate as a visible leader for change in Dorchester County. Economic intimidation and retaliation was one means by which opponents suffocated black leadership and activity across the South. Mr. DeLee worked for the federal government as a laborer at the Charleston Naval Weapons Station. His employment outside the county at a federal agency insulated the DeLees from local and even state economic reprisals. Furthermore, Victoria DeLee never was employed for wages during the majority of her years of civil rights practice. She was able, however, to transport registrants and voters, to attend movement workshops and meetings across the county and state, to host myriad volunteers in her home (providing them with meals and often shelter), to travel across the county organizing and executing numerous types of work, and to perform a variety of other activities. These practices not only required time away from the couple's ten children, but they also consumed the family's financial resources. Mr. DeLee's work provided the financial means for Mrs. DeLee's practice.

Mr. DeLee's willingness to stay at home released Mrs. DeLee from many mundane family and household responsibilities. Moreover, he guarded the place to which Mrs. DeLee returned daily after battles outside against repression. "Well," DeLee recalls, "my husband always would stay home. He stay home to protect the house." When the two of them were at home during the evening they sometimes alternated, but more often Mr. DeLee alone stayed up awake for long hours to ensure their survival. "[M]e and my husband set to the back door," DeLee says. "He'd set down on the thing like that there in the door," she continued, "in the back where he could look and see the cars coming from this side, and cars coming from that side. . . . 'Cause where we was living at, we'd have to see which way they was coming from."[61] Acknowledging the importance of her spouse's support of her as leader, DeLee says of her husband, "I feel like that I owes him a lot because of all this struggle."[62]

CONCLUSION

Victoria DeLee persisted because she saw "God in front leadin' all of us" in the work.[63] Like other black religious women community activists she saw congruity between responsibility to the community and religious responsibility. DeLee and such other women activists presumed that God supported their mundane practice. This responsibility expresses a "take charge" attitude in the face of conventional obstacles to black community prosperity. The women acted out of their relationship with God, whom they understand as faithful to them, and, therefore, as being with them in all circumstances. They responded to God's faithfulness by being faithful to God through their consistent efforts to preserve their community and to work for a better society.

Notes

1. Dorothy Sterling, *We Are Your Sisters: Black Women in the Nineteenth Century* (New York: Norton, 1984), pp. 151, 265; Evelyn Brooks Higginbotham, *Righteous Discontent: The Women's Movement in the Black Baptist Church 1880–1920* (Cambridge: Harvard, 1993), p. 124; Remarks of Marian Wright Edelman, Annual Meeting, the American Academy of Religion, November 1998, Orlando, Florida.

2. Audre Lorde, *Sister Outsider* (Freedom, California: Crossing, 1984), p. 42.

3. Victoria Way DeLee, interview by author, 8 August 1992, Ridgeville, South Carolina. Tape recording.

4. Laughlin MacDonald, "An Aristocracy of Voters: The Disfranchisement of Blacks in South Carolina," in *South Carolina Law Review* 37 (Summer 1986): p. 557.

5. Alrutheus Ambush Taylor, *The Negro in South Carolina during Reconstruction* (Washington, D.C.: The Association for the Study of Negro Life and History, 1924), pp. 188–89. Taylor reports of the Klan's "whipping and otherwise intimidating inoffensive Negroes and white men solely because of their political affiliations," often resorting to arson and murder. These included the 1868 murder of B.F. Randolf, a black state senator from Orangeburg; James Martin, a white Republican legislator from Abbeville; and freedman Tabby Simpson of Laurenceville and Johnson Glascoe of Newberry.

6. MacDonald, p. 571.

7. MacDonald, pp. 568, 570–72; John Hope Franklin and Alfred A. Moss, Jr., *From Slavery to Freedom: A History of Negro Americans*, sixth ed. (New York: McGraw-Hill, 1988), p. 232ff; I.A. Newby, *Black Carolinians: A History of Blacks in South Carolina from 1895 to 1968* (Columbia: University of South Carolina), p. 282; George Brown Tindall, *South Carolina Negroes: 1877–1900* (Columbia: University of South Carolina), p. 239ff.

8. One means by which southern states disenfranchised African Americans was by legally restricting party politics to whites. In 1944, the Supreme Court ruled in favor of the NAACP which argued that the Texas state law excluding African Americans from Democratic party primaries violated the Fifteenth Amendment. This decision opened the way for challenging white primaries across the South. See John Hope Franklin and Alfred A. Moss, Jr. *From Slavery to Freedom: A History of African Americans*, seventh ed. (New York: McGraw-Hill, 1994), p. 356.

9. S.C. Code of Laws, *Statutes at Large* (1956) #741, 1747; Ibid., #920, 2181; "Propose Open NAACP Roll: Bill Would Require Group to File List," *The State* (25 January 1957); S.C. Code of Laws, *Statutes at Large* (1957), 216, 247.

10. "Monthly Report" (Columbia: The South Carolina Council on Human Relations, March 1957), Southern Regional Council Files, Atlanta University Center Special Collections. Several families from Clarendon County were among those participating in the coterie of cases argued before the Supreme Court by the NAACP resulting in the 1954 Brown decision.

11. Mrs. Victoria Way DeLee, interview by author, 4 July 1988. Tape recording, Ridgeville, South Carolina.

12. Mrs. Victoria Way DeLee, 4 July 1988; Trillin, Calvin, "U.S. Journal: Dorchester County, S.C.—Victoria DeLee—In Her Own Words," *New Yorker* 47 (27 March 1971): p. 86.

13. Ibid.

14. DeLee 4 July 1988; Also, Mr. Thomas H. Ross, interview by author, Dorchester, South Carolina 11 March 1994.

15. DeLee, 4 July 1988; Trillin, p. 86.

16. See Katie G. Cannon, "Moral Wisdom in the Black Women's Literary Tradition," in *The Annual of the Society of Christian Ethics* (1984), pp. 176–77; and "Resources for a Constructive Ethic in the Life and Work of Zora Neale Hurston" in *Journal of Feminist Studies in Religion* I (Spring 1985): p. 46. Also see Maya Angelou, *Gather Together in My Name* (Toronto: Bantam, 1974), pp. 78–79.

17. DeLee, 4 July 1988; Trillin, p. 86.

18. DeLee, 8 August 1992.

19. Ibid.

20. Ibid.; Trillin, p. 86.

21. DeLee, 8 August 1992.

22. Trillin, p. 86.

23. Ibid. DeLee says a dispute about the pastor between factions in the church effectively destroyed the congregation as a place where they felt comfortable to worship.

24. Full name of the denomination is The House of God (the Church of the Living God, the Pillar and Ground of Truth, Inc.). The denomination was established around 1903, by itinerant preacher, now designated denominational founder, elder, and saint, Mary Magdalena Lewis (later Tate) whose pentecostalism may have been connected with the California Azuza Street revivals near the same time. See General Assembly of the Church of the Living God, *The Constitution Government and General Decree Book* (Chattanoga: New and Living Way Publishers, 1923) and *75th Anniversary Yearbook: The Church of the Living God, the Pillar and Ground of the Truth, Inc., 1903–1978.*

25. DeLee, 8 August 1992.

26. Ibid.

27. See Cheryl Townsend Gilkes, "The Role of Women in the Sanctified Church," *The Journal of Religious Thought* 43 (Spring-Summer 1986) for a discussion of independence and fervor of women community workers of the "sanctified" churches.

28. Mrs. JohnEtta Grant Cauthen, interview by author. Telephone tape recording, Charleston, South Carolina, 8 April 1994; DeLee, 4 July 1988.

29. DeLee, 4 July 1988.

30. Ibid.

31. Ibid., Trillin, pp. 86–87.

32. "Question is Posed on Halting NAACP Activity in State," *Charleston News and Courier* (9 July 1956).

33. Heidi Sinick, "Dealing for the Poor," *Washington Post* (8 February 1971), sec. B, p. 1.

34. Mike Daniel, "Hollings Says He'll Stop FBI Probe," *Charleston News and Courier* (29 September 1961), sec. A, p. 1.

35. "Report of the Secretary of State to the General Assembly of South Carolina," in *Reports and Resolutions of South Carolina for Fiscal Year Ending June 30, 1959* (Columbia, S.C.: State Budget and Control Board, 1959), p. 222.

36. "S.C. Voter Registration History: 1956 to 1979," in *Reports and Resolutions of South Carolina for Fiscal Year Ending 1979* (Columbia, S.C.: State Budget and Control Board, 1957), p. 447.

37. South Carolina State Conference of the NAACP, Souvenir Program, "Testimonial Honoring Parent Plaintiffs and Their Children in the Clarendon County Case Against School Segregation," Liberty Hill A.M.E. Church, Summerton, South Carolina, 17 June 1951; quoted in Barbara Woods Aba-Mecha, "Black Woman Activist in Twentieth-Century South Carolina," Ph.D. Diss., Emory University, 1978.

38. "Governor Says S.C. 'To Resist Integration,' " *Richmond News Leader* (4 November 1955).

39. W. D. Workman, Jr., "No Integrated Schools for S.C., Says Report to White House Meet," *Charlotte Observer* (17 November 1955).

40. "Hollings Praises Assembly for Segregation Actions," *The State* (28 May 1960). Also see "Two Attack S.C. Segregation Statute Change," *The State* (5 May 1960).

41. "Negroes Are Turned Away at 2 Dorchester Schools," *Charleston News and Courier* (27 August 1965); Jack Bass, "44 School Districts Open; 41 Have Compliance Plans," *The State* (26 August 1964), sec. D, p. 1.

42. Office of Education, U.S. Department of Health, Education, and Welfare and U.S. Commission on Civil Rights, "Status of School Desegregation in Southern and Border States," an occasional report, March 1966, Southern Regional Council Files, Atlanta University Center Special Collections.

43. *DeLee* v. *Dorchester County School District Three*, CA#66-183 (USDC S. Carolina 1966).

44. See, for example, "NAACP Asks Protection for Woman," *The State* (25 July 1969), sec. B, p. 4.

45. DeLee, 4 July 1988. Also see United States Commission on Civil Rights, *Political Participation* (Washington, D.C.: Government Printing Office, 1968), p. 117.

46. Roosevelt Geddis, Ridgeville, to Richard Detreville, Dorchester, 13 January 1969, South Carolina Council on Human Relations Files, The South Caroliniana Collection, University of South Carolina.

47. Attendance List, Conference on Education Desegregation, Southern Regional Council Files, Atlanta University Center Special Collections.

48. See *DeLee* v. *Dorchester County School District Three*, "Motion to Add Parties," 11 December 1967; DeLee, 4 July 1988; Mordecai Johnson, Florence, to Selected Persons with S.C. School Cases, 8 October 1969, South Carolina Council on Human Relations Files, The South Caroliniana Collection, University of South Carolina.

49. Ibid; Mordecai Johnson interview; *DeLee* v. *School District Three*; Attorney Fred Moore, Charleston, to Paul Anthony, Atlanta, 3 March 1970, Southern Regional Council Files, Atlanta University Center Special Collections.

50. "Hemphill Raps 'Political Rumors,' " *Charleston News and Courier* (18 July 1969), sec. B, p. 6; McCollum, Matthew D./Paul Matthias/South Carolina Commission on Human Relations, Columbia, S.C., (telegram) to President Richard Nixon, Washington D.C., 26 June 1969, South Carolina Council on Human Relations Files, The South Caroliniana Collection, University of South Carolina.

51. Mr. Hayes Mizell, former field worker, American Friends Service Committee, interview by author, 18 June 1993. Tape recording, New York, New York.

52. Mr. Hayes Mizell, 10 June 1993; "Mitchell Reassures Protesters," *The State* (2 July 1969), sec. A, p. 1; "30 'Occupy' Attorney General's Office," *The Washington Post* (2 July 1969), sec. A, p. 4; "The Administration: Tenuous Balance," *Time* (11 July 1969), p. 14–15; "Civil Rights: A Debt to Dixie," *Newsweek* (14 July 1969), p. 23.

53. "NAACP Asks Protection for Woman," *The State* (25 November 1969), sec. B, p. 4.

54. DeLee, 8 August 1992.

55. DeLee, 4 July 1988.

56. Ibid.

57. Ibid.

58. Ibid.

59. Ibid.

60. Ibid.

61. Ibid.
62. DeLee, 28 September 1991.
63. DeLee, 8 August 1992.

Further Readings

Cannon, Katie G. "Resources for a Constructive Ethic in the Life and Work of Zora Neale Hurston." *Journal of Feminist Studies in Religion* I (spring 1985): pp. 37–51.

Crawford, Vicki, Jacqueline Rouse, and Barbara Woods, eds. *Women in the Civil Rights Movement: Trailblazers and Torchbearers, 1941–1965*. Bloomington: Ind. University, 1993.

Grant, Joanne. *Ella Baker: Freedom Bound*. New York: John Wiley, 1998.

Fleming, Cynthia Griggs. *Soon We Will Not Cry: The Liberation of Ruby Doris Smith Robinson*. Lanham Md: Rowman and Littlefield, 1998.

Higginbotham, Evelyn Brooks. *Righteous Discontent: The Women's Movement in the Black Baptist Church, 1880–1920*. Boston: Harvard, 1993.

Hine, Darlene Clark, ed. *Black Women: An Historical Encyclopedia*, Volumes One and Two. New York: Carlson, 1993.

Lee, Chana Kai. *For Freedom's Sake: The Life of Fannie Lou Hamer*. Urbana: University of Ill. 1999.

Riggs, Marcia Y. *Awake, Arise, and Act: A Womanist Call for Black Liberation*. Cleveland: Pilgrim, 1994.

Robinson, Jo Ann Gibson. *The Montgomery Bus Boycott and the Women Who Started It*. Knoxville: University of Tenn. 1987.

4

Mother Guru: Jnanananda of Chennai, India

CHARLES S. J. WHITE

PART I: INCEPTION

I first met Her Holiness Satguru Swami Shri Jnanananda Saraswati in the summer of 1976. An American who had traveled around India for several years as a Hindu monk took me to have her *darshan* (literally, "to look at her" but also "to share her spiritual presence"). At that time I was trying to gather material for a lecture on women's leadership roles in Hinduism. Jnanananda was very cooperative in telling me about herself, and I looked forward to a time when I might talk with her again. In the fall of 1978 I returned to Madras, hoping to meet with her for a longer time, but I was able to speak with her only once. She was absorbed in almost constant *samadhi*, or mystical trance, and was not giving interviews. Finally, in March of 1979, I returned to Madras once again and was able to speak with

CHARLES S. J. WHITE holds a Ph.D. in History of Religions from the University of Chicago. He is Professor Emeritus of Philosophy and Religion of the American University in Washington, D.C. He has done research in India off and on for more than thirty years and among other things has studied contemporary Indian gurus. He is the author of the monographs, *The Caurasi Pad of Sri Hit Harivams* (Honolulu: University Press of Hawaii, 1977); and *Ramakrishna's Americans: A Report on Intercultural Monasticism* (Delhi: Yugantar Prakashan, Ltd., 1979); among other works he is the co-author of *Joseph Campbell: Transformations of Myth Through Time* (San Diego: Harcourt Brace Jovanovich Inc., 1990). He contributed the chapter, "Indian Developments: Sainthood in Hinduism," to *Sainthood: Its Manifestations in World Religions* (Los Angeles: The University of California Press, 1988 and 1990). His recent publications include: "The Remaining Hindi Works of Sri Hit Harivams," *The Journal of Vaisnava Studies*, Fall 1996 and "Muhammad as Spiritual Master," in *The Quest*, August 1998. He is currently engaged in the editing of the catalog for "The Vaisnava Literature [Microfilm] Conservation Project," in cooperation with the Adyar Library in Chennai, South India.

Jnanananda several times during a six-week period. During these interviews I learned much about her life and experiences, as well as her attitudes towards many things, both worldly and spiritual. I also watched her give advice to many of her devotees, who come to her with a variety of questions and problems.

A WOMAN GURU

Ma (a familiar form of "mother"), or Satguru (a title meaning "true guru"), is quite unusual among Indian women, for she is both a guru and a *sannyasi*. In order to appreciate Ma and her interviews, it is necessary to know something about these two important religious roles. The guru is perhaps the most influential religious specialist in Indian culture. As religious teachers, gurus usually have no official positions at local temples and may conduct no ceremonies at all. Instead they counsel their disciples and teach meditation and spiritual understanding. The bond between a disciple and his or her guru is very strong; when the disciple finds the proper guru, complete commitment should follow. A *sannyasi* is one who has taken a formal vow renouncing all worldly life, including family ties and possessions. Such a vow, in effect, means death to one's former life. This renunciation allows full-time pursuit of spiritual goals and fosters spiritual development. Such vows have been common in India from ancient times to the present.

In India, not all gurus are *sannyasis*, nor are all *sannyasis* gurus. However, though notable exceptions have occurred throughout Indian history, usually women do not take on either role. In fact, Jnanananda is the only woman ever allowed to take *sannyasa* vows by the present Shankaracharya of Kanchipuram who, as a chief teacher of classical *Advaita* Hinduism, is one of the most authoritative and important religious figures in South India today.[1] This exception was granted because the Shankaracharya recognized her as a fully realized *jnani*—one who knows experientially through mystical states of consciousness the deepest truths of Advaita Hinduism. She had attained this state while in her worldly life, during which she had been married and had raised five children. It is to be expected that one whose realization of truth is so deep will be a guru and teach spiritual discipline. In fact, Jnanananda already had students in her worldly life before she took the *sannyasa* vow.

PRELIMINARY DISCUSSION

I had arranged to attend Ma's *darshan*, at which she would see her devotees, on Friday, March 9, 1979. The *darshan* was to begin at 5:30 P.M. We parked our cycles inside the gate and were greeted by one of several young men devotees who were to help during the evening *darshan*. The spark of religious fervor in their eyes, their expectant attitude, and a kind of nervousness signaled the familiar feeling of being in the proximity of a saint. Toward the rear of the compound was a low shed that had been converted into a reception area and prayer hall. A large photograph of Satguru was suspended on the back wall, with a red light, covered with flowers, hanging above it. In this room we waited with others to see Ma. When our turn came, we ascended the outside staircase of the bungalow and went through a door directly into the room where Ma was sitting on a mat covered by a small orange carpet.

One of the first impressions one has of Jnanananda is of her wide, frank smile. Many of her photographs depict her this way. Now, as part of her *sannyasa* vow, she has given up symbols of human vanity, such as long, well-groomed hair, jewelry, and saris. She wears instead an ochre cloth around her body and a thick paste of ashes on her forehead and on her arms, where the paste forms horizontal stripes. She has cut her hair short. Her pictures show that, before she put on the ascetic habit, she was a beautiful woman. The beauty is still there, but it impresses one as being more a reflection of her spiritual state. A lilting chuckle sometimes ripples behind her comments. One feels a radiant, peaceful joy in her presence.

As she greeted me, she asked where I had been since the previous November. Then she asked me what I would like to discuss with her now and made reference to the questions I had left with her at our previous meeting. She said she would set up an appointment to go over them. Almost without interruption from these preliminaries, she began speaking from a spiritual viewpoint. She uses vigorous, idiomatic English with a clear accent. Her manner is completely natural, homey, motherly. Her hands make sweeping graceful gestures. She appreciates her listener's catching on to what she says and will throw back her head and laugh heartily when others show that they find her comments amusing.

She said near the beginning of the conversation, "My work is growing slowly, but it will become very big. The world is ready for it—needs it before chaos encompasses everything. I teach the path of surrender, whatever your walk of life is and whatever you are doing. I followed that path and underwent terrible *tapas* [austerity] for many years. But the Divine spoke to me constantly. I never had a guru. Everything came from within. For years I had this most terrible burning sensation, *mahabhava*, all over my body. I tried every kind of medication—ayurvedic,[2] homeopathic, and allopathic. Can you imagine it? Some doctors even gave me injections for it!

"The Divine Command would come to me: 'From today onward, you fast.' It never said 'until next Tuesday'! It went on indefinitely. Eventually the starvation turned to dysentery, and blood came out.

"You know I had disciples twenty-five years ago in my worldly life. So that is nothing new. I directed them even when I was in the householder stage. You may wonder why I stayed so long in that stage. Partly it was for the children. The Divine spoke to me and said that my children were to be extraordinary. Two of them have been working closely with me. Eventually they will become *sannyasis*. My youngest daughter, when she was only five, observed voluntarily the full day's fast of *Shivaratri*—not even taking water.

"Really, I didn't require initiation by the Shankaracharya. It came as a Divine Command. He was touring and came to the city where I was living then. I went to the place where he was staying. You know they never receive women. But he did receive me. Then the impulse came to me. I asked him if he would come to my house. (They never go to private houses.) He smiled and said, 'You want me to come to your house? Where do you live?' I gave him my address, and we fixed the day. About two hundred people had gathered there on the appointed day. But I was unconcerned. I have no need of a guru, I was only following instructions. When he arrived at my house, I was upstairs. Up to that time I had been talking to people around me but when he arrived, I fell into *samadhi*. There was no one to receive him at the gate. So he simply walked into the drawing room and sat down. Then I 'woke up' and came downstairs. He stayed for a short while and then went away. But, I repeat, I did not feel the need to call upon him to become my guru although he did give me *mantra-diksha* [initiation into a sacred Sanskrit phrase used in meditation], which is something they normally never do for women. That was on the previous occasion.

"It was the Divine Command that led me to ask for *sannyasa*. It was not a necessary thing for me, since my *tapas* and spiritual training were already complete. In fact many people did not like the ambiguity of a woman being initiated by the Shankaracharya. But now that they see what I am like and what my tendencies are, there is less resistance."

I asked, "Will these young men you are initiating into *sannyasa* work with you?"

"Yes, to some extent. I may call them for some work. The first one I have had initiated, Sadashva Giri (a former Indian airforce officer), I have sent to an *ashram* [religious community] some 180 kilometers from here. He still has a great deal of *tapas* [austerity] and *sadhana* [spiritual practice] to complete."

"Do you plan to train any women for *sannyasa*?"

"It is not a question of men and women. I am looking for the best material, and so far these young men have been most suitable."

MA'S OWN SPIRITUAL EXPERIENCE

At another interview—in fact nearly the last I had with her—Ma Satguru talked more about the trance state of *samadhi*, which was such an important ingredient in her role as guru. When I came to see her on April 4, 1979, her elder son told me that she had been in *samadhi* more or less continuously for the past few days. He said that I might find she was having difficulty answering questions. When I sat down in front of her for *darshan*, I could sense the difference, so to speak, in her level of consciousness. With a kind of sympathetic response, I even felt myself carried away by her self-absorption and did not much want to pursue a conversation. But we both made an effort, and I was able to gather a few comments.

She said that she had experienced this deep absorption many times ever since she was a child. She added that when one is finally fixed in it, there is no more ego. Now that absorption is always the background of her consciousness. *Samadhi* is an experience without content and yet is not empty. It is complete fullness. "In that state I used to ask myself, 'Where am I?' Then I would try to think of myself at some point, but I immediately felt myself to be at the opposite point. In short, it is a feeling of being simultaneously everywhere. But there is no perception of the physical world. The physical world is dissolved in the unity."

She said that in a way she had been different from others from childhood. She had never been distracted by the things that trouble most people—problems of self-control, for example. Even as a young girl she had entered a *samadhi*-like state, "I knew that I was standing by a sea. At first there were others with me, then I was alone. The waves rose up, and I felt they would wash me away. I was afraid, but later I fearlessly experienced complete immersion in the waves. In my early journeys into *samadhi* I sometimes saw the moon shining on a completely darkened ocean. This, the Shankaracharya told me, is one of the signs of the true *jnani*. I also experienced, and still experience, a blinding white light in this state.

"At one point many years ago, when I was attaining what I did not know then was the highest level of classical yoga, I thought I was going mad. In fact, they were ready to take me to a mental hospital. But the Divine Voice told me to go to a nearby book stall. There, on a particular shelf and in a particular book, was the writing on the page that directed me to consult a description of the advanced yogic realization I was experiencing."

At present, teaching seems to be Ma's major occupation. She stays mainly at home and performs no religious ceremonies. Congregational meetings, a part of her routine in the past, have been temporarily suspended. For the time being, Ma seems to be concentrating on her personal relationships with disciples and on the counseling of those who seek to come within her circle.

QUESTIONS AND ANSWERS

In several other interviews I was able to ask her questions that I thought would help bring out more clearly her teaching, life experience and special slant as a woman. On other occasions I was permitted to listen as she gave interviews and advice to some of her students or to others who sought her counsel. Many of her comments during these interviews are typical of any contemporary Indian guru, female or male. Only on some questions specifically about women does any special "woman's slant" come through.

On March 15, 1979, I had a two-hour private interview with Ma Satguru. I report my questions and her answers.

Q *"Do you find the public life of the spiritual teacher distracting?"*

A "There is no distraction for one who is completely realized. [*Realized* is a term employed in discussions of Indian spirituality to refer to one who is identified entirely with God.] But premature publicity is very dangerous. It can increase conceit and arrogance and also egoism. Without the Divine Command one should not teach."

Q *"Can the guru communicate directly with the hearts and minds of the disciples?"*

A "Quite a lot depends on the state of mind, or consciousness, of the disciple. Through faith, complete surrender, and openness on the part of the disciple I am fully accessible. One thought from such a disciple penetrates my own consciousness, and the response is instantaneous. I may be anywhere. The disciple may have difficulty in seeing me physically, but that doesn't mean that help and communication are not available."

Q *"What form has your* sadhana *taken since your vow of* sannyasa *in May 1975?"*

A "I do no special meditation or *puja* [worship]. I am always lost in God. There is no need for anything else."

Q *"Does the Satguru perform miracles?"*

A "The question of miracles is a fascinating one to the general public. All I can say is that 'miracles'—if that is the right word—have happened to my devotees. For example, there was a young *sannyasi* who came to see me. I was giving him instruction in meditation and the theory of *advaita.* One night he was on his way here, arguing with himself whether he should think of me without form or with form as the Goddess Rajarajeshwari. His mind was so absorbed in the question that he didn't see the motorcycle bearing down on him on the dark road. Just then the answer overcame his hesitation. 'Think of her as the Goddess Rajarajeshwari!' At that very moment the motorcycle struck him, but he put up his arm defensively, and the vehicle was 'miraculously' deflected to one side. He arrived here more or less in a state of shock and with some scratches on his arm but otherwise unhurt."

Q *"How can we know who is the true guru? How do we choose when different gurus teach different paths?"*

A "Very few of the so-called gurus are fully realized. Some may have achieved partial realization. Generally speaking, when the *chela* [disciple] is ready for the guru, the guru comes. No true guru will promise instantaneous enlightenment. When one finds the true guru, one should surrender completely. Think of it as schools and universities. There are classes and classes and classes and teachers for all of them. There are also subjects that certain individuals should not enter into."

Q *"It has been the tradition, especially among orthodox Hindus in South India, to regard women as unsuitable candidates for spiritual initiation or leadership while they are menstruating. After all, there are strong objections to menstruating women here; they have to sleep in a separate room and cannot even do the cooking. What is your view about this?"*

A "I think such ideas are foolish and wrong. It shouldn't make any difference.

Of course there are emotional differences between men and women, but these do not relate to self-realization. Yet, this tradition has its good points, too. It really gives the woman a needed rest. And I think that was its main purpose."

Q *"What should be the spiritual goal of modern Indian and Western women?"*

A "My teaching is the same for everyone. It is summed up in the principles of absolute *truth, purity, dharma,* and *ahimsa.* Truth contains them all, but purity emphasizes moral perfection or morality, while *dharma,* or righteousness, has more to do with responsibility to duty. Of course, *ahimsa* means nonviolence. All who wish to practice complete self-surrender—my way of *nish-kama karma* [action without desire]—must adopt these principles."

Q *"Are men and women exactly equal in spiritual characteristics?"*

A "Have you ever seen the statue of Shiva Ardanari [a Hindu god]? He is depicted in two sexes but one body. It is primarily at the gross physical level that we must perceive precise distinctions. When the male and female elements are completely developed and complement each other in the same individual, the soul is fully realized. It is certainly true that men and women have different characteristics. The woman tends to be more emotional, also motherly and loving; whereas the man is more intellectual, perhaps braver. But we cannot rely absolutely on these distinctions. For myself I no longer feel that I inhabit a body of particular sexual gender. In fact, I sometimes refer to myself with the masculine pronouns."

Q *"Your younger married daughter mentioned that you are from the Nayar caste in Kerala. This caste has practiced inheritance through the female line. Hence women have great status in your caste. Do you think this background gave you more confidence to pursue your spiritual path independently?"*

A "Well, you must remember that I hardly lived in Kerala. My father was the deputy general manager of the Southern Railway—during British times, the highest office that an Indian had ever held in the Southern Railway. We lived luxuriously in Madras, with a large house, many servants, and so on. I was educated in Catholic convents and did very well in certain subjects. I was always very good in English; it was even predicted in my natal horoscope. As a child I adopted a strict code of behavior for myself, although I could also be mischievous. My motto came to be—I preferred the German form—*Ich dien,* 'I serve.' When I was a young married woman, I became quite good at music, photography, and gardening. I played the *vina* [a string instrument] and once performed on All India Radio. But God stopped everything. For a long period of my life—even in the midst of my householder duties—He required complete seclusion of me. That whole time I was being trained by the Divine Voice. I had visions, including one of Jesus with a dazzling sacred heart that shot rays of power throughout my body. I just mention these facts by way of background. It may be that the great dignity generally accorded women in Kerala influenced me, if indirectly. Also, the literacy rate among the people of Kerala is the highest in India. Even the servants are always reading books and newspapers. So we are accustomed to the pursuit of knowledge.

"It may also be true that women find it a little easier to come to me than to a man. They can talk over their personal problems with me without shyness. In fact, the Shankaracharya has sent a number of women to me in this regard, since he himself does not advise women disciples."

THE *DARSHAN* EXPERIENCE

On March 29, 1979, Satguru granted me a great privilege in allowing me to sit with her on the first of two evenings while she gave *darshan* to her Indian disciples individually or in small, mainly family, groups. In all, I saw and listened to about forty persons during those exchanges. At least for now Ma is able to see personally most of the people who approach her. What an experience of relief this intimate discussion of problems must be to hard-pressed individuals who discover Ma, the loving mother, in the torturing crosscurrents of Indian life! Nevertheless, she does not always say what one would prefer to hear. For Satguru may also be regarded by her disciples as the incarnate goddess, Rajarajeshwari. Westerners could probably identify with this approach more fully if they thought of her as an incarnation of the Blessed Virgin Mary. I don't believe Ma would consider it wrong to do so. Her motherliness, therefore, is in a different category altogether from ordinary human motherliness.

The first person to come in was a young man, about college age, whom I had seen waiting outside. To me nothing seemed to be wrong with him. After prostrating before Ma, he knelt and with a fervent, pleading smile asked her for help in getting a job. "With your grace, mother, I will get it. Please help me. Please."

Jnanananda replied, "But how many jobs can I help you get? After three months you always quit. You have to learn to stick to one job. Are you still taking your medicine?"

"Yes, mother. With your grace, I know I can get the job."

When he had left, she said, "You know, he is a mental case. He cannot keep a job. He is heavily medicated with tranquilizers. It is too bad."

A pretty young woman knelt before Ma. She spoke in a very low voice, so that I could not hear all of the conversation. At one point Ma said, "You must continue to pray at all costs, even when you feel that you cannot. Pray mechanically, if nothing else. This ultimately will help you to overcome your depression and despair."

By the end of the interview the woman was sobbing quietly and saying, "Please help me, mother. Please help me." Jnanananda smiled and closed her eyes with an expression of deep peace. When she opened her eyes again, she gave a handful of *vibhuti* (sacred ash) on a banana leaf to the young woman, who prostrated and then left. (Ma gave some kind of *prasad*, a sacramental substance—water, for example—that has been blessed by the god or the guru, at nearly every *darshan* that I came to. Besides *vibhuti* she gave rock candies or toffees. Once she gave me a small bunch of bananas. It is also the custom for those coming to have *darshan* to give a gift to the guru—things such as fruit, coconut, flowers, incense sticks, or money. Trays were placed in front of Ma to receive these offerings.)

An elderly white-haired Brahman lady, dressed in the elegant dark-colored sari of her class, spoke to Ma for some time. At one point Ma sat back, smiled broadly, and said in a loud voice, "How can he go wrong or fail as long as I am here? There is nothing to worry about." The woman, I learned later, had been asking about her son, who was undergoing intense *sadhana* (spiritual discipline) under Ma's guidance. The woman had with her a large, rectangular envelope whose contents she seemed to be discussing with Ma before she placed it on one of the brass trays for the reception of offerings. Ma told me afterward that the woman had brought her a deed of gift for a house but that she didn't know whether she would accept it.

A girl of about twelve came with her mother. Ma chatted pleasantly with them in Tamil. The emotional ambience had become relaxed and domestic. At one point the girl took out her pen and placed it on the tray in front of Satguru, who smiled indulgently, picked up the pen, and handed it back to the girl. Afterward she laughed and said that the girl wanted a special blessing for the pen, which she was going to use to write her examinations.

A plumpish middle-aged woman with several teeth missing came and sat in front of Ma. She spoke enthusiastically, smiling, frowning, and using gestures. Ma said afterward that the woman complained of her family life. She was a widow with three sons and three daughters, but she couldn't get along with her children. She lamented that her daughters-in-law had thrown her out of the house. She wanted to come to live with Ma and take the vows of a *sannyasi*, but Ma had to tell her no. She was not ready for that life and would not be in this incarnation.

An athletic looking man in his late twenties or early thirties came in and prostrated full length on the floor (as do most of the male devotees) before Satguru. Then he stood and beamed at her for a few minutes as they talked quietly. He was one of her close disciples, Satguru revealed after he had left. He worked for the Defense Department and now rose daily at 4:00 A.M. to practice an hour of meditation before going to work. She said that the aftereffects of the meditation gave him a feeling of happiness throughout the day.

A middle-aged father and mother and their grown daughter came shyly forward. Most of the discussion after the preliminary bows and prostrations had to do with the man's job prospects. He had been offered a new job. Ma told him not to take it unless he received an appointment letter and by no means to resign from his present job until he received such a letter. His aged mother, who was blind, lived about 200 kilometers away and would not leave her house. Satguru told him that they must do something to look after her welfare—either their daughter could go to stay with her grandmother or the wife should. They reverted to the question of the job. The man said he didn't think he should change jobs until he had collected the annual bonus, which was due to be paid at the end of March. Ma agreed with him. He mentioned that negotiations had begun to marry his daughter to someone. Horoscopes had been exchanged, and they were harmonious, but there was nothing definite yet. They left, with the father making elaborate and prolonged, full-length prostrations. When they were gone, Ma said that the man was very naive about his employment and had lost several jobs because of this. The daughter had no push and wouldn't go out to work even though she had graduated.

The next man, short, his face twisted with emotion, prostrated and squatted on his heels before Ma. He tried to smile, but there was a bitterness in his words. "I did everything you told me to." Ma had a stern look on her face and said nothing. He opened his mouth crookedly. Satguru said, "I have told you many times that nothing can happen without complete surrender. You haven't surrendered completely." The man clenched his teeth in a last attempt at a smile and went away.

Satguru commented, "That man is very well read in Indian spirituality—he knows the philosophies by heart—but doesn't know how to practice a line of it. He is very stubborn. He and his wife are separated legally, and the wife has custody of the child. He wants my help to regain custody of his son, but nothing can happen without complete surrender to God."

A young society lady swept in, an air of hurry about herself. She was wearing a pair of glasses with fashionably owlish frames and a sari with a large pattern in the current mode. When she was seated in front of Ma, she began immediately to talk. "I have just come from a journey of two-thousand-plus miles," she said. "I hurried here as fast as I could, and then last night you wouldn't admit me."

"We have changed the schedule now," Satguru said. "*Darshan* is only on Tuesdays and

Fridays—otherwise I wouldn't have any time at all to myself."

"But tonight," the woman interrupted, "after so many delays, they have made me wait until nearly the end of the *darshan* time. Ma, I think you are trying to cut me off!" She looked the part of a petulant ingenue in a Hindi film.

Ma smiled—wanly, I thought. "But it's the same sort of thing. Don't you see? If we don't take people in order, there can be great trouble. As it is, the volunteers have a difficult time restraining some of the people who come here to see me. There have been rows. I have to be perfectly fair—it's only right, anyway—first come, first served! You must have arrived after the others. And what about your plans?"

"We are supposed to go to the States. I don't want to go, but he [her husband] wants me to go. I don't know what to do. Who will look after the dog?"

"If he wants you to go," Ma said, "you should go—to please him. When do you leave Madras?"

"Tomorrow morning, for Hyderabad. There is another wedding. Then back north." The woman, somewhat subdued, departed after placing an offering of money in one of the trays.

A SEEKER FROM THE WEST

On other occasions I went to Ma with Westerners who wanted spiritual guidance. Although the questions are someone else's they could be mine or those of any seeker, Indian or foreign. Her answers reveal many of her religious teachings. After I had introduced my twenty-four-year-old friend from South America, Satguru began to speak without waiting for the first question.

"One must surrender completely to God. There is no alternative. In the morning one should spend some time in prayer and meditation in whatever form is suitable to one's chosen deity. Then one should turn one's attention to the day's work or activity. No one can be without activities, but they should be done in such a manner that the mind's attention may still be focused on God. The object is always to surrender completely to God. I suggest various paths, depending on temperament. Not everyone is ready for self-inquiry or for the practice of deep religious teachings. If one has not achieved a good deal of self-control at the lower level and doesn't have some degree of mental discipline, then such attempts are mere mockery. They can lead us into delusion. If we are not ready for them, they may affect our health and cause high blood pressure. I'll tell you a story. An old *sannyasi* came to see me. He claimed to have developed a good deal of realization. I had a question about that. I asked him whether he usually ate polished rice or unpolished rice. He said he usually ate polished rice. I told him to switch to unpolished rice and come to see me after a week. When he returned, I asked him how he had been. 'Very sick,' was the reply. You see, his body still had such a hold on him that even such a simple change in diet was enough to throw him off. I went for years with only about one hour of sleep a night, engaged in terrible fasts; now I don't even know whether the next day I shall eat anything. For days now I have been on a liquid diet.

"So, use your simple prayer and try to purify your mind. When certain thoughts, distracting thoughts, enter the mind—they should not be entertained there—remember that they can be managed and controlled by substituting prayer, a *mantra*, or thoughts of God. God realization should be one's entire goal in life, and everything else should be secondary. All else in the world pales alongside God realization. As you come closer to it, the valuable things of the world will draw you less because they will be less attractive. You should become aware of the passage of life from childhood on to old age. Nothing lasts—the joys, the sorrow. So much is fated—the result of past *karma*. We cannot avoid anything. But the attitude toward events, the type of attention we give to them, these are within our control. That is where we exercise our freedom. Do you understand?"

"Yes," my friend said. "I think I do understand what you say. It is difficult, but I agree with it. I have a couple of questions, though."

"Yes."

"First of all, I was wondering about studies. Should we continue our studies? What relation do these have to God realization?"

"As I said," Ma replied, "you have to do something. You should continue your studies in the normal course of things but turn your mind as much as possible toward God. As with all outward activity, you may reach a point at which you are no longer capable of continuing in the old way. That is the time to stop—when the things of themselves automatically fall away."

"I have another question," the young man went on. "It is about the sex side of life. It doesn't bother me too much, but I wonder how I can completely control my sexual desires."

She answered, "The first thing to remember is that your case is nothing rare. Most people are in the same situation. They choose between being married and being single. On the whole, from the point of view of a religious life, it is better to be single. Marriage inevitably draws you toward the world and its problems. The way toward divine love eventually cancels out the loves of the lower nature. You must love God and desire divine union to such an extent that you want to shed tears of longing. We all have a higher and lower nature. The higher nature, when it becomes more developed, tends to triumph over the lower nature. Marriage for some people is necessary—as the Bible says, 'It is better to marry than to burn.' But married life is difficult, it is like a three-legged race!" (She laughs.) "You can't go very fast. Those who have purified their lives can rise very rapidly toward God realization. There is another thing, too. I rarely answer direct questions about sex. These answers generally come from within. Sex is an intensely personal matter."

. . .

Over the weeks, months, and years that I have been meeting Ma, I have felt increasingly attracted to her. What part of my attraction has to do with her being a woman? I think most people would like to have a mother like her—without apparent inner conflicts, dignified, wisely admonitory, and, at the same time, completely accepting. But beyond that, as far as I can tell, her spiritual knowledge stems from a profound inner life that seems to illuminate general human experience, a man's as well as a woman's. True, she has a powerful personality, and this is especially meaningful at a time when women are seeking leading roles in all areas of human endeavor. But Shri Jnanananda Saraswati, the guru-goddess, will be most attractive to anyone, female or male, who wants to know about the depth of the spiritual reality from one who is amazingly articulate in stating her perception of it.

PART II: A DIALOGUE

In the spring of 1998, I reestablished contact with Satguru Jnanananda Saraswati and was able on May 16 and 17 to attend two public *darshans* in her present ashram (*Pitham*) in the Mylapore section of Chennai (formerly Madras). Satguru's son now functions as her chief disciple and manager of the ashram's activities. He is a bearded man in his mid-thirties, a sharp contrast with the teenage boy I remembered from twenty years ago. Other committed disciples—the *Sevarthis*—also assist in the work. Ma herself has not changed much in physical appearance and is notable still for her broad, engaging smile and her delight in humor and laughter. She still wears the ocher-colored robes of a dedicated celibate, and has close-cropped hair; but she has modified the *tilak*, or religious mark that she places on her forehead, to indicate that she is now combining the Vaishnava path with the Shaivite Advaita.

Her address on Brindaban Street is appropriate to her new religious emphasis, for Brindaban is the renowned North Indian shrine of Lord Krishna, one of the most popular deities of the Vaishnava path. The blue-painted gate of her bungalow also reminds us of Krishna, the Blue-skinned Lord. At intervals Ma has spent long periods of time, even years, in seclusion. But recently, and fortunately at the time of my present visits to India, she has again opened her doors. Hundreds of devotees attend her discourses and discussions—and it seems as though the present quarters might one day be inadequate to hold the crowds. In spite of that, Satguru is reluctant to accept financial donations on a large scale to expand her premises. Her personal religious style, with long retreats and disengagement from human contact, moves her to accept contributions only from an inner circle of her most devoted followers. Indeed, she has declined bequests of land and other properties.

In October and November of 1998 I was once again in Chennai with questions I had prepared as the basis for a dialogue. Ma graciously received me for a private interview on two occasions. Through the prepared questions and the spontaneous discussions on those days, I hoped to provide a kind of update to the materials presented in the prior section. The reader will find questions, set out in italics, and Ma's answers in regular type. Occasionally, I interject a comment. This, too, is indicated by italics. Quotation marks are used for quotations within Ma's speech.

Q *Since our last interviews, almost twenty years ago, what significant changes have developed in your role as guru and teacher of the spiritual way: For instance, though I tried to meet you, during my occasional visits to Madras (Chennai), I could not find out where you were. Did you spend some years in total seclusion?*

A When we first met, I was teaching more or less on the lines of Advaita [nondualism] only. There were many people who were coming to me—throngs. There were a lot of personal questions, things like that. But then, afterward, there were periods when I would go into seclusion. Now the last time was for about four and a half years. I would live in one room, and I would come to the next room to have my dinner and go back. I would stay inside. There was no fresh air and light, but I never missed anything. People used to come and go. A group of ladies had come from America—they would see only lady teachers—and they came here and invited me. Many other persons from other ashrams in the south wanted me to help them, to guide them. But I said, "It is not yet time. I can't see them. I can't see anybody. You can't break it when something is going on. It is being done on another dimension; so, as it is just growing, I can't just break it. It has to grow by itself, fulfill itself, and then I'll be told that I can go and give *darshan* to people."

Q *What is your experience of Advaita? Do you sleep and wake up? They talk of samadhi. What is samadhi? What is your experience like?*

A I just grew into it, and *samadhi* used to come many, many years ago. This may have been about thirty to thirty-five years ago. Then I used to be totally unconscious; then I used to wake up. That used to go on regularly for about one year. I would just lean back or just lie down. It would look as though I was deeply asleep or something like that. Then there are different types of *samadhi*. In *Laya*, they say that the mind leaves connection with the world and goes to another dimension and, yet, has not reached the highest level—just a higher level and stays in a half-sleepy, half-drowsy state and, yet, has left this world also.

Then, there are many more, like that which is called the *Saguna Samadhi*, when you realize the Personal God. The next one is the Impersonal, the *Nirguna*. But above this you go into all *That*; you realize all *That*; you become master of it, and then you came back into the world to work. That is called the *Sahaja* state. You would have reached that state, you are in that state, but you still continue to work as though you are an ordinary human being, fulfilling all the needs, obligations and duties of that level. I never bothered about which stage I had reached until some very highly advanced *Sannyasis* or *Yogis* said that she is in that *Sahaja* state.

Q *Do people still ask you about their personal problems?*

A Yes, they still do! Hundreds of them still come. They still come, but most of them who are familiar to me have been coming [for a period of time]. But now I have taught them how to surrender to God. The second stage of the Teaching has taken place now. The first stage was Advaita. Now I am teaching *Sharanagati* or surrender. It is very easy to say, "I surrender," but what do you surrender? How far can you take it? How far are your duties there? I teach them from the Bhagavad Gita.

[You see] each age has its own way of expressing itself. In Kaliyuga it is that of speed—supersonic planes and satellites. Speed is the attribute of this age, covered by darkness, and Avidya or ignorance, which makes persons think or do evil. The tendency to evil is much more prominent in this age than in any other age. So therefore it is not possible for anybody to think on the lines of the Jnana Marga: "I am not the body, etc." Nowadays, the only thing you can do is a mixture of all the Yogas and that is *Surrender*. In surrender you do your duty and leave the results to God. You don't want the results. When you look forward to the results then the trouble starts. . . .You get that freedom; you continue to do your duty; and as you go on praying to Him and surrendering to Him, you find that you get more and more calmness and self-control. When your senses are under control, you find that you are a totally different person and find it easier to live life.

Q *Do you think that personal existence continues after death?*

A Definitely. I happened to see Rajiv Gandhi like that—Indira Gandhi's son. In spite of the violent death he had had, I saw him just as he was. He was blasted in a very cruel manner. He was a good man, such a good man—a very kind man—and a gentleman to his fingertips. I was in seclusion at the time, but, yes, I saw him. He came to me. Immediately, [after the explosion] he was standing over the body, for some time in his form really. And for some days after that I could see beautiful valleys, mountains, rivers. Quietly he was walking in all that happily. The type of soul will not come near me unless it is a good soul. It will get frightened and go away. [People are worried about life after death], but there is nothing to be worried about. You just pass on to another dimension, where, perhaps all your problems may cease: no illness, no disease, nothing like that. I always tell this to the people who come here, the devotees.

Q *What is your view of the many current deities of the Hindus?*

A Hinduism is the most universal of all the religions, and it understands that there are different grades of people and all the souls are in different states of evolution. You cannot give Mahavishnu, who is *sattvic* [calm, peaceful, preserving] to a person who has got a lot of *rajas* [passionate action and feeling]. They'd prefer to have Shiva or Parvati; so according to each one's tendencies, *Purvajanman* [previous-birth] tendencies, the deity is chosen.

Q *You speak of being guided by the Divine Command. How does that happen? Is it a thought?*

A It is not really a thought; it just comes. Sometimes there is a command. Most of the time, as you grow closer to God, all your thoughts, words, deeds and feelings are God's. You don't have to ask Him; it comes naturally, it comes naturally. He talks through you; He acts through you; He feels through you. So you cannot be wrong. You must come to that Highest Level—only then you can trust yourself: that I am not a human being, but that God has entered into me and that human-being ego has merged into Him. Only then can He take over. There cannot be two inside; there can be only one. Either it is God or you!

Q *How can it be explained to someone who wonders what it means?*

A I did not have fear of anything, very fearless I was. Then by the time I was twenty-eight or thirty-one this incident took place. My children, both of the boys and their younger sister—she is now married and gone to Malaysia—the three of them were playing. I was told, "don't let the children play outside in the garden. Bring them inside." You can see how difficult that might be! But, luckily, they were obedient. They were very happy. There were lots of toys and they were playing inside. It was very, very hot. Their father had gone to the factory; he was working in a magnesite factory. He was about to come back. It was nearly six in the evening and it was very, very hot. We were living in the [company] quarters there, very nice quarters, just outside the factory; and I said, "Can I go outside and sit there?" God said, "No, sit inside. Don't go outside." It was very hot, and I felt as though I was burning. After about half an hour I said, "Can I go and put a chair in the garden and sit in the cement square in the middle of the garden? I won't go into the garden itself. I'll just sit in the square."

God said, "Don't open the door and go out!" I was wondering why. I had that trust that there must be some reason for God to say something like that. So I thought, "Okay." I was walking around, played the radio, etc. The children's father was coming down the road and he stopped and spoke with the people next door. I heard them telling him,

"Mr. Achan, you don't know what happened. Just look at this."

"What happened?"

"See for yourself."

I looked from the open window and I couldn't see anything. I saw them bending down and examining something.

He came inside and said, "Do you know what happened?"

"No, I wanted to go out, but God asked me not to go out."

"Do you know what you missed? No wonder God told you not to go out! Go there and see and you will find a five-foot cobra!"

It was a black one, a very rare and poisonous type. And this man—a very young couple they were—had been coming on their motorbike [his wife was riding behind] and the headlights fell on the snake, coming out of our house from the cement square, where I wanted to sit, and going there into our area. He told his wife to bring a big rod. She got it; by that time it had crossed the hedge and was entering his garden. He hit it on the head and killed it and dragged it and kept it in front of his house and stretched it out.

"See," he said, "what has come from your garden, from the cement square, and it was just coming out, and if I had not been here, I don't know what would have happened to your family or mine."

I learned later, in a book by Annie Besant, that murderers . . . and such cruel souls are cursed and born as cobras. They bite and kill or they bite and they are killed, and then go on in a cycle like that for a long time. For a long time they have to work out the evil that they did. I was shocked when I read it. Really! I couldn't believe it, you know. So much of truth!

There is a promise in the Gita, that even a most wicked sinner, if he surrenders to Me [Lord Krishna] and has resolved rightly—from then on I will take him in hand. He will be purified and will become My devotee. You see the Hope that He holds out even to the worst of them. For some of them there is no Hope. It is no use telling them, but we can do our best to change the rest of them.

EPILOGUE

It seems to me that there is some change in the presentation of Satguru's spiritual views today as compared with the prior interviews. Of course the Shaivite to Vaishnavite shift in emphasis is important. Her comments also have a richer texture, are more nuanced, and at times a touch somber. But, as in her last statement, she continues to brim with Hope. She is filled with the reality of God to Whom *Sharanagati* (surrender) is the solution to all of life's ills and the promise of a better life after death.

This short summary will have to suffice for now until the publication of the complete discussion I had with Ma. This will appear from the Jnana Advaita Pitham and may eventually be ordered from the address at 13 Brindaban Street, Mylapore, Chennai, 600 004, India.

Notes

1. *Advaita* Hinduism teaches the essential oneness of the soul (*atman*) and the Absolute (*brahman*). The material world in relation to that oneness is a mere slide show.

2. *Ayurvedic* medicine, using primarily herbal potions and ointments, is the traditional Indian medical practice; its origins lie in ancient, even prehistoric times.

Further Readings

Nikhilananda, Swami. *Holy Mother: Being the Life of Sarada Devi, Wife of Sri Ramakrishna and Helpmate in His Mission*. London: George Allen and Unwin, 1963.

White, Charles S. J. "The Hindu Holy Person." *Abingdon Dictionary of Living Religions*. Nashville, Tenn.: Abingdon Press, 1981.

———. "The Indian Situation: The Saints and Holy Ones." *Sainthood: Its Manifestation in World Religions*, ed. by Richard Kieckhefer and George Bond. Berkeley, Calif.: University of California Press, 1988.

———. "Jidda Krishnamurti." *The Encyclopedia of Religion*. New York: Macmillan, 1987.

———. *Ramakrishna's Americans: A Report on Intercultural Monasticism*. Delhi: Yugantar Prakashan Ltd., 1979.

———. "The Sai Baba Movement: Approaches to the Study of Indian Saints." *Journal of Asian Studies* 31, no.4 (1972): 863–78.

"Swami Muktananda and the Enlightenment Through Shakti Pat." *History of Religions* 13, no. 4 (1974): pp. 306–22.

II

WOMEN CALLED BY SPIRITS

Shamans and Savants

We who have been raised in some of the more formal Western traditions are accustomed to think that people choose to take up a religious career or to join a religious movement of their own volition, as did Dorothy Day and Victoria Way DeLee in the examples described in this book's first section. But the examples of Julia and Jnanananda in that same section show us a different situation. These two extraordinary women were chosen rather than choosing. The sacred powers honored in their own traditions summoned them to their religious callings. Throughout the history of the world's religions, women have often been called upon by spirits, deities, or other sacred powers to perform tasks not part of women's usual roles, as their cultures define these. Sometimes this call and the role change that results are part of a dramatic breakdown and breakthrough that radically alters the life of a woman who experiences such a summoning, rearranging family relationships or withdrawing the woman from her family altogether. At other times, changes are more modest and the shifts in the woman's relationships are far less visible. We shall see examples of both the dramatic and the subtle in this section.

The women of this section, many of whom it refers to as "shamans," practice modern survivals of perhaps the oldest category of religious leadership role in which women are known to have achieved prominence. Shamans come in two types: those who venture into other realms via out-of-body travel to heal and bring back special knowledge, and those who, by possession, accomplish the same goals. Both types were important in much of ancient East Asian religion, and in both women have been quite important. But the possession type has survived best, and provides us with all of this section's examples.

In our more dramatic example of this possessive type of female shamanism, the Korean women of Chapter 5 explode out of their prescribed roles as subordinate wives and mothers into virtual role reversals within their families. This dramatic change is sparked by a breakdown, during which a woman becomes unable to function as her culture demands. Korean folk society then diagnoses her as one chosen by the spirits to be a shaman, a psychic advisor and healer sought out by other Koreans who will pay for the aid they receive from her. Although her family—and herself—usually resist, she must take up this role, for her life depends on it. The decision to accept it entails very high costs, for she and her family will be outcasted as a result of making it. Yet it also results in fundamental changes in her life. Not only does she emerge as a much stronger person in a role better suited to her; she has also resolved the difficult family situation that had sparked her initial breakdown.

In comparison, the several examples of Chinese women in Chapter 6 who respond to the call of spirits have much less dramatic stories, and do not experience the permanent role reversals found among the Korean shamans. They work, however, in similar ways, offering counseling, comfort, and social healing. Thus, the author of this chapter argues, they aid in achieving a central goal of Chinese religious and cultural practice: preserving harmony within the family, or restoring family harmony that is threatened or lost.

The motif of shamanic calling will reappear as well in several later chapters of this volume. Astute readers will spot it, for example, in Chapter 14, where an author describes the experiences of a woman who founded one of Japan's many new religious movements. Also scattered throughout the volume are several other examples of women entering into altered states of consciousness or being possessed: Julia and Jnanananda, whom we have already met (Chapters 1 and 4), Hindu women devotees of Krishna dancing on the beach at his Puri temple (Chapter 9), Garifuna women celebrating funeral rituals (Chapter 10), the Senegal prophet Alinesitoué (Chapter 15), Mother Ann Lee of the Shakers (Chapter 22), and Vodou priestesses of Haitian descent in Brooklyn (Chapter 23).

5

Possession Sickness and Women Shamans in Korea

YOUNGSOOK KIM HARVEY

Korea has a long-standing tradition, probably reaching into prehistoric times, of women serving in the religious role of *mudang*, or shaman. Two different types of *mudang* are found in Korea. The first is a kind of family priestess whose role is usually inherited. The second may be called a "professional" shaman, whose services may be engaged by anyone willing to pay a fee. Unlike the family priestesses, these professional shamans acquire their role through individual experiences of spirit possession and subsequent rites of initiation conducted by qualified professional shamans. The professional shamans can enter into trance states and are believed to possess supernatural powers, which they use to perform a variety of services for the clients who have hired them. Although some professional shamans are men, the overwhelming majority are women.[1]

To understand the position of present-day shamans, some historical background is nec-

---

YOUNGSOOK KIM HARVEY was born in Korea and came to the United States at the age of seventeen. She studied, worked, and lived on the East Coast and Hawaii. When this study was written, she was serving as Associate Professor of Anthropology at Chaminade University and as Assistant Clinical Professor of Psychiatry at the University of Hawaii School of Medicine. She wrote a monograph on *Koreans in Hawaii*, and also *Six Korean Shamans: the Socialization of Shamans*, from which the material in this chapter was selected (see Further Readings at the end of the chapter). We deeply regret to inform our readers of Dr. Harvey's untimely death in 1983.

Author's Note An earlier version of this article was presented to the 76th annual meeting of the American Anthropological Association, Houston, Texas, 1977, as part of the session on Religion, chaired by Ruth Wangerin. I am indebted to Dr. W. P. Lebra for reading the manuscript and suggesting certain changes. Responsibility for the article, however, rests with myself alone.

essary, for the institution of professional shamans resulted largely from actions taken under the Yi Dynasty (1392–1910). The Yi Dynasty government was founded by neo-Confucian scholars and government officials, who were fanatically determined to bring about a total and radical reform of Korean society. To its founding fathers, the Yi government represented the political triumph of neo-Confucianism, which was seen as the design for rational society. Its exponents immediately launched a comprehensive national program of social reform in which shamans and shamanistic cults were quickly identified as foremost targets of attack. The new regime saw shamanism as appealing to nonrational aspects of humanity; thus, for a rational society to be achieved, it had to be eradicated.

Initially the government attempted to isolate shamans from the populace by banning them from cities and towns and penalizing government officials who failed to keep them out. Such government efforts to stamp out shamanism and replace it with neo-Confucianism resulted in merely driving it underground. In no small part, the program of eradication failed because neo-Confucianism could not minister to the emotional and religious needs of the people. Eventually the government recognized the futility of its program and shifted its policy from total eradication of shamanism to severe restrictions aimed at containing it. Although the government allowed shamans to exist, it licensed them for purposes of taxation and then officially ascribed the social status of outcastes to shamans and their families. This outcaste status had the effect of severely restricting shamans' ability to use their influence and economic power for personal or family social mobility.

Since the fall of the Yi Dynasty in 1910, subsequent governments, including the present one, have continued the traditional policy of persecuting shamans to some degree. Thus, shamans and their families continue to suffer the ostracism directed against outcastes in Korea. Notwithstanding, professional shamans have been, and continue to be, in persistent popular demand to serve as religious functionaries and ethnopsychiatrists. Clients call upon them to find out whether their ancestral spirits are comfortable, to arrange reunions between the dead ancestors and the living descendants, to pick auspicious days for weddings or burials, to reveal causes of marital and family strife and to advise on their resolution, to perform rituals that guarantee continued prosperity, to open up the "gates of good fortune" for those in difficult circumstances, and to heal those who are broken in body or soul.

In the life of a professional shaman, *sinbyŏng* ("possession sickness") is a crucial experience. It often causes great hardship both to the victim and to her family, but it is also a crucial prerequisite to becoming a shaman. Given the disadvantages of the shaman role in Korean society, it seems that *sinbyŏng* may actually be a face-saving mechanism that permits Korean women to acquire the shaman role and their families to accept it. At the same time *sinbyŏng* reflects tensions within the family. Its diagnosis and subsequent cure, which occurs when the shaman role is assumed, relieve some of those tensions.

Sinbyŏng, represented by two Chinese ideographs—*sin* (spirit) and *pyŏng* (sickness)—is the term that Korean researchers of shamanism use to refer to a range of bodily, mental, and behavioral symptoms that, in the Korean folk view, are a supernatural summons to the afflicted that she should assume the shaman role. Koreans view *sinbyŏng* as the most critical prerequisite experience to becoming a professional shaman. The decisive symptom for the diagnosis of *sinbyŏng* is a possession state in which the afflicted person experiences hallucinations and manifests inappropriate behavior. Koreans say that such behavior is the result of possession by spirits.

The Korean folk terms for *sinbyŏng*—*sin-chip'yŏtta* and *sin-naeryŏtta*—in fact focus on the possession state as the critical element in *sinbyŏng* experience and can be translated literally as "caught by spirits" and "spirits have descended," respectively.

Symptoms of *sinbyŏng* are at first vague and, therefore, difficult to diagnose. Initially the symptoms are physical. At first, victims have feelings of listlessness and later complain of many or all of the following conditions: anorexia, circulatory distresses such as extreme coldness and/or numbness of hands and feet, diarrhea, faintness or dizziness, headaches, aches in the joints, insomnia, nausea, palpitations of the heart, respiratory congestion experienced as "heaviness of the heart" or "tightness of the chest," acutely painful ringing in the ear, sudden fevers, and weight loss. These physical symptoms do not respond to treatment by the usual home remedies, Chinese herbal medicine, or modern Western medicine and are eventually compounded by mental and behavioral symptoms.

Mental symptoms generally include auditory and/or visual hallucinations and strange dreams, which later prove to have been prophetic of the shaman role destined for the victim. Behavioral symptoms include a variety of actions that would be judged inappropriate or shocking, such as bathing in midwinter with cold water in an open courtyard in direct violation of female modesty and sensible health-care practices, traveling in the cheapest public conveyances in warm weather dressed in extravagantly luxurious winter clothes, or stopping strangers on the streets and telling them their fortunes. Worst of all, as far as the community is concerned, victims may speak too frankly and accurately about things going on in the community that would normally not be openly discussed. They may, for example, say that the chronic illness of a young housewife is due to bottled-up resentment toward her abusive mother-in-law or toward her husband, who will not curtail his gambling or extramarital affairs. Or they may refer to the well-known, but never publicly discussed, history of a man who repeatedly fails in his business ventures and puts the blame for his failures on the disturbance created in his household by his nagging wife. They sometimes reveal adulterous affairs among neighbors that, in all likelihood, everyone has known about but no one has openly acknowledged.

Behavioral symptoms are usually the last to emerge; they ultimately invite the diagnosis of *sinbyŏng* because of their socially disruptive nature. Typically, people are either angered or frightened by these behavioral symptoms. They will think that the women who display them are morally reprehensive or "crazy," with the latter perhaps the more common response. In fact, according to the Korean folk view, it is extremely difficult to differentiate the shaman recruit in possession state, or *sinbyŏng*, from a "crazy" person. Very frequently the diagnosis of *sinbyŏng* is first seriously considered when the victim starts to act as though she were insane.

As the two Chinese ideographs representing the term imply, Koreans believe that *sinbyŏng* is of supernatural origin. Its outcome, on the other hand, is thought to depend on human responses to it. The victims who suffer *sinbyŏng* cannot be blamed for it personally, nor are they free to deny it. Any attempt to resist or deny the call, it is believed, will inevitably invite life-threatening supernatural retaliation on the victims, their families, or both and is therefore ultimately meaningless. Resistance only intensifies *sinbyŏng* and makes it last longer. Furthermore, if the victim dies without assuming the shaman role, the role will be transferred to another member in the lineage, either at once or in the future. If, on the other hand, the victim accepts her calling, she can obtain immediate relief and protect her kinfolk from potential supernatural harm. Thus, refusing to become a shaman can be viewed as an act of futile selfishness on the part of the victim, while assuming it can be interpreted as an act of altruism that will protect others at the same time it alleviates the victim's own suffering.

However, because a shaman in the family brings that family outcaste status, the decision making becomes complicated. Here another folk belief may furnish further motivations for the family to urge that the victim accept her shamanic calling. Koreans believe that, when spirits are searching for humans to possess and use as their mediums, they are particularly attracted to individuals whose *maŭm* (heart/soul) has been "fractured" by experiences of exploitation and tragedy caused by others. Implied in this belief is the suspicion that families of *sinbyŏng* victims may have predisposed them to possession by mistreating them. Such suspicion places the families of victims in a socially embarrassing and psychologically defensive position within the community. It makes them more vulnerable to the implied moral obligation to rescue the victims from *sinbyŏng* as well as to their obligation to urge the victims to assume the shaman role. At the same time, their willingness to assume outcaste status in order to relieve the *sinbyŏng* victim of her affliction makes the family seem altruistic, thus countering the possible suspicions about its earlier treatment of the victim.

In analyzing the life histories of six women shamans, I have traced the spiraling development of their *sinbyŏng* through at least the following phases: (1) The victim experiences severe conflict between her sense of self and her housewife's role, as well as significant conflict with important members of the family, such as her husband, mother-in-law and/or sister-in-law. (2) The victim attempts to cope with these conflicts but feels overwhelmed and helplessly trapped by them. (3) The victim falls ill with vague symptoms and is given "time out." (4) The illness persists, and the family reduces or completely eliminates its normal demands on the victim while mobilizing its resources to rescue her from her sickness. (5) Under these circumstances, the victim recovers and resumes her usual functions. (6) Now reassured by her recovery, her family reassumes old patterns of interacting. (7) The cumulative strain of living with the conflicts again becomes unbearable, and the victim again becomes sick. This oscillatory process may be repeated several times, as it did with all of my informants, until an impasse develops between the victim's repeated illness and her family's rescue efforts. At this point of impasse, the attending shaman diagnoses the victim's afflictions as *sinbyŏng*.

In one case history, this process took twenty-eight years and two marriages. When she was seventeen, Namsanmansin was forced into an arranged marriage. She tried several times to sabotage the marriage by running away but was caught each time; the last time she was kept a prisoner in her room until the wedding. She felt so violated by the marriage that she refused to consummate it for four months, and when the consummation occurred, she felt raped by her husband. She had not consented; he had simply overpowered her physically one night. When it became apparent that she was pregnant, she tried valiantly to accept her marital role and even to excel in some of her tasks. To her dismay, she found that she simply could not put her "heart into it," and she fell ill with vague symptoms in a recurrent pattern. She had hoped that her child's birth might change things, but she felt no emotional attachment to him when he was born. He was conceived, she says, as a result of rape.

In quick succession, she had two more babies, both girls. The first was stillborn, and the second died when two years old. Namsanmansin felt numb after her daughter's funeral, for she had become fond of the girl, whereas she still felt estranged from her son. Shortly after her daughter's funeral, she began to feel ill again with the same symptoms she had had before, but this time they were much more severe. Her parents-in-law finally called in a shaman to attend her, after the treatments of the Chinese herbalist and the modern doctor from town proved totally ineffective. The shaman declared that Namsanmansin was suffering from *sinbyŏng*, thereby confirming rumors that had been whispered for some time among the elderly women of the village. Namsanmansin's parents-in-law urged her to accept the call and put an end to her own afflictions and the drain on the family's resources. However, the prospect of becoming a shaman was so horrifying to Namsanmansin that she fled from the house that very night and became a peddler in a distant town.

Within a year, she was living in common-law marriage with a North Korean refugee who had a young son. She was very much in love with him and wanted to have their union legalized in marriage, especially after the birth of a daughter. However, her "husband" already had a wife, who had remained in North Korea to look after his aging parents when he fled with their son to South Korea during the Korean War. Although Namsanmansin understood the circumstances of her "husband's" resistance, she herself could not accept being a common-law wife and the mother of a "bastard." She was determined to legalize their relationship.

Knowing that her common-law husband dreamt constantly of big business ventures but lacked the capital for implementing any of them, she underwrote his first big business scheme by adroit investment of her own savings in several mutual aid societies. Shortly afterward they were legally married. However, when his business became stabilized and generated enough income for her to quit her business and become the conventionally ideal Korean wife and mother, her husband became involved in a series of extravagant extramarital affairs that eventually brought financial ruin to them. In the meantime Namsanmansin fell ill with symptoms similar to those that had once been diagnosed as *sinbyŏng*. She consulted a shaman and was told that she was destined to become a shaman. However, she recovered from her illness when her husband's financial ruin was complete and the family was on the brink of starvation. She was a capable businesswoman and soon was able to subsidize her husband's business venture again.

This pattern repeated itself many times during their marriage, until her husband's erratic and extravagant behavior with women finally placed them in such dire financial straits that Namsanmansin had to abandon their fourth child, a month-old girl, at the gate of a prosperous-looking house that she had picked out some weeks before when she feared she might have to give up her baby. She felt she could not care for an infant as well as provide for the older children. She broke down again shortly thereafter. This time, however, she did not recover from her illness and was not able to go to her husband's and children's rescue, as had been the pattern before. Instead, she sat staring into space and hallucinating intermittently for six months, completely oblivious to the needs of her family. Her husband tried all of his previously effective ploys and strategies to motivate her to return to business; but this time he failed completely. Desperate, he called in a shaman who, like others before her, diagnosed Namsanmansin as suffering from *sinbyŏng*.

When they owned nothing more that could be sold, Namsanmansin herself suggested that she must become a shaman, that she was so predestined, and that all the afflictions that she and her family suffered had been for the purpose of breaking her will and making her accept her calling. Her husband acquiesced, especially since the spirits possessing his wife were identified as those of his own ancestors. In 1973, when I last visited her, Namsanmansin had, in two short years after her decision to accept the shaman role, built up a moderately thriving practice in Seoul and was supporting her children and her chronically unemployed husband. Her husband, for his part, totally accepted his dependence on his wife as a predestined "curse" that befalls husbands of shamans. He still talked about going into business for himself and hoped that his wife would underwrite him just once more. She no longer gave him substantial amounts of money, keeping him on a daily allowance doled out just before he left home to join his cronies for yet another idle day.

The developments that typically occur after *sinbyŏng* diagnosis are as significant as those that precede the diagnosis. In general, post-*sinbyŏng* developments involve drastic changes in the previously conflict-ridden relationships between the victim and her family. These new developments manifest themselves in several ways.

First, the mutual antagonisms between the daughter-in-law and her family are eased. Her family drops or suppresses any suspicions it might have harbored about the victim's faking illness to avoid work. In her eyes, the family must also be absolved of any responsibility for the illness, because it has accepted the implied accusation and consented to the proper remedy, despite the liabilities that will be suffered by its members.

Second, since both the victim and her family are now viewed as fellow victims of supernatural phenomena that are beyond their control, a new bond of mutuality emerges between the victim and her family. This bond offers them new possibilities for collaboration as they respond to the diagnosis of *sinbyŏng* and the shaman role it implies for the victim. This happened with five of the six informants I worked with. The sixth returned to her mother's family for support. These reconciliations can be quite dramatic. In one case, a shaman had initially been evicted from her mother-in-law's house when she became a shaman. But the verbal taunts and physical abuses that her children, as children of a shaman, had to endure from the other children in the neighborhood finally brought reconciliation between her mother-in-law and herself. One day the mother-in-law happened upon one of her grandchildren who was crying piteously because her playmates hurled insults at her about her shaman mother. The grandmother became so angry that she picked up a piece of firewood and chased after all the children, shouting insults about their parents and daring the whole neighborhood to come out and face her. She finally took her crying grandchild by the hand to her daughter-in-law's house and made peace with her "for the sake of the children."

Third, the diagnosis transforms the afflictions of *sinbyŏng*, albeit retrospectively, into "sensible" and "meaningful" experiences for the victim and her family. They can now "see" that their suffering had a purpose. For another shaman in my sample, the official diagnosis enabled the entire family to live more comfortably with the fact that they had survived the previous winter by begging on the streets.

The spirits possessing the victim are extremely important in changing the relationship between the shaman and her family. They must be consulted about any actions taken concerning the *sinbyŏng*, its termination, and the victim's assumption of the shaman role. With their entrance into the family situation, the possessing spirits transform the previously dyadic power relationship between the new shaman and her family into a triad, with themselves in the controlling position. However, since the new shaman alone, among the family members, has direct access to the spirits, judgments will be at least somewhat susceptible to the needs and interests of the shaman. Since the possessing spirits are often ancestral ghosts from the lineage of the victim's husband, the coalition between the shaman and her possessing spirits is very powerful. Other family members are quite helpless in this situation, for in Korea descendants do not generally deny the advice and counsel of their ancestral ghosts or ignore their demands.

Thus, it is clear that, once the diagnosis of *sinbyŏng* is acknowledged, the old patterns of interaction within the family cannot be resumed. Metaphorically, one could say that *sinbyŏng* is analogous to the spirits' "kidnapping" the victim from her ordinary but conflict-ridden role within the household. The spirits, from their position of superiority, then bargain for the ransom they demand, which is that the shaman recruit must serve as their medium and that, additionally, her family must support her in this role.

The experience of another shaman I interviewed illustrates well the changes in family relationships that occur after the *sinbyŏng* diagnosis is accepted and the shaman role is assumed. When she publicly accepted the call to become a shaman by receiving clients, this woman initially saw thirty to forty visitors a day. She would begin shortly after dawn and work almost nonstop until nine or so every evening. Her husband had to take over most of her housekeeping and child-caring chores. He and his daughters prepared the family's food; he would call her in at mealtimes to feed the baby. Her mother-in-law, distressed beyond description by the sight of her son doing women's work, began to come over and relieve him of many of these tasks. Today the mother-in-law not only supervises the general housekeeping chores of her older granddaughters but also takes full charge of all the hired women who prepare ritual food for her daughter-in-law's shamanistic activities. Thus the roles have been completely reversed, not only between the shaman and her husband but also between the shaman and her mother-in-law.

Such a reversal of power positions is common among the families of shamans, and the former victim often eventually achieves de facto household headship. As a shaman, she bargains with her family from a position of strength based on her earning power, spiritual superiority, and recovered health and self-confidence. This change in the family's power structure is much more pronounced, if, as is usually the case and was with five of my informants, the family's economic resources have been exhausted in the course of her *sinbyŏng*. Circumscribed by their outcaste status, the members of her family tend in such instances to become almost totally dependent on her for economic support.

I suggest, therefore, that *sinbyŏng* is a symptomatic representation of an impasse in both the victim's conflicted self-image and in her friction-ridden relationship with her family. When *sinbyŏng* results in her assuming the shaman role, she and her adversaries in the family are extricated from the impasse. Thus they can remain together as a family unit by redefining their roles. This solution, however, begets other problems. Members of the shaman's family are permanently held hostage by their fear of supernatural retaliation and by the social stigma of their outcaste status. The shaman, on the other hand, must deal with the social and personal sacrifices that her family must make. Furthermore, she suffers the frustration of not being able to use her power to restore them to their proper standing in society.

Note

1. Male shamans are considered by Koreans as marginal men and were customarily expected, until about three decades ago, to practice transvestism. They are not necessarily homosexuals.

Further Readings

Harvey, Youngsook Kim. *Six Korean Women: The Socialization of Shamans*. St. Paul, Minn.: West Publishing Company, 1979.

Janelli, Roger L. *Ancestor Worship and Korean Society*. Stanford, Calif.: Stanford University Press, 1982.

Joe, Wanne J. *Traditional Korea: A Cultural History*. Seoul: Chung'ang University Press, 1972.

Kendall, Laurel. "Korean Shamanism: Women's Rites and a Chinese Comparison." *Religion and the Family in East Asia*, ed. by George A. DeVos and Takao Sofue. Berkeley, Calif.: University of California Press, 1984.

———. *Shamans, Housewives, and Other Restless Spirits: Women in Korean Ritual Life*. Honolulu: University of Hawaii Press, 1985.

Lee, Jung Young. *Korean Shamanistic Rituals*. The Hague: Mouton, 1981.

Yu, Chai-shin and Richard Guisso. *Shamanism: The Spirit World of Korea*. Berkeley, Calif.: Asian Humanities Press, 1988.

6

Harmonizing Family and Cosmos: Shamanic Women in Chinese Religions

RANDALL L. NADEAU

INTRODUCTION

One late fall afternoon ten years ago in central Shanxi Province, a procession of mourners bearing a vermillion palanquin filed slowly across a dry field of denuded birches and broken sorghum stalks. Though dressed in hemp robes and playing a wailing dirge, the mourners were not carrying a corpse to the burial ground, but were rather transporting a bride to her new home, some fifteen miles away, where she was to join her husband's family and its ancestral line. Behind the beaded curtains of the sedan chair appeared the bride's form: an ancestral tablet inscribed with her name and the date of her death.

This was the third time I had seen this young woman. Two weeks before, I had been witness to her sudden death. Waiting for a bus to the city, I watched a steady stream of bicyclists returning home from work in the early evening. The sun was low in the sky. Though shrouded by the fine dust of the north China plain, it burned a fiery yellow. A trucker, driving too fast and blinded by the harsh light, came crashing down the hill and struck a

---

RANDALL NADEAU received his M.A. in Religion from Princeton University (1980) and his Ph.D. in Asian Studies, specializing in Chinese Religions, from the University of British Columbia (1990), under the direction of Daniel Overmyer. He has published research on popular religious literature, deity cults, and folk religion in both China and Japan, as well as methodology in the study of folk religion and Buddhism. Currently he is conducting research on self-mutilation in Chinese popular religion and completing a bibliographic study of Chinese research on religion. Since 1990, Nadeau has been teaching at Trinity University in San Antonio, Texas, where he offers courses on Chinese and Japanese religions, the Buddhist tradition, popular religion in comparative perspective, gender and religion, and methodology in the study of religion.

bicycle with such force that its rider was thrown a hundred feet. She had been killed instantly.

Several days later, I had seen her funeral cortege passing by, and here I was again, on an auspicious day, observing her wedding procession on the same road, carrying the ancestral tablet beyond the crematorium to her permanent home as a wife and newest member of her conjugal family. Upon arrival at her new home, she would be given in marriage to her fiance, her ancestral tablet standing in her place. Later, her husband would take a living, second wife, who would bear his children and provide descendants not only to his family, but to the deceased first wife as well, to care for her spirit for generations to come.

Our story begins here—with a death and a marriage—because funerals and weddings are rites which establish and preserve harmony. Harmony is the most fundamental Chinese value, and is the focus of every religious tradition: folk, Taoist, Confucian, and Buddhist. The cosmic and social harmony maintained by ritual creates peace and blessings for all of the participants and their beneficiaries, whether human or divine.

Proper burial restores harmony between the living and the dead, ensuring that kinship relations are not irreparably broken by death (an inherently disruptive event). Care in siting the grave, as well as presentation of offerings to the dead by living descendants fulfill obligations incurred at birth—they are a repayment for the gift of life itself. In the case of the young unmarried woman, who had not yet had the opportunity to bear the children who would care for her in death, special measures were required. Her spirit wedding was a rite of harmony and pacification, ensuring that the young woman would have descendants to sustain her, and not wander as a hungry ghost seeking to avenge her untimely death.

These rites of burial and marriage included the participation of two religious professionals: one male, one female. The first was a geomancer, or "*feng-shui* master," dressed in traditional flowing robes and bearing the attitude of a Confucian scholar. He sited the placement of a marker (in much of China, close to urban centers, burial of the dead is not permitted by law), ensuring that the deceased would be comfortable and that her surviving family would be protected from harm. The other was a shamaness, consulted late at night on the day of the wedding. Ordinary in bearing and appearance, working from her two-mat home in a tiny rural hamlet, she spoke directly with the dead girl, assuring her anxious mother that her daughter was content and grateful to have been given in marriage to another family.

The contrasts between the geomancer and the shamaness are representative of contrasts between male and female participation in Chinese religious life. The geomancer worked by day; the shamaness by night. The geomancer employed guidebooks and a *feng-shui* "classic"; the shamaness was, in all likelihood, illiterate. The geomancer bore a "gentleman's" air, and carried the robes and spectacles of a distinguished, classical tradition; the shamaness worked from a spare room, wearing frumpy pants and blouse. The geomancer enjoyed an audience of men—father, brothers, fiance, and village head; the shamaness an audience of one—the girl's grieving mother. Nevertheless, both of these religious professionals sought a common goal: establishing family and cosmic harmony in the face of a profoundly disruptive event.

FAMILY

For virtually all Chinese, men as well as women, the center of religious life is the home. From the home radiate moral values, spiritual beings, and ritual action. The primary moral tie is the tie between parents and children, and moral consciousness begins with training in *hsiao,* filial piety. The most revered of all spiritual beings are the family ancestors, and their ritual veneration is a regular occurrence, with offerings of incense, rice, meat, and fruit every morning at the family altar and on anniversary days at the family gravesite. Periodic rites at local shrines and temples are equally for the benefit of family: its health, harmony, and preservation. If the family is broken, by death or separation, there is danger: the threat of dissatisfaction, disruption, and disease caused by spirits who have lost their place. If the family is broken, every effort is made to restore and reharmonize its members. The function of the rites of marriage is to establish connection; the function of the rites of burial is to restore connection, to mend a breach. Chinese religion is, first and foremost, family religion, and the cult of the ancestors heals what has been broken by death.

Because the family is primary, all other relationships are derivative. Outside the home, community life is based metaphorically upon family relationships. The way one acts towards others is analogous to the way one has learned to treat one's parents and siblings. Moreover, in the supernatural realm, the gods and spirits worshipped by the community are embedded in familial webs, with kinship ties to one another and to the "descendants" who worship them: Chinese gods are addressed as "Mother," "Grandpa," "Big Sister," and "Little Brother." Community rites—from imperial investitures to temple fairs—establish bonds of identity described in terms of family connection: birth, adoption, marriage, and brotherhood. State, village, and temple all employ the language of family, but never replace it. Family itself is first: the model by which all social and religious interactions are judged.

The literati Confucian tradition is often credited with the Chinese prioritization of family, but domestic life and the cult of the ancestors penetrates all of Chinese religion. Long before the emergence of Confucianism, the earliest writing—inscribed in the Shang Dynasty on "oracle bones" from the hips of sheep and oxen, and on the plastron shells of tortoises—records communications between rulers and their ancestors, seeking advice and intercession: good weather, successful hunts, right decisions. And today, to the extent that Confucianism is "dead" or requires a millennial revival, the foundation of family can also be said to post-date Confucianism, as it remains the center of value for Chinese at home and abroad. While it is true that the Confucian tradition systematized the cult of the family and gave articulation to its values, the Chinese family is not a Confucian creation and may long outlive Confucian teachings.

The domestic cult is also more fundamental than the other two of China's so-called "great traditions," Taoism and Buddhism. Confucian critics accused their Taoist and Buddhist rivals of being anti-family—as no epithet could be more damning—but this is far from the case. The earliest Taoist classics, the *Book of Chuang-tzu* and the *Tao te ching,* give much more weight to natural kinship than they do to artificial (communitarian or nationalistic) relationships; the burgeoning Taoist sects of the medieval period, as well as sectarian movements of late imperial and modern times, aimed their conversion efforts at whole families and created new family relationships within their ranks; and priestly rites of the present day link families and communities both ritually and spiritually.

Even Buddhism, which in its Indian origins advocated separation from family, was explicitly "pro-family" in its Chinese transformation. We see this in the fact that Chinese Buddhism has been predominantly home-based. It is explicit in advocating love of family, and, for most Chinese, Buddhism is intimately associated with the family at times of greatest need: Buddhist priests conduct funerary rites for the benefit of the recently deceased and thus serve the cult of the ancestors. The path of monastic renunciation has been chosen rarely and most often in cases of family loss, as a substitute for family. Far from "denying family," Chinese Buddhist monasteries reconstitute family relationships, giving monks and nuns a common surname (*Shih*—familiar to many Westerners in its Vietnamese pronunciation, *Thich*), and creating new kinship ties as brothers and sisters. Also, unlike Theravada monasteries in Southeast Asia, Chinese monasteries feature a shrine hall for fathers and mothers, and carry on the daily domestic offerings of the household.

Among all human relationships, the vertical/generative always took precedence in China over the horizontal/affiliative, reflecting a general cultural bias in favor of nature over artifice. Thus the parent-child relationship was emphasized over the husband-wife relationship, the latter patterned after but always secondary to the former. This is reflected in the private writings of the scholar-official class (the "Confucian" intellectuals), who wrote of their mothers without fail and at length, but rarely if ever of their wives. The parent-child bond remains preeminent today, in spite of the cultural influence of the West, which emphasizes relationships of choice (friendship and marriage) over relationships of destiny or descent. For Chinese, relationships between parents and their children are the most definitive of personal identity.

GENDER ROLES

Confucianism was less instrumental in establishing the home as central than it was in delineating the boundaries between inner and outer, and in separating clearly and distinctly the inner sphere of woman's lives from the outer sphere of men's lives. A man's sphere of value and activity extended beyond the home, while a women's life was bound to it. There is a tendency in the West to view this as an expression of hierarchy, but it is important to remember that the primacy of home and family was a cultural value shared by men as well as women. Most literati men, if their poems and private writings are to be trusted, would much rather have "stayed at home" in preference to an official career. Men often expressed envy for their wives and mothers, simply because they remained at home. Even today, when gender-based identities are less narrowly defined, Chinese feel more "free" at home, better able to "be themselves," to be happy. What could be more fulfilling than living at home and sustaining the most central institution of Chinese culture, the family? Just as the veil, in the view of its defenders, gives a woman a greater sense of freedom and self-respect in the Arab world, so too the domestic life of the "inner chambers" has been, for generations of Chinese women, primarily an arena of self-fulfillment, not burdensome confinement.

As in most traditional societies, women have borne the heaviest responsibility for the perpetuation and maintenance of the family, and throughout Chinese history, a woman's identity was defined almost exclusively in relation to her immediate kin: as daughter, wife, daughter-in-law, sister-in-law, mother, mother-in-law, grandmother. For innumerable women throughout Chinese history, home was the right and natural place to be, such that the main source of personal anxiety was the anxiety of failure as a daughter or mother. Marriage into a family with a boorish husband or disapproving mother-in-law could never have been as grave as the loss of one's parents before marriage or the failure to bear sons, for to be an unmarried daughter without parents or a married wife without a son was the source of the most profound distress. Every cultural resource—education, work, religion—was first expended on the basic goals of creating and maintaining kinship, to marry and bear sons.

Life in the inner chambers was socially complex. A young girl in imperial China lived within a domestic system dominated by women. Among the elite, these may well have included her mother, her father's concubine or second wife, sisters of the same mother and father, half-sisters of the same father borne by a concubine or second wife, the wives and concubines of her father's brothers, their daughters, and her father's own mother and grandmother. Even in smaller families, a girl would have been taught precisely how to behave towards each member of the household, and these lessons would have been applied in parallel when she entered a new family as a young bride. Her domestic responsibilites ranged from weaving and sericulture, to management of family funds. She also participated in daily religious rites of the ancestral cult, as well as prayer to local deities at neighborhood temples and regular participation in community festivals.[1]

The idea that women belonged at home, and that their lives were bound by the intricate ecology of the "inner chambers," while men defined themselves primarily in interaction with other men who were not kin, became sharper over the course of Chinese history,[2] especially as governmental service and commercial trade expanded increasingly across country and provincial boundaries. The examination system, instituted in the first centuries of the Common Era, was national in scope, meaning that successful candidates travelled farther and farther from home at each level. Success in the exams ensured a career in public service, carried out in provinces some distance from one's own home in order to ensure national over local allegiance. Consequently, education provided not only "opportunity," but exposure to the world at large, and the writings of the scholar-official elite often took the form of travelogues, documenting local histories and customs far from home.

The outwardly oriented male sphere required education; life in the inner chambers did not. For women, education was a luxury and an indicator of family wealth, and although literati women are included among China's greatest poets,[3] their writings focussed characteristically upon home and family. The subject of most poetry by women is family ties: parents, husbands, and children.

However, despite the fact that Chinese culture and gender roles predisposed women to remain illiterate in the inner chambers, nevertheless, women *do* make literary and public appearances, as we shall see in the remainder of this chapter. They do so at the behest of the spirits, for spirits are more powerful than social conventions, and can overturn them in some circumstances.

SACRED WRITINGS OF INSPIRED WOMEN

For most women of the past in China the ability to write was so rare that it was considered miraculous. Look at the story of Seng-fa, a remarkable nun who died in 505 C.E. at the age of sixteen, as recorded in a Buddhist catalogue compiled by the monk Seng-yu only ten years later.[4] Seng-yu's catalogue, the first comprehensive list of Buddhist scriptures in Chinese, lists twenty-one works attributed to the young girl: composed between 499 and 505, when she was between the ages of nine and sixteen, they totalled twenty-eight fascicles. Seng-yu did not trust the girl's abilities, or find the texts credible, and so he listed them in his "Registry of Doubtful Scriptures." He explains:

> The titles listed above were produced by the young daughter . . . of Chiang Pi, a scholar of the Grand Academy of the late Ch'i Dynasty. At the time when she was still losing her baby teeth (accounts say she was 8 or 9 years old), there were occasions when she would close her eyes and sit in meditation, reciting these scriptures. It is said by some that she ascended to heaven to receive them; others claim that they were

given to her by spirits. Her speech was fluid and effortless, as if she had practiced ahead of time. She let others write down what she recited. And then she would suddenly stop. Ten days after the first of each lunar month, the same thing would happen again, just as before.

From this description, it would appear that Seng-fa could not write—she composed her scriptures literally by reciting them in trance. Seng-yu refers to the case of a Lady Ting in which inspired speech was set down on paper by the medium herself:

> Long ago, at the end of the Chien-an reign period of the Han Dynasty (196–220 C.E.), the wife of a man named Ting of Chi-yin [in modern Shantung Province] could suddenly, as if struck by a seizure, speak in a barbarian tongue, and would request paper and pen and compose texts in a foreign script.

Seng-yu comments in closing:

> Searching back into antiquity, there was never a time when such things did not exist. But the texts are unorthodox and were not translated by Buddhist masters. So I have assembled them together under the category of doubtful scriptures.

Later cataloguers also excluded Seng-fa's works from the canon, describing them as "false" or "suspect." They reiterated Seng-yu's phrase that Seng-fa "practiced ahead of time," and concluded that her acts "had nothing to do with spirits."[5] They argued that her receptivity to suggestion was attributable simply to "a weakness in the passions of women."[6]

Throughout Chinese history, this "weakness in the passions of women" has made women particularly receptive to the influence of gods and spirits, aiding them in the practice of divination both oral and written.[7] In contemporary Taiwan, girls between the ages of eight and fifteen are chosen by gods and spirits to compose scriptures for the Unity Sect (*I Kuan Tao*). They are called "savants"—*T'ien-ts'ai, Ti-ts'ai,* and *Jen-ts'ai* ("Heavenly," "Earthly," and "Mortal" savants)—and the composition of scripture by automatic writing is termed "wielding the phoenix." A sect history describes the procedure:

> When the offerings at the altar have been made, the three Savants take their places. The Heavenly Savant grasps a wooden brush; the Earthly Savant takes up paper and pen; and the Mortal Savant holds a rake. Each stands on one side of a tray of sand. . . . In silent worship, they request the Immortals and Buddhas to draw near. After a short time, in response to the will of Heaven, the spirits approach the altar, via the Mysterious Gate; they come to rest upon the person of the Heavenly Savant, and, moving the wooden brush with a flourish, they begin to write. Usually they begin with a poem of five- or seven-character lines, in anywhere from eight to sixteen verses. The brush itself announces the Buddha's name. . . and the assembly receives him by kneeling in worship and pronouncing ritual incantations, as a show of respect. During this reception, the spirit temporarily suspends moving the brush. Then, the audience rises and draws near, and the spirit resumes writing.
>
> In most cases, the text written by the spirit is in verse, of 5, 7, or 10 characters per line. A 7-character verse might read,
>
> The wind approaches the water's surface, awakening the potential for enlightenment.
> The moon approaches the mind of Heaven—the Way is here!
>
> First appear the four characters, "The wind approaches the water's surface." The Mortal Savant sees this, and immediately announces the phrase in a loud, clear voice, at the same time smoothing out the sand in the box with her rake. The Earthly Savant,

in the meantime, having seen the characters in the sand and having heard the words pronounced by the Mortal Savant, promptly records them in writing. Immediately the spirit writes the next three characters, "awakening the potential for enlightenment," and again the Mortal Savant makes the announcement and the Earthly Savant records the characters in writing. And in this way the writing continues. . . .

Once the text is complete, the spirit retreats from the Mysterious Gate and departs, and only then does the Heavenly Savant regain consciousness. While wielding the Phoenix, the Heavenly Savant feels nothing whatsoever. So, the poetic verse of the Flying Phoenix is written by the Immortals and Buddhas using the hand of the Savant; it can be said to be a spiritual composition. . . .

In most cases the teachings revealed by the spirits take up about one thousand characters, and can be completed in less than an hour. . . .

The teachings revealed by the spirits encompass all things. . . They move us deeply, and we can only sigh in admiration.[8]

The sectarian manual goes on to discuss the qualifications and character of the Heavenly Savant. She must be "pure in thought, supremely clean in character, without a hint of vice." Though she is taught the peculiar calligraphy of revelation, sectarians insist that she lacks the education required to compose the scriptures without divine assistance.

In the spirit-writing session that I observed, the god spoke through the Heavenly Savant with a message of reconciliation after a divisive local election. The congregants who benefited from this revelation were urged to begin a process of communal healing, and to lead by example: by practicing virtue and avoiding vice, working hard, and maintaining harmonious relationships within their families. Though the means of expression were extraordinary, the message from these shamanic girls was explicitly domestic and communal.

It is remarkable to see the similarities between the shamanic performances of Seng-fa in 499 and the spirit writing of girls the same age some 1500 years later! At the conclusion of the session, I was invited to the home of the "Heavenly Savant" by her father, who had assisted in the rite. The sixteen-year-old girl—I will call her Aiyun—appeared wan and dehydrated. The spirit-writing performance had lasted over two hours, and the close, sticky air of a summer afternoon in southern Taiwan had sapped her strength. During our interview, she sat quietly in the family's traditional "four-square" courtyard, sipping orangeade, and her father spoke for her.[9]

He recounted that Aiyun had begun her training as a "Mortal Savant" (of medium, reader, and recorder, the Mortal Savant is the reader) from the age of nine. This Savant is not in trance, though from my observation the interpretation of written characters inscribed in sand by the mediumistic Heavenly Savant is at least as mysterious as the possession itself. He insisted that she had had no education in Classical Chinese, and, even at sixteen, could not have learned in any conventional sense to write in the elegant style of the revealed texts.

"Why did you want to become a Savant?" I asked Aiyun.

The question may have been inappropriate. There was an awkward silence. "I didn't," she replied.

Her father explained. "She was very resistant from the beginning. She doesn't like it, and at first she didn't want to do it. This kind of thing is hard, and she is so tired that sometimes she can't get up for days. At school, some of the other girls keep their distance, and my daughter complains that she doesn't have friends. But the gods are powerful, and she can't resist them." Despite Aiyun's desire for an ordinary childhood, the pressure from the gods and the community of believers was too great.

After several years as an Earthly Savant, Aiyun experienced her first shamanic possession, and has served as the group's spirit-writing Heavenly Savant for the past two years. Soon, she will be replaced by one of the younger girls, as she is nearing the age when her powers will diminish.

I asked her father about the "grandmothers who speak to spirits"—older shamanesses who ply a nightly trade of shamanic intercession with ghosts and ancestors in village and neighborhood temples. Aiyun's father scoffed. "Oh, they really are low-class. They can't read and write at all, and they're just a mouthpiece for minor spirits, with all that gutteral groaning and spitting. Our Savants are courtly and refined, and they have to be pure." The Savants are obviously unmarried, and, I suspect, pre-adolescent, though I did not inquire directly.

SHAMANS AND THEIR CLIENTS

These women who write through the power of the spirits can be viewed in the larger context of shamanism—both male and female—in Chinese culture. The history of female shamanism is older still than Seng-fa, dating long before the Common Era. Shamanism in ancient China most commonly took the form of deities and spirits possessing receptive human beings. Female mediums were called *wu,* a word related to "dancing," and ancient poetry suggests that it was the beauty and grace of the shamaness's dance that made gods choose and possess her.[10] These spirit mediums were women who participated in various aspects of the religious life of the court: invoking the descent of the gods, praying and dancing for rain, and ceremonially sweeping away harmful forces.

With the establishment of Confucian values as the standard of orthodoxy by the Han Dynasty, the ecstatic shamanism of earlier times was actively discouraged—in fact, punishable by death. Shamanism blurs the boundaries that the Confucian tradition seeks to clarify. Confucius is recorded as saying, "Revere the ghosts and spirits, but maintain a proper distance." And, with the emerging consensus that women's religious lives should be limited to the home, the culture pushed charismatic women to the peripheries of society. This is still largely true today, as the "grandmothers who speak to spirits" operate from darkened temples in back alleys in the middle of the night, and young girls like Aiyun are seen—and see themselves—as peculiar and out of place.

Shamanesses link the living and the dead. The anthropologist Jack Potter describes "grandmothers who speak to spirits" in the New Territories of Hong Kong:

> They act as intermediaries between the villagers and the supernatural worlds of heaven and hell. . . . [The mediums] send their souls to the supernatural world, where they communicate with deceased members of village families. They also know how to recapture the souls of sick village children, and they can predict the future. They take care of the souls of girls who die before marriage, and protect the life and health of village children by serving as . . . fictive mothers.[11]

Potter writes that several of the women he interviewed became shamans after the deaths of their own children. The spirits of these children were among their helpers.

Unlike Aiyun, who serves a community of believers, Chinese shamanesses are typically consulted by families, reinforcing the cultural link between religious women and family life. In most instances, the mediums are consulted when families are faced with medical crises, and clients are presented with pharmaceutical prescriptions in addition to counseling. The shamanesses communicate directly with the dead, and are often possessed by the parents and grandparents of their clients. Disharmonies within the physical body are explained in terms of disharmonies within the extended family, and can be healed with the restoration of proper relations between the living and the dead.[12]

At the Temple of the Eastern Peak in Tainan, Taiwan, shamanic rites are performed on a nightly basis, with as many as a dozen mediums working at a time. I have fieldnotes for a number of individual sessions with the shamanesses at the temple, in interviews conducted by a female research assistant, Ch'iu Shu-chen.[13] Typically, families consulted the medium for the purpose of physical healing, often for a relative ill at home. The medium, possessed by the spirit of a deceased parent or grandparent, provided a medical prescription, but also admonished her descendant-clients to heal conflict within the family, and to provide better care (more frequent and more abundant offerings and propitiatory rites) for the dead.

But I had also heard scintillating tales of the patronage of clients from Taiwan's underworld: gamblers, thieves, and prostitutes. I was told that there were temples that catered especially to these nefarious customers. One night, only an hour before sunrise, Shu-chen and I visited such a temple, along the canal between Tainan and Anping, and observed a shamanic counseling session with two young women who had just finished a night's work at one of the hundreds of *karaoke* bars that have appeared in the last decade. "K-TV" clubs are extraordinarily popular throughout East Asia: originating in Japan, they have spread and multiplied in Korea, China, Taiwan, Hong Kong, and overseas Asian communities. They principally, though not exclusively, serve men. Customers pay for rooms by the hour, and are provided with a television monitor and stereo, wine and beer, snacks, and either male or female companionship, depending upon the clients' tastes.

The two women visiting the Anping Temple on a warm summer night were seeking counsel from the dead through a shamaness working late and alone. They were dressed in sequined blouses and translucent slacks, damp from perspiration and spilled beer, looking tired and disheveled. Though the consultation was performed on behalf of one of the women (we'll call her Mei-ying), it was her friend who opened up to Shu-chen as I retreated to the outer halls of the temple. Mei-ying had just returned to work after some weeks in reclusion, after terminating a pregnancy. The child had been fathered not by a client (in the age of AIDS, prostitutes are extraordinarily careful to protect their health), but by her lover, an occasional pimp and petty thief who had lost all of his money gambling at cards.

Abortion in China does not carry the same moral weight that it does in the West. Both the fetus and the newborn infant are considered part of the mother, physically and spiritually, and are not fully formed or "complete" until weaned, usually at eighteen months. Hence abortion, and even infanticide, is not regarded as the killing of a whole or independent person. Nevertheless, the souls of dead infants must be cared for, and special Buddhist rites are performed after an abortion or miscarriage for their benefit.[14] Mei-ying had suffered greatly as a result of her love affair. Not only had her lover squandered all of his money, but he had demanded that Mei-ying support his gambling addiction by aborting their child, in order to maintain the sizeable weekly income that she earned at one of the gaudy K-TV palaces along the Anping Canal. It was these anguishing events that had brought Mei-ying to the temple, to address her sense of imprisonment, betrayal, and powerlessness.

The shamaness was possessed that night by the spirit of the aborted infant, bawling and cooing like a newborn child. Though she offered no tangible advice to her client, Meiying appeared to be comforted by what she interpreted as the child's acceptance of his fate. Though the abortion had not been freely elected, at least the act of "visiting her child" through the intermediary of the shamaness had been deliberate, restoring not only the connection between mother and child, but also the active choice of a ritual performance in contrast to the passivity and absence of choice that characterized Mei-ying's romantic life. A break, both spiritual and material, had been mended.

Female shamans are powerful and efficacious. They are consulted when individuals and families face crises that cannot be resolved by ordinary means. They restore harmony, especially harmony within families that have experienced disruption due to abandonment, death, disease, or dissention. In spite of this important role, shamanesses are largely invisible, operating in liminal spaces and times: in small temples or rural settings, late at night.

SHAMANISM AND SELF-MORTIFICATION—MALE AND FEMALE

Today, the most visible shamans in China, Taiwan, and Hong Kong are men. They are "barefoot masters" who are possessed by powerful gods and practice exorcistic rites at temple fairs and community-wide celebrations.[15] Anyone who has ever attended a temple festival in Taiwan, Hong Kong, Singapore, or rural South China has undoubtedly been shocked by the spectacle of the barefoot mediums. Slightly dressed, dancing in a repetitive gait, they strike themselves on the back, arms, chest, and forehead with knives, skewers, swords, and other instruments of torture. They are possessed by gods such as the Emperor Supreme of the Dark Heavens, the Three Grandfather Kings, the Grandfather Prince, and the Emperor Supreme of the Eastern Hell. In Mandarin, they are called *ji-t'ung* (in southern dialects *dang-ki*), meaning "divining boys." It is at religious festivals that they are most visible, for it is on these occassions that they perform gruesome acts of self-mutilation. The Dutch ethnographer J. J. M. DeGroot observed one such performance in nineteenth century Amoy, and the same can be seen today:

> He parades in a state of delirium which proves that the god is in him . . . . Long daggers stand implanted deep in his cheeks and upper arms, so that the blood drips out . . . . At times he looks unconscious; then suddenly he hops, runs, spins around, and rolls from side to side, inflicting bloody wounds on his back with his sword or with a ball studded with sharp iron points.[16]

The "barefoot masters" represent the lowest tier among Taoist religious professionals, and though they create a colorful scene, they are reviled by their superiors, the Celestial Masters. Celestial Masters commune only with the heavenly immortals who have not experienced the stain of death.

In keeping with the fact that in ancient China women were central in public shamanism, Kristofer Schipper has written that Taoist functionaries at all levels were once equally divided between men and women, and that women once enjoyed equal status with men. Significantly, the earliest evidence of shamanic self-mutilation recorded by DeGroot involved a performance by two female *wu* in the Chin Dynasty (265–420 CE). The *History of the Chin* reads: "Chang Tan and Ch'en Chu drew out daggers, cut their tongues, swallowed the daggers, and spat fire."[17] This was in the context of an ancestral sacrifice. It is descriptive of the self-mortifications conducted by spirit mediums to the present day. However, such acts are rarely if ever seen among female shamans, and I know of no public performance of self-mortification by a woman.

Though self-mortification is now rarely practiced by Chinese women in public, it is an abiding religious practice of the inner chambers. It is interesting, however, to see how ancient public shamanic self-mortification has been transformed in the context of women's central and powerful role in the inner chambers. For women bound to the home, the primary virtue is loyalty to family, expressed in daily acts of filial piety. One of the most dramatic means employed by women both to express and to fulfill their filial duty is to cut their flesh to heal the illnesses of their husband's parents or their own parents. From medieval times forward, tales of "exemplary women" have recounted such acts of self-mortification: heroic daughters and daughters-in-law drawing blood, excising slices of skin and organs to feed the sick. Today such cases are rare, though they appear now and then in the news (and can be seen in Amy Tan's *Joy Luck Club* as well as the movie based on it), but hundreds of cases are reported in the dynastic histories and local gazetteers of imperial China. Though the practice seems to have started among the elite, it was common to all strata of society, and for many poor and illiterate women, these acts earned them a rare place in written history, not to mention the blessings of gods and ancestors.

I have studied hundreds of such cases, and traced their medicinal origins to the earliest book of medicine, quoted in the *Herbal Pharmacopia* (*Pen-ts'ao shih-i*) of the eighth century—which enumerates the benefits of consuming various parts of the body to cure illness—and their religious origins to bodhisattva tales of self-sacrifice translated from Sanskrit into Chinese in the early period of Buddhist growth in China. These early gestures of filial piety were carried out by both men and women, but by the late imperial period almost exclusively by women. Though in most cases the wounds were superficial, some were quite severe and must have been excruciating: drawing blood, slicing flesh from the hip or thigh, extracting portions of the liver or kidneys, gouging an eye. We are assured by their male chroniclers that these women enjoyed the protection of gods and ancestors, and did not suffer: blood clotting of itself, the heroine feeling no pain, the exercise even having the miraculous effect of actually lengthening, not shortening, her life. That these were religious acts can be seen in the rituals of their performance, the invocations to household deities, and the blessing of healing conferred by the spirits.

This example comes from a text that was used for the education of young girls in the seventeenth century, the *Illustrated Twenty-four Tales of Filial Piety for Women:*

> There was once in Hsin-ch'eng, Chiang-hsi Province, a woman of the Ch'en family married to Wang Tsung-lo. While her husband was serving as an official in another province, her mother-in-law, with the onset of old age, became gravely ill. The wife burned incense day and night, praying to Heaven. She vowed to shorten the destined years of her own life to lengthen her mother-in-law's lifespan.
>
> A physician said, "This old-age malady is difficult to cure. Only dragon liver and phoenix marrow can save her."
>
> The wife said to herself, "Dragon's liver is impossible to come by. Why not use my own liver in its place?" Thereupon, praying for blessings from the God of the Kitchen, she took up a knife and cut into her belly, extracting a slice of her liver. Of this she made a broth, which she served to her mother-in-law. Her mother ate it, and found it delectible.
>
> She asked, "What is this?"
>
> The wife equivocated. "It is the liver of sheep."
>
> When her mother-in-law finished eating, her illness was immediately cured.
>
> Even though the wife felt no pain, the blood of her wound flowed without ceasing.

All of this was spied out by her husband's younger sister, and the story spread quickly throughout the whole family. When the mother-in-law learned that the wife had sliced her own liver, she cried bitterly and soothed her. The mother-in-law lived another twelve years before she died.

When the provincial governor Duke Chou heard of this, he presented a placard for the Wang family gate. It read, "Such marvelous filiality reaches all the way to Heaven!"

Subsequently, the wife enjoyed a lifespan of 108 years. Her sons and grandsons numbered five generations under the same roof. On the day of her death, she gathered the family together, saying, "I am about to ascend into the heavens. The Golden Boy and Jade Girl have come to welcome me!" Thus speaking, she departed.[18]

However difficult we may find it to take such a story at face value, all of the most significant moral and religious values taught to women in traditional China appear in it: the anonymity of the heroine (we know her only as a daughter of Ch'en and wife of Wang) and of her act (it is done in secret, humbly shielded from her mother-in-law and witnessed inadvertently by a sister through a crack in the door); the ritual and religious dimensions of the performance (accompanied by invocations to the Kitchen God and rewarded with blessings of health and long life by the gods and spirits); and, most important, continuation of the family line (the good fortune of seeing, with her own eyes, many generations of male descendants). Still, it is important to emphasize that this powerful, efficacious act was culturally marginal (as we have seen, the marginalization of women in roles of religious power is one of the abiding effects of the Confucianization of Chinese culture): hidden, secretive, anonymous. At the same time, it was culturally central: restoring health and reinforcing the bonds of marriage and family.

CONCLUSION

Shamanism, female shamanism in particular, is highly ambivalent in Chinese religion and culture. The Confucian tradition, which had a large hand in molding Chinese values, has frowned upon shamans for more than 2,000 years. Nevertheless, the spirits are powerful; male and female shamans of various types still do their work, despite being socially ostracized. For female shamans, this situation is especially difficult. They should be in the inner chambers, but the spirits pull them out into the public sphere, even if in marginalized aspects of the public sphere. As we have seen, women helped by the spirits who do their work in the privacy of the inner chambers or the context of a religious movement are more respected in Chinese culture than those who work in public. Herein lies the central paradox for Chinese female shamans. Culture wants them in the inner chambers but the spirits want them out. This paradox is resolved both by severely marginalizing female shamans, who are even more ostracized than their male counterparts, and by giving them the role of restoring lost family harmony.

In every case that I have described in this chapter—the Shanxi shamaness who comforted the mother of an unmarried daughter suddenly departed, the two spirit-writers (the young nun Seng-fa and the teenage "Heavenly Savant" Aiyun), the Anping shamaness possessed by an aborted infant, and the wife who mortified herself to save her husband's mother—religiously gifted women were at once peripheralized by their culture and at the same time contributed greatly to its maintenance and cohesion. The Shanxi shamaness was old, poor, and unremarkable, and her consultation was conducted late at night. Potter's "grandmothers who speak to spirits," the mediums of Taiwan's Temple of the Eastern Peak, and the medium of the temple on the

Anping Canal also work late at night, in quiet, obscure temples, and serve clients from both the *yang* and the *yin* social worlds. The spirit-writing Seng-fa and Aiyun are "literate" shamans, but they too are marginalized by the surrounding culture: in the first case with dismissive judgments as to the "spurious" provenance of the inspired texts, and in the second case by the fact that the inspired writing is sponsored by a new religious movement, the *I-kuan Tao,* which has been banned by martial law for most of its existence. Wife Wang acts in secret, and her story would never have been known at all if not for a grateful, observant sister-in-law. Yet despite this marginalization, all of these women play central roles in Chinese religious and cultural life: healing, restoring, harmonizing, building families and communities.

The *Tao-te ching* says that the Tao works "in places where no one deigns to dwell" and this describes women's religious power for most of Chinese history. But perhaps it is this marginalization which gives shamanic women their remarkable sacred power, a power generated and regenerated by the convergence of *yin* forces: female gender, darkness, poverty and low social station, communication with the dead (particularly infants, unmarried girls, and other spirits who have departed prematurely), sadness, illness, and loss. While the domestic cult of the ancestors and the classical traditions of the "Three Religions" have confined women to the "inner quarters," women's religious participation has remained vital and powerful both at the heart and on the peripheries of Chinese culture, on the boundary lines between inner and outer, private and public, country and city, "cult" and "religion," night and dawn, the dead and the living.

Notes

1. For a detailed description of the domestic life of women in imperial China, see Patricia Ebrey, *The Inner Quarters: Marriage and the Lives of Chinese Women in the Sung Period* (Berkeley: University of California Press, 1993).

2. Indeed, women in ancient times seem to have enjoyed greater independence and a far higher social status outside the home than they did after the Han. See Lisa Raphals, *Sharing the Light: Representations of Women and Virtue in Early China* (Albany: State University of New York Press, 1998).

3. For an excellent recent study, see Susan Mann's *Precious Records: Women in China's Long Eighteenth Century* (Stanford: Stanford University Press, 1997).

4. *Ch'uan tsang chi chi* (Collection of Records Concerning the Tripitaka), by Seng-yu (515 CE), *Taisho Tripitaka* (T), vol. 55, no. 2145, pp. 39b–40c.

5. *Ta T'ang nei-tien lu* (Catalogue of T'ang Dynasty Sutras), by Tao-hsüan (664 CE), T55.2149.264c.

6. These views are attributed to Chang Fang, author of the *Li tai san pao chi* (History of the Three Treasures in Successive Reigns), T49.2034.22–129, but I have not yet located the references. They are cited in the *Ta Chou k'an ting chung ching mu lu* (Chou Dynasty Catalogue of the Sutras), by Ming-ch'üan (695 CE), T55.2153.415c; *Ta T'ang nei-tien lu* ibid., 264c. For further discussion of the strange case of Seng-fa, see Emil Zürcher. "Perspectives in the Study of Chinese Buddhism." *Journal of the Royal Asiatic Society of Great Britain and Ireland* 2 (1982): pp. 165–66; and Kogen Mizuno, *Buddhist Sutras: Origin, Development, Transmission* (Tokyo: Kosei, 1982), p.119.

7. Spirit mediums are vehicles of communication for families and their ancestors. Their pronouncements are rarely set down in writing. On the background of female shamanism, see J.J.M. DeGroot, *The Religious System of China: Its Ancient Forms, Evolution, History, and Present Aspect; Manners, Customs and Social Institutions Connected Therewith* (Leiden: E.J. Brill, 1910), Volume VI, pp. 1187–1341. On the participation of women in divination and spirit writing, see Hsü Ti-shan, *Fu-chi mi-hsin ti yen-chiu* (Studies of the Belief in Spirit-Writing) (Taipei: T'ai-wan shang-wu yin-shu kuan, 1980): and David Jordan and Daniel Overmyer, *The Flying Phoenix: Aspects of Chinese Sectarianism in Taiwan* (Princeton: Princeton University Press, 1986), esp. pp. 36–88. I am currently working on histories of women at the popular level who have been recipients of divine revelation.

8. Su Ming-tung. *T'ien tao kai lun* (Outline of the Way of Heaven) (Tainan: T'ien-chü shu-chü, 1978), pp. 186–87.

9. The interview was conducted in Tainan, Taiwan on August 24, 1986 by myself and a

Mandarin-Taiwanese interpreter. Aiyun and her father could understand my questions in Mandarin, but answered in Taiwanese. Subsequently a transcript of their responses was prepared by the interpreter.

10. See David Hawkes, *The Songs of the South: An Ancient Chinese Anthology of Poems by Ou Yuan and Other Poets* (London: Penguin Books, 1985). Indeed, in modern Korea, shamanesses still attain possession through dancing. See Laurel Kendall's *Life and Hard Times of a Korean Shaman* (Honolulu: University of Hawaii Press, 1988).

11. Jack M. Potter, "Cantonese Shamanism," in Arthur P. Wolf, ed., *Studies in Chinese Society* (Stanford: Stanford University Press, 1978), pp. 321–45.

12. Shamanic healing as a restoration of cosmic harmony is a major theme of Arthur Kleinman's work. See especially *Patients and Healers in the Context of Culture* (Harvard University Press).

13. It was important for me to rely on a female assistant for a number of reasons: first, the researcher and her informants share the same ethnic and cultural identity; second, in most cases, both the shaman and her client are women, and often the crises which have brought these women to the temple are private matters; finally, the interviews were by necessity conducted in Taiwanese, the only dialect spoken by a number of older or uneducated residents of southern Taiwan. I am grateful to Ch'iu Shu-chen for her careful work in conducting, recording, and transcribing the interviews upon which this discussion is based.

14. Japanese funerary rites for these "water babies" are described in detail by Helen Hardacre and William LaFleur in two excellent studies. Helen Hardacre, *Marketing the Menacing Fetus in Japan* (Berkeley: University of California Press, 1997); William LaFleur, *Liquid Life: Abortion and Buddhism in Japan* (Princeton: Princeton University Press, 1992).

15. These public shamanic rites are well described by Donald Sutton in several monographs. On the relative status of the "barefoot masters" in the history of Taoism, see Kristofer Schipper, *The Taoist Body* (Berkeley: University of California Press, 1993).

16. DeGroot, p. 984.

17. Ibid., p. 1212.

18. Woodblock print from the *Nü-tzu erh-shih-ssu hsiao t'u shuo* by Wu Chia-yu (fl. 1850–1910). Illustration reprinted from Jonathan Chaves, *Harvard Journal of Asiatic Studies,* 1986.

Further Readings

Ahern, Emily. "The Power and Pollution of Chinese Women." Margery Wolf and Roxane Witke, eds., *Women in Chinese Society,* Stanford: Stanford University Press, 1975, pp. 193–214.

Cahill, Suzanne. "Performers and Female Taoist Adepts: Hsi Wang Mu as the Patron Deity of Women in Medieval China." *Journal of the American Oriental Society* 106 (1986): pp. 155–68.

Cass, Victoria. "Female Healers in the Ming and the Lodge of Ritual and Ceremony." *Journal of the American Oriental Society* 106 (1986): pp. 233–40.

Grant, Beata. "The Spiritual Saga of Woman Huang: From Pollution to Purification." David Johnson, ed., *Ritual Opera, Operatic Ritual.* Berkeley: University of California Press, 1989, pp. 224–311.

Harrell, Stevan C. "Men, Women, and Ghosts in Taiwanese Folk Religion." Carolyn Walker Bynum, Steven Harrell, and Paula Richman, eds., *Gender and Religion: On the Complexity of Symbols.* Boston: Beacon Press, 1986, pp. 97–116.

Levering, Miriam. "The Dragon Girl and the Abbess of Mo-shan: Gender and Status in the Ch'an Buddhist Tradition." *Journal of the International Association of Buddhist Studies* 4 (1982): pp. 19–35.

Paper, Jordan. "The Persistence of Female Deities in Patriarchal China." *Journal of Feminist Studies in Religion* 6 (1990): pp. 25–40.

Reed, Barbara. "Taoism." Arvind Sharma, ed., *Women in World Religions.* Albany: SUNY Press, 1987, pp. 161–81.

Sangren, P. Stevan. "Female Gender in Chinese Religious Symbols: Kuan Yin, Ma Tsu and the 'Eternal Mother.' " *Signs* 9 (1983): pp. 4–25.

Schuster, Nancy. "Striking a Balance: Women and Images of Women in Early Chinese Buddhism." In Y. Y. Haddad and E. Findley, eds., *Women, Religion, and Social Change.* Albany: SUNY Press, 1985, pp. 87–111.

Seaman, Gary. "The Sexual Politics of Karmic Retribution." In E. Ahern and H. Gates, eds., *The Anthropology of Taiwanese Society.* Stanford: Stanford University Press, 1981, pp. 381–96.

Wolf, Margery. "The Woman who didn't Become a Shaman." In *A Thrice-Told Tale: Feminism, Postmodernism, and Ethnographic Responsibility.* Stanford: Stanford University Press, 1992, pp. 93–126.

Yu Chun-fang. "Feminine Images of Kuan-yin in Post-T'ang China." *Journal of Chinese Religions* 18 (1990): pp. 61–89.

III

IN THE WINGS

Rituals for Wives and Mothers

Unlike the women of extraordinary calling who enliven many pages of this volume, the women in this section are primarily involved in everyday concerns. In five of these studies, there is little tension between their religious and their mundane lives. Rather, their religious concerns often validate these women's ordinary concerns and help to give them meaning. In the sixth case, religion helps women bear the frustrations of their everyday lives. At least in terms of sheer numbers, these are probably the more common patterns of women's religious lives.

One of the least known aspects of women's everyday religious lives relates to the many rites and ceremonies that women celebrate on their own. Yet these rituals are as much a part of the religious milieu as are the much-better publicized rites and gatherings of men. Often women will organize them, prepare for them, and celebrate them, with little or no male participation or intrusion. It is important for us to review these practices, because, more than any other aspects of women's religious lives, they reflect women's most common concerns and experiences. Virtually any woman in most traditional cultures could find something in the descriptions included here that would parallel some significant aspect of her own religious world.

We have offered six samples from four cultures. Although the heritage of Hindu women's rites and festal occasions was rarely studied before the time of this book's first edition, it offers an exceptionally rich sampling of women's practices. The first three chapters in this section describe three very different types of rituals practiced by Hindu women in different regions of India. These three chapters show how rich women's ordinary religious world can be even in a culture like India's, in which men control so many public and formal religious practices and institutions. Childbirth provides a significant religious occasion for women of central India as it does for women in other regions of the world. Chapter 7 allows us to share in this experience. Chapters 8 and 9 describe how wives and mothers of a north Indian village engage in numerous rituals to protect their families and household interests and how middle-aged women of a village near the eastern Indian coast protect their husband through a month-long discipline in which they joyfully worship the deity Krishna.

In many cultures death seems as much a special women's province as birth. Chapter 10 carries us halfway around the globe to Central America to witness another group of older women who organize and celebrate traditional rituals of mourning.

The two final chapters of this section describe practices connected with cults of saints in Iran and Morocco. In a practice popular in pre-revolutionary Iran, women of all ages made requests to the Muslim saints. These requests were related to their various domestic concerns; as part of this practice, women also vowed to provide a ritual meal for their friends if the request was met. Though sometimes criticized, these vows and feasts were important occasions for women, both socially and religiously. In Morocco, the saints are also important in women's religious lives, even though the saints and their sanctuaries are not part of official Islam. In this case, the tombs of saints serve as a place of refuge and solace for women overtaxed by the demands and stresses of their family roles.

7

Golden Handprints and Red-Painted Feet: Hindu Childbirth Rituals in Central India

DORANNE JACOBSON

The cry of a newborn child sounds faintly from within the thick mud-plastered stone walls of a house in an Indian village. Barely audible in the night air, this tiny cry gives evidence of a major event in the lives of those who dwell within the walls of that house.

While this birth is but one of about 80,000 that occur each day in India (some 29 million every year), it is the focus of much concern, some of which is manifested in a set of rituals performed by women before and after the arrival of the baby. Centering on the infant and its mother, these rituals involve kinswomen of the baby, other women of the village, and, tangentially, some men. The rituals serve a number of purposes: they announce the baby's arrival to the world, magically strengthen and protect mother and child from evil influences, mark the passage of mother and infant from one stage of life to another, provide the new mother with approval and support, contribute to women's

DORANNE JACOBSON received her Ph.D. in Anthropology from Columbia University and is currently Director of International Images, Springfield, Illinois. She has focused her anthropological research on changes in women's roles in Central India, where she has conducted research for a total of more than six years over the past three decades. She has published two books on India and more than thirty articles on women, the family, development, and religion in India. She is also a widely published photographer.

Author's Note: The data on which this chapter is based were collected during three years of field research in India (1965–1967, 1973–1975), as well as several shorter periods of research in the 1980s and 1990s, including a month in 1999. I am grateful to the American Institute of Indian Studies, the National Institute of Mental Health, and the National Endowment for the Humanities for support for research and writing. For their essential assistance, I wish to thank the residents of Nimkhera village and Ms. Sunalini Nayudu, Dr. Leela Dube, Dr. Suzanne Hanchett, and Dr. Jerome Jacobson.

sense of solidarity with other women, and publicly recognize women's vital roles in perpetuating and enhancing the prosperity of the family and the larger community. In a culture in which women typically enjoy fewer privileges than men, the rituals serve to remind women—and men—of the fact that women, after all, produce children, the one thing without which no kin group or society could long exist.

This chapter discusses the Hindu practices and rituals surrounding pregnancy and childbirth that are observed in Nimkhera, a village in Madhya Pradesh State, Central India. These rituals, summarized in Table 1, are primarily life-crisis rites, also known as rites of

Table 1 *Summary of Childbirth Rituals and Practices in Nimkhera Village, Madhya Pradesh*

Occasion or Timing	Ritual and Practice	Sociological Interpretation
Pregnancy	Minimal restrictions on food and activity	Gradual separation of pregnant woman from group
Delivery and 3-day pollution period (*Sor*)	Strong restrictions on food and activity	Definite separation of mother and child from group; recognition of their lineage membership
Day of birth	Placement of the *charua* pot; special foods for the new mother	Psychological support for the new mother
Evening after birth	*Charua* songfest	Announcement to village of the birth; tacit public recognition to new mother; symbolic sharing of her fertility
3 days after birth	Lifting of 3-day pollution period (*Sor*); ritual cleansing	First step in reintegration of mother and child into group
7–10 days after birth	*Chauk* ceremony: blessing of mother and child; worship of sun and water pots; folk birth control	Recognition and support of the new mother; introduction of mother and child to outside world; symbolic extension of her fertility
	Chauk songfest	Announcement to village of infant's successful completion of most dangerous period of life
	Grass Celebration (*Duba Badhai*): celebration of birth of first son; gift distribution	Display of generosity; averting of envy
About 40 days after birth	Well Worship	End of postpartum pollution period; final reintegration of mother into group; symbolic extension of her fertility to village water supply
2 1/2 or 5 months after birth	First feeding of solid foods	A milestone in the child's growing individuality
No set time	*Pach* gifts from mother's natal kin	Recognition of importance of kinship ties with maternal relatives
No set time	Head shaving (*Mundan*)	Final separation of child from physical attachment to mother; acknowledgement of importance of mother's care for child's survival; introduction of child to life outside the home

passage, centering on a major transition in the lives of the newborn infant, its mother, father, and other kin. Typically, in all cultures, rites of passage—ceremonies marking birth, coming of age, marriage, and death—note momentous changes in the lives of individuals. In basic outline, rites of passage are remarkably similar the world over. Those undergoing a major transition are formally separated from their old status and routines and enter a sacred, often hazardous, transitional state. They assume their new roles, frequently in isolation. Finally, a ceremonial reintegration into the larger society recognizes their changed status and resulting changes in social relationships.

In Indian childbirth ceremonies, although the infant is important, most of the ritual focuses on the parents, especially the mother. Childbirth rituals are unique in the degree to which they are the domain of women in a culture where men often seem to dominate. The contrast is seen, for example, in a Hindu wedding; when the bride is given to the groom and his family, a male Brahman priest chants Sanskrit verses and directs the rites, while veiled women sing on the sidelines. In childbirth rituals, however, men play only minimal supporting roles. Giving birth is a skill in which no man can claim expertise. This is the heart of the domestic sphere, the women's domain par excellence. In dramatizing one of women's most vital roles, the rituals contribute to harmonious cooperation among women brought together to live in the patrilineal joint family, the key social unit in rural India.[1]

NIMKHERA VILLAGE AND THE CULTURAL SETTING

Nimkhera village is situated in Raisen District, about fifty miles east of Bhopal, the capital of Madhya Pradesh, geographically India's largest state. The village is similar to hundreds of others in the region. The population of the village was 621 in 1974 and 760 in 1999. Approximately 85 percent of the villagers are Hindu and 15 percent Muslim. The villagers belong to eighteen different ranked Hindu castes and four Muslim caste-like groups. Several of the village men work outside Nimkhera, but most villagers derive their support from the abundant crops of wheat and other cultigens grown on the village fields.

Raisen District is almost completely rural, and most of its villages are relatively small. The district has a relatively low population density and has traditionally been underdeveloped agriculturally and educationally. Within the past few years, increased use of tubewells, irrigation, tractors, electricity, pesticides, and fertilizer, and the growing of new Green Revolution crops have brought agricultural change and increased prosperity to the region. Rural educational facilities have expanded significantly. Twenty years ago, fewer than one-tenth of district females could read, but at present approximately one-fourth are at least minimally literate (compared with approximately half of males). As in many other parts of India, there are fewer females than males (900 females per 1,000 males), reflecting the special physical hazards to which girls and women are subject in a region where good medical care can be difficult to obtain. The rate of infant mortality has traditionally been high but is currently declining.[2] Television is now becoming extremely popular here, as it is throughout India.

In the local village setting, Hindu parents arrange the marriages of most girls in their mid to late teens, and most boys before age twenty-two. The age of marriage has risen—just a generation ago, village girls were usually married before puberty and boys before twenty. The young couple—usually strangers to each other—do not normally begin living together until after the consummation ceremony, which may occur at the time of the wedding or from one to three years later. Dressed in fine clothes, ornamented with glistening jewelry, and modestly cloaked with a white shawl, the weeping bride is led from her parental home and borne in a tractor-drawn trailer, jeep, bus, or taxi to her marital home, usually in a village one to forty miles distant from her parents' home. There she meets alone with her husband for the first time. She begins to spend much of her time in her husband's home as the lowest-ranking member of his joint family. However, most women enjoy long, refreshing visits in their natal homes until late in life.

In most joint families, the young wife is expected to observe purdah: she stays inside the house most of the time and veils her face from her elder in-laws. Moving about outside the home without strict chaperonage is likely to lead to aspersions being cast upon her moral character. She is usually responsible for winnowing grain, cooking, and other time-consuming domestic chores. Some women—usually not the youngest brides—go to the village well twice daily to bring back heavy pots of water atop their heads. Women's duties also include gathering cow dung and shaping it into cakes for cooking fuel, as well as plastering and painting the house and courtyard. Many women work in the fields and perform a multitude of other tasks. Women of high-status families are much more circumscribed in their movements than are poorer low-status women, who may have to seek laboring jobs outside the home. But even women of low socioeconomic status must carefully guard their reputations through modest demeanor and face-veiling.

In this region, as in much of rural India, village women have little independent political and economic power. They can influence family members within the home, but they are strongly discouraged by every cultural norm from participating in political activity outside the domestic realm. Among rural Hindus, most land and real estate is owned by men and inherited by sons rather than wives or daughters. For most women, access to wealth and economic support is obtained primarily through their relationships with the men who control important material assets. Under Indian law, women may claim legal rights of ownership in land and buildings, but in fact, demanding these rights from her male kin could cause a woman to be ostracized by her relatives—for most women, a price too high to pay.

All over India, millions of women, particularly in urban areas, are seeking higher education and finding fulfilling employment outside the home. Women have achieved high political office at local and national levels, and businesses and the professions are studded with the glittering accomplishments of talented women. As television spreads its messages throughout India, village women are becoming increasingly aware of lifestyles alternative to their own. In Nimkhera, two married women of the village are working as part-time primary school teachers in local government-sponsored programs. A substantial percentage of village children, both boys and girls, are attending classes in the local primary and secondary schools. Nonetheless, for the women of Nimkhera and of hundreds of thousands of other Indian villages, traditional roles emphasizing female modesty and self-effacement remain essential to daily life.

In Nimkhera, as in much of North and Central India, a young bride is addressed by her elder in-laws not by her personal name, but by the term *Dulhan,* or Bride. The word politely emphasizes the woman's status as a treasured yet low-ranking member of her husband's family, a person whose expected role is to silently follow the commands of her elders, uncomplainingly carry out household duties, and produce children for the lineage.

In 1993, India adopted a constitutional amendment that set aside a third of all seats on local elected village councils, or *panchay-*

ats, for women. Similarly, a third of the council chief, or *Sarpanch,* positions were reserved for women. The Nimkhera *Sarpanch* position is reserved for a woman—and Shanti Devi, the wife of an important village man—who would otherwise have been elected himself—was chosen for the post. In her late thirties, the mother of five children, educated to the fifth standard, she veils her face when attending meetings, where she is accompanied by her husband. She "feels shy" to speak out before the older men from whom she must veil her face. Still, her tenure has not been without accomplishment: government workers have come to Nimkhera to drill new drinking water wells and to pave village lanes with stone, as per her requests, emphasized by her dynamic husband. Since she has been the incumbent of this important post for a few years, one might have thought that her village neighbors would hold her in some awe and address her as "Leader." But the hold of traditional family obligations and female modesty standards remains firm; her fellow villagers address Shanti Devi as they do all young wives *"Dulhan."*

Indeed, whether she is titular village chief, teacher, or an ordinary member of an unremarkable family, for a woman, her prime role is to be a mother, particularly a mother of sons. Every girl receives early training in child care, and girls love to carry young children about. A young woman is brought as a bride into her husband's family to produce children for the family. Through bearing children she finds social approval, economic security, and emotional satisfaction. Every young bride knows of old women who lack children, their houses empty of sons and grandchildren, with no young hands to depend upon for support and aid. Even having daughters is not enough, for daughters marry and go to live with their husbands' kin. Adoption is possible only under very limited circumstances. Fortunate older women are those who are protected and fed by loving sons and cared for by respectful daughters-in-law. The message is clear: to be barren brings grief, to bear children brings joy. Thus every bride looks forward to becoming pregnant. Even women with several children are usually happy about new pregnancies. Abortion is rare, and until recently contraception was very seldom practiced. Within the past few years, a small proportion of village mothers, having given birth to several children, have had tubal ligations in government clinics. The infant mortality rate in the region has traditionally been quite high and is only now coming down. Thus, the disinterest in birth control is not surprising.[3]

Childbirth rituals are almost the same for a baby boy as for a baby girl, but the greater enthusiasm surrounding rituals for boys shows a strong bias in favor of sons. Women say they love boys and girls the same. After all, they say, they suffer equally painful birth pangs for both. "But we feel great pleasure if a son is born," one woman said. "A son remains part of our family. A daughter will belong to others."

Throughout the birth rituals, certain materials appear again and again as symbols, expressing cherished values and desires. Cow dung is commonly used for cleaning and purifying. Produced by the sacred cow, dung is used daily in the form of dried cakes for cooking fuel. As a paste that dries to form a resilient film, it is used to plaster earthen walls and floors. Only women make cow-dung cakes and apply cow-dung paste. Golden turmeric, used in many Hindu rituals, is especially noticeable in ceremonies involving women. Wet turmeric is used to help effect transition from one state to another, and in childbirth rituals it also symbolizes female generative powers. Items of red and russet hue are often part of women's rituals along with the turmeric; these, too, symbolize female fertility. Wheat and objects used by women to produce wheat foods appear frequently—hardly surprising in this area where wheat is literally the staff of life. Chilis, lentils,

Photo © Doranne Jacobson

The Goddess and Golden Handprints

To thank the Goddess Narbada Mai for the gift of a son, a woman makes upright handprints in golden turmeric paste at the base of the goddess's temple at Hoshangabad, Madhya Pradesh. Handprints in cow-dung paste, pointing downward, have been left by women asking the goddess for a son.

and salt, classic accompaniments to a meal of wheat breads, are also evident. Brown sugar and the more expensive puffed white-sugar candies are highly desired treats used in many rituals and also distributed at births and weddings to express the joy of the family. Water is a key symbol signifying both purification and fertility. In this region, the water supply is limited throughout much of the year, and the vital link between water and survival is keenly felt by the villagers. Since one of women's particular duties is to bring water into the house, women and water are often connected in ceremony and symbol.[4]

PREGNANCY

Since women's overriding concern is to produce offspring, no effort is spared to encourage pregnancy. Brides who remain childless too long are given every opportunity to be with their husbands by night and to worship

Matabai, the village Mother Goddess, a manifestation of the powerful Goddess Durga, by day. The childless wife also offers special oblations to Lord Shiva or fasts every week in honor of the Goddess Santoshi Mata. Concerned relatives may take her to visit the shrines of other deities of the region, particularly the temple of the Goddess Narbada Mai, the much-revered river goddess who flows as the Narmada River through Central India. Silently begging the goddess for a son, the woman wets her hands with cow-dung paste and makes inverted handprints on the base of the goddess's temple. If her prayers are answered, she gratefully returns to make upright handprints in golden turmeric on the temple and to make other offerings to the goddess. The childless woman may also visit a shaman, or medium, who will divine the cause of her problem and seek to cure it. The shrines of such mediums are thronged by worshippers, many of whom return to express their thanks for newly born offspring. A few villagers also consult women gynecologists.

Generally, failing to conceive is regarded as a feminine defect. A childless daughter-in-law is criticized and may be replaced. Barrenness may be seen as punishment for sins committed in a past life or as the result of educating a girl too highly. Husbands are virtually never blamed for childlessness, despite the fact that most villagers believe that a baby grows out of the man's seed alone, developing like a plant's seed in the fertile field of the womb. On the other hand, a woman is not blamed if she gives birth to babies who die; people say that it was not in her husband's fate to have living children. Anything pertaining to sexuality is a matter of "shame" in much of India, especially in the North and Central regions, and young women—and men—are often quite uninformed about human biology, sexual practices, and fertility regulation.[5]

Once she suspects that she is pregnant, the happy young woman shyly refrains from mentioning the joyous news to anyone. She delicately leaves it to others to notice that she has not observed the usual monthly pollution period, is sometimes nauseous, or is widening at the waist. Her husband and other relatives gradually recognize the situation, and she begins to receive special treatment. In later pregnancies, a joking neighbor may euphemistically inquire, "Have you been eating *mung* lentils?" These lentils are said to cause one's stomach to swell.

The pregnant woman is advised not to eat certain foods that are regarded as possibly harmful to the baby, and she may be given special delicacies. A major concern is shielding the expectant woman and her unborn child from malevolent magic and spirits. The pregnant woman is encouraged to remain home as much as possible. She is not allowed to wander about after dark, for fear of evil spirits. The woman may wear a tiny jacknife on her belt: a sharp iron object wards off ghosts and spirits. She also does not wear the usual auspicious substances with which women paint themselves, for fear that they may attract an evil spirit. A pregnant woman stays shut up inside her house during an eclipse of the sun, since her appearance would be an "offense to God," and the child would be born with a defect. Conservative villagers feel that sexual relations should be avoided for the latter months of pregnancy. A few very conservative women believe that a pregnant woman should not be photographed, for fear of an unseen danger to her or her child. These protective practices serve to gradually set the pregnant woman apart and to inform others of her special and valued condition.

Particularly for the first birth, the woman must be at her husband's rather than her parents' home for delivery. If a woman bears her first child in her parental home, it is strongly believed that misfortune or tragedy will befall her relatives. For example, one young woman bore her first child in her natal home, and villagers shook their heads knowingly when her teenaged brother suddenly died the next day. Furthermore, a woman giving birth is almost never attended by her

Photo © Doranne Jacobson

Waiting for her Baby

A pregnant young Brahman wife separates wheat from chaff with a winnowing fan as she awaits the birth of her first child. Wheat and the winnowing fan will be used to bless her infant almost as soon as it is born.

mother but by her female in-laws. A young woman would find shame in flaunting her pregnancy—clear evidence of her sexuality—before her mother, and instead must be comforted by the women of her husband's home, where sexuality is an expected part of her wifely duties.

DELIVERY

When labor begins, the prospective mother is suddenly and radically separated from others. In Hindi, the language of the region, a woman who is in labor or has just given birth is called a *jachcha*. A *jachcha* is in a highly polluted and polluting state, similar to that of the lowest untouchable castes. Anyone who touches her or her newborn infant becomes ritually polluted and must take a bath before touching others. Therefore, when labor begins, the *jachcha* retires to a little-used room or curtained-off area, separated from all other members of the household. A man of the family is sent to call the midwife.

The midwife (*dai*) who delivers most babies in Nimkhera lives in a nearby village. Like traditional midwives in much of India, she belongs to a very low-ranked caste, because of the ritually defiling nature of her work. Four generations of women in her family have been midwives. She has received some training in modern methods and sterile technique at the district hospital, but she all but ignores this training in her practice. A nontraditional nurse, trained in midwifery and employed at a government health station in a nearby village, is also available. This post is usually filled by a Christian woman from the southern state of Kerala, to whom ritual-pollution concepts are relatively unimportant or even irrelevant. The traditional midwife's fees are lower than the government nurse's, and her methods are more familiar, so most villagers call the nurse only in a very difficult case.[6]

During labor, some women undo their buttons, braids, knots, and trunk locks to "open the way" for the baby. The *jachcha* may be fed water in which the idols in the village temple have been bathed. This sacred water is said to alleviate labor pains and bring about a speedy delivery.

Inside the dimly lit birth room, the *jachcha* squats on the cow-dung-plastered earth floor and clings to a rope or house post. If delivery is difficult, the midwife or nurse may encourage her to lie on her back. One woman from her marital family and the midwife are with the *jachcha*. The assisting relative hands things to the midwife and watches to make sure that the midwife does not perform magic on the *jachcha*. No matter how great the pain, the *jachcha* is expected to endure the pangs of labor stoically. Silence is ideal, low moans are tolerated, but shouting or crying are strongly disapproved of and ridiculed.[7] One woman who had been in labor for nearly twenty-four hours was seen crying and clutching her husband in a desperate embrace. The village women gossiped for weeks about this shameless indiscretion. Furthermore, the woman giving birth is expected to retain her modesty as much as possible by draping her sari adroitly, and she should take care not to soil any garments or bedclothes, since the Washerwoman[8] objects to laundering cloth defiled with uterine blood. In childbirth, as in other facets of life, restraint is the keynote.

Finally, the baby emerges. No exclamations or cries of delight are heard; only a quiet statement is made: "It's a boy," or "It's a girl." Emotions are kept in check; to compliment or admire the baby would surely draw the evil eye.[9] A man with a watch is asked the time, so that an accurate horoscope can be prepared later. Otherwise, no announcement is made.

The midwife lays the slippery babe on a rag on the earthen floor while she waits for the placenta to appear. Thus, after emerging from its mother's womb, the child's first resting place is the earth upon which the child will depend for sustenance. As Ruth and Stanley Freed have pointed out, a Hindu's life is bracketed by being placed upon the earth at birth and again just before death. The soul of the infant, having been reincarnated from a previous existence, comes from the land of the dead, and the body of a deceased person is returned to the earth through the cremation process. Importantly, the earth is conceptualized as a mother goddess, symbolic of creation and fertility, and together with water, the source of all life.[10]

Once the placenta appears, with scant care for aseptic technique, the midwife ties a string or bit of rag around the umbilical cord and cuts it with a sickle or an old razor blade. The act of cutting the umbilical cord is considered to be extremely polluting and is done only by the midwife. Even if the midwife's arrival is delayed for hours after the birth, the cord is left uncut until she arrives.

After the mother and child are cleansed with a warm-water sponge bath, the newborn baby is placed for a moment in a winnowing fan along with a sharp metal object, such as a knife or a sickle, and a handful of uncooked wheat, lentils, salt, and red chilis "to make the child's mind sharp." The food items are those considered essential to even the simplest meal and help insure that the child will always have access to these crucial comestibles. The sharp metal object is later placed near the head of the bed shared by mother and infant, to keep evil spirits and ghosts at bay during this dangerous period of transition.

The midwife then digs a shallow hole in the earthen floor near the mother's cot and buries the placenta and severed umbilical cord there to keep them safe from the clutches of malevolent magicians. (It is believed that a bit of placenta, manipulated magically by a childless woman, could help that woman produce a healthy child but would cause harm to the original baby.) A smoldering piece of cow dung is placed over the spot; the fire is kept burning for several days to warm and purify the new mother and to protect the vulnerable vestiges of the birth from harmful influences.

The midwife scrapes up the other remnants of the birth from the floor and later discards them. Then she plasters over the area with a new layer of purifying cow-dung paste. A broken earthen pot is put beside the mother's bed for a urinal, as she will not leave the birth room for several days. The birth sari is given to the Washerwoman to be laundered (and thus purified). The midwife may give the new mother an oil massage. Still in a very polluted state, not to be touched by anyone other than the midwife and assisting relative, the sequestered mother and child rest, wrapped in old clothes. Outsiders are not invited to see the baby, and even when the midwife makes follow-up calls on the mother, the baby is covered with a cloth to avoid the evil eye (and, unknown to the villagers, extra germs). The fear of illness or death striking the baby is so strong that no visitors, and not even the parents, ever openly admire the child. Instead, they exaggerate complaints about the baby's health.

CEREMONIES FOLLOWING DELIVERY

On the day of the birth, a small ceremony is held for the new mother. At an auspicious time, selected by the family Brahman priest, an herbal tea is ritually brewed for the mother. Only women of the extended family are invited to this event. The sister of the baby's father purifies an area of the floor with cow dung, and, using wheat flour, draws an auspicious design (*chauk*) on it. Then a special new clay pot, called a *charua,* is decorated with red paint, cow dung, turmeric, and grass, filled with water, special herbs, medicines, and fruits and set atop the design. After that, five or seven women from the family carry the pot into the kitchen, where the child's father's sister places it over the family cooking fire. The reddish herbal tea that results is the *jachcha*'s main drink for many days. When the new mother wants water, she must drink it warm, and for some time, she avoids spicy foods in favor of bland porridge. The women of the family prepare special strength-giving *laddus* for her—spherical sweets packed with butter, brown sugar, almonds, shredded coconut, dates, ginger, raisins, caraway seeds, and many medicinal ingredients. These items are very expensive, but under the circumstances, miserly in-laws can hardly balk at providing them.

That evening a woman's songfest is held at the home of the new infant. These songfests bring women together as women to celebrate a uniquely female achievement and to honor the new mother. Women and girls from the neighborhood—or the whole village—are invited by the Barber woman on behalf of the host family. As darkness settles over the village, the women gather in the *jachcha*'s courtyard to talk, spread news, reminisce about other pregnancies and other births, and sing special childbirth songs. The *jachcha* and the infant remain hidden and unheard in their polluted isolation, but they can hear the sounds of the gathering.

Most of the birth songs refer to the *jachcha* and the pain she has suffered, as well as to tensions between the new mother and the in-laws with whom she lives. A typical song is the lament of a woman in labor, with her husband away, and her mother-in-law and husband's sister providing her with no help or sympathy. None of the songs center on the child, presumably to avoid the evil eye, but in a few songs the child is referred to as "jewel-like." In one song, Lord Krishna's adoring mother is singing a lullaby to her beautiful divine infant. Thus, indirectly, women can express the joy they feel in holding their own precious babies—their one great consolation for having to live among unfamiliar and often unloving in-laws. Listening to the conversation and to the songs, young girls at the songfest receive early training in what to expect when they reach childbearing age. As refreshment, the singers receive sugar candies and also swollen boiled wheat, suggestive of the *jachcha*'s formerly swollen body and hence symbolically extending her fertility to the other women.

The infant is not normally suckled immediately after birth, but women say they wait until a priest designates an auspicious moment for the first nursing. This usually occurs within a day or two of the birth and is typically at about the time when the mother's milk comes in. Feeding a baby with a bottle of cow's milk is extremely rare, and is done only when the mother dies or completely fails to produce milk herself.

For three days after the birth, the new mother and child are in an especially great state of pollution, "because nine months' menstrual blood comes out at a baby's birth." During these three days, called *Sor,* no one but the midwife touches the mother and infant. All members of the baby's father's family are also polluted, though less so than the mother and child. Even if the baby is born away from its paternal home, members of the patrilineage are still polluted and should not engage in fully normal social interaction or worship of the deities. This pollution observance emphasizes to kinsmen the significance of the arrival of a new member of the kin group. At this time, the father of the baby may glimpse it but not hold it. Any physical contact whatsoever between husband and wife is forbidden during these three days, and they may not have any intimate contact for forty days. If a new father wished to show some affection at this time for his wife and new baby, rules of pollution, etiquette, and shame about matters related to sexuality (such as spousal interaction and birth) would prevent him from doing so, particularly in the presence of any onlooker.

During *Sor,* mother and child are given sponge baths and oil massages each day by the midwife. Then, on the third day after the birth, a ritual, Sor Lifting (*Sor Uthana*), ends this state of greatest impurity. At a time selected by the family priest, the midwife breaks the mother's old glass bangles, polluted by the birth, off her wrists. She rubs the mother with an ointment of turmeric, wheat flour, oil, and water to cleanse her skin. The baby is rubbed with a ball of turmeric and dough and given an oil massage. Then the midwife gives both mother and child complete purifying baths (the mother's first real bath since the birth), and they don clean clothes. Other family members also bathe. The bedding and dirty clothes are either washed by the Washerwoman or thrown away. The midwife purifies the birth room by applying cow-dung slip to the floor and up onto the base of the walls.

After *Sor*, since the new mother has moved a step closer to her normal state, the untouchable midwife no longer takes care of her. Instead (if the new mother belongs to a non-untouchable caste), the middle-ranking village Barber woman now takes over. The Barber woman cuts the new mother's nails and applies another layer of cow dung to the floor of the room. If the new mother wants to become pregnant again soon (as is often the case if she has just given birth to a girl), she asks the Barber woman to apply the cow-dung slip so that it covers only a narrow band at the base of the walls. But if she wants to postpone her next pregnancy, she asks the Barber woman to smear the slip higher on the wall. Women members of the family apply cow dung to the other floors of the house and replace all earthen water pots (which are porous and hence considered polluted by the birth) with new pots. The sickle used to cut the umbilical cord is purified with fire by the blacksmith.

After this purification, the members of the kin group, as well as the infant, emerge in a clean and renewed state. The new mother can now enter the main room of the house and be touched by others, but she is still not pure enough to engage in normal household tasks. In particular, she avoids cooking and any jobs involving contact with dampness. In fact, she should not even wash her own baby, for fear of her catching cold. Also, she still avoids eating certain foods. Not until forty days—usually expressed as one-and-a-quarter-months—after the birth will she achieve a completely normal state.

THE CHAUK CEREMONY

The major ritual following childbirth is the *Chauk* ceremony, held about a week to ten days after the birth. The exact time is selected by the Brahman priest according to astrological calculations. The *Chauk*, or Square, takes its name from the auspicious four-sided design drawn in wheat flour to mark the central location of the ritual.

The infant's father's sister (paternal aunt), who should be present for the occasion, plays an important role in the *Chauk* ceremony. Through this role she reaffirms her involvement in the home of her birth and the importance of her continuing bonds with the family of her parents and brothers. If she is not available, another female relative—usually a young girl—can substitute. If the infant is a boy, the aunt makes two bas-relief wall designs out of wet cow dung, one on each side of the house's main door. Otherwise, the *Chauk* ceremonies are the same for boys and girls.

In the late afternoon, after the wall designs have been made, the Barber woman arrives to prepare the mother for the *Chauk*. She bathes her, cuts her nails, does her hair in fresh braids, and fits new mirror-studded lacquer bangles on her wrists. The baby too is bathed.

The *Chauk* ceremony itself takes place at dusk, around six or seven o'clock. It is a private ceremony, normally attended only by women and girls of the household and by the Barber woman, who physically guides the new mother through the ceremony. Boys and men are usually excluded.

The aunt uses cow dung to cleanse a spot on the floor in the center of the main room of the house, just in front of the door, and then draws the *Chauk* design in wheat flour on the spot and arranges other ritual paraphernalia. The new mother appears, her face covered by a veil, and sits down on a wooden platform, which has been placed over the design, facing the door of the house. She is wearing all her fine jewelry and best clothing, over which she wears a white cover-all shawl. Held in the crook of her right arm and completely covered with her sari and shawl is her baby, dressed in new clothes that were blessed by having a maiden step on them. (A young maiden, or *kanya* is regarded as an auspicious representative of the Mother Goddess, through whose blessings the infant was produced and will be protected.)

The Barber woman rubs the mother's feet with wet turmeric and, using red paint, draws an auspicious design on them. Garbed in finery, modestly cloaked in white, with only her ornamented hands and gold-and-red painted feet protruding, the new mother looks as she did when she first arrived at the door of the house as a bride on the occasion of her consummation ceremony. Then she stood outside the door, facing the house, with her white veil tied to her new husband's shawl, while he stood on the wooden platform. Now, holding her baby, she sits on the platform inside the door, facing out. In her new role as mother she is fulfilling the promise that was inherent in her role as bride.

Guided by the Barber woman, the baby's father's sister holds a platter filled with ritual paraphernalia and stands before the veiled mother and child. With her finger she carefully paints a turmeric swastika (an ancient Hindu auspicious design) on the white cloth over the woman's head and on the cloth over the baby. The swastika on the mother's head is said to help ensure that she will enjoy a long married life. The swastika over the baby is intended to "keep her lap full of babies." The aunt then slowly swings the brass platter back and forth over the woman's head, in an arc from one shoulder to the other, five or seven times. As she moves the platter, she puts her hand over the glittering oil lamp and then onto the mother's shoulders and the baby, blessing them. This gesture, called *arti,* is a key feature of the worship of deities by their devotees and in addition to being an act of adoration may also provide protection from the evil eye.

Carrying her baby, the mother rises from her seat over the auspicious design on the floor and goes out the door. She quickly turns and hands the baby back in through the door to a relative who puts the baby in a wheat-filled winnowing fan and covers it with a cloth. As it was just after birth, the infant is again placed upon the grain which will sustain it throughout life, in the woven bamboo winnowing fan, the device to be used by the baby's mother to clean grain for meals to feed the child for years to come.

Out in the dark courtyard, the Barber woman guides the new mother through several additional rituals, one of which is believed to determine how long it will be before the new mother conceives again. She herself makes the determination when she throws lumps of food eastward "as an offering to the sun." The farther she throws them, the longer it will be before her next pregnancy. In another part of the rite, the new mother worships and blesses the family water supply by placing her own golden handprints—symbols of her fertility—on the family water pots. She then reenters the house.

The entire *Chauk* is performed without any particular verbal expressions or prayers. Formalized ritual utterances are the province of the male priests in the ceremonies they run. Women's rites involve doing, not talking, except for their songs.

In the *Chauk* the woman clearly emerges in her new role as mother of a child and as a woman who has fulfilled her duty to her marital lineage. Leaving the door of the house with her baby, both mother and child make a

Photo © Doranne Jacobson

The Chauk Ceremony & Red-Painted Feet

Dressed in fine clothing, a new mother sits on a small wooden platform over a *Chauk* design, as a Barber woman applies red paint to her feet in auspicious patterns. Cradled in the mother's lap is her infant daughter, completely covered with a new cloth to protect her from evil influences. The baby's father's sister blesses the mother and child with auspicious symbols and gestures. Watching and learning the elements of this important women's ritual is a young daughter of the family, at right.

formal entry into the outside world. The *Chauk* stresses the beneficent and creative powers of the female. In her new role as a child-producing member of the household and lineage, the mother is reminded that she upholds the strength of the family group through chaste behavior and devoted motherhood. Much depends on her.

Although the *Chauk* has brought them a step closer to normal life, the mother and child are still in a state of vulnerable transition. They are shrouded by layers of cloth and darkness throughout the ceremony, and the child must not even glimpse the lamplight. They remain sequestered for the rest of the forty-day postpartum period. The infant is not individualized to the point of being given a name. Although it has survived the most dangerous days after birth, its grip on life is still not deemed to be a sure one.

That night, after the *Chauk* ritual itself is over, many women are invited to a *Chauk* songfest. If the family is prosperous and high-ranking, a drummer is hired to announce the beginning of the event, and a crowd of perhaps forty women and girls gather in the courtyard to sing childbirth songs. The mother and child are still not seen or heard from. Here too, as in almost all other situations involving childbirth, the new father is not at home and is nowhere to be seen. The women sing the usual songs, many of which stress a woman's alienation from her conjugal kinfolk. One song, about Bemata, a goddess who gives babies to women, declares:

> As a scorned basket is useful in carrying cow dung,
> A scorned daughter-in-law is useful in producing sons.

After the singing, sweets are distributed to the guests, to be tied up in the ends of their saris to be taken home with them. Silently, the women guests modestly pull their saris over their heads and disperse into the dark lanes of the village, each quietly slipping into the doorway of her own home for the night.

The birth of a first-born son in a prominent and prosperous family may be marked with a special celebration, to which all the villagers are invited. This celebration, held on the night of the *Chauk* celebration, is called *Duba Badhai* (Grass Celebration) in reference to the sacred *duba* grass that the village Barber sticks in the turbans of the male guests as a blessing. The men sit and chat while the women, sitting separately, sing. Guests may give money or clothing to the Barber to be presented to the baby.

To the sound of beating drums, the celebrating family distributes gifts—clothes and money to the family Brahman priest and his wife, the family guru (religious teacher) and his wife, the village temple priest and his wife, the Barber and Barber woman, the Sweeper woman, the Potter woman, and even the Tanner woman. Sisters and daughters of the family often receive clothing. All the male guests are given lumps of brown sugar or sugar candies, and the women receive sweets and boiled wheat. In the privacy of the courtyard, away from the eyes of the men, women guests may dance in celebration. In addition, women of the higher castes may be feasted as special guests on the *Chauk* day. The family head may also present cows to the village tailor, the Barber, the Sweeper, and, as an act of religious merit, to a poor maiden. All of this largesse reaffirms the family head's position as a prominent and generous person and suggests that the newborn infant may follow in his footsteps. The generosity also helps to fend off envy, as the good fortune of the family in having a new male member is shared with others.

After the *Chauk*, the mother can again eat most normal foods; in addition, she may continue to eat the special foods that are prescribed for new mothers. She can now do many routine household tasks, such as cleaning grain and sweeping. But she should still refrain from fetching water or touching wet cow dung, for fear she might catch a chill. For the same reason, she does not take a full bath again until forty days after the birth. Because

Photo © Doranne Jacobson

Enjoying Their Children

Sisters-in-law delight in playing with each others' children on the occasion of a Hindu festival. Each of these women has known the sorrow of losing babies, and they treasure their living sons and daughters.

she is still somewhat polluted, she does not enter the kitchen or cook, except sometimes for herself on a small stove outside the kitchen. Grinding flour, too, is usually avoided. She does not participate in any worship services for gods or goddesses or touch the household's holy images. Except for going out to eliminate at the edge of the forest or fields, she stays home. Very poor women, however, may not be able to afford so many days of idleness and may return to their jobs in the fields much earlier.

WELL WORSHIP

Finally, the postpartum pollution period ends about forty days after the birth. The exact date is set by a Brahman priest. The mother bathes, her room is cleansed with cow dung, and her clothes and bedclothes are washed again. She is now ready to resume normal life. The return to normalcy is marked in some castes with a ritual called Well Worship (*Kua Puja*). In some of the middle-ranking castes, women perform the Well Worship ceremony after the birth of a first child, and Brahman women perform it after the birth of every child. Women of other castes may perform a tiny ceremony at the well side before drawing water for the first time, or they may not bother with any ceremony at all.

For her Well Worship, the bejeweled and white-shrouded Brahman mother proceeds at night to the village well, preceded by a drummer and accompanied by the Barber woman, a few women members of her household, and a few relatives and neighbors. After a fairly complex ritual in which the new mother makes auspicious diagrams at various points around the well's rim, she pushes ritual offerings into the well, draws some water in the household water pots, and carries it home. Women who have gathered there sing and receive sugar treats. The well is circular and deep, and with its life-giving water supply, suggestive of the woman's reproductive tract, so essential to the continuation of the family. Worshipping the well may represent symbolic respect for the otherwise frequently disrespected female body. Additionally, and perhaps more obvious to all, through her auspicious contact and special offerings pushed into the well, the new mother symbolically extends her fecundity to the village water supply. The woman's transition to her new status as the mother of her child and her reintegration into the normal life of her family and community are now complete.

THE CONTINUING CYCLE OF CEREMONIES FOR THE CHILD

The ceremonies following the Well Worship center on the child, its gradual achievement of individuality, and its relationships with others. In an event known as the *Pach* ceremony, held at any convenient time within the first few months after the birth of a first child, members of the mother's natal family arrive at her marital home with gifts of clothing, jewelry, toys, and perhaps even a fancy cot for the baby. The visitors also ceremonially present clothing to the child's parents and other men and women of the child's paternal household. Thus, the bond between a child and its mother's parents, its mother's brother, and other maternal relatives is acknowledged and strengthened. At the same time, the importance of the link between a woman's natal family and her conjugal kin is recognized. When they leave, the visitors take the new mother and the baby home with them for a lengthy stay. Most children and their mothers visit their maternal kin often, and some children live in their maternal uncle's home for years at a time.

A small ceremony is held when the child is fed solid food for the first time—generally, at two and one-half months for a girl and five months for a boy. Tiny portions of wheat breads, fritters, sweet milk-and-rice pudding, or other foods (ideally, thirty-six varieties of food) are fed to the child from a silver rupee coin by the child's paternal aunt or a stand-in. The aunt then receives a present from the baby's father. The child usually continues to suckle until it is about two years old, gradually increasing the amount of solid food it consumes.

The naming of a child is celebrated ceremonially in some parts of the world, but in Nimkhera it is a quiet affair, done whenever the family tacitly accepts that the child may remain alive. Some children are called by nicknames throughout their lives, such as Kallu, "Blackie," Halke, "Little Guy," Guddi, "Dolly," etc. Others use formal names, often chosen with the help of a priest consulting his Hindu almanac. These names frequently include the appellations of deities, perhaps in the hope that the honored deities will protect the children so named.

At some time in the first year or two of life, a child's head must be ritually shaved to remove the polluted "birth hair." Among many high-caste families in Nimkhera, the Head-Shaving ceremony (*Mundan*) is held near the Matabai (Mother Goddess) shrine. The mother and child are dressed in nice clothes; accompanied by female relatives, neighbor women, and the Barber couple, they parade to the shrine in late morning. An auspicious design is made on the ground in front of the shrine. The mother sits on a wooden platform over the design, with her baby cradled in her lap. A worship service (*puja*) is performed; then the Barber shaves the baby's head with a wicked-looking straight-edged razor, and the baby's head is anointed with turmeric paste, usually by the mother. The hair cuttings are collected in a patty of raw wheat-flour dough, to be saved and thrown into a sacred body of water as an offering.

The head-shaving is the first fully public ceremony involving the child and serves to introduce the child to the village Mother Goddess and to the village. While the earlier rites are performed in dark protective privacy, the head-shaving ceremony takes place in open sunlight. Here, for the first time, a male (the Barber) representative of the world outside the home acts as the child's attendant. The simple *puja,* with offerings put into a small fire, is typical of scores of other rituals involving male participants. This ceremony mediates between the dangerous period of infancy and the less dangerous period of childhood. With the removal of the birth hair, the child is finally separated physically from the mother and achieves individuality. Offering the hair to the divine may act to consecrate the child and help protect him or her from harm. The mother's anointing the child's head with turmeric is a blessing, a visible symbol of a belief often stated by village women: "A child needs his mother's hand over his head; then he grows fast, sustained by her love." Not until the child's wedding, when he or she steps on the path to parenthood, will the child again be rubbed with turmeric. Then the child—bride or groom—will be anointed with the golden ointment by young women of the family, while the mother protectively holds her hand on the child's head.

CONCLUSION

In Nimkhera, childbirth rituals are performed very frequently, since more than twenty-five Hindu infants are born in the village each year. Approximately every two weeks, the women of the village are involved in the rites and practices surrounding new motherhood. Childbirth rituals are certainly the most frequently performed life-cycle ceremonies, and among all Hindu ritual observances in Nimkhera, only the short daily worship services held in the temple and at some homes and shrines outnumber them. In a situation in which modesty and fear of unseen evil forces militate against public discussion of childbirth, these ceremonies provide public recognition to women as they contribute their procreative capacity to the family and to society. Indeed, except for her wedding, there is virtually no other situation in which a woman can legitimately achieve recognition at all. Ideally quiet and—in her marital home—veiled and secluded, the woman is the center of attention only in new motherhood. The never-ending sequences of childbirth ceremonies continually tell her that, above all, women should be mothers and that only in motherhood will she find satisfaction.

Within the family-oriented village society, there is little room for following individual preferences. All must work together for the family's strength. Women must dutifully carry out their assigned tasks in the home and in the fields and, most importantly, make their unique contribution of new members for the group. As anthropologists Yolanda and Robert Murphy have written, "The woman remains the custodian and perpetuator of life itself. Those who would question the worth of this trust must first ask if there is anything else in human existence that has an ultimate meaning."[11]

Notes

1. Childbirth rituals have been described elsewhere for various regions of South Asia. Of particular interest is a detailed account by Therese Blanchet, *Meanings and Rituals of Birth in Rural Bangladesh: Women, Pollution and Marginality* (Dhaka: University Press Ltd., 1984), in which the author compares Hindu and Muslim practices and relates these to differing concepts of interactions between humans and the divine. Another detailed discussion relating practices to religious ideas is by Ranjeet Singh Bajwa, *Semiotics of the Birth Ceremonies in Punjab,* Series in Semiotics and Literature, 9 (New Delhi: Bahri Publications, 1991). A classic early ethnographic account is Helen Gideon, "A Baby Is Born in the Punjab," *American Anthropologist* 64 (1962) pp. 1220–34. Perhaps the most thorough and insightful discussion of childbirth rituals in India is found in Ruth S. Freed and Stanley Freed's monograph, *Rites of Passage in Shanti Nagar,* vol. 56, part 3, Anthropological Papers of the American Museum of Natural History (New York, 1980).

2. Madhya Pradesh ranks third-highest among Indian states in rural birth rate (36.4 per thousand, compared with 32 for the country) and rural infant mortality rate (124 per thousand, compared with 98 for the country), according to 1989 figures from the Office of the Registrar General, Vital Statistics Division, summarized in Ashish Bose, *Population of India: 1991 Census Results and Methodology,* (Delhi: B. R. Publishing Corporation, 1991), pp. 52–54. In Nimkhera, increased access to health care, including government-sponsored inoculation programs for pregnant women and infants, is helping to improve maternal and child health.

3. In some areas, infant mortality has dropped to almost zero, but this is not yet the case in Raisen District or its environs. Pauline Kolenda has documented recent dramatic declines in maternal and child mortality—and in the birth rate—in a large North Indian village. See Pauline Kolenda, "Fewer Deaths, Fewer Births; Decline of Child Mortality in a U.P. Village," *Manushi: A Journal About Women and Society,* no. 105 (March-April 1998), pp. 5–13.

4. For a detailed discussion of the intertwined themes of femininity, fecundity, water, and rivers, see Anne Feldhaus, *Water and Womanhood: Religious Meanings of Rivers in Maharashtra* (New York, Oxford University Press, 1995).

5. The linkage between women's lack of crucial reproductive knowledge and their pervasive lack of control and autonomy over their own generative capacities, and to women's subordination in general, is cogently explored by Miriam Sharma and Urmila Vanjani in "Engendering Reproduction: The Political Economy of Reproductive Activities in a Rajasthan Village," in Alice W. Clark, ed., *Gender and Political Economy: Explorations of South Asian Systems* (Delhi and New York: Oxford University Press, 1993), pp. 24–65. Other articles in this volume are also pertinent to this issue.

6. Links between rural Indian women's lack of political and economic power, poor maternal and child health care, cultural values associating birth with ritual pollution, and illiterate low-status local midwives are carefully analyzed in Patricia Jeffery, Roger Jeffery, and Andrew Lyon, *Contaminating States and Women's Status: Midwifery, Childbearing and the State in Rural North India* (New Delhi: Indian Social Institute, Monograph Series, 22, 1985). Most traditional midwives are paid very little for their services—a few rupees, a few items of clothing, some grain, and some sugar, for example. Nontraditional birth attendants expect larger payments and most are unwilling to perform pollution-removing cleanup services deemed essential by Hindu villagers.

7. No painkillers are used. Indian women could benefit greatly from knowledge of Lamaze childbirth techniques, in which a series of breathing exercises directs the pregnant woman's mind away from feelings of pain or discomfort.

8. The terms "Washerwoman" and, later, "Barber woman," have been capitalized in this chapter because they designate the women's caste groups as well as the service that they perform. The term "midwife," however, designates only a woman performing a service. Midwives belong to a number of different castes.

9. Excellent sociological and ecological analyses of the evil-eye beliefs found in many parts of the world are presented in Clarence Maloney, ed., *The Evil Eve* (New York: Columbia University Press, 1976).

10. See R. Freed and S. Freed, *Rites of Passage in Shanti Nagar,* op. cit., p. 357.

11. Yolanda Murphy and Robert F. Murphy, *Women of the Forest* (New York: Columbia University Press, 1974), p. 232.

Further Readings

Agarwal, Bina. *A Field of One's Own: Gender and Land Rights in South Asia.* Cambridge: Cambridge University Press, 1994.

Balakrishnan, Radhika. "The Social Context of Sex Selection and the Politics of Abortion in India." In Gita Sen and Rachel C. Snow, eds., *Power and Decision: The Social Control of Reproduction.* Harvard Series on Population and International Health; distributed by Harvard University Press, 1994.

Bumiller, Elisabeth. *May You Be the Mother of a Hundred Sons; A Journey Among the Women of India.* New York: Fawcett Columbine, 1990.

Falk, Nancy Auer. *Women and Religion in India: An Annotated Bibliography of Sources in English 1975–92.* Kalamazoo: Western Michigan University, 1994. [Review—D. Jacobson, *Journal of Asian Studies* 55, no. 1 (1996) 191–93.]

Flint, Marcha. "Lockmi, An Indian Midwife." In Margarita Artschwager Kay, *Anthropology of Human Birth.* Philadelphia: F. A. Davis Co., 1982, pp. 211–19.

Hanchett, Suzanne. *Coloured Rice: Symbolic Structure in Hindu Family Festivals.* Delhi: Hindustan Publishing Corporation, 1987.

Jacobson, Doranne. "A Reverence for Cows." *Natural History* 108, no. 5 (June 1999) pp. 58–63.

———. "India: Social Systems." In James Heitzman and Robert L. Worden, eds., *India: A Country Study,* 5th ed., Area Handbook/Country Studies Series, Washington, D.C.: The Library of Congress, 1996, pp. 231–93.

———. "Women's Work in a Central Indian Village" (article and photographic essay). In S. Raju and D. Bagchi, eds., *Women and Work in South Asia: Regional Patterns and Perspectives.* London: Routledge, 1993, pp. 158–79.

———. *India: Land of Dreams and Fantasy.* London: W.H. Smith, 1992.

———. "Gender Relations: Changing Patterns in India." In Myron L. Cohen, ed., *Asia: Case Studies in the Social Sciences.* Armonk, N.Y.: M.E. Sharpe, 1992, pp. 46–66.

———. "Studying the Changing Roles of Women in Rural India." *Signs: Journal of Women in Culture and Society* 8, no. 1 (1982) pp. 132–37.

———. "Purdah and the Hindu Family in Central India." In H. Papanek and G. Minault, eds., *Separate Worlds: Studies of Purdah in South Asia.* Columbia, Mo.: South Asia Books, and Delhi: Chanakya Publications, 1982, pp. 81–109.

———. "The Chaste Wife: Cultural Norm and Individual Experience." In Sylvia Vatuk, ed., *American Studies in the Anthropology of India.* New Delhi: American Institute of Indian Studies and Manohar Publications, 1978, pp. 95–138.

———. "Flexibility in Central Indian Kinship and Residence." In Kenneth David, ed., *The New Wind: Changing Identities in South Asia.* World Anthropology, Sol Tax, General Editor. The Hague: Mouton, 1977, pp. 263–83.

———. "Purdah in India: Life Behind the Veil." *National Geographic Magazine* 152, no. 2 (August 1977) pp. 270–86.

———. "Songs of Social Distance. Women's Music in Central India. *Journal of South Asian Literature* 11, nos. 1–2) (1975) pp. 45–69.

Jacobson, Doranne, and Susan S. Wadley. *Women in India: Two Perspectives.* Columbia, Mo.: South Asia Books, and New Delhi: Manohar Book Service, 1999.

Jeffery, Roger, and Patricia M. Jeffery. "Traditional Birth Attendants in Rural North India; The Social Organization of Childbearing." In Shirley Lindenbaum and Margaret Lock, eds., *Knowledge, Power, and Practice: The Anthropology of Medicine and Everyday Life.* Berkeley and London: University of California Press, 1993, pp. 7–31.

Jeffery, Patricia, Roger Jeffery, and Andrew Lyon. *Labour Pains and Labour Power: Women and Childbearing in India.* London: Zed Books, Ltd., and New Delhi: Manohar, 1989.

Jeffery, Patricia, and Amrita Basu, eds. *Appropriating Gender: Women's Activism and Politicized Religion in South Asia.* New York and London: Routledge, 1998.

Kolenda, Pauline. "What Really Causes Fertility Decline?" *Economic and Political Weekly* (24 January 1998), pp. 163–65.

8

Hindu Women's Family and Household Rites in a North Indian Village

SUSAN S. WADLEY

Slap! Slap! The sound of the winnowing fan being beaten reverberates through the house and courtyard as Jiya, the mother, rids the family living quarters of evil spirits and chases away poverty. It is late on a dark night, the no-moon light of the month of Kartik (October–November), and everyone else is asleep. Earlier in the evening the entire family has celebrated Divali, the Hindu festival honoring Lakshmi, the goddess of prosperity. Divali is also known as the Festival of Lights because Lakshmi is called to homes throughout India by lighting rooftops and windows with clay lamps. It is a joyous festival, also celebrated with fireworks and special foods. But even though the main celebration is over and the family is sleeping, Jiya performs this one last task. As is the case for many other women's calendrical rituals in north India, she, as the eldest female in the family, has to protect her family's health and welfare.

SUSAN S. WADLEY, Ford Maxwell Professor of South Asian Studies and Professor of Anthropology at Syracuse University, received her Ph.D. in Anthropology from the University of Chicago in 1973. Her research interests range from women's ritual and folklore to regional epic traditions to socioeconomic change, especially as it affects women in rural north India. She has published several books and numerous articles on women, folklore, and rural north India.

Author's Note: I conducted the research on which this paper is based during 1967–1969, 1974–1975, 1983–1984, and 1998, and was supported by grants from the National Science Foundation; the South Asia Committee, the University of Chicago; the American Institute of Indian Studies; and the Smithsonian Institution. I also wish to thank my colleagues Barbara D. Miller, William Houska, and Bruce W. Derr, whose insights and suggestions aided me in writing this paper. Last, the women of Karimpur deserve the most thanks. I can never repay them for their hospitality and kindness; I only hope that I do them justice.

Whereas men's rituals are aimed primarily at general prosperity or good crops and at the world outside the house itself, women's rituals focus more specifically on family welfare and prosperity within the walls of their homes. In this chapter I will examine how women deal with these concerns by discussing the calendrical cycle of rituals practiced by the high-caste Hindu women of Karimpur,[1] a village of North India.

Karimpur is located approximately 150 miles southeast of Delhi. In 1968 it had a population of 1,380 divided among 22 hierarchically ranked castes, whereas in 1994, it has a population of 2522 divided amongst 22 hierarchically ranked castes.[2] These caste (*jati*) groups remain endogamous and are associated with a traditional occupation, though most men practice some form of farming or labor to make a living. Moreover, for ritual purposes, the castes are ranked in a hierarchy based in part of conceptions of purity and pollution and in part on economic well-being. Jiya belongs to the highest-ranking group, the Brahman caste. In Karimpur, members of this caste, though nominally priests, are actually farmers. Even in the 1990s, they dominate the village ritually and economically. Most people in Karimpur live by farming, although increasing numbers of men are migrating to nearby cities for jobs in the new Indian economy. Others work as day laborers in the district headquarters ten miles away. A few have salaried jobs as clerks, schoolteachers, or librarians. Of those still reliant on farming, the men work the fields with their bullock-drawn plows or one of the four tractors now found in the village, while the women process the food through winnowing, husking, grinding, and cooking. Women work in the fields only rarely, and it is a sign of a family's low status if the women work outside of the home.

Approximately half of Karimpur's population, in both the 1960s and 1990s, lives in joint families—families in which sons, sons' wives, and grandchildren all live with the parents. Married daughters live with their husbands or husbands' families in other villages and only periodically visit the home of their birth. Most of the women in Karimpur, especially wealthier and young married women, follow *purdah* restrictions. In north India *purdah* requires that females should be secluded in their family courtyards and houses. When outside these quarters, they must cover their heads and faces with their saris or shawls. Even inside they must cover their faces before their husbands and husbands' older male relatives—fathers, uncles, and older brothers. These rules are still firmly adhered to in the village, especially around ritual occasions, but women who travel outside of the village are less likely to maintain veiling before strangers.

Essentially, men and women in Karimpur occupy separate worlds. For the most part, women, especially those who are high caste and/or wealthier, live and work in their homes and have little mobility within the village, though they may move between the village and the nearby town. The physical structure of Karimpur houses is important in understanding women's activities. Most homes are built of mud or baked bricks and have an outer room with a verandah adjoining the village lanes. Behind this room is an open courtyard with one or more rooms attached to it. This courtyard and the rooms around it form the women's world. Men must cough or otherwise announce their presence before entering it. Within the confines of their homes, women process grains, cook, clean, care for children, visit with neighbors (who come by crossing over rooftops rather than by using the "public" lanes), weave baskets, knit, and celebrate their rituals. Men use the courtyard primarily for eating and bathing. They entertain their guests on the front verandah or in the outer room. Much of the time, the men sleep there as well.

In many aspects of life, even in the content of songs and the way they are sung, men and women express their separate worlds, worlds which remain largely separate even in the 1990s. It is not surprising, then, that women's desires, as expressed in their rituals, are those of their world—the household—while men's concerns are focused primarily on the outer world. Since the world affects women differently than it does men, women's symbols of hope and prosperity are also different from men's symbols. On a more theoretical level, we could say that the calendrical rituals of Karimpur express women's most vital moods and motivations. Whether by beating the winnowing fan on Divali night or by worshipping a banyan tree during Marriage Worship or by offering milk to snakes, women in Karimpur symbolically, yet very powerfully, state the longings and ideas that are vital to their women's world. They express these longings and concerns in the twenty rites they perform every year. Of these twenty rituals performed by women, three involve directly worshipping male relatives. In these rituals the male relative is actually the deity worshipped, and offerings are made directly to him. Four rituals involve the worshipping of a deity for the protection of a particular family member. Another four annual rituals are concerned with obtaining protection for one's family in general. Nine more rituals seek household prosperity. (See Chart A for a complete list of these rituals.)

Before going on to examine these rituals in detail, three points should be clarified. First, living human beings can be, and often are, deities in Karimpur, as are plows, snakes, bullocks, and wheat seedlings, in addition to the normally recognized pantheon of mythological gods and goddesses. The basic rule is that any being that a person considers more powerful than himself or herself in any particular realm of life can become an object of worship. Thus for any given individual the religious pantheon of Karimpur is potentially enormous, since it could consist of all other beings. Moreover any action that is undertaken because of another being's power (*shakti*) is religious action. The implications of this point for women's religion will become clearer later.

Second, all the rituals listed in Chart A are performed by women and/or girls. None of these rites requires the services of a priest or other religious specialists (who are almost exclusively male). All the rules for proper worship and all the stories and songs that accompany worship used to be orally transmitted from women to women for women's use, although now some women may read a pamphlet containing the ritual story. But since fewer than 30 percent of adult women are literate, many households have no one to read.

Third, women in Karimpur practice three major forms of religious activity: *vrat* (fasts), *puja* (worship), and *bhajan* (devotional singing). Fasting implies greater devotion than that associated with mere worship. Worshipping means honoring the deity as one would a guest: food is presented, the image may be bathed and perfumed, and new clothes are given. To further symbolize her humble subordination to the deity, the worshipper then eats the god's leftover food (*prasad*). The third ritual form, devotional singing, is both entertainment and serious religious activity. Women's religion in north India is primarily devotional. The deities are worshipped with love and respond with boons for the devotee. Devotional singing often accompanies the worship.

I will examine in detail five of the twenty rites practiced by women. I will also look in depth at those aspects of the women's world that give meaning to their ritual actions. The five rituals to be discussed are Brother's Second, Marriage Worship, Lampblack Mother, Snake's Fifth, and the Festival of Lights. Male kin—brothers, husbands, and sons—are the focus of the first three; general family health is sought in the fourth, and family prosperity, in the fifth.

Chart A *Women's Rituals in Karimpur*

Deity Worshipped	Name of Festival	Purpose	Date*
Worship of Kin			
Brother	Tying on Protection (*raksha bandan*)	Obtaining his protection	Savan 2:15 (July–Aug.)
Husband	Pitcher Fourth (*Karva chauth*)	Obtaining his protection	Kartik 1:4 (Oct.–Nov.)
Brother	Brother's Second (*Bhaiva duj*)	Obtaining his protection and his long life	Kartik 2:2 (Oct.–Nov.)
Worship on Behalf of Kin			
Savitri Banyan tree	Marriage Worship (*barok ki puja*)	Long life of husband	Jeth 1:15 (May–June)
Gauri	The Third (*tij*)	Brother's welfare	Savan 2:3 (July–Aug.)
Devi	Nine Nights (*neothar*)	Happy marriage for girls	Kuar 2:1–9 (Sep.–Oct.)
Siyao or Sihayo Mata	Lampblack Mother (*siyao* or *sihayo Mata*)	Having sons; children's welfare	Kartik 2:1 (Oct.–Nov.)
Worship on Behalf of Family			
Devi	Goddess Worship (*Devin ki puja*)	Protection for family	Chait 2:9 (Mar.–Apr.)
Snakes	Snake's Fifth (*nag panchmi*)	Deliverance from snakes	Savan 2:3 (July–Aug.)
Krishna	Cow Dung Wealth (*gobardhan*)	Protection for family	Kartik 2:1 (Oct.–Nov.)
Devi	Goddess Worship (*Devin ki puja*)	Protection for family	Chait 1:8 (Mar.–Apr.)
Worship for Prosperity			
Grain, Vishnu	Grain Third (*akhtij*)	New crops, shelter	Baisakh 2:3 (Apr.–May)
Devi guru	Asarhi (*asarhi*)	Protection from rains	Asarh 2:15 (June–July)
Hanuman	Eternal Fourteenth (*anant chaudas*)	Protection	Bhadon 2:14 (Aug.–Sep.)
Lakshmi	Elephant Worship (*hathi ki puja*)	Wealth, fruits	Kuar 1:8 (Sep.–Oct.)
Lakshmi	Festival of Lights (*divali*)	Wealth	Kartik 1:15 (Oct.–Nov.)
Vishnu	Awakening Gods (*deothan*)	Prosperity	Kartik 2:11 (Oct.–Nov.)
Vishnu	Full Moon of Kartik (*Kartik purnamashi*)	Wealth	Kartik 2:15 (Oct.–Nov.)
Shiva	Shiva's Thirteenth (*Shiva teras*)	Protection	Phagun 1:13 (Feb.–Mar.)
Holi Mata Krishna	Holi	Crops. removal of evil	Phagun 2:15 (Feb.–Mar.)

*The religious calendar in India is reckoned by lunar months, with each month divided into a dark half (full to new moon) and a light half (new to full moon): this column specifies the date by month, then half (1 = dark half. 2 = light half), then day within the half (1–15).

BROTHER'S SECOND

Brother's Second occurs in the fall, two days after the Festival of Lights. On this day women worship their brothers, if the brothers are present in the village, or images of their brothers, if they are not present. To understand the ritual significance of brothers, we need to learn why brothers are important to Karimpur women. To do this, we shall focus on the roles and activities of women, for it is what women are and do that makes their brothers so important.

Two crucial factors in the lives of Karimpur women affect their relationships with their brothers. First, all girls must marry out of the village of their birth (village exogamy); second, they must marry into families considered to have higher ranks than their own (hypergamy). As a result of becoming a part of her husband's family and hence "taking on" his higher status, a married woman has higher status than her own brothers, father, and other natal kin. Because of his lower status, her father should not visit her new relatives or receive any hospitality from them. Yet, since women of north India, especially those of higher castes, may not travel alone (at least until very recently), some male relative must fetch her from her husband's home when she makes her annual visit to her natal home. Normally, brothers are entrusted with this task. Hence a woman's brothers symbolize her links to her natal village. They bring her back for her first visit after her marriage, and they come at times of distress or bring gifts when a child is born or married. This cultural rule makes a great deal of sense. Given that, as recently as the 1960s, the Indian life span was approximately forty-four years for males, it is the brother and not the father who will more likely live to carry out these tasks; only rarely would a woman's father be alive into her middle age.

Conditions of life in a husband's household, as well as stereotypes about it, add to the brother's significance. In rural north India, all marriages are arranged by the male kin of bride and groom. Neither the girl or the boy will have ever seen the other before the wedding day itself, and even then *purdah* restrictions require that the bride be cloaked in heavy shawls. The wedding takes place in the bride's home. Afterward the groom and his male relatives (traditionally no female relatives can take part in the journey from one village to the other) remove the bride from the family that she has known since birth and take her as a complete stranger to her new family. Here she is a *bahu* (wife) and is subordinate to all until either she has a child or a yet younger "wife" is added to the family. As a servant to her elder, her mobility circumscribed by the rules of *purdah*, and under the control of a mother-in-law, the woman sees her husband's home as a trying and often lonely and unhappy place.

In contrast, the time spent in her father's home, ideally at least one month a year, gives a woman joy, happiness, and a feeling of being loved and cherished. While she is again a daughter, not a wife, *purdah* restrictions are lifted, childhood friendships are reestablished, and freedom from imprisonment in service relationships with everyone above her is gained. Thus the emotional tone of a woman's life undergoes a complete turnabout when she moves from one house to the other. Many women's songs recognize this fact, particularly those of Savan, the rainy-season month when daughters should return home. Swings are hung in trees, and daughters of all ages gather to sing of swinging in the cool monsoon air gazing at the green fields and listening to the peacock. Many of the Savan songs lament the fate of women whose brothers did not bring them home, as in this excerpt:

> Oh my sister, have the neighborhood dyer
> color me a brightly colored shawl,
> One neither torn nor dirty . . . .
> Oh my sister, my brother hasn't yet come,

Oh my sister, my brother hasn't yet come,
Oh when I went to draw water, oh listen when I was sent to fetch water,
Oh listen, a traveler came into the lane.
Oh listen, someone told me of their brother.
Oh listen sister, my brother hasn't yet come.
Oh listen, my mother-in-law and sister-in-law spoke harshly to me.
Oh listen, someone is crying, eyes filled with tears.
Sister, my brother hasn't yet come . . . .
Oh listen, someone is coming, oh sister, my brother.
Oh listen someone with a turban like a god's.
Oh sister, my brother has come.

A brother's importance is further enhanced by his gift-giving role. Beginning with engagement gifts and ending only when she dies, a woman's natal family is expected to give gifts to her husband's family. Gifts should be given yearly and also on special occasions, such as the birth of a child and children's marriages. For example, the mother's brother provides his sister's children with their wedding clothes. Gifts are especially important during the first years of marriage, when gifts from the bride's family, given via the brother, are almost like bribes to ensure that the bride will be well treated in her new home.

Brothers are necessary for women's long happiness. A girl without a brother is considered only slightly better off than a widow. In north India, toe rings are used as wedding rings marking a woman as married. Most village women wear two sets of toe rings, one set for the husband and one for the brother. A woman who is widowed will take off the set for her husband, but keep those for her brother, for he is her second refuge and protector. A girl with many brothers is most fortunate and brothers shelter their sisters from afar. Thus, in the rituals called Brother's Second, The Third, and Tying on Protection, women work to ensure the health and welfare of their protectors.

In the fall, after the Festival of Lights, sisters worship their brothers by putting an honorific *tika* (auspicious mark) on their foreheads and by offering them food, especially sweets, and water. The brother responds by giving his sister gifts of money or clothing, symbolizing his protection for the coming year. When the brother is not present, his sister draws a figure of him in flour paste on the courtyard floor and offers food and water to the image. Some women also make a figure out of cow dung that represents their brothers' enemy. They crown this figure with thorns, take it to the door of the house, and smash it with a rice pestle. Having thus demolished their brothers' enemies for the year, the women conclude their ritual.

Although ritual actions during Brother's Second suggest that the sister seeks the brother's protection, stories told in connection with the rite emphasize that in fact the sister protects the brother. She destroys his enemies for him and thus ensures him a long life. There are two common stories.

Story 1

Once upon a time, a brother came to his sister's house to take her to his marriage. She made food for him in the middle of the night, but by accident she ground a snake into it. When later she discovered that the cakes she had prepared were bad, she promptly replaced them. Having saved him from the poisonous food, she learned of a thorn (*sahe*) that would rid him of all misfortunes. So, when he got married, she put *sahe* thorns on all the offerings and used them at all the ceremonies, thus giving everybody the impression that she was mad. She even insisted on sleeping in the same room as the bride and groom. When a snake sneaked into the room and tried to bite her brother, she killed it and saved him and his bride. Thus, she shielded her brother from many troubles. When she told her story, she was highly praised. So all sisters worship their brothers and ask for their brothers' long life.

Story 2

Yamuna, a goddess, and Yamraj, the god of death, were sister and brother. Every day Yamuna went to her brother's house and gave him food. One day Yamraj came to Yamuna's house instead. This day was the second day of the light half of Kartik (the day of Brother's Second). Seeing her brother, Yamuna greeted him with reverence and great happiness. After worshipping him, she gave him food. Yamraj was very pleased by her signs of respect and gave her gifts of ornaments and clothes. When he left, Yamraj said, "Sister, I am very pleased with you. Ask any boon. I will fulfill all your wishes." Yamuna said, "Brother, if you are truly pleased with me, come every year on this day and I will feed you. And may a long life be given to those people who go to their sisters and take food on this day." Saying, "It shall be this way," Yamraj left, and Yamuna's every wish was fulfilled.

These stories highlight the main elements of a brother's importance to a Karimpur woman. In the first story, the brother has come to fetch his sister, and she in turn seeks his long life. In the second, the brother not only visits his sister but also gives her gifts. We have seen how important both these elements are to Karimpur women.

MARRIAGE WORSHIP

However important a brother may be, the husband is even more important to a woman's general happiness. A variety of factors, both religious and social, contribute to a husband's importance.

According to Hindu teachings, a good woman is devoted to her husband. The ideal wife is Sita, heroine of the Ramayana, an epic widely read and known throughout India. In the Ramayana, Sita follows her husband Rama into twelve years of exile in the forest. She is kidnapped by a demon, whom Rama eventually destroys. When Sita's virtue is questioned, she mounts a lighted pyre to prove her continued chastity. The gods recognize her purity, and the flames do not burn her. The Ramayana's message is explicit, as illustrated by this quotation from the version commonly read and recited in Karimpur:

> [A sage's wife speaks to Sita]
>
> Though a husband be old, diseased, stupid, or poor, blind, deaf, bad-tempered or in great distress, yet if his wife treats him with disrespect, she will suffer all the tortures of hell. This is her one religious duty, her one vow and observance—devotion in thought and word and deed to her husband's feet. . . . The wife who honestly fulfills her wifely duty wins salvation with the greatest ease, but she who is disloyal to her husband, wherever she be born, becomes a widow in her early youth.[3]

Thus a woman's hopes for salvation also depend on her marriage.

Traditional Hindu teachings also deal with women who are widowed. Ideally, the high caste widow should commit *sati* by throwing herself on her husband's funeral pyre; this actually occurred quite rarely even in the past. However, by committing *sati*, the widow eliminated two problems: her own inauspicious presence and potential charges of unfaithfulness. Upper-caste widows traditionally were not allowed to remarry, and the sad status of widowhood was displayed for all to see. Widows could no longer wear jewelry; they had to wear plain cotton saris, and their heads were shaved. They could not attend marriages, childbirth celebrations, or other auspicious occasions. In fact, even today, widows are often considered to be witches or carriers of the evil eye.[4]

The conditions of the extended family also make a husband vital to a woman's happiness. Although a husband should not intercede with his mother on his wife's behalf, having a husband around to note mistreatment is considered crucial for a woman's protection. A popular myth associated with the goddess Santoshi Mata reiterates this theme. According to this myth, the husband went to a foreign land to make his fortune. Meanwhile his wife was abused by her mother- and sisters-in-law. The goddess herself intervened on behalf of the wife, but fair treatment was meted out only when her husband returned.

Since Hindu women believe that husbands are necessary for their own religious salvation and for a better day-to-day life, it is not surprising that women direct much of their yearly religious activity toward them. Three rituals directly concern husbands. *Barok ki puja* (Marriage Worship) seeks the husband's long life. Young girls perform *neothar* (Nine Nights) in order to secure a future good husband. Performing *karva chauth* (Pitcher Fourth) seeks to have the husband protect his wife, while incidentally asking for his long life. These rites differ from rites honoring brothers in that the two performed by married women (Marriage Worship and Pitcher Fourth) are deemed absolutely necessary. They are part of a wife's duty (*dharma*). For a woman to be a *pativrat* (worshipful wife)—a state requiring chastity, virtue, and the worship of one's husband—these two rites must be performed.

In Marriage Worship, which occurs during the hot season, women seek long lives for their husbands. The Hindi name for this ritual is revealing—*barok ki puja. Barok* literally means "the gifts given to the groom's family by the bride's relatives at the time of marriage." In this ritual the gift given to the groom's family is his long life. And only a faithful, worshipful wife can give this gift. On this day, women fast and worship the goddess Savitri and a banyan tree in order to ensure a long married life, health for their husbands, and many sons.

The well-known story of Savitri captures the essence of this important celebration. I give a summary here.

> A daughter, Savitri, named after the goddess, was born to a wise king. When the time came for her marriage, her father told her to choose her own husband. She selected Satyan, son of King Dumtsen, who had lost his kingdom and his eyesight. Satyan cared for his parents by collecting firewood in the jungle. Later, a great sage told Savitri about Satyan's fate. He said that Satyan was a very great man but that he would live only one year. Nevertheless, Savitri married him and served him and his parents well. Three days before he was due to die, she started fasting, and on the third day she insisted on accompanying him to the forest. There, under a banyan tree, he died and Yamraj (the God of Death) came to take him. Savitri followed. Eventually Yamraj noticed her and tried to send her back, but she refused to go. Noting her devotion, Yamraj allowed her one wish—anything but her husband's life. She asked for King Dumtsen's kingdom and eyesight. Her wish was granted. Again she followed, and again she received a boon—a hundred brothers—because she was a true and faithful wife. Yet another boon was given—one hundred sons. Still Savitri followed. Yamraj again stopped her, and she said, "Having a hundred sons without a husband is not right. How can I, a true and faithful wife, have a hundred sons if I have no husband?" Outwitted, Yamraj conceded defeat and returned Satyan to life. His father's kingdom was restored, and eventually Savitri gave birth to one hundred sons.

By worshipping Savitri, the women honor their marriages and claim recognition as loyal and faithful wives. As they well know, those who worship their husbands and worship on behalf of their husbands will be rewarded. The truly devoted wife can even save her husband from the arms of the god of death. Wifely duties and worldly happiness are intertwined in this ritual.

LAMPBLACK MOTHER

In their worship of Lampblack Mother (Siyao Mata), women seek the welfare of a third set of important kin—their sons. Having sons is considered vital by women for several reasons: sons are needed to perform the ancestral rites, they provide "insurance" in one's old age (especially crucial if a woman should be so unfortunate as to become a widow), and they also make up the family labor force. Equally important is the emotional support that sons provide. Daughters marry and leave home, but sons remain. And whereas in rural India husbands and wives are not supposed to have close emotional attachments, mothers and sons have the strongest emotional affinity of any kinship pair. It has been noted that Indian women's devotion to their sons surpasses that to their husbands.

> For a young Indian wife, her son in a quite literal sense is her social redeemer. Upon him she ordinarily lavishes a devotion of an intensity proportional to his importance for her emotional ease and social security. Even when a woman has several sons, she cherishes and protects and indulges them all to a degree not usually known in the Western world.[5]

This joy in sons is reflected in the songs women sing to honor their sons' births:

> Jasuda gave birth to a son, bliss spread in Gokul.
> Came outside the call for the midwife:
> The midwife cut the cord, bliss spread in the palace.
> Now the queen gave birth to a son, bliss spread in Gokul.

Women's desires for sons are expressed in the ritual known as Lampblack Mother, in which women express their desire for sons and also seek their sons' continued welfare. At dawn on the morning following the Festival of Lights, women rise early to perform their rites before beginning the day's work. Mornings are chilly in October. While everyone else sleeps, the married women gather, shivering, at designated spots felt to be auspicious to their family—most often the site or doorway of the ancestral home. They make a rough figure of a cow with a heap of fresh cow dung. Then a lamp is lit, and a silver coin is immersed in the lamp's oil. Finally a spoon is held over the lamp to collect the soot (lampblack), which is applied around the eyes of children to ward off evil spirits. Symbolically Lampblack Mother is the cow mother, who in this case is clearly related to women's fertility. After these preparations the women in turn take a bunch of sacred grass and, while "sweeping" it behind them with one hand, say, "Give me wealth. That which is bad, run away." They then each take a *puri* (fried bread) and, while holding it under their saris at the womb, say, "Siyao, don't give daughters, give sons. Keep all well in the next year." Or, if they already have sons, they say, "Keep my sons alive and give them many children." After each woman in turn has sought the goddess's favor, the rite ends with a short session of devotional songs.

Stories told during this ritual are about women who have no sons. In the stories someone tells the unfortunate woman about Lampblack Mother and how to worship her. She does so and has many healthy children. To the Karimpur women having many healthy sons is extremely important. Equally important is their belief that the goddess will give them sons and will help them keep their sons healthy.

SNAKE'S FIFTH

On *nag panchmi* (Snake's Fifth) women ask the snakes to keep away from their families. This ritual takes place in July during the monsoon season. Because of flooding, snakes often seek refuge—on higher land—in many cases inside someone's house. As a result, snake bites increase.

Early in the day, women draw a picture of snakes on the wall of the house. These symbolic snakes are offered milk (believed to be a favorite food of snakes) and flowers. The oldest woman in the family usually makes these offerings. The snakes are asked not to harm family members. The rite itself is brief, and generally no songs and stories are associated with it. Similarly, the request itself is less weighty than those made to other deities.

FESTIVAL OF LIGHTS

I have already described how Jiya concludes the Festival of Lights: it is enlightening to put her activities in a larger context. The Festival of Lights is widely celebrated throughout India. Preparations are made for several days. Houses are repaired and freshly whitewashed, new clothes and ornaments are bought, and sweets and special foods are cooked. Most of the day itself is spent in further preparations. The potter has brought numerous tiny clay lamps that must be filled with oil. The cotton brought by the cotton carder is made into wicks. The courtyard is cleansed once more with a fresh layer of cow dung.

Finally darkness descends. While the women and children arrange the unlit lamps on an auspicious square marked on the courtyard floor, the head of the household, with his wife at his side, worships Lakshmi, the goddess of prosperity. This ritual takes place in the small walled space forming the family "kitchen." This area is the heart of the home, and family heads often conduct their rituals in it. Here, in sacred space, Lakshmi is entreated to visit the household during the coming year. To encourage Lakshmi's arrival, clay lamps are then lit and placed around rooftops, in windows, and on or near items that could benefit from Lakshmi's gift of prosperity, such as the cattle yard, a student's books, or the granary. Where a lamp burns, Lakshmi's way is lit. To spell out the invitation to her, fireworks, rockets, sparklers, and pinwheels are set off. Men dominate these activities. But men cannot deal with the spirits of the house—the women's world. Hence, when all other activity ceases, Jiya bangs her winnowing fan and shouts, "Get out, poverty" as she roams the courtyard and rooms where her family sleeps. This act, dealing with the immediate family and house, is women's work. Her husband and sons have sought Lakshmi's protection, but she must ensure that evil spirits are chased from the nooks and crannies of *her* house.

CONCLUSION

Hinduism is nominally a male-dominated religion. According to the Sanskrit scriptures, women cannot study the most sacred texts or engage in rituals without their husbands. Furthermore, the most important rituals should be performed by a male religious specialist—the Brahman priest. Yet, as the evidence from Karimpur shows, women regularly engage in religious activity that requires no male specialists. Devotional religion (*bhakti*) as practiced in much of India does not require priests. The rites of Karimpur's women are all devotional in character, and therefore they can be conducted by women.

By studying these rituals, we can see which ones are most important to Hindu women. Only in the case of three rituals performed for specific relatives does each woman perform her own ritual herself. The female head of the family conducts two more general rites for all the other women. Two of these five rituals involve fasting—Brother's Second and Marriage Worship. The fast for Marriage Worship is longer and more rigid. Ritual preparations, including the making of special foods, are more demanding for Brother's Second, Marriage Worship, and the Festival of Lights. Thus, it is clear that Marriage Worship is given the greatest weight, followed in order by Brother's Second, Lampblack Mother, and Snake's Fifth. The Festival of Lights is an anomalous case, because it is actually a family ritual in which men also play an important role.

In all these rituals, women, who should ideally be submissive and passive, become instead active. Such rituals may give psychological support to the women themselves, because they allow women to have active control of events rather than depend completely on their male kin. Ritually, only a wife or a sister can really save a husband or brother from death; only Jiya can in fact finally chase poverty out of her house. The rituals performed by Karimpur's women clearly reflect the women's social world—the world of the family and household. Their attempts to have active control over these most important facets of their lives may in fact be most critical for our understanding of Karimpur women's rituals.

Notes

1. Karimpur is a pseudonym given this village before I first did research there. This paper is based on research spanning the period 1967 through 1998. The village has been described in William Wiser and Charlotte Wiser, *Behind Mud Walls* (Berkeley: University of California Press, 1972) and in my writings, see especially *Shakti: Power in the Conceptual Structure of Karimpur Religion* (Chicago: University of Chicago Department of Anthropology, 1975) and *Struggling with Destiny in Karimpur,* 1925–1984. (Berkeley: University of California Press, 1994).

2. Some 8 percent of the population migrated out between 1984 and 1998. Before that, permanent migration was rare. For information on social change and caste ranking, see Wadley, 1994, especially Chapter 6.

3. W. Douglas P. Hill. *The Holy Lake of the Acts of Rama* (London: Oxford University Press, 1952), pp. 297–98.

4. For more on the status of the widow in Karimpur, see Susan S. Wadley, "No Longer a Wife: Widows in rural North India." In P. Courtright and L. Harlan, eds. *Marriage from the Margins* (New York: Oxford University Press, 1995), pp, 91–118.

5. David Mandelbaum. "The Family in India," in *The Family: Its Function and Destiny* (New York: Harper and Brothers, 1949), p. 104.

Further Readings

Archer, William G. *Songs for the Bride: Wedding Rites of Rural India.* New York: Columbia University Press, 1985.

Babb, Lawrence Alan. *The Divine Hierarchy: Popular Hinduism in Central India.* New York: Columbia University Press, 1975.

Goodwin, Raheja, Gloria and Ann Grodzins Gold. *Listen to the Heron's Words: Reimaging Gender and Kinship in North India.* Berkeley, Calif.: University of California Press, 1994.

Harlan, Lindsey and Paul B. Courtright, eds. *From the Margins of Hindu Marriage: Essays on Gender, Religion and Culture.* New York: Oxford University Press, 1995.

Jacobson, Doranne and Susan S. Wadley. *Women in India: Two Perspectives.* New Delhi: Manohar Books, 1999.

Wadley, Susan S. "The Katha of *Sakat.* Two Tellings." *Another Harmony: New Essays in the Folklore of India,* ed. by Stuart H. Blackburn and S. Ramanujan. Berkeley, Calif.: University of California Press, 1986, pp. 195–232.

———, ed. *The Powers of Tamil Women.* New York: South Asia Series, Foreign and Comparative Studies Program, Syracuse University, 1980.

———. "Vrats: Transformers of Destiny." *Karma: An Anthropological Inquiry,* ed. by Charles F. Keyes and E. Valentine Daniel. Berkeley, Calif.: University of California Press, 1983, pp. 147–62.

———. *Struggling with Destiny in Karimpur, 1925–1984.* Berkeley, Calif.: University of California Press, 1994.

———. "Charlotte Wiser's 'Srimati': Gender and Caste Relations in a North Indian Village in the 1920s." *Manushi,* no. 127 (1998), pp. 16–23.

9

The Ladies of Lord Krishna: Rituals of Middle-Aged Women in Eastern India

JAMES M. FREEMAN

During an anthropological study of a village in Orissa, India, some years ago, I became fascinated by the *habisha* rituals associated with the Jagannatha temple in the pilgrim town of Puri. These rituals, performed mainly by women, are remarkable for the intense religious fervor they inspire, for their grace and beauty, and for their complex symbolism. Despite the importance of these rituals for women, no existing description of the Jagannatha cult gives the *habisha* more than passing mention.

The *habisha,* like many Hindu rites, is a *brata* (or *vrata*) rite—a vowed observance. Historically, vows have been an important part of Hindu ritual life for centuries. People make vows mainly to secure something in this world, such as progeny, wealth, good fortune, health, fame, or long life; sometimes people make vows to secure something in the next world; and occasionally, as in the *habisha* rites, people make vows to gain something both in this world and in the next. Some vows last only a day; others, a lifetime. But whether

JAMES M. FREEMAN (Ph.D. Harvard) is Professor of Anthropology at San Jose State University. He is the author of thirty-five articles and four books, of which the best known are *Untouchable: An Indian Life History* and *Hearts of Sorrow: Vietnamese-American Lives.* He has won several book and writing prizes, including the American Book Award and the Outstanding Book Award of the Association for Asian American Studies. His research has been funded by grants and fellowships from the American Institute of Indian Studies, the Social Science Research Council, the Center for Advanced Study in the Behavioral Sciences at Stanford, the National Endowment for the Humanities, the National Science Foundation, and the Alfred P. Sloan Foundation. At present, he is completing a book on unaccompanied refugee children (*Seeking Asylum and the Disruption of Childhood*) and is working on a long-term collaborative project with C. Darrah and J. English-Lueck that focuses on work, family, and daily life in Silicon Valley.

they be long or short, failure to fulfill a vow is said to lead to dire consequences. Hindu scriptures known as *puranas* contain detailed descriptions of rules for vow makers. Among others, these rules include fasting, worshiping of gods, frequent purificatory baths, sexual abstinence, refraining from drinking water and from chewing betel nuts, and not sleeping during daylight hours. Proper fulfillment of vows not only brings the vow maker the rewards that he or she seeks but also invests that person with great spiritual power. For example, a virtuous wife who fulfills certain vows is said to gain the power to prevent the death of her husband—a power that plays an important role in *habisha* rites.

In the village that I studied, which is located three miles from Bhubaneswar, the capital of Orissa, the rite that people call *habisha* seems to be a combination of many vows and ceremonies. The village rites that I witnessed differed significantly from descriptions found in both Western and Indian literature on the topic. In particular, although written sources state that the *habisha* is especially a widows' rite, the village women informed me that widows were not supposed to perform *habisha* rituals, and, in fact, I found that they rarely did so. Most *habisha* participants were menopausal women whose husbands were still alive. Although several women informed me that their main purpose for performing *habisha* rites was to protect their husbands, they also revealed other important religious motivations. In general, the village women's *habisha* rituals were far more elaborate than already available descriptions might suggest.

My principal research in the village consisted of taking a census of each household and collecting life histories from a number of villagers. Two of the women who narrated their life histories to me in their native language of Oriya described the complex details of their *habisha* rituals. Tila Sahu, the younger of the two women, was fifty-five years old, married, and a member of the Confectioner caste. She was lively and talkative, and, when she discovered my interest in her *habisha* rituals, she offered to show me how she performed them and urged me to photograph them. In October–November, 1971, I witnessed Tila's performance of these rites.

The older woman, Padma Bewa, was the seventy-year-old widow of a temple priest. She introduced herself to me one morning by pulling me into her tea shop and offering me some sweets. When, at my suggestion, she later narrated her life history to me, I learned that she had followed the *habisha* fasts as well as many others for thirty years, stopping only a year earlier, when her husband had died. Because she was a widow, she believed that she should no longer perform the rituals. Nevertheless, she did tell me in great detail her recollections of the ceremonies that she had performed in the past.

Both women, who were deeply religious followers of the Jagannatha cult, spoke of their *habisha* experiences, especially their pilgrimages to Puri, as high points of their lives. Every year Padma Bewa and Tila Sahu, as well as many other elderly middle- and high-caste Orissan women, would observe *habisha.* For a period of thirty-five days in October–November, women vow to the deity Jagannatha (a form of Vishnu or Krishna) that they will perform purificatory rituals and fasts to protect their families or to improve themselves spiritually. During the *habisha* rites, women worship Jagannatha as the young Krishna, the cow herdsman surrounded by his female devotees, or *gopis* (milkmaids). Frequently they create ephemeral, stylized, but intricate and individualized rice-powder paintings of the god and his followers. Replicating the activities of the *gopis,* the devotees churn milk, offer Krishna coconuts and cowrie shells, and dance ecstatically to demonstrate their devotional love of Krishna.

Whenever possible, the rite concludes with a forty-mile pilgrimage to the temple of Lord

Jagannatha in the holy city of Puri. One of the holiest and most famous shrines in India, this temple is best known for its annual chariot festival in July, which draws over 100,000 pilgrims. However, the religious cult of Jagannatha is also the focus of many other ceremonies like the *habisha* throughout the year.

HABISHA RITUALS OF TILA SAHU AND OTHER VILLAGE WOMEN

Because *habisha* rituals are expensive and often inconvenient for other family members, Tila Sahu, like all prospective vow makers, asked and received permission from her family before beginning her *habisha* vows. Six days before the month of Kartik (October–November), I watched a barber trim Tila's fingernails and toenails as a preliminary act of purification. After bathing, Tila summoned a Brahman family priest who customarily performed ceremonies for her family.

To purify Tila further, the Brahman—a tall, thin man—sprinkled cow-dung water on her head. The Brahman then turned to me and said that people ought to purify themselves for *habisha* vows by drinking *panchagavia,* "the five holy substances of the cow"—milk, curds, clarified butter, urine, and dung—but that nowadays few people did it. After putting on a new sacred cloth, Tila offered her Brahman priest gifts indicating that she would be his disciple and follow his instructions on the performance of the rituals and that she would listen to his daily recitation from a sacred book during the month of Kartik. She also promised to fulfill her vows of fasting, purification, and sexual abstinence.

On the following day Tila Sahu began the predawn bathing and purificatory rites of the *habisha* devotee. With nine other elderly and middle-aged Hindu women, only one of whom was a widow, she walked slowly into the chilly waters of the village pond. Facing north, waist deep in the water, they called out to three deities—Brahma, Vishnu, and Maheswar (Shiva)—asking them to witness their *habisha* vows. Turning east, the most sacred and auspicious direction, each woman scooped up a handful of water and called to all the holy rivers of India, venerated as Goddesses, to attend the women's sacred activities. Each woman threw this sanctified water over her head and body and then bathed. Facing south, the direction of death, sin, and pollution, each woman called to her ancestors to take a holy bath and witness the sacred events. Turning west, the direction symbolizing the completion of auspicious rituals, the women offered water to the deities of the ten directions (the cardinal directions, the ordinal directions, the zenith, and the nadir). Finally each woman dipped beneath the water three times, each time calling to the god Vishnu. The water of the pond was especially purifying because it was the water of a sacred place where the village deity had been bathed.

Dawn had nearly arrived as the women scooped up handfuls of mud and climbed out of the village pond. They shivered in their thin, wet, clinging saris as the biting October wind whipped past them. On the stone steps above the pond, the women, following Tila's lead, patted the mud into little images of Damodar, a form of the deity Vishnu as a child, and then uttered prayers and sprinkled offerings of flowers and water over them. Standing and facing east, they offered prayers to the rising sun. Next they prayed to the *tulasi,* the holy basil plant sacred to Vishnu, that grew in a stone pot on the steps. Finally they entered the village temple next to the pond, where they waved burning wicks in tiny clay oil lamps before each of twenty-six deities and chanted songs describing their desire to merge their souls with the souls of the deities.

I asked Tila why none of the women were young. She replied, "A *habisha* woman should be fifty years or over, so that menstruation has stopped. A woman who menstruates becomes 'untouchable' for four days and must stop her vow activities during that time. While she is impure, another person who is pure performs the rituals for her. A woman gets more *dharma* [merit] if she starts her vow rituals while her husband is alive, but she receives *papa* [demerit] if she performs the *habisha* while menstruating."

The other women smiled and nodded in agreement. They were in a joyous mood, as befit the occasion. It was the beginning of their holy period of one-meal-a-day fasting, praying, and purifying themselves—a period when, as they pointed out to me, they put aside animosities and jealousies and ceased gossiping, turning instead to cooperation, expressions of good will, and religious devotion.

The women went to their homes and cooked their meals. During the *habisha* they would eat only once a day, before sundown, or not at all if they so desired. Tila had previously collected the white unparboiled rice, required for ritual practice, which would be her main food during her *habisha* days. (Rice used for everyday purposes is often partially cooked before final boiling.) Besides rice, she could eat only certain other foods considered to be pure: a variety of lentil, green plantain, taro, cucumber, ginger, and custard apple. The devotees were supposed to prepare their own meals, which had to be boiled. No spices were allowed, but each meal had to contain clarified butter, a substance considered holy because made from cow milk.

After cooking her meal, Tila bathed again in the village pond and waved burning wicks at the deities of the temple. When she returned home, she washed her legs, hands, and face. Next she sprinkled water containing holy basil leaves—the sacred food of Vishnu—around the food pots and into the food, transforming it into Vishnu's *prasad,* (sacred food).

Then she ate, talking to no one but silently uttering the name of Vishnu at each bite. The *habisha* food is considered even more sacred than ordinary sacred food, so much so that the Brahman family priest, who ordinarily must not eat food cooked by persons of castes lower than his, regularly eats the food cooked by his *habisha* disciples. After offering some food to the Brahman, Tila gave the rest to her husband and son, as well as her daughter and granddaughter, who had come for a visit.

Tila observed purificatory rules not only when she ate or bathed but when she performed other activities as well. She avoided touching and talking to untouchables and lowcaste people. If she stepped on human urine or feces or on the feces of animals such as dogs, chickens, or goats, she bathed and sprinkled cow-dung water on her head. She was supposed to avoid gossiping and arguing, as well as begging and borrowing. At all times she carried with her two nuts representing Krishna and his brother. Throughout the day she prayed to these symbols of God and sang prayers to Vishnu that she had learned over the years by listening to others. "The month of Kartik is a religious month," she said. "Affection for God comes in that month. During Kartik I never feel away from God but devote my days to God."

On the first day of the month of Kartik, the full *habisha* ceremonies began. After bathing in the pond and praying in the village temple, Tila and the other women brought ritual articles to a holy basil plant in the front yard of the house where Usha, the Brahman woman, lived. Donated by the women's husbands, these articles were offerings for the ceremonies honoring Krishna. While Usha directed the collection of the articles, Tila, using colored powders made from rice, charcoal, turmeric, and vermilion, created a picture around the holy basil plant. She drew Krishna in the form of Jagannatha, his brother Balabhadra and his sister Subhadra. Then she added a large *garuda* bird (the symbolic vehicle of Vishnu), footprints of Lakshmi, the goddess of wealth and wife of Vishnu (Jagannatha), and two bodyguards. She completed her picture with a ladder leading to the sea of eternity, a lotus plant (associated with

Lakshmi), and a conch shell and a discus, symbols of Vishnu.

Usha, the leader, began praying. She made the ululating *hulahuli* sounds that women utter at auspicious or holy occasions. The others then followed with other *hulahuli.* While ringing a bell, Usha threw offerings of flowers on the holy basil plant and water from the conch shell onto the sacred food. Then she raised her eyes to the sun and prayed. The other women presented their offerings by placing them in a brass plate that all of them held together, and they made the *hulahuli* sounds as they held onto the plate.

Then the women reenacted the familiar legend of Krishna and the milkmaids. One woman in the role of a milkmaid churned milk in a small clay bowl. Tila, playing the role of Radha, the chief milkmaid and divine lover of Krishna, placed the pot of churned milk on her head. The women, holding hands, formed a circle, danced, sang loudly, and clapped their hands, imitating the devotional worship of the milkmaids for Krishna. One of the women, in the role of Krishna, reenacted the practical jokes he played on the milkmaids—hiding their clothes while they were bathing in the river, moving the boat that would ferry them across the river, and delaying its return. Pretending not to know who he was, the milkmaids loudly criticized the boatman until he revealed himself as Krishna, beloved to all of them. One of the women, in the role of Krishna's mother, played with her son and tried to prevent his mischievous pranks, while the other milkmaids danced, sang, and laughed noisily.

To end the ceremony, the women placed flowers and sacred water on the sides of one another's faces and on the tops of their heads. Then they prostrated themselves, touched their foreheads to the mound around the holy basil plant, and dispersed.

Each day Tila and the other women performed their Krishna dances and games, increasing the tempo of the singing and dancing, twirling and leaping around the holy basil plant. Except for myself, adult males were not permitted to watch.

On the final day Tila presented her Brahman family priest with a gift of cloth and food. The next day she invited her immediate family and relatives to a feast of goat-meat curry, reversing her month-long diet of bland vegetarian food. While all her relatives were sitting together and eating, Tila announced, "I have fulfilled my vow. God should bless me. I should receive that for which I performed my vow."

Padma Bewa, the old widow, did not participate in the *habisha* rituals on this occasion. "For thirty years I followed the rites of many vows, including *habisha,*" she said to me, "but after the death of my husband, I forgot all about them. Women observe their vows until their husband dies; then they stop, as I did. This is what women should do. My *habisha* was for my husband [to protect him]. When I first started *habisha,* I did it only occasionally, fasting for twenty of the thirty days, eating only one meal of white rice at night. My husband was a temple priest. He often observed the *habisha* rites because the pilgrims he served would appoint him to perform *habisha* for them for five, seven, or even twenty-one days—sometimes even for the entire month. So I vowed to perform the full *habisha* ritual with him, even though it was improper because I was too young. But our village deity had appeared to me in a dream and ordered me to do it, so I knew it was all right." Padma Bewa did continue to observe some vows for her son. "These days I carry out several fasting vows to protect my son. I will do this until my life ends."

THE RELIGIOUS EXPERIENCES OF TILA SAHU

Tila Sahu, the Confectioner's wife, said to me with regret that she had visited Puri only twice in the month of Kartik but that both visits had been memorable experiences. "Thirty years ago I visited Puri during *habisha* for the first time," she said. "I longed to participate, but I just watched others. I was not in *habisha* because I was too young—a new wife without children.

"Ten years ago during the month of Kartik I went to Puri to see a dance in the temple of Lord Jagannatha. I hardly saw it because of the thousands of people there. Although I had traveled to Puri with relatives, I stayed alone that night in the temple. I watched how different *habisha* people worshiped. They became ecstatic, and in their devotional fervor they forgot all about the world. They tried to merge their souls into that of the deity.

"When morning came, I returned to my uncle's house in Puri. Then I bathed in the temple's tank. Afterward I went with my relatives to the Gate of Heaven on the beach where the dead are cremated. We saw several women doing their *puja* [ritual]. I joined in and sang for them a *habisha* song that the milkmaids sang when Jagannatha and his brother went to help the king of Puri fight a war against the king of the south. All the *habisha* people were surprised at how much I knew. They happily pulled me into the center of their group, dressed me as Radha, and dressed another woman like Krishna, while the others became milkmaids for the drama. We danced and sang on the beach, and the others praised me. Many groups of women were singing and dancing; one after another they invited me to dance and sing with them. I continued for twelve hours.

"I returned home by bus. In the village we dance and sing but not like in Puri. Men and women in the village criticize *habisha* people because, they say, it is improper to sing and dance publicly. Those villagers are wicked. They have no power of devotion."

I asked Tila why she longed to go to Puri and why she performed her village *habisha* rituals so faithfully. Tila said that she had been trying to reach God since her childhood. When she was eleven years old, she met a *babaji,* an ascetic holy man of marvelous powers, who lived in a forest dwelling near her village. She brought him an offering of milk, sent by her mother. The *babaji* blessed her. "From that day," she said, "my religious devotion increased, and I wanted to serve that *baba.*" She returned each day with offerings of milk. Her mother, a devout woman, excused Tila from her ordinary household tasks so that she could serve the *babaji.* "I was happy because I preferred to be with the *babaji* than to do household chores," said Tila. "So every day I went, and after a while I didn't need friends to go with me and play. I became very familiar with the *babaji,* like a disciple. The *babaji* never let the shadow of a mature or married woman fall across him. He ate sour meditation medicine to bind his body [prevent sexual discharge]."

Tila said that the holy man used his religious powers to help villagers appease the Goddess Bimala so that she would not burn down their villages in the dry season. According to Tila, his powers astonished people. "What can I say about that *baba*?" said Tila. "I was too young at that time. I did not follow any religious faith. I did not learn anything from him. I did not receive any remarkable abilities or magical powers. So when I think about him, I feel very unhappy. Tears come to my eyes. What a powerful deity I lost! You can't imagine his qualities and abilities!"

Tila served the holy man for three years. Then, when she was fourteen years old, a marriage proposal came to her house from a family in a nearby village. She was married soon after. After staying for a few days in her husband's house, she returned to the home of her parents. She said, "That evening I remembered about the *baba* and decided to visit him the following morning. In the middle of the night, however, the *babaji* came and sat near my head. He said, 'Tila, look at me well; this is the last time you will see me. No matter how much you want to, you can never visit me again. You are married, so you must stay away. If you come near me, I'll beat you and drive you away!' I cried and suddenly woke up. I never saw my *babaji* again. I heard that four months later he left the forest and that two months after that he left his mortal body. Since that time I have been searching through my *habisha* vows for someone like the *babaji.*"

THE RELIGIOUS EXPERIENCES OF PADMA BEWA

Padma Bewa, the old widow who had performed her *habisha* rituals in Puri for thirty years, usually walked to that holy city. Each year Padma and about fifty or sixty women from her village, carrying their small grandchildren, their own food, and some cooking utensils, trudged the forty miles from their homes to the city of Puri, stopping and praying at holy shrines along the way. A couple of elderly men usually went with them. At Puri the women first visited several shrines and performed the prescribed purificatory rites. Then they walked to the beach and joined other groups of women who were singing, swaying, and dancing. When Padma joined them, she was swept up in wild exultation and lost all sense of self, time, and place. "While bathing or dancing," she said, "I never felt tired. I was so happy from being in Puri that I felt no weariness." Some villagers returned home after one or two days; Padma usually stayed on the beach for many days and sometimes during the entire month fasting, praying and dancing.

I asked her how she had become a religious person. Padma said that from childhood she had believed strongly in various gods and goddesses. As a young childless wife, she visited temples all over Orissa, praying that the deities of those temples would bless her with a child. Although her prayers went unanswered, her faith remained strong. As she grew older, she visited various shrines whenever she could afford to. She planted fruits and plants sacred to different deities, and in her yard she worshiped Lord Vishnu's holy basil daily. Each day she prayed to two gods and to twelve goddesses, all forms of the Mother Goddess.

She said, "I prayed to them to pull me to their feet. I desired to visit their shrines. I thought about nothing but gods and goddesses. I enjoyed listening to the stories from the *puranas* [old books]. Each night, when I had no other obligations, I gathered with other women at the house of a Brahman woman who could read. She read us stories from the old religious books.

"From her I learned about the powers of the gods and goddesses. I learned that by prayer and devotion people can receive whatever boons they wish. I had always had religious feelings, but now they grew in my heart more and more. I attended the nightly readings regularly because I liked it so much. I liked all of the gods and goddesses.

"Then one night I had a dream in which Sri Lokanatha, one of Puri's deities, said, 'Why do you delay visiting Lord Jagannatha at Puri? You have never seen him. You should go and visit him.' I told my husband about my dream, and I persuaded him to come with me. That was my first trip to Puri. Soon after, I began going each year for *habisha.*

"One year during *habisha,* while we were bathing on the Puri beach at the Gate of Heaven, the undercurrent took one of our women, swallowing her body into the womb of the sea. Although she was very old, we still cried at her death. We sent a woman back to our village to inform the drowned woman's son.

"When he arrived, he ran into the sea to drown himself, but the fishermen pulled him back. We tried to cheer him up, saying that, because his mother had been pious, she had received the gift of dying in the holy abode of Vishnu and Lakshmi. We tried to convince him that his mother's death was a significant and noble one and that her fortune had guided her to die in this most sacred place, next to the Gate of Heaven, where the soul could reach heaven without any death ceremony.

"The next morning all of us *habisha* women looked for the body along the seashore. Late in the morning a wave washed her onto the beach. Her son held her body and cried, and so did we. Then we collected bamboo and branches, carried her to the Gate of Heaven, and cremated her.

"During those two days, instead of eating one meal a day, we ate nothing. How could we eat, thinking of the death of one of our companions and the sorrow of her son? We all prayed to Lord Jagannatha that he would bless us so that we might meet a death like that of our companion. But we are unfortunate. How can we get that sort of death?

"Several people from that group have since died, but all of them died in the village. Several times I have dreamed that I died in Puri and that I saw my own funeral procession and ceremony. I liked that death. So every year I want to go to Puri to die, but only God knows whether I will be able to die in Puri."

THE SIGNIFICANCE OF *HABISHA* AS A HINDU RITUAL

Habisha rituals, like practically all Hindu rituals, are concerned with the opposing themes of purity and pollution. This was evident in Tila Sahu's performance of her month-long vow as she sought to increase purity and avoid pollution and polluting substances even more than usual. Closely linked with the concern about purity and pollution is a concern to increase the auspicious and to drive away the inauspicious—a concern that runs through most Hindu rituals. In rituals that enhance the auspicious, such as the *habisha,* marriages, and many calendrical celebrations of deities, worshipers acquire a high degree of ritual purity (eliminating more pollution than usual) in part by using purifying substances. Then, as Tila Sahu did, they share their high state of purity with their families by giving them sacred food. Thus auspiciousness radiates from the woman performing *habisha.* As part of the same theme, the *habisha* rites end with an abrupt reversal that returns the *habisha* worshipers to their ordinary state; they cook and share with their relatives a meal of goat-meat curry that, like all meat, is much less pure than the diet permitted during *habisha.*

Habisha rituals, like all Hindu rituals, also involve sacred space and sacred time. Villagers like Tila Sahu and Padma Bewa believe that the region in which they live is itself a sacred space, and they replicate this space in their rituals. When the *habisha* followers make rice-powder paintings of deities, they, in effect, create a sacred altar. The women believe that, by purifying themselves and praying, they draw together the divine powers within themselves. They then transfer these powers to the inanimate pictures, bringing them to life as the deity, who is invited to the ritual as a friend. All Hindu worshipers engage in rituals to bring deities to life, whether in temples, houses, or, as the *habisha* women did, out in the yard next to the holy basil plant. The *habisha* worshipers are involved not only with sacred space but also with sacred time. The month of Kartik is a special holy time that heightens religious consciousness and releases worshipers from ordinary daily activities. The women deliberately drop what they consider to be bad behavior, such as gossiping and quarreling, and try to be cooperative. More importantly, during this month women engage in behavior that is normally forbidden—emotional public displays of dancing, singing, and worship.

Habisha rituals fit neatly into the complex of theistic, devotional Hinduism. The beliefs and activities of the women closely parallel practices in devotional Hinduism that have usually been studied and discussed by Western scholars as performed by men. The *habisha* women worship Vishnu, a popular deity of contemporary Hinduism, who has many forms and hundreds of different names. They identify most closely with the north-Indian deity Krishna, one of the most widely known forms of Vishnu. In Orissa, however, Krishna and his legends have been merged with Jagannatha, "Lord of the World," a local deity probably of tribal origins who has his own distinctive traditions, stories, and art forms. The women's worship of Krishna through art and ritual is typical in Hinduism. The women who make the powder paintings create individualistic representations that are part of a distinct regional style of women's ephemeral art (the paintings are rubbed away and recreated each day of the ritual). However, the paintings also contain symbols that are widely recognized throughout India—the conch shell, the *garuda* bird, the footprints of Lakshmi, and the discus. The women also retell and reenact, through dance and drama, all the beloved stories of Krishna and Jagannatha.

THE SIGNIFICANCE OF *HABISHA* IN THE LIFE CYCLES OF WOMEN

Habisha is performed most often by menopausal, married, upper-caste women. All three adjectives are crucial to understanding the significance of *habisha* in women's life cycles.

Only upper-caste women are allowed to, or have reason to, perform *habisha*. To understand why, we must remember that one of the main stated reasons for performing *habisha* is to keep husbands alive. This is important to high-caste women both because of the difficulties an upper-caste widow faces and because of her economic dependency on her husband. A high-caste woman from the village of Tila Sahu and Padma Bewa most often remains at home, without outside employment, supported by her husband's family. Once widowed, she becomes inauspicious, an object of scorn and a source of potential sexual scandal. She is expected to remain at home doing household chores, faithful to her deceased husband. But often she is assumed to be secretly involved with other men. Ordinarily, she must not attend auspicious rituals like marriages, and she may participate only in penance and purification rites. No wonder these women want to keep their husbands alive!

By contrast, women from low and untouchable castes are not expected to perform the *habisha* rituals. Many of these women live in poor households, become wage earners outside of the house, and consequently have greater economic independence from their husbands than do high-caste women. Furthermore, lower- and untouchable-caste widows are not expected to remain faithful to their deceased husbands; instead, they are allowed to remarry and frequently do so.

Almost all of those who perform the full thirty-five-day ritual are older wives, not yet widowed, who no longer menstruate. This suggests that the *habisha* marks an important transitional stage in the life pattern of a high-caste Hindu woman of Orissa—the stage between menopause and widowhood—and meets her distinctive needs. The most important question is why the *habisha* has become a ritual for older wives rather than younger ones. If *habisha* is performed in part to protect husbands, why do young high-caste wives of childbearing age rarely perform the full *habisha* rituals, waiting instead until they become fifty years old? Surely young high-caste wives have as much at stake in keeping their husbands alive as do older wives. Whether young or old, a high-caste widow becomes inauspicious, is not allowed to remarry, and usually suffers greatly.

There are at least five possible reasons why younger women usually do not perform *habisha.* The first, which Padma Bewa and Tila Sahu stressed, is that young wives will be menstruating during some of the days of the full *habisha.* Women in such a condition are considered polluting and should not perform the ceremony themselves, although it would be permitted to have the rites performed by a proxy during the days of actual menstruation. Second, young wives may be prohibited from performing the full *habisha* also because public singing and dancing are considered particularly inappropriate, if not scandalous, behaviors for young women. By contrast, women beyond the age of childbearing are allowed much greater freedom in speech and action. Third, the *habisha* is an expensive, time-consuming ceremony. Young women, who have a greater workload than older women in a joint household, are less likely to be released from their daily chores for thirty-five days than are older women, whose daily tasks are not as time consuming. Fourth, historically the rites were performed by widows and have only recently become rites for older married women. Enough of their previous association with inauspicious widows may linger on to make the rites seem inappropriate for young, childbearing women. Fifth, with improvements in nutrition and health care, particularly for higher-caste and wealthy people, fewer husbands die young. The wives of young men may not consider their husbands to be as vulnerable to harm as do older women who are married to older men. The older wife, on the other hand, has strong reasons for performing the *habisha* ritual. Recognizing their aging husbands' increasing vulnerability to disease and death, elderly women make and fulfill *habisha* vows to forestall the dreaded onset of widowhood with all its negative implications, including the expectation that they will no longer perform *habisha.*

These menopausal wives are in a unique phase of their life cycle—a phase that allows and encourages them to engage in such rituals for the first time in lives. It is also a phase that almost demands that they perform *habisha,* because through *habisha* they hope not to lose the status of older wives by becoming widows. Also, they are at a moment in their lives when they have passed through the stage of childbearing, which is associated with the polluting conditions of childbirth and menstruation. Menopause gives a woman greater ritual purity (absence of pollution) and frees her from the numerous ritual proscriptions placed on women of childbearing age. Thus it is easier for older women to perform a ritual that will intensify their purity. Furthermore, menopausal women are released from many social obligations required of younger women. They enjoy the highest degree of domestic, social, and ritual freedom that any adult Hindu woman ever knows. Thus they have the time and the energy to perform *habisha* rites. The opportunities afforded to *habisha* women, who have completed all their worldly obligations, are similar to those offered to men who have completed their worldly occupations and can withdraw into a stage of the life cycle that is more concerned with spiritual growth. This parallel is quite important in the study of women's life cycles.

There is, however, a negative side. Menopausal women are increasingly vulnerable. The performance of marriage duties and childbearing—historically the primary functions of Hindu women—are mostly things of the past. More important, their husbands are aging, a fact that increases the threat of widowhood, with its concomitants of pollution and inauspiciousness. Thus these women have a great stake in prolonging this relatively free and fortunate phase of their life cycle. Consequently, they are increasingly concerned about husband and family protection, as well as with their own spiritual purification.

The *habisha* has, therefore, come to symbolize an unusual period of freedom from men and their demands, as well as from the social obligations and ritual prohibitions that men ordinarily impose on women. But such freedom comes at the cost of increased vulnerability to widowhood. Although the women perform the rituals in part to protect their husbands, they perform the rituals mainly for themselves. The *habisha,* by reversing ordinary behavior, gives these women the opportunity to look after their own spiritual development before the ritual prohibitions of widowhood again limit their religious expressions.

Further Readings

Babb, Lawrence. *The Divine Hierarchy: Popular Hinduism in Central India.* New York: Columbia University Press, 1975.

Das, S. R. "A Study of the Vrata Rituals of Bengal." *Man in India* 32 (October–December 1952) pp. 207–45.

Eschmann, Anncharlott, et al., eds. *The Cult of Jagannath and the Regional Tradition of Orissa.* New Delhi: Manohar Books, 1978.

Freeman, James M. "Trial by Fire." *Natural History Magazine* 83 (January 1974) pp. 54–63.

———*Scarcity and Opportunity in an Indian Village.* Prospect Heights, Ill.: Waveland Press, 1985 (1977).

Kane, Pandurang Vaman. *History of Dharmasastra.* Vol. 2, part 1. Poona: Bhandarkar Oriental Research Institute, 1941.

———*History of Dharmasastra.* Vol. 5, part 1. 2d ed. Poona: Bhandarkar Oriental Research Institute, 1974.

O'Malley, L. S. S. *Puri District Gazeteer.* Patna: Government Printing Press, 1929.

10

Garífuna Women and the Work of Mourning (Central America)

VIRGINIA KERNS

In 1840 an Englishman named Thomas Young traveled through several of the Garífuna (Black Carib) settlements that lie along the coast of Central America. In his *Narrative of a Residence on the Mosquito Shore,* published several years later, he mentioned that the Garífuna, practicing Roman Catholics, took great pains to see that their children were baptized. But even then they also held ceremonies for their dead that were not sanctioned by the Church. These death rites were (and still are) misunderstood by outsiders, who suspected that the Garífuna engaged in "devil worship" and even cannibalism on these occasions. They did not, as is clear from Young's account of the "feast" that he attended in one community. Apparently he was unaware of the religious significance of this mourning ceremony, known as *dügü.*

Today women are very prominent in dügü and the other death rites. Their participation seems to be a long-standing feature of Garífuna religious life. In his brief account Young pointedly remarked that the women "in great numbers" danced and sang at the "feast" and that the men were concerned with sharing "strong spirit," or rum—a necessary ingredient of any death rite even today. Older women

VIRGINIA KERNS holds a Ph.D. in Anthropology from the University of Illinois and is currently Professor of Anthropology at the College of William and Mary. She is the author of *Women and the Ancestors: Black Carib Kinship and Ritual* (Urbana, Ill.: University of Illinois Press, 1997, second edition) and co-editor, with Judith K. Brown, of *In Her Prime: New Views of Middle-Aged Women* (Urbana, Ill.: University of Illinois Press, 1992, second edition).

Author's Note: I wish to acknowledge the generous support of the Fulbright-Hayes Commission and the Wenner-Gren Foundation for Anthropological Research, which made my fieldwork possible.

organize most of these ceremonies; they contribute their labor to the time-consuming preparations, and their expertise to the actual performance. Aside from singing and dancing, they also assume major ritual roles. In theory, any adult may take part in any of the major death rites; in fact, it is largely older women who choose to do so.

During 1974–1975, and again in 1976, I observed and took part in dozens of death rites in several communities in Belize. Like Thomas Young, who had witnessed one of these ceremonies well over a century before, I was struck by the prominence of women, and especially older women, as ritual performers. The following account is based on my field research in Belize in the mid-1970s. On a return trip in the mid-1990s, I found that ritual life continues to flourish, and that uninformed outsiders (most recently Evangelical missionaries) continue to speak of it as "devil worship."

COMMUNITIES IN BELIZE

The Garífuna have an unusual history, too complex to relate in detail here, which explains the fact that they speak Carib, an Amerindian language, although they are also obviously of African descent. The first of those to settle in Belize entered the territory early in the nineteenth century. Today there are six Garífuna settlements in Belize, ranging from villages of several hundred to towns with several thousand inhabitants. These are the northernmost of the more than fifty settlements scattered along the low and sandy coastline of the Caribbean Sea. Eighty thousand or so Garífuna live in these communities in Belize, Guatemala, Honduras, and Nicaragua.

In Belize, the villages are rural and quite isolated, but the people who live in them are not peasants. Today farming provides relatively little food or income. Some men work at nearby plantations and return home to their families on a frequent and regular basis. Many other men and young women work as unskilled laborers all over the country, coming home only occasionally. Most of the older people who live in these villages are men and women who cannot find work, either because of physical disability or, in the case of women, because of age discrimination in the labor market. The government of Belize sets no compulsory retirement age, and, because of a chronic shortage of male labor, most men can find jobs as long as they are physically able to work. Some are employed into their sixties and even early seventies. Fewer jobs exist for women, especially for those who are older. After the age of forty or fifty a woman finds it very difficult to obtain any regular employment aside from the lowest-paying kinds of domestic work. Most older women must depend on others for support—either their grown children or, if they are married, their husbands.

While marital relationships are relatively unstable, the Garífuna consider the parent/child bond to be perpetual, one that even death cannot sever. Deceased men and women may request private or public offerings from their children and other descendants. Older women—the daughters and granddaughters of the dead—usually see to these offerings, as well as to the other mourning ceremonies.

DEATH AND RITUAL

Beliefs about the supernatural are highly syncretic and quite intricate. Villagers believe that a plethora of spirits, both human and nonhuman, frequent the local landscape. Most of the nonhuman spirits are entirely hostile to the living, while the spirits of lineal kin can either protect or harm their living descendants. Interaction between the living and the dead is highly reciprocal. If the living neglect their dead kin, they can expect to suffer for it: their ancestors may cause them to sicken and even to die. The only protection against such misfortune, and the only cure for it, is careful attention to the needs and demands of the dead.

The needs of the dead are met through ritual. Two rites, deemed to be absolutely necessary, are held after the death of any adult. These are the wake (and burial) and the ninth-night wake, which is a major ritual and social occasion.[1] Three additional minor mourning ceremonies may be held. These are *tagurun ludu,* which ends the period of formal mourning by close kinswomen of the deceased; a ritual bathing, *amuidahani;* and a requiem mass with a small "feast" afterwards. The dead typically request these last two ceremonies through dreams, often within a year or two of burial. Finally, spirits also occasionally ask for two other major rituals, *chugu* and *dügü,* voicing their requests by speaking through a shaman. As shown in Table 1, they may request these as soon as a few years or as long as half a century after death.

The three intermediate rituals listed in Table 1 are minor ones. They last for only a few hours and attract no more than one or two dozen participants, most of them older women who live in the community. Minor ceremonies also entail far less expense than the major rites, which draw larger and more heterogeneous crowds, including visitors from other communities. Several hundred women and men may attend ninth-night wakes and *dügü.* Despite the differences in scale, all mourning rituals share the same serious purpose—satisfaction of the dead and protection of the living. But the usual ambience is not solemn; they are festive occasions enjoyed by the living as well as, it is believed, by the dead. Rituals are also work. The preparations require the efforts of at least several women and sometimes of several dozen women.

THE WORK OF MOURNING

The sound of women wailing is the first public signal of a death in a Garífuna village. Kinswomen of the deceased begin their

Table 1 *Sequence of Death Rites*

Rite	Timing
Beluria (wake) and *abunahani* (burial)	Obligatory, within 48 hours of death
Arisaruni (novenas) and *beluria* (ninth-night wake)	Obligatory, usually within 2 or 3 weeks of death
Tagurun ludu (end of mourning ceremony)	Obligatory, 6 months or 1 year after death of parent or spouse
Amuidahani (bathing the spirit)	Obligatory if requested, usually within several years of death
Helemeserun hilaña (requiem mass) and *efeduhani laugi lemesi* (feasting after mass)	Obligatory if requested, usually within several years of death
Chugu (feeding the dead)	Obligatory if requested, usually more than 10 and less than 50 years after death
dügü (feasting the dead)	Obligatory if requested, usually more than 10 and less than 50 years after death

customary display of grief as soon as they hear of the death, and they continue to wail at intervals until burial the next day. Preparations for the wake are under way almost immediately. Women of the community, who volunteer their help to the bereaved family, start to prepare the food that they will serve at the wake.

While a few elderly women work in private preparing the corpse for burial, several men hastily construct a coffin. When the wake begins after dark, the coffin is finished and has been placed in the main room of the house. Men, women, and children go there to view the body, and many of the adults linger to express their "appreciation" of the deceased. The men speak eloquently but briefly, the women speak more tearfully and at greater length. When they wail, they eulogize the deceased and lament the death.

People are subdued as the wake begins. Some men sit together and gamble; others converse. Women talk quietly among themselves or help to distribute food and rum. The size and conviviality of the crowd grow in proportion to the amount of rum that the women pass around. Later in the night a few men begin to drum on wooden crates, providing the musical background for the traditional dances that are staple ingredients of nearly any public occasion in Garífuna communities. Men and women of all ages join in these dances. If the wake is a "good" one, with a generous supply of food and rum, many of them will remain throughout the night. Even if refreshment is in short supply and most of the people depart early in the night, older women will keep their vigil by the body until dawn.

The next day people gather briefly in the church to pray. Then a procession of women, children, and a few men follows the male pallbearers and coffin to the burial ground. As the men lower the coffin into the grave, kinswomen of the deceased begin to wail again. One or two of the women may be so overcome with grief that other women and men must physically support them and help them away from the site.

In most cases novenas for the deceased begin on the first or second Friday after burial. Following Roman Catholic tradition, this nine-day period of prayers assures repose for the soul and separates the dead person from the living. Shortly before dusk each day, ten or fifteen older women gather to say prayers at the house where the ninth-night wake will be held. The leader of the prayers, who may be either male or female, must be fluent and literate in Spanish, the preferred medium for novenas.

People explain that the ninth-night wake is a kind of farewell party for the dead man or woman, who "resurrects" on the third day after burial and then wanders about aimlessly, "bothering" the living, unless given a proper send-off to the next world. Many of the older women who have attended the novenas also help with food preparation on the Saturday of the ninth-night wake. They finish their work before dusk and then attend the final prayers, held inside the house at 8 P.M., at midnight, and at dawn on the following morning. Outside the house a crowd of men and women enjoy themselves during the night, singing and joining in the traditional dances performed on festive occasions. After the midnight prayers women serve the food they have prepared; the people who attended the midnight prayers are fed first, then those outside the house. The women also distribute rum throughout the night. After the prayers at dawn, they abruptly tear down the novena altar while kinswomen of the deceased wail briefly one final time. This marks the end of the ninth-night wake.

Close kinswomen of the deceased do not take part in dancing on this occasion, nor do they join in any festivities for some time after it. As part of the formal mourning observances prescribed only for women, they abstain from all such merrymaking and put aside their normally colorful clothing for more somber dress. This period of formal mourning continues for six months or a year after the death, depending on the woman's relationship to the deceased.

Tagurun ludu, which literally means "throwing off the mourning cloth," is a ceremony that marks the end of these observances. On the day before this end-of-mourning ceremony, women prepare food for the occasion. Shortly before dawn on the appointed day, the mourning women enter the church for brief prayers. Accompanying them is a throng of older women, and perhaps a few men. After the prayers end, the crowd leaves the church and gathers on the beach to watch the mourning women ritually bathe. Each woman has a female partner whom she has selected to walk with her into the sea. Linking their arms together, and fully dressed, the pairs wade out beyond the breakers. There the companions of the mourning women submerge them completely, then help them up, repeating this twice again. After the third submersion they leave the water and walk home. As each of the mourning women stands in the doorway, about to enter the house, other women grasp the back of her wet dress. With a sudden pull, they tear the garment open and away from her body. The woman removes her underclothing, screened from public view by the women clustered around her, and then walks to another room to dress. There she and her kinswomen, who have shed their mourning dresses in the same manner, all put on brightly colored new garments and jewelry, adorning themselves for the first time since their relative's death. In the same room, by a burning candle, the women place a small plate of food and some rum as an offering for the spirit of the deceased. In the main room of the house a few begin to serve food, and later rum, to the twenty or thirty older women who have assembled there. After they eat, the women begin to sing *abaimahani* songs—songs of remembrance that the women themselves compose to sing on such occasions. Outside the house there is the inevitable crowd of spectators—young women, men, and children—that gathers during any ritual event.

Occasionally, perhaps even before the end-of-mourning ceremony, the deceased appears in a dream to a relative, requesting a bath. The journey to the next world is long and arduous, and spirits of the dead often desire the refreshment of a bath. *Amuidahani* is held in response to this request. The day before the ceremony a few kinswomen of the deceased prepare the necessary food. The next morning, in the predawn darkness, a small group of people gathers by the house where the deceased man or women lived. Some of them are close relatives of the deceased, and the remainder are older women who are interested in the event. Standing by a shallow pit, which represents a grave, each of the men and women in turn throws a bucket of water into it. Addressing the spirit by the appropriate kin term, they say simply, "Here is water for your bath." Then they fill the pit with sand, and some of the women begin to distribute the food and rum to the others. The *abaimahani* songs of remembrance, and later some festive singing and dancing, follow. Inside the house the women have set some food and rum next to a burning candle as an offering to the spirit.

Like the preceding ceremony, a requiem mass is held if a spirit requests it in a dream. After the mass older women, and perhaps a few old men, gather at the house of the woman who arranged the mass. Then, as a small "feast," food and rum are served. The women usually sing the remembrance songs for some time and then perhaps add other traditional songs and dances. In a back room of the house a small offering of food and rum for the spirit stands beside a burning candle.

Chugu and *dügü* differ from the preceding ceremonies in many details of performance; but, as in the other ceremonies, older women are very prominent, and an individual spirit is the focus of ceremonial attention. In most cases a series of misfortunes precipitates the elaborate offerings of *chugu* and *dügü.* One person, or a number of relatives, may fall seriously ill or develop some chronic sickness. The afflicted person is usually an adult and is more often female than male. Only a shaman can identify the particular ancestor who is responsible for the misfortune; having done so, the shaman tries to determine what sort of offering the spirit wants. Although shamans may be either male or female, those in Belize are mature women, over the age of forty.

Chugu is a one-day event, an elaborate offering of food and prayer. Throughout the day a shaman leads prayers, alternately addressing them to God, the Virgin Mary, Christ, and the afflicting ancestor. Women prepare the food, which is usually offered in the afflicted person's house. The offerings of fish and meat, bread, fruits, and vegetables are set on tables in the morning and left there during the day for the spirit to eat. Other older women in the community represent their children and grandchildren by bringing smaller offerings, usually a single plate of food, for their own ancestors. *Chugu* is a quiet event, without drums or dancing. The music is limited to remembrance songs, which the older women sing.

All the mourning ceremonies entail some "feasting"—sharing food and drink among the living and, usually, offering food and drink to the dead. In the minor ceremonies, and some of the major ones as well, the food is quite simple: bread, coffee, and rum. But *dügü* far eclipses the other ceremonies, both in the lavishness and in the length of the feast. Moreover, unlike the other rites, *dügü* takes place in a temple, not in an ordinary house, and the ancestral spirit may request that a new temple be built for the occasion. Preparations sometimes require as much as a year's work. The organizer, nearly always an older woman, must collect the necessary funds and foodstuffs for *dügü*: a hog, great quantities of cassava bread, dozens of chickens, gallons of rum, and various other staple items. A rather small portion of this food is offered to the spirit and then buried or discarded at sea. The sponsors of the ceremony distribute most of the food among the living. Some is given as a gift to the drummers and to those who helped to procure and to prepare food for the occasion. Women cook the rest and serve it to the dancers at *dügü.*

A *dügü* typically lasts for three days and nights. Each day several older women prepare the food; the nights are devoted to dancing, drinking, and dining. These festive qualities do not obscure the serious purpose of *dügü.* Like *Chugu,* its stated purpose is to appease an ancestor who is afflicting the living. This ancestor is the guest of honor, so to speak, at the ceremony; the dancing and offering of food are intended to placate the spirit and thus to cure the afflicted person. Other spirits of the dead also attend *dügü,* at the invitation of the ancestor for whom it is held. These spirit guests require offerings, albeit very small ones, from their own descendants. To neglect them is to court future misfortune at their hands. The older women who provide the small offerings serve as intermediaries between their living kin and their ancestors.

Women typically outnumber men ten to one as singers and dancers in the temple; there they perform eight or more dances of placation to the ancestor each night of *dügü.* Led by the shaman, to the accompaniment of drums, they sing to the spirit, whom they address as *nagütu,* "my grandmother," regardless of the spirit's gender. Between the dances of placation, they sing songs and perform other dances specific to *dügü.* At midnight they stop to share a meal and then continue to sing and dance until dawn.

Possession by ancestral spirits, usually occurring in the early hours of the morning, is a distinctive feature of *dügü.* As the drummers and most of the dancers pause briefly to rest, one or two dance on, having been possessed by a spirit guest. Those possessed are usually women. Very few men, aside from the drummers and some of the sponsors of the ceremony, participate in the dancing and possession. Some men say that they depend on their kinswomen to represent them to the ancestors. More men choose to stand outside the temple as transitory spectators than to enter it and dance. The few men who do enter the temple rarely linger for more than an hour or two, in contrast to the many women who remain through the night.

OLDER WOMEN IN RITUAL

Older women figure in the whole gamut of death rites in a number of important ways. They organize and provide most of the necessary labor and expertise for the events, and they represent their kin in certain ones. In many rituals they predominate as singers and dancers. Religious specialists are typically women, whether they are shamans or simply women who are consistently sought out as advisers because of their knowledge about the various rites.

Why older women predominate in ritual life is something that the Garífuna, including the women themselves, can explain only in personal terms. Although they insist that anyone may take part in the death rites, they say that women, and especially older women, simply happen to take greater "interest" in them. They do not explain this interest as an inevitable outcome of declining activity at home. No one suggests that older women "have more time" for ceremonies, and, in fact, many of the most active women have very heavy domestic responsibilities.[2] Nor do people see older women as being "cleaner" than younger women or spiritually better suited for these activities. It is true that menstruating women are supposed to avoid public gatherings in general and rituals in particular. But many young women scoff at the idea that they attract malevolent spirits when they menstruate, and some claim to disregard any monthly restriction. More to the point, few of them choose to participate in mourning ceremonies, aside from wakes and ninth-night wakes, even when they are not menstruating. As a rule, women begin to take active part in ceremonial life after their mothers cease to do so (either because of death or extreme infirmity). This may be before or after they reach menopause, in their mid-to-late forties.

There is no specific age at which women beging to participate in mourning ceremonies, but their interest seems to develop slowly with age. Many young women are openly skeptical about the need for some of the ceremonies. They confess to little interest in them, and they lack the ritual knowledge and skills that their mothers or grandmothers possess. Standing outside a temple during *dügü,* watching the older women dance inside, young women and men routinely admit that they do not even understand the meaning of the songs being sung. Most older women, in contrast, are true believers who are well versed in the large body of belief and protocol associated with the death rites. By their own accounts, their expertise and personal belief grew slowly over the course of many years, primarily through observing and occasionally taking part in the ceremonies. Many concede that they were once skeptics themselves. But over the years, they explain, they saw cures effected by shamans and by ritual means; they witnessed countless cases of possession, or, more startling and convincing, they experienced it themselves. This cumulative evidence finally persuaded them that what they had once questioned, as some of their own daughters and sons now do, was in fact true.

To take a broader view of these personal experiences, women, as they age, may well be more easily persuaded of the importance of ritual. The whole pattern of Garífuna life, and especially the interdependence of generations, seems to "predispose" older women to take interest in the death rites. As a women's personal circumstances change with age—as her children grow up and her parents die—the ceremonies assume greater meaning for her. She can no longer depend on her mother to represent her in ritual; now she must represent herself, and her children and grandchildren as well.

Moreover, like her mother before her, the older woman increasingly depends on her daughters and sons for support. And while there is no law that compels their support, morality demands it, and women do their best to encourage it. For the Garífuna, a moral person is a generous and responsible one who honors the obligation to "help" kin, in whatever manner necessary. An immoral person is a stingy and negligent one. As young mothers, women instill the traditional values of generosity and sharing in their children; from a very tender age a child's refusal to share brings swift punishment. Later in life, when their sons and daughters are grown, women organize the rituals that express these values. In many of the death rites the living make offerings to the ancestors: they tangibly demonstrate concern for the well-being of their (deceased) elders. Two of the ceremonies, *chugu* and *dügü,* show how elder kin, even after death, can punish neglect.

Whether older women consciously recognize that their position of dependence parallels the ancestors' is debatable. But they obviously find the entire moral thrust of ritual life more meaningful than men or young women do. For older women the traditional values represent survival, and it is scarcely surprising that they take such interest in ceremonies that express them.

Older women do consciously recognize a very practical reason for taking part in death rites. They consider ritual activity to be one of a number of caretaking services that they can provide for their grown children in return for economic support. By organizing and cooperating in these ceremonies, they claim to protect their sons and daughters and grandchildren from possible harm at the hands of neglected ancestors. Of course, this amounts to self-protection as well, since a woman's own economic welfare is so closely bound to her children's productive abilities and, ultimately, to their general health and well-being.

Paradoxically, the economic dependence of older women helps to explain not only their interest in these rituals but also their ability to organize them. Only these women have the economic and social means to stage the elaborate and expensive ceremonies with any degree of ease. Despite the fact that they are excluded from the labor market, older women potentially have greater economic resources at their disposal than other adults because they are entitled to contributions from their grown children. All the major rituals are quite expensive, and a man or a single household usually finds it impossible to meet the expense. When an older woman assumes responsibility, as is usually the case, the expense is divided among a number of sponsors—her grown daughters and sons. Older women also have the "human capital" that is often required. Female cooperative labor, which is indispensable to any major ritual undertaking, is founded on reciprocity. Any older woman who has helped others when they organized events can expect their help in the future when she needs to organize a mourning ceremony. Women work to create an elaborate and enduring network of mutual obligations with other women, and they draw on this network as necessary.

It bears repeating, in closing, that both men *and* women, by cultural consensus, are equally eligible to take part in nearly all of the rituals. Yet for the most part only women, and more specifically older women, choose to participate in them. A whole array of very concrete circumstances—women's lifelong caretaking roles based on a principle of female responsibility for lineal kin, the loss of a family representative in ritual when their own mothers die, increased economic dependence in later life—all induce them to join in these activities. Social circumstance everywhere shapes the personal experiences and colors the perceptions of individuals, and in many societies it affects male and female, or young, and old, in different ways. Among the Garífuna the differing life experiences and perceptions of women and men, of old and young, are manifest in the pattern of ritual activity.

Notes

1. The Garífuna hold only a very simple wake and burial for an infant or child who dies. There are no further mourning ceremonies for them.

2. Many older women foster some of their grandchildren, whose parents work in other districts or even abroad. Rather few live in households without any dependent children.

Further Readings

Gonzalez, Nancie L. *Sojourners of the Caribbean: Ethnogenesis and Ethnohistory of the Garífuna.* Urbana, Ill.: University of Illinois Press, 1988.

Kerns, Virginia. *Women and the Ancestors: Black Carib Kinship and Ritual* (second edition). Urbana, Ill.: University of Illinois Press, 1997.

———. "Structural Continuity in the Division of Men's and Women's Work among the Black Carib (Garífuna). *Blackness in Latin America and the Caribbean,* ed. by Norman E. Whitten, Jr. and Arlene Torres, pp. 133–48. Bloomington, Ind.: Indiana University Press, 1998.

Kerns, Virginia and Judith K. Brown, eds. *In Her Prime: New Views of Middle-Aged Women* (second edition). Urbana, Ill.: University of Illinois Press, 1992.

Khan, Aisha. "Migration and Life-Cycle among Garífuna (Black Carib) Street Vendors." *Women's Studies* 13, no. 3 (fall 1987) pp. 183–98.

Macklin, Catherine L. "Garífuna." *American Immigrant Cultures: Builders of a Nation,* ed. by David Levinson and Melvin Ember, vol 1., pp. 303–10. New York: Simon & Schuster Macmillan.

Sered, Susan Starr. *Priestess, Mother, Sacred Sister: Religions Dominated by Women.* New York: Oxford University Press, 1994.

11

The Controversial Vows of Urban Muslim Women in Iran

ANNE H. BETTERIDGE

Relatively little has been written in the West about Islamic ritual. Scholarly attention has been devoted largely to Islamic history and textual traditions, while the religious life of the Moslem has gone unstudied. Still less has the religious life of Moslem women been the object of study. This results not only from lack of interest in women's activities; for the most part these activities are inaccessible to the Western male researcher. Even what a Moslem man knows of women's religious activities is usually restricted to his experience with women of his own family, particularly during his childhood.

As a woman anthropologist studying Islamic ritual in Iran, I have been able to observe and participate in a wide range of ceremonies in which women take part. Women's religious activities are not a pale imitation of those engaged in by men. In addition to the formally enjoined participation in prayer and pilgrimage, women are significantly involved in marriage-contract ceremonies, funeral observances, pilgrimages to local shrines,[1] and in the making and fulfilling of vows, including the preparation of special foods having religious significance.

ANNE H. BETTERIDGE (Ph.D. Anthropology, University of Chicago) is currently Executive Director of the Middle East Studies Association of North America (MESA). MESA is based at the University of Arizona, where Dr. Betteridge is affiliated with the Center for Middle Eastern Studies as a faculty member. Her research interests included women in Middle Eastern society, especially Iran, women and Islamic ritual, and women in Iranian immigrant communities.

Author's Note: This chapter is based primarily on research conducted in Shiraz, Iran, between December 1974 and November 1976. The second rowzeh and ritual meal described in the article was attended in June 1977.

Men usually belong to formal religious organizations. These may be connected with a mosque or local shrine, or they may be occupationally based. Women, often lacking the extradomestic existence of men, are less likely to belong to organized groups that meet outside the home on a regular basis. This is not to suggest that women's activities are unstructured. Rather, women tend to use informal means in organizing and communicating with others about any ritual event. Women's ritual events are usually held in the home; news of them is spread through informal networks of family and friends. Women regard word of mouth as an effective means of publicizing a gathering. It is thought that news about gatherings for women should not be placed in public view. The large numbers of women attending the gatherings, and the still larger numbers aware of them, attest to the correctness of the women's assumption; formal publicity is unnecessary.

Even women's religious education has traditionally been informal. Although girls may now attend religious schools in the theological center of Qom in Iran (as of 1976), this was not true in the past. Thus, for example, the one woman in Iran currently to reach the highest Shi'a Muslim clerical rank of *mujtahid* was educated at home by private tutors.[2] Some girls' schools do exist; like parochial schools in the United States, they place great importance on teaching religion in addition to the usually required subjects. Also, many knowledgeable older women, often those whose children have grown or who are childless, conduct classes in Qoran reading and principles of religion in their homes.

Such women may also function as leaders in the various religious ceremonies sponsored by women. As is the case with the ceremonies themselves, these women do not announce themselves publicly. They dress no differently from the laity, while male clergy can readily be identified by their robes and turbans. Women do not have to signal their status by outward means; they know who among them is knowledgeable in religious matters and who occupies a position of clerical eminence.

The majority of Iranians adhere to the Shi'a sect of Islam. It is distinguished from the more common Sunni sect by dispute over rightful succession to the leadership of the Islamic community. Shi'a Muslims, unlike Sunni Muslims, believe that the Prophet's successor should not have been elected and that the Prophet Mohammad intended to appoint Ali, his trusted companion, cousin, and son-in-law, as the next leader of Islam. Ali was the first in a sequence of twelve leaders, or Imams. The Imams are regarded as having had the ability to interpret divine law for Shi'a society. The twelfth and last Imam disappeared when he was a child but is regarded as still alive. Shi'a society now awaits the return, when God wills, of the twelfth Imam. Until his return, religious leaders are responsible for interpreting and administering divine law.

The esteem and affection in which the Imams are held give a distinct character to Shi'a Islam. Popular ritual practices, addressed to the Imams and their relatives, recount the sufferings that these holy individuals endured during their lifetimes. Such rites are performed in addition to the formally prescribed ritual duties of daily prayers, fasting, and pilgrimage to Mecca. These popular practices are not obligatory, but are considered religiously commendable.

Among important Shi'a popular rituals is the *rowzeh,* a ceremony of great significance to many women. The *rowzeh* is a very common ritual attended by people of all social classes. Men and women, either at one gathering or in single-sex assemblies, convene to hear a sermon and to mourn for the cruelly slain members of the Prophet's family. The sermon may concern any topic of the speaker's choice, but it always ends by recounting the tragedies that befell the Imams. *Rowzeh* ceremonies emphasize especially the third Imam's martyrdom at the Battle of Kerbela. This last part of the *rowzeh* provokes great sadness and mourning activity among members of the audience. Both men and women weep, beat themselves, and call out to the Imams and their relatives. In general, the women are far more demonstrative than the men, sobbing and beating their thighs, heads, and chests. At *rowzehs* attended exclusively by women, the reciter of *rowzeh* is often a woman. Women who recite at these ceremonies are known for their ability to read Arabic well and often for their religious learning. In many cases they are the same women who conduct religious classes for women and children in their homes.

In theory, the *rowzeh* provides an opportunity for communicating religious ideas and history to the audience. In practice, however, the *rowzeh* has come to serve other functions, which have made it the center of often heated controversy. This has been especially true of the women's *rowzehs,* which are criticized not only by men but by many of the more devout and better-educated women. Objections focus on both the mercantile attitude reflected in making *rowzeh*-connected vows and the tendency to emphasize social aspects of the ceremony rather than sincerely expressing devotion to God.

Both objections require more explanation. The first objection involves the fact that often, in recent times, the *rowzehs* have been used as vehicles for registering personal requests with God. In return for attending the ceremony and mourning for the Imams, people hope that such requests will be answered. This is particularly true of women's *rowzehs,* which are often performed in connection with a vow. Vow making has a prominent place in women's religious activities; a woman may vow that, if a particular request is granted or a difficulty remedied, she will sponsor a specific kind of religious ceremony. One woman has illustrated this for me by saying that, if one's child were in a car accident, one might make a vow to sponsor a ceremony on condition that the child recover. Another woman cited her own vow: "I asked that my youngest son, about thirty-two years old, should get married. I declared it in my own heart, and that this should happen within the month, by the first of Ramazan. If my request is answered, then I will fulfill my vow." Should her petition go unanswered she is under no obligation and can make another vow.

Because of what is felt to be their basically emotional nature and because of their involvement in the home, women are charged with the care of domestic and personal problems. Nevertheless such ritual transactions are readily viewed by some as perverting the true nature of Islam. One Shirazi woman, well educated in religious matters and very much opposed to most *rowzehs* and vows, says that practices like these make the relation between humans and God "commercial." Rather than requesting strength of character and other kinds of spiritual help from God, people have come to expect material rewards—children, spouses, employment, houses, health—and are prepared to pay for these goods by fulfilling vows. The objection is made that ceremonies are not sponsored out of religious feeling but as payment for services rendered. The relationship is contractual, not devotional.

To understand more fully the second common criticism—that women performing *rowzeh* also engage in socializing (or "recreation," as one priest has called it)—it is perhaps easiest to examine one type of *rowzeh* in performance. One of the most heated controversies about women's *rowzeh* concerns a vow called *sofrehye Hazrat-e 'Abbas.* If the woman's request is granted, the woman who made this vow is obliged to give a ritual dinner along with a *rowzeh* in the name of a very popular saint of Shi'a Islam, 'Abbas, the son of the first Imam and younger half-brother of the second and third Imams. Because of his youth and the tenderheartedness shown in his compassionate deeds in warfare, this saint is regarded as more easily approachable than his brother, the third Imam. He has, as a young shrine helper told me, "less endurance": he cannot bear to refuse and is hence more likely to answer the pleas of distraught believers. Still another informant referred to 'Abbas by his title—"the gate to needs," or "the path by which one can achieve one's desires." Hence a wide variety of petitions can be addressed to him; virtually any kind of request can be made in connection with a promise to sponsor a rite in the name of 'Abbas.

The *rowzeh* and *sofreh,* or ritual dinner given in the name of 'Abbas, have a set form and menu, although they can be done in a more or less elaborate fashion. The ritual dinner is given in the home. Its date and time are important; either major religious holidays or Mondays are preferred, and it is usually held in the late afternoon and early evening. The ceremony may begin with a reading of a long prayer in Arabic. I was told that this prayer assures a favorable divine response to any needs or requests that those attending the ritual dinner might have. Following this, the *rowzeh* leader will deliver a sermon, ending with a *rowzeh* about the martyrdom of 'Abbas. During this time the women will have been sitting around a white cloth. When the *rowzeh* is finished, special foods are placed on this cloth, and everyone begins eating.

The ritual meal provides an opportunity not only for the hostess to celebrate the successful conclusion of her vow but for her guests to make their own vows as well. Generally, this is done by lighting a candle. A hostess may provide a metal tray filled with sand to hold the candle. Alternatively, individual candles in candlesticks may be placed on the white cloth for guests to light if they wish.

Thus described, this religious observance seems straightforward enough. The major source of criticism centers on the way it is put into practice. The ritual meal may also be an occasion for showing off finery, gossiping, bawdy storytelling, singing, and dancing. Needless to say, the fine spread of food is also greatly enjoyed. Furthermore, the occasion is undoubtedly used for social competition. For example, a woman who conducts classes in religion for girls and women told me that she had once received invitations to two such celebrations to be given on the same day at the same time. They were to be held on opposite sides of the street by wives of two brothers; clearly, it was a contest.

I attended my first ritual dinner and *rowzeh* given in the name of 'Abbas on the eve of the Prophet's birthday in the company of my friend Homa and her mother. The hostess was a local doctor's wife. I was somewhat surprised when I was told to put on my best clothes and jewelry; I knew that the entire ceremony would include *rowzeh* and had assumed that black clothes would be appropriate. We left at about 5:45. I took my see-through *chador* (veil) for the first time, feeling somewhat uneasy about it.

We parked the car, put on our *chadors,* then entered the house. As we walked through the door, Homa took a deep breath and happily announced, "I smell food." The hall was filled with shoes, much jazzier than those I was used to seeing gathered in a hall when a *rowzeh* was in progress. Near the door to the living room was a metal tray filled with sand, with lighted colored candles standing in it. I was told that any woman who wished to make a vow could light a candle and place it in the tray.

As Homa's mother disappeared into another section of the living room, we took our seats on the floor along the back wall by the door. The entire floor was spread with white cloths decorated with vases of flowers. Some of the food was already set out. Homa started eating the pickles immediately; she had them polished off by the time the *rowzeh* was over. No one else was eating, however, and I later learned that Homa's action had brought a scolding from her mother.

Reading in Arabic was in progress when we entered. The *rowzeh* leader sat at the juncture of the two sections of the L-shaped room. A low wooden table, spread with a lovely cloth, had been placed in front of her. I recognized her as Khanom-e Rohani, a *rowzeh* leader whom I had seen previously at a different ceremony in town. Her veil was down around her shoulders throughout the reading and *rowzeh.* She was dressed in black, and her hair was parted in the middle. She looked very severe in comparison to the other women. They were made up, wearing colorful suits and dresses; most of them had on printed or light-colored veils. It was hot in the room; one very pregnant woman fanned herself vigorously throughout the ceremony.

Two women at the head of the room took turns reading in Arabic. Khanom-e Rohani corrected their reading and would sometimes take over for a while. I was surprised to see a young, very pretty, and well-dressed woman with frosted hair take her turn reading from the text. Her reading was loud, nasal, and forceful; I noticed that her hand shook as she read. When not reading, she followed along in her text, unlike the other women. Most of the guests did not have prayer books and spent their time sitting, watching the children they had brought along, and talking among themselves. Homa asked me if this was my first time at such a ceremony. When I told her it was, she assured me that I would get whatever I wanted.

From time to time the children interrupted. Some tried to snatch packets of *ajil*—a special vowed food consisting of nuts and candies—from the tray where it was stored. Homa frightened off one little girl by shouting in a gruff voice, "Don't touch it!" As the girl ran shaking to her mother, Homa tossed two packets of *ajil* over to her. While the women around me laughed, the *rowzeh* leader joined in by asking everyone to send a blessing for the child.

The *rowzeh* leader then gave a brief sermon. She reminded all the women that on the Day of Judgment each must answer for herself and be responsible for her own actions. One cannot get any outside help and must bear the weight of one's own deeds. Her speech included recitations of two brief prayers in Arabic, each repeated five times; all those present joined in repeating the prayers. Following the prayers, the *rowzeh* leader asked all the women to say the response, "*amin*" (amen), in unison. Several women by the back door continued talking throughout the sermon; they were not in the least fazed by the *rowzeh* leader's fierce glances. A series of blessings was recited for those who had read in Arabic and for the mothers and fathers of those who were present. Every now and then the *rowzeh* leader would encourage the women to be vociferous in their blessings. Homa responded very loudly. At one point she was busy teasing the children and just managed to come in at the end for the last phrase. When the *rowzeh* leader began to speak about the happy occasion of Mohammad's birth, some women began to cry, pulling their veils down over their eyes.

The *rowzeh* leader then told the lady of the house, "You can turn the lights out now," something that I had never seen before in an Iranian ritual. Once the lights were off, she launched into a *rowzeh* about 'Abbas, recounting the details of his bravery and martyrdom. The women sat in the dark sniffling and weeping. Very shortly the *rowzeh* wound to a close, the lights were turned on, and our hostess removed the table in front of the *rowzeh* leader.

In the break that followed, Homa told me that the year before the *rowzeh* leader had been very entertaining. She had told all those present that any woman who did not make love with her husband when he wanted to would be hung by her breasts in hell. Homa's apt comment to the women seated around her had been, "If a man doesn't make love with his wife when she wants to, what do they hang him by?" Homa said that last year's *rowzeh* leader had been invited by mistake; the hostess had heard her complimented undeservedly and had invited her on the basis of what proved to be false praise. A woman across the way laughed when she heard the story and told that she had come this year in hopes of hearing the same woman speak. An older woman next to me, the mother of one of Homa's friends, told me not to believe what the woman had said about wives being punished in hell, because it probably wasn't true. She was afraid that I might take it seriously and didn't want to see Islam so misrepresented.

At that point the food began to arrive—platters of chicken, rice, and flatbread. Homa managed to wangle from the hostess some of the tasty crust at the bottom of the rice. The sweets came soon after. Homa advised me to take out my plastic bag; it turned out that a good-sized plastic bag had been neatly folded and placed under everyone's plate. We were served several kinds of cookies and candy, then fruit; all the participants popped the sweets into their bags. After the fruit had been passed the first time, Homa told me to hide my bag behind me so that they wouldn't realize we had been served. I did as she recommended and, sure enough, we were served again, ending up with twice as much as our fair share.

I noticed that Homa's mother had come back for yet another round of food. She wasn't talking with anyone, just quietly stuffing her bag. She poured the excess oil off a plate of *halva,* scooped all of it onto a piece of bread, rolled it up, and tucked it into the bag. She later told me that she had wanted to take the chicken from a plate in front of her but had restrained herself; a few minutes later it had disappeared into the bag of the *rowzeh* leader.

The ritual meal was over. As we prepared to leave, Homa captured a final plate of *halva* and a pair of daffodils that she later gave to me. As she offered an extravagant thank-you and good-bye to the *rowzeh* leader, her mother was talking the hostess out of the last of the exceptionally good soup. Driving home, Homa congratulated her mother on their haul; they had gathered more than enough to feed Homa's brothers that evening. Like many other guests, we had removed our veils on leaving; most of the guests were doctors' wives or doctors themselves and wore their veils only for special religious occasions.

The basic framework of the ritual meal with its *rowzeh* provides a great deal of opportunity for elaboration; thus each celebration tends to have its own distinctive style. This can be seen in a second ritual meal I attended. This time the ceremony was held on the eve of the thirteenth of Rajab, birthday of the first Imam. The meal's sponsor was a woman from a family well known as members of a Sufi order. I attended with Simin, a friend visiting from Teheran, and her mother; a friend of Simin's mother had arranged the invitation.

This time the ritual meal was for men and women; men were seated in the house and women in the courtyard. This had been covered with a canvas tent, while green lights, crepe paper, and metallic garlands were draped between and through the branches of the courtyard's trees. The ground was covered with carpets spread with white cloths set for dinner. My friend Simin commented that this was a very well laid out and classy affair. She drew my attention to the fact that no plastic had been spread over the white cloths, a tacky measure practiced by some who give such dinners. Other aspects of the setting were also very richly embellished, but with more of an attempt to evoke the religious theme of the occasion than was the case with the first ritual meal I attended. A finely woven carpet with a picture of 'Abbas on horseback hung on the courtyard wall; a picture of Ali was above it. Black-and-white postcards portraying 'Abbas on horseback had been placed on top of each china plate on the white cloth. Ali was represented on a gold-colored coin placed to the right of each setting. When dinner was served, we would also find the names of members of the Prophet's family inscribed in icing on cakes. The white cloths were strewn with one-rial coins and silver candy balls that women gathered up during the course of the evening to take home for their children. Green candles stood on the white cloth for the use of any woman who might wish to make a vow.

As befitted a mixed occasion, the principal invited speakers were men. They spoke from a porch at the far end of the courtyard, facing the house, and their sermons were broadcast through a loudspeaker. The first man delivered a general sermon, assuring us that we would all get whatever we wanted; he concluded with a traditional chanted remembrance of 'Abbas' suffering on the field of Kerbela. The second, an esteemed priest known for his mystic inclinations, chose to tell us about Islam's famous women. He referred to the womb of Ameneh bearing the Prophet as a shell containing a pearl and recounted the stories of other famous women in the early history of Islam: the Prophet's first wife, Khadijeh, his daughter Fatimah, wife of the first Imam Ali and mother to the second and third, and, finally, Husain's sister Zainab, who had been present at the Battle of Kerbela. The priest next turned to the subject of Ali's search for a suitable wife after the death of Fatimah: she had to be lovely, intelligent, and able to bear him fine sons. Ali's search ended when he married Omm ol Banin, who subsequently gave birth to 'Abbas and six other sons. This time the speaker did not follow with the usual account of 'Abbas' death; for the lament had already been performed by his predecessor. The last man to recite chanted beautiful verses about Ali; Simin knew all the words and chanted along softly, crying as she chanted.

One striking feature of the evening was a brief speech by the hostess, in which she told her own reasons for sponsoring the ritual dinner. She said that she had been very sick during the month of Muharram. On the day of 'Ashura (the tenth of Muharram, anniversary of Imam Husain's martyrdom), she had made a vow to Ali and 'Abbas that she would sponsor a ritual meal and *rowzeh* in the name of 'Abbas on Ali's birthday if she recovered. She explained that she had made this vow rather than any other because it would provide a chance for all her friends to get together. In so saying, she acknowledged the dual social and religious function of the ritual meal. Simin, who had given the same ceremony some years before, confirmed our hostess's estimation of the ceremony's social virtues. Women begin working together at least a week ahead and enjoy themselves in preparing for the meal. In fact, many of the women present had helped our hostess to get ready for the celebration. Some also served during the dinner, while others brought flowers or cakes and boxes of sweets to be served after dinner.

The formal part of the ceremony ended as a friend of the hostess read her own poem in honor of Ali. The dinner was served and cleared, with plastic bags stuffed as before. Then the evening's socializing began in earnest. A tray was handed to a very plump and jolly friend of our hostess. She began to beat on the tray, dance around, and sing gay, bawdy songs, much to the delight of the clapping audience of women, who joined in the refrains. Gradually some of the women, including our hostess and her poet friend, began dancing, each in turn. During the singing and dancing, many of the women got up from their places and moved around to visit friends. They caught up on the news, found out who had married, who had had children and how many, who had been sick, and on and on. This continued until people started to leave.

The preceding descriptions should give some idea of why a Shirazi plaster worker I know told me that the ritual meal is not "real Islam." He said that he had a relative too poor to keep a decent carpet underfoot but that the same person had spent some 10,000 *toman* (about $1,500) to sponsor a *rowzeh* and ritual meal in the name of 'Abbas. He himself charged that the ritual was being pushed by low-level priests in search of a free meal; he could also not see why such money should be spent in serving persons whose bellies were already full. A devout woman of my acquaintance has called such events "silly ladies' parties." She objects to the way women pounce on their food and stuff their plastic bags. She herself no longer attends them, describing the behavior of those who attend as "disgusting."

In general, however, one finds a striking difference between men's and women's responses to the ritual meal and similar women's ceremonies. Men may condemn women for their display, overeating, and gossip and yet are often willing to tolerate such practices. The reason is unflattering: women's excesses and failings are attributed to their more "emotional" nature, while men's own ritual practices are seen as being more "rational." In effect the men are saying that women's ceremonies are abused but that this can't really be helped. Women, on the other hand, are much more likely than men to press for "reform" of these ceremonies.

The women's ceremonies can also find intelligent defenders. My friend Simin is an example. She agrees that this occasion can be misused, but she does not find this a reason to condemn the practice as a whole. Simin sponsored the entire ceremony, both *rowzeh* and ritual meal, when her aunt returned from the United States, where she had successfully undergone a serious operation. Her aunt and her friends, many of them members of her Qoran reading group, attended the ritual. In this way Simin was able to celebrate her aunt's recovered health in the company of good friends, most of whom shared her religious views. In answer to the charge that the ritual meal is irreligious because it gives food to people who are not in need, Simin told me that, as part of her vow, much of the food prepared for the ritual meal was given away to the poor. She had cooked special large pots of rice with this in mind and had them distributed at a local shrine. Simin feels that her actions were properly devout, but she also thinks it important that she could share with friends the happy resolution of a worrisome event in her life.

A popular Shirazi *rowzeh* leader annually sponsors three weeks of *rowzehs* in his home during the month of Sefar. One morning I was surprised to hear him condemn the practice of women's vows and ritual meals in the course of his sermon. His remarks provoked a furor among the women who were listening that day. During sermons in his home on succeeding mornings, quite a few women interrupted to question the *rowzeh* leader himself and other speakers about their views on women's vows. The women were very fond of the practice and reluctant to give it up; they argued with each of the male preachers in turn during the next few assemblies, always defending the ritual meals. I had never seen a stronger audience reaction to any sermon topic in Iran.

Since so much can be said against the way the vow is currently practiced, we must consider why some women remain so firm in its defense. The women's ritual meals are a major part of the social lives of many Iranian women. As Robert and Elizabeth Fernea say about an Iraqi ceremony that is very similar to the Iranian ceremonies I studied, religious gatherings offer women "one of the few community-sanctioned opportunities for meeting socially in each other's homes, in groups that cut across the ordinary kin grouping and which include representatives from all segments of the community."[3] In Iran it is true that women of educated families and upper-class groups are no longer very restricted in their visiting patterns and movements about town. But, especially for lower-class women and for those who come from more traditional families, religion offers a much-needed opportunity to assemble. It is also one of the few occasions in which a sizeable amount of money can be properly spent on a women's gathering. Once a vow has been made and answered, a woman is bound to fulfill it; her family will support her financially in completing the obligation.

Chapter 13 of this volume describes the situation of women in one Iranian village. I am struck by the absence of group ritual occasions for women there. Women seem to be isolated in their homes, have little religious education, and seldom gather, lest they be accused of frivolity and laziness. Their lives are the more desolate for lacking communal gatherings.[4]

It is perhaps unfortunate that women are obliged to justify their socializing by placing it in a religious framework. However, this is a common feature of women's religious lives in much of the Middle East. Only modern, educated, or upper-class women can move about easily in a secular context. Such women are divided in their opinions about women's vows and ritual meals. Those with deep religious orthodoxy tend to oppose these ceremonies. However, because it is easier for them to get together in nonreligious settings, it is also easier for them to condemn the practice of women's *rowzeh* and ritual meals. Such practice does not play as important a part in their social lives as it does for most women, who favor it. Other upper-class women, less orthodox in temperament and background, see no contradiction in holding a festive social event in connection with a religious ceremony. What, in their view, is wrong with combining religion and enjoyment?

What is actually at stake in these controversies over women's ceremonies is the definition of the proper boundaries of religion. Overall in Iran, women's religious activities fall into several categories, ranging from the more contemplative and intellectual quests to group-oriented social affairs such as those I have described. Members of either group may be equally sincere in their religious motivations, but they are defining religion differently. While some women define religion in a strict and formal sense as a way of life and thought centering around certain beliefs and commandments, others may agree with this view but include a more social dimension as well. For many women religion pervades all aspects of social life, as witnessed by the variety of occasions on which vows may be made. To separate religion from social life would be to make a distinction not recognized in practice by many Islamic women.

The opportunity to gather on religious occasions and combine fellowship with worship is not to be condemned out of hand. It is in the nature of much religious practice to draw people together and to promote understanding and sympathy among them. That such occasions provide a chance to visit with friends is part and parcel of the nature of women's religious lives in traditional Islamic society. Women share many common problems: the effort to find a good husband and bear a child, the threat of barrenness and children's sickness, and hopes for the success of their children and husbands. Women often seek resolution to these problems through religious means and celebrate such resolutions through group activities. Many of those who participate in a given ritual share certain beliefs and, by sharing them, support one another's faith. As an outside observer, one may distinguish social activities and see their place in religious behavior. However, in the daily course of women's religious lives, the two are so interwoven that their conjunction seems correct, desirable, and even necessary to many women who join in ritual activity.

Notes

1. Fatima Mernissi has described women's visits to local shrines in Morocco in her article "Women, Saints and Sanctuaries," which follows in this volume.

2. A *mujtahid* is one learned in religious sciences whose learning and abilities have been formally recognized and certified by the Shi'ite religious leaders (*'ulama*) of the time. A *mujtahid* is unique

in having the right to make independent decisions in the interpretation of religious law. This distinguished woman, now in her eighties, is Khanom-e Amin; she received her degree of *ejtehad* on the basis of her writings, which were read by the *'ulama* then centered in Najaf, Iraq.

3. Robert and Elizabeth Fernea, "Variations in Religious Observance among Islamic Women," in *Scholars, Saints, and Sufis: Muslim Religious Institutions Since 1500,* ed. Nikki R. Keddie (Berkeley: University of California Press, 1972), pp. 394–395.

4. See Erika Friedl, "Islam and Tribal Women in a Village in Iran," in this volume.

Further Readings

Betteridge, Anne H. " *'Aqd*" (marriage contract). In Ehsan Yarshater, ed., *Encyclopaedia Iranica,* vol. 2 (London: Routledge & Kegan Paul, 1982), pp. 189–91.

———. "*Arusi*" (wedding celebration). In Ehsan Yarshater, ed., *Encyclopaedia Iranica,* vol. 2 (London: Routledge & Kegan Paul, 1982), pp. 666–70.

———. "Domestic Observances: Muslim." In Mircea Eliade, ed., *The Encyclopedia of Religion* (New York: Macmillan, 1986).

———. "Gift Exchange in Iran: The Locus of Self-Identity in Social Interaction." *Anthropological Quarterly* 58, 4 (October 1985): pp. 190–202.

———. "To Veil or Not To Veil: A Matter of Protest or Policy." In Guity Nashat, ed., *Women and Revolution in Iran* (Boulder, Colo.: Westview Press, 1983), pp. 109–28.

Haeri, Shahla. "Of Feminism and Fundamentalism in Iran and Pakistan." *Contention: Debates in Society, Culture, and Science* 4 (Spring 1995): pp. 129–49.

Hegland, Mary Elaine. "A Mixed Blessing: The *Majales,* Shi'a Women's Rituals of Mourning in Northwest Pakistan." In Judy Brink and Joan Mencher, eds., *Mixed Blessings: Gender and Religious Fundamentalism Cross Culturally* (New York: Routledge, 1997), pp. 179–96.

———."Flagellation and Fundamentalism: (Trans)forming Meaning, Identity, and Gender Through Pakistani Women's Rituals of Mourning." *American Ethnologist* 25, 2 (May 1998): pp. 240–66.

———. "Gender and Religion in the Middle East and South Asia: Women's Voices Rising." In Margaret L. Meriwether and Judith E. Tucker, eds., *Social History of Women and Gender in the Modern Middle East* (Boulder, Colo.: Westview Press, 1999), pp. 177–212.

Jamzadeh, Laal, and Margaret Mills. "Iranian Sofreh: From Collective to Female Ritual." In Caroline Walker Bynum, Stevan Harrell, and Paula Richman, eds., *Gender and Religion: On the Complexity of Symbols* (Boston: Beacon Press, 1986), pp. 23–65.

Kamalkhani, Zahra. *Women's Islam: Religious Practice Among Women in Today's Iran.* London: Kegan Paul, 1997.

Torab, Azam. "Piety as Gendered Agency: A Study of Jalaseh Ritual Discourse in an Urban Neighbourhood in Iran." *Journal of the Royal Anthropological Institute* 2 (1996): pp. 235–51.

12

Women, Saints, and Sanctuaries in Morocco

FATIMA MERNISSI

. . . The next morning I went to see my mother. I had a snack with her and the children and then I went to spend the day at the Marabout [a sanctuary]. I lay down there and slept for a very long time.

Q *Do you go to the Marabout often?*

A Yes, quite often. For example, I prefer to go there on the days of *Aïd [religious festivals]. When one has a family as desperate as mine, the shrine is a haven of peace and quiet. I like to go there.*

Q *What do you like about the shrine? Can you be more precise?*

A Yes. The silence, the rugs, and the clean mats which are nicely arranged . . . the sound of the fountain in the silence. An

---

FATIMA MERNISSI was formerly Professor of Sociology at Muhammad V University at Rabat, Morocco, and has also held a research appointment at Morocco's Institut Universitaire de Recherche Scientifique. Among her many writings on Muslim women translated into English are *Beyond the Veil: Male-Female Dynamics in Modern Muslim Society, Doing Daily Battle: Interviews with Moroccan Women, The Forgotten Queens of Islam,* and *Dreams of Trespass: Tales of a Harem Childhood.*

Author's Note: Gathering of historical data on saints, mainly female saints, was done with the collaboration and critical supervision of the Moroccan historian Halima Ferhat, a Maitre de Conférence at the University Mohammed V.

enormous silence where the sound of water is as fragile as thread. I stay there hours, sometimes whole days.

Q *The day of Aïd it must be full of people.*

A Yes, there are people, but they are lost in their own problems. So they leave you alone. Mostly it's women who cry without speaking, each in her own world.

Q *Aren't there any men at the shrine?*

A Yes, but men have their side, women theirs. Men come to visit the shrine and leave very quickly; the women, especially those with problems, stay much longer.

Q *What do they do and what do they say?*

A That depends. Some are happy just to cry. Others take hold of the saint's garments and say, "Give me this, oh saint, give me that. . . ." "I want my daughter to pass her exam . . ." [she laughs]. You know the saints are men, human beings. But sometimes, imagine, the woman gets what she asks for! Then she brings a sacrifice . . . she kills an animal and prepares a meal of the meat and then offers it to the visitors. Do you know Sid El Gomri?

Q *No.*

A [laughs] Salé is full of shrines . . . full, full. You know, there is a proverb, "If you want to make a pilgrimage, just go around Salé barefooted . . ." [laughs]. They do say that . . . . All of Salé is a shrine. There are so many that some don't have names [laughs]. My father is a native of Salé. He knows the shrines and talks a lot about them. When you are separated from someone or when you have a very bad fight, the saint helps you overcome your problem. When I go I listen to the women. You see them tell everything to the tomb and mimicking all that took place. Then they ask Sid El Gomri to help them get out of the mess. They cry, they scream. Then they get hold of themselves and come back, join us, and sit in silence. I like the shrine.

Q *Are you ever afraid?*

A Afraid of what? In a shrine, what a question! I love shrines.

Q *And when do you go?*

A They are shut in the evenings except for those that have rooms, like Sidi Ben Achir, for example. You can rent a room there and you can stay a long time.

Q *Rent a room for how much?*

A Oh, fifteen dirhams.[1]

Q *Fifteen dirhams a night?!*

A No, for ten dirhams you can stay as long as you like, even a month. You know, they call Sidi Ben Achir a doctor. Sick people come with their family; they rent a room and stay until they are well. You know, it's not Sidi Ben Achir that cures them, it's God, but they think it's Sidi Ben Achir.

Q *Can anybody rent a room?*

A Not any more. Now you have to have the authorization of the *Mokkadem* [local officials]. They want to know where you live and be sure that you are really sick. Once a woman rented a room and told them she had a sick person, but it was her lover. Since then they've made renting rooms more difficult.

Q *Are there young people your own age at the shrine?*

A Yes, but they don't come for the shrine, only for the view. A lot of young men from the neighborhood come to the shrine for picnics during the spring and summer. You should see the shrine then: the Hondas, the motors roaring, the boys all dressed up, the girls with short skirts, all made up and suntanned. It's beautiful. It's relaxing . . . the silence inside of the shrine, and life outside . . . it's crawling with young people. You know they have even made a slide in the wall that goes down to the beach. I will show it to you when we go. It's faster. You jump off the rampart, go down the slide and you're on the beach. You know some people come to the shrine during the summer for their vacations instead of going to a hotel where you pay ten or fifteen dirhams a day. In the shrine a whole family pays fifteen or twenty dirhams a week or month. It's especially the people who live outside of the city and come from far away, the north, the south, all corners of Morocco. For them the shrine is ideal for vacations. The old people can pray and the young can go to the beach. In the summer I meet people from all over Morocco. It's as if I were in Mecca, but I'm in Salé! You must come and see it. We can go in the summer if you want, it's more pleasant. You don't have to come to pray, you can just come and look. I told you, when I go to the shrine its not to pray. I never ask for anything. When I want something I'll ask God directly, but not the saint . . . he's a human being like I am.

This except from an interview with a twenty-year old maid, who works in a luxurious, modern part of Salé and lives in its *bidonville* section, suggests the great variety of experiences which take place in the sanctuary according to individual needs. Although they vary throughout the *Maghreb* (North Africa) from a humble pyramid of stones to a pretentious palace-like building,[2] all sanctuaries have one element in common: the saint's presence is supposed to be hosted there, because it is his tomb, a place he inhabited, or the site of an event in his life. The sanctuary testifies to the saint's welcomed presence in the community, but as an institution in a dynamic developing society it also reflects the society's economic and ideological contradictions.

SANCTUARIES AS THERAPY

For women, the sanctuary offers a dramatic contrast to their subordinate position in a bureaucratic, patriarchal society where decision-making positions are held by men. In the courts and hospitals, women hold a classically powerless position, condemned to be subjects, receptacles of impersonal decisions, executors of orders given by males. In a public hospital, the doctor is the expert, the representative of the bureaucratic order, empowered by the written law to tell her what to do; the illiterate woman can only execute his orders. In the diagnosis process, she expresses her discomfort in awkward colloquial Arabic and realizes, because of the doctor's impatience and irritation, that she cannot provide him with the precise, technical information he needs. Moreover, the hospital is a strange, alien setting, a modern building full of enigmatic written signs on doors and corridors, white-robed, clean, and arrogant civil servants who speak French for all important communications and only use Arabic to issue elementary orders (come here, go there, take off your dress, etc.).

In comparison to the guardians who stand at the hospital's gates and in its offices, the saint's tomb is directly accessible to troubled persons. Holding the saint's symbolical drape or another object like a stone or a tree, the woman describes what ails her, and it is she who makes the diagnosis, suggests the solution or solutions which might suit her, and explains to the saint the one she prefers. Saints know no French and often no literate Arabic; the language of this supernatural world is colloquial dialects, Berber or Arabic, the only ones women master. The task of the saint is to help her reach her goal. She will give him a gift or a sacrifice only if he realizes her wishes, not before. With a doctor, she has to buy the prescription first and has no way of retaliating if the medicine does not have the proper effect. It is no wonder, then, that in spite of modern health services, women still go to the sanctuaries in swarms, before they go to the hospital, or simultaneously, or after. Saints give women vital help that modern public health services cannot give. They embody the refusal to accept arrogant expertise, to submit blindly to authority, to be treated as subordinate. This insistence on going to saints' tombs exemplifies the North African woman's traditional claim that she is active, can decide her needs for herself and do something about them, a claim that the Muslim patriarchal system denies her. Visits to and involvement with saints and sanctuaries are two of the rare options left to women to *be,* to shape their world and their lives. And this attempt at self-determination takes the form of an exclusively female collective endeavor.

In the sanctuaries, there are always more women than men. They speak and shout with loud voices as if they are the secure owners of the premises. Men, although allowed in, often have to shorten their *Ziara* (visit) because they are overwhelmed by the inquisitive and curious looks of ubiquitous female visitors. Women gather around each other at the saint's supposed tomb and feel directly in contact with a sacred source of power that reflects their own energies. Distressed and suffering, these women have a very important bond: the will to find a solution, to find a happier balance between themselves and their surroundings, their fate, the system that thwarts them. They know they are *wronged (Madluma)* by the system. Their desire to find an answer to their urgent needs is a desire to regain their rights. That other women are in exactly the same situation creates a therapeutic network of communication among them.

When a woman enters the sanctuary, she goes directly to the tomb, walking over the stretched feet of sitting women, the stretched bodies of sleeping women. If women have already cried and screamed, they often lie in a fetal position with their heads on the floor. The newly arrived woman will put her hand on the tomb, or on the drape over it, and will explain her problem either in a loud voice or silently. She might go into great detail about her son who failed his examination or was driven away from her by his bride. When describing an intimate fight with her husband, the woman will mimic what happened, name the actors, explain their gestures and attitudes. After she has expressed her needs, she will come to sit among the other women. Eventually, they will gather around her, ask her more details, and offer her the only expertise these women have: experience in suffering. Outraged by her situation and encouraged by this female community, the woman may fall on the floor and scream, twisting her body violently. Some women will rush to her, hold her, hug her, soothe her by talking to her about their own cases and problems. They will massage her forehead, cool her off with a drink of water, and replace on her head her displaced headgear or scarf. She recovers quickly, regains her composure, and leaves the scene to the next newcomer. Undeniably therapeutic, the sanctuary stimulates the energies of women against their discontent and allows them to bathe in an intrinsically female community of soothers, supporters, and advisors.

SANCTUARIES AS ANTIESTABLISHMENT ARENAS

It is primarily as an informal women's association that the sanctuary must be viewed. It is not a religious space, a mistake which is often made. Most saint's sanctuaries are not mosques. With very few exceptions, they are not places where official orthodox Muslim prayer takes place. As Derminghem remarks,

> In principle, the *cubba* is not a mosque (*Mesjid*) where one does *soujoùd,* the prostration of ritual prayer (*çala*), even less so, the *Fam',* the cathedral mosque where Friday service is held. One can do the *dou'a,*

> prayer of supplication and optional invocation, but not the *sala,* sacramental prayer before a grave.[3]

The institution of saints that is enacted in the sanctuary has an evident antiorthodox, anti-establishment component which has been the object of a prolific literature. But studies of the woman-saint relation have placed excessive emphasis on its magical aspect. Western scholars who investigated the institution were fascinated by the "paralogical" component of the "Moroccan personality structure" and the importance of magical thinking patterns in the still heavily agrarian Moroccan economy and paid little attention to what I would call the phenomenological aspect, namely, what the practitioners themselves derive from their involvement with the saint and the sanctuary.

Such practices have also been interpreted as evidence of the mystical thinking of primitives as opposed to the secularity of the modern mind. As Mary Douglas points out,

> Secularization is often treated as a modern trend attributable to the growth of cities or to the prestige of science, or just to the breakdown of social forms. But we shall see that it is an age-old cosmological type, a product of a definable social experience, which need have nothing to do with urban life or modern science. Here it would seem that anthropology has failed to hold up the right reflecting mirror to contemporary man. The contrast of secular with religious has nothing whatever to do with the contrast of modern with traditional or primitive. The idea that primitive man is by nature deeply religious is nonsense . . . . The illusion that all primitives are pious, credulous and subject to the teaching of priests or magicians has probably done even more to impede our understanding of our civilization.[4]

Women, in particular, who are always the ones to be kept illiterate (and 97 percent of rural Moroccan women still are),[5] are described as simple-minded, superstitious creatures, incapable of sophisticated thinking, who indulge in esoteric mysticism. This view of women has gained even greater support with the advent of the development and nascent industrialization in Third World economies. If women in industrialized societies are granted some capacity for rational thinking, women in Third World societies are still described as enthralled in magical thinking, despite the fact that their societies are leaping into a modernity enraptured with rationality, technology, and environmental mastery.

SAINTHOOD AS AN ALTERNATIVE TO MALE-DEFINED FEMININITY

Far from magical, a visit to a saint's tomb, an ongoing relation with a supernatural creature, can be a genuine attempt to mediate one's place in the material world. Interaction with the saint can represent an effort to experience reality fully:

> The sacred is the real *par excellence,* at one and the same time power, efficiency, source of life and fertility. The religious desire to live within the sacred is in fact equivalent to the desire to be in objective reality, not to be paralyzed by endless and purely subjective experience, but to live in a world which is real and efficient, and not illusory.[6]

At bottom, women in an unflinchingly patriarchal society seek through the saint's mediation a bigger share of power, of control. One area in which they seek almost total control is reproduction and sexuality, the central notions of any patriarchal system's definition of women, classical orthodox Islam included.[7] Women who are desperate to find husbands, women whose husbands have sexual problems, women who have lost their husband's love or their own reproductive capacities go to the saint to get help and find solutions. One of the important functions of sanctuaries is precisely their involvement with sexuality and fertility. Indeed, if power can be defined as "the chance of a person or a number of persons to realize their own will in a communal action, even against the resistance of others, who are participating in the action,"[8] then women's collaboration with saints is definitely a power operation. Excluded from ritualistic orthodox religion, women walking in processions around saints' tombs express their quest for power in the vast horizons of the sacred space, untouched, unspoiled by human authority and its hierarchies:

> Some pale young girls throw red flowers into the spring, others sugar or honeycombs, so that their voice may become sweet, spiritual, persuasive. The women who throw musk dream of being loved. . . . None goes to the spring without henna, without benjamin. While burning her green or red candle, the virgin says, 'Master of the spring, light my candle' which means 'marry me,' or else 'give me splendid health.' The power to which they speak is capable of granting them all the goods of the world: life, strength, fortune, love, children.[9]

Now this quest for power that underlies the woman-saint relation is further confirmed by the fact that there are women saints who occupy a preeminent place and who specialize in solving problems of sexuality and reproduction.[10] They assume what Freud would certainly have called a phallic role and function. Some female saints go beyond the stage of penis envy and reverse traditional patriarchal relations: they are the ones who give penises to men suffering from sexual disturbances; such is the case of the Algerian female saint, Lalla Nfissa.[11] But this is not their only function. Unlike the emphasized passivity of women in the material, real world, supernatural women lead intensively active lives, perform all kinds of acts, from benign motherly protection to straightforward aggression, such as rape of men.[12] These women in the supernatural realm do not respect the traditional Muslim sexual division of labor which excludes women from power in religion and politics. In the supernatural realm, women may refuse to assume domestic roles and play active roles in both religion and politics.

In one of the most respected saint's biographies, the thirteenth-century *At-Tasawwuf Ila Rijal At-Tasawwuf,*[13] the biographer, Abu Yaqub At Tadili, makes no specific reference to the fact that some saints were women: they enjoy exactly the same rights and privileges and assume the same characteristics as male saints. At one point, a woman saint, Munia Bent Maymoun Ad-Dukali, says, "This year, hundreds of women saints visited this sanctuary." At another, a male insists that, "In Al Masamida [a region], there were twenty-seven saints who have the power to fly in the air, among whom fourteen are women."[14]

Female saints seem to fall into two categories, those who are saints because they were the sisters, wives, or daughters of a saint[15] and those who were saints in their own right.[16] Many of these saints have strikingly "unfeminine" personalities and interests. Imma Tiffelent, for example, literally fled her domestic condition:

> Not wanting to marry, Imma Tiffelent took the shape of a dove, escaped, and became a prostitute. . . . Twenty-seven young men disappeared after having loved her. Then she became an ascetic, in a hut, at the top of the mountain. . . . Ragged, unkempt, she preached religion in the valley, returned to her hut, shed even her rags, lived nude, and prophesied. It is forbidden to touch the trees around her grave, to kill the birds, to take the partridge eggs from the nest.[17]

The same identical flight from patriarchal "womanhood" can be seen in Sida Zohra El Kouch, "who was as wise as she was beautiful, resisted Moulay Zidane, died a virgin, and was visited only by women."[18] No less important, a prolific body of literature shows a number of female saints played important roles in the political arena.[19] One of the most famous is certainly the Berber saint Lalla Tagurrami, who played a strategic role in her region's history as a referee in conflicts between tribes and between tribes and the central authority.[20] Politically, she was so influential and successful that the king imprisoned her:

> As she was among the most beautiful girls of the village, she was sought after for marriage, but refused all suitors. . . . Her reputation as a saint grew and extended far. The sultan wanted to meet Lalla Aziza and asked her to come to Marrakesh. Once there, she continued to distinguish herself by her piety and the good she did. She was very honored, but her influence became so great that the sultan took offense and had Lalla thrown into prison. She was poisoned and died.[21]

It is of course possible that her fate was devised by myth tellers to discourage other women from taking such paths.

MALE SAINTS AS ANTIHEROES

Male saints, on the other hand, were profoundly concerned with what we would call a housework issue: how to eat without exploiting somebody else's work. Most analyses of the saints' lives fail to emphasize their constant preoccupation with food and its preparation; that they walk on water, fly in the skies, are given more weight than their efforts not to exploit the traditional domestic labor force available—women. Around this question clustered all other issues, such as the repudiation of possessions, privileges, political power, and the condemnation of wars and violence, the very characteristics of a phallocratic system.

Most saints fled urban centers and their sophisticated exploitative lives, tried hunting, fishing, gathering, and cooking for themselves.[22] Some fasted as often as they could[23] and trained themselves to eat very little; one went as far as to feed himself on one mouthful.[24] Still others had supernatural help which ground their own wheat or simply which gave them food.[25] They all tried to do without housework and to avoid food cooked by others,[26] and they also tried, to the community's dismay, to perform daily domestic chores themselves, such as taking the bread to the neighborhood oven.[27] One of the most famous of saints, Bou Yazza, went so far as to assume the appearance of a female domestic and to serve a woman for months.[28]

Some saints have families and children, some abstain and live in celibacy. But those who marry are unsuccessful fathers and husbands and live like embarrassed heads of families who can't provide properly for their dependents.[29] Others, especially elderly saints, did not hesitate to renounce their marital rights when these appeared to be totally opposed to the woman's happiness.[30] They definitely did not play the patriarchal role well. Among those who did not marry, one saint explained he was afraid to be unjust to his wife;[31] for him, apparently, marriage was an unjust institution to women. Another said he saw a beautiful woman walking down the street and thought he was in paradise; she was exactly like a *houri,* females provided to good Muslim believers in paradise.[32] Although he secluded himself because he was afraid females would turn him away from God,[33] he did not identify them with the devil, as classical Muslim ideology does, but with paradise, the most positive aspect of Muslim cosmogony.[34] Another saint fainted when he found himself alone with a woman in a room,[35] an unmasculine gesture to say the very least. Indeed, all these fears are not those of a self-confident, patriarchal male.

Like the women who come to visit their sanctuaries, a large number of saints were of humble origin and were involved in manual or physical activities as shepherds, butchers, or doughnut makers.[36] Others had no jobs and lived off nature, eating wild fruits, roots, or fish. Some saints were learned men, even judges, who refused to use their knowledge to obtain influential positions and accumulate wealth, or even to teach,[37] and encouraged illiterates to be proud of their illiteracy. Like the women in the sanctuaries, however, many of them were illiterates. They reminded their communities, which respected them, of their illiteracy,[38] perhaps in order to demystify knowledge as a prerequisite for decision-making positions. Moulay Bou Azza made a point of not speaking literate or even colloquial Arabic.[39] Moulay Ábdallah Ou Said, for example, tried to practice a teaching method for the masses "without the intervention of written texts."[40] Although it shocked the learned mandarins, the illiterate female saint Lalla Mimouna constantly insisted she did not use the customary complicated Koranic verses in her prayers because she did not know them. "Mimouna knows God and God knows Mimouna"[41] was the prayer she invented. This resistance to hierarchical knowledge is a persistent characteristic of saints' lives and their battles, which finds sympathy with the oppressed of the new developing economies: the illiterates, who are predominantly women. It is, therefore, no wonder that in the disintegrating agrarian economies of the Maghreb, sanctuaries, among all institutions, are almost the only ones women go to spontaneously and feel at home in. The sanctuary offers a world where illiteracy does not prevent a human being from being a wholesome, thinking, and reasonable person.

The psychic and emotional value of women's experience in sanctuaries is uncontested and evident. Sanctuaries, which are the locus of antiestablishment, antipatriarchal mythical figures, provide women with a space where complaint and verbal vituperations against the system's injustices are allowed and encouraged. They give women the opportunity to develop critical views of their condition, to identify problems, and to try to find their solution. At the same time, women invest all of their efforts and energies in trying to get a supernatural force to influence the oppressive structure on their behalf. This does not affect the formal power structure, the outside world. It has a collective therapeutic effect on the individual women visitors, but it does not enable them to carry their solidarity outside, to affect the system and shape it to suit their own needs. For these needs spring from their structural economic reliance on males and on the services they must give them in exchange: sex and reproduction. The saint in the sanctuary plays the role of the psychiatrist in the capitalist society, channeling discontent into the therapeutic processes and thus depriving it of its potential to combat the formal power structure. Saints, then, help women adjust to the oppression of the system. The waves of resentment die at the sanctuary's threshold. Nothing leaves with the woman except her belief that her contact with the saint triggered mechanisms which are going to affect the world, change it, and make it suit her conditions better. In this sense, sanctuaries are "happenings" where women's collective energies and combative forces are invested in alienating institutions which strive to absorb them, lower their explosive effect, neutralize them. Paradoxically, the arena where popular demonstrations against oppression, injustice, and inequality are most alive become, in developing economies, the best ally of unresponsive national bureaucracies. Encouragement of traditional saints' rituals by administrative authorities who oppose any trade unionist or political movement is a well-known tactic in Third World politics.

Notes

1. A dirham is roughly equivalent to $0.20 (U.S. dollars).

2. Emile Derminghem, "Les Edifices," in *Le Culte des saints l' Islam maghrébin* (Paris: Gallimard, 1954): p. 113.

3. "En principe, la cubba n'est pas une mosquée, Mesjid, où l'on fait le soujoùd, la prosternation de la prière rituelle, çala, encore moins, la Jam', la mosquée cathédrale où se fait l'office du vendredi. On peut faire la dou'a, prière de demande et d'invocation facultative, mais non la sala, prière sacrementale devant un tombeau." Ibid.

4. Mary Douglas, *Natural Symbols: Exploration in Cosmology* (New York: Random House, Vintage Books, 1973), p. 36.

5. *Recensement général de la population et de l'habitat, 1971* (Rabat: Direction de la statistique, Ministère de Planification, 1971), 3:5. The illiteracy rate is evaluated to be 75 percent for rural women between the ages of ten and twenty-four and between 93 percent and 97 percent for older women.

6. "Le sacré c'est le réel par excellence, à la fois puissance, efficience, source de vie et de fécondité. Le désir de l'homme religieux de vivre dans le sacré équivaut en fait à son désir de se situer dans la réalité objective, de ne pas se laisser paralyser par la réalité sans fin des expériences purement subjectives, devivre dans un monde réel et efficient et non pas dans une illusion." Mircea Eliade, *Le Sacré et le profane* (Paris: Gallimard, 1965), p. 27.

7. Fatima Mernissi, *Beyond the Veil* (Cambridge, Mass.: Schenkman Publishing Co., 1975), esp. the chapter entitled, "The Traditional Muslim View of Women and Their Place in the Social Order."

8. Max Weber, *From Max Weber, Essays in Sociology,* trans. and ed. with an introduction by H. Gerth and C. Wright Mills (New York: Oxford University Press, 1958), p. 180.

9. "Des jeunes filles pâles jettent dans la source des fleurs rouges, d'autres du sucre, des rayons de miel, pourque leur parole devienne douce, spirituelle, persuasive. Les femmes qui y lancent du musc rêvent de se faire aimer . . . nul ne s'y rend sans henné, sans benjoin." En brûlant son cierge vert ou rose, la vierge dit, "Maître de la source, allumesmoi mon cierge" ce qui veut dire "mariez-moi," ou encore "donnez-moi une santé brillante." La puissance à laquelle on s'adresses est capable de donner tous les biens de ce monde: vie, force, fortune, amour, enfants." Desparmet, "Le Mal magique," in Derminghem, p. 44.

10. Léon L'Africain, *Description de l'Afrique,* trans. from Italian by A. Epaulard Adrien (Paris: Maison Neuve, 1956), p. 216; and E. Doutté, *Magie et religion dans l'Afrique du Nord* (Alger: Typographica Adolphe Jourdan, 1908), chap. 1, p. 31.

11. Derminghem, p. 43.

12. Vincent Crapanzano, "The Transformation of the Eumenides: A Moroccan Example" (unpublished manuscript, Princeton University, 1974), and "Saints, Jinns and Dreams: An Essay on Moroccan Ethnopsychology" (unpublished manuscript, Princeton University, Department of Anthropology).

13. Abu Yaqub Yusuf Ibn Yahya At-Tadili, *At-Tasawwuf Ila Rijal At-Tasawwuf; vie de saints du sud Morocain des V, VI, VIIIème siècles de l' Hègire. Contribution à l'ètude de l'histoire religieuse du Maroc,* ed. A. Faure (Rabat: Editions Techniques Nord Africaines, 1958). I will refer to this work as *Tasawaf* and cite the number of each saint's biography.

14. *Tasawaf,* no. 160, p. 312; no. 209, p. 397.

15. See *Tasawaf,* no. 240, p. 431; no. 7, p. 70; no. 25, p. 111; and Derminghem, Lalla Mimouna, p. 68; Lalla Aicha, p. 125, Mana Aicha, p. 107.

16. See *Tasawaf,* no. 160, p. 312, no. 209, p. 397; no. 207, p. 394; no. 210, p. 398; no. 167, p. 331.

17. "Ne voulant pas se marier, Imma Tiffelent s'échappa sous forme de colombe et se fit prostituée dans la montagne. . . . Vingt-sept jeunes gens disparurent après l'avoir aimée. Puis elle devint ascète, dans une hutte, au sommet de la montagne . . . déguenillée, hiruste, elle prêche la religion dans la vallée, revint à sa hutte, quitte même ses haillons, vit nue, prophétise. Il est interdit de toucher aux arbres autour de sa tombe, de tuer les oiseaux, de dénicher les oeufs de perdrix." Trumelet, "Blida," and "Saints de l'Islam," as quoted in Derminghem, p. 53.

18. "qui fut aussi savante que belle, resista à Moulay Zidane, mourut vierge, et n'est visitée que par les femmes." Derminghem, p. 49.

19. Jacques Berque, *Structures sociales du Haut Atlas* (Paris: Presses Universitaires de France, 1955), p. 296.

20. Ibid., pp. 281, 286.

21. "Comme elle était parmi les plus belles jeunes filles du village, ell fut recherchée pour le mariage, mais refusa tous les prétendants. La réputation de sainte de la jeune fille en grandit et s'étendit au loin. Le sultan voulut connaître Lalla Aziza et la fit demander à Marrakech. Elle s'y rendit et continua dans la ville à se faire remarquer par sa piété et par le bien qu'elle faisait autour d'elle. Elle fut très

honorée, mais son influence devint tellement grande que le sultan en prit ombrage et Lalla Aziza fut jetée en prison. Elle mourut empoisonnée." Ibid., p. 290.

22. *Tasawaf,* no. 73, p. 186; no. 67, p. 170; no. 13, p. 88; no. 87, p. 217; no. 12, p. 86; no. 59, p. 162.

23. *Tasawaf,* no. 68, p. 76; no. 96, p. 228; no. 33, p. 124.

24. *Tasawaf,* no. 25, p. 111.

25. *Tasawaf,* no. 93, p. 223; no. 63, p. 171; no. 54, p. 156.

26. *Tasawaf,* no. 62, p. 166; no. 132, p. 184.

27. *Tasawaf,* no. 93, p. 224; no. 77, p. 197; no. 162, p. 321.

28. *Tasawaf,* no. 77, p. 200.

29. *Tasawaf,* no. 92, p. 222; no. 51, p. 152; no. 48, p. 144; no. 34, pp. 125–26.

30. *Tasawaf,* no. 99, p. 233; no. 56, p. 158.

31. *Tasawaf,* no. 45, p. 141.

32. *Koran,* Sourate 44, verses 53–54.

33. *Tasawaf,* no. 84, p. 214.

34. Abu Hasan Muslim, Al-Fami' As-Sahih (Beirut: Al Maktaba at Tijaria, n.d.), 8:130.

35. *Tasawaf,* no. 94, p. 224.

36. *Tasawaf,* no. 10, p. 79; no. 26, p. 115; no. 96, p. 228.

37. *Tasawaf,* no. 17, p. 95; no. 69, p. 178; no. 6, p. 69.

38. *Tasawaf,* no. 93, p. 223; no. 77, p. 197.

39. V. Loulignac, *Un Saint Berbère—Moulay Bou Azza; Histoire et légende* (Rabat: Hesperis, 1946), 31:29.

40. Jean Chaumel, *Histoire d'une tribu maraboutique de l'Anti-Atlas, le Aît Abdallah ou Said,* vol. 39, ler et 2éme trimestre (Rabat: Hesperes, 1952), p. 206.

41. Derminghem, p. 69.

Further Readings*

Davis, Susan Schaefer. *Patience and Power: Women's Lives in a Moroccan Village.* Cambridge, Mass.: Schenkman Press, 1983.

Fernea, Elizabeth, ed. *Women and the Family in the Middle East: New Voices of Change.* Austin: University of Texas Press, 1985.

Mernissi, Fatima. *Beyond the Veil: Male-Female Dynamics in Modern Muslim Society.* Rev. ed. Bloomington and Indianapolis: Indiana University Press, 1987.

———. *Le Maroc raconté par ses femmes.* Rabat: Société Morocaine Editeurs Réunis, 1984 (translation forthcoming by The Women's Press, London).

———. "Virginity and Patriarchy." *Women and Islam,* ed. by Azizah al-Hibri. Elmsford, N.Y.: Pergamon Press, 1982.

———. "Zhor's World: A Moroccan Domestic Worker Speaks Out. *Feminist Issues* 2, no. 1 (1982): pp. 3–31.

———. "Women and the Impact of Capitalist Development in Morocco." *Feminist Issues* 2, no. 2 (1982): pp. 69–104.

Rassam, Amal. "Women and Domestic Power in Morocco." *International Journal of Middle East Studies* 7, no. 2 (1980): pp. 171–79.

Smith, Jane I. *Women in Contemporary Muslim Societies.* Lewisburg, Pa.: Bucknell University Press, 1980.

* Selections primarily from a list compiled by Mary Jo Lakeland for the 1987 edition of Dr. Mernissi's book *Beyond the Veil* (Bloomington, Ind.: Indiana University Press).

IV

OUT OF THE SHADOWS

Women in Male-Dominated Systems

Several of the studies included in the preceding sections refer to the special obstacles that women confront when they act within religious or cultural systems that normally justify patterns of male domination. This section gathers together a number of studies that focus especially on these obstacles.

Chapter 13 continues the exploration of ordinary women's religious lives begun in the preceding section but shows how religion can alienate women instead of providing them with an avenue of self-expression and validation. Muslim tribal women of a village in Iran live with traditional and male-defined religious ideals and norms that they cannot possibly hope to meet. They also find little opportunity to participate in public religious life. Their situation invites comparison with that of the urban Iranian women discussed in Chapter 11, who, like them, confront some degree of misogyny and exclusion. But the outcome is different, for the urban women have created an alternative religious life of their own, while the tribal women seem more prone to conclude that religion is "made for men" only. It should be noted that both these situations involve the same Shi'a sect of Islam in Iran. Thus we see that it is quite difficult to make blanket judgments about how a given religion affects the lives and attitudes of women, since much depends on subtle local variations.

The next three chapters are quite different, for they follow ventures of extraordinary women. Furthermore, from one point of view all might be considered success stories, for the women studied in these chapters all challenge conventional expectations to create a new kind of place in the world for themselves. However, in each case the greater system in which they are embedded eventually reasserts its claims and undercuts their achievements.

In the middle of the twentieth century, a middle-aged Japanese countrywoman named Sayo Kitamura declared herself the instrument of God, chosen to usher in a new divine age. The "new" religion that she founded still thrives in Japan as well as in a number of other countries. Sayo herself achieved an extraordinary personal liberation through her experiences and career as founder. Nonetheless, the inevitable dilemmas caused by her own teachings as well as by traditional patterns of religious and managerial leadership seem to ensure that men will eventually dominate her movement and shape its direction.

During the same turbulent years when Sayo began to preach in Japan, a much younger woman of West Africa named Alinesitouê began to receive revelations teaching her how to heal her people's imbalance and to bring her country much needed rain. She also inadvertently launched a revolution that brought her country's colonial rulers down upon her. Arrested and exiled by them, she died in a detention camp. This did not end her story, however, for she now lives on as a national hero. Moreover she launched a tradition of women prophets who continue the efforts to heal their people that Alinesitouê herself began.

Our fourth study of this chapter assesses the history of the order of Buddhist nuns in India. For more than a thousand years the order provided refuge for Indian women who found the everyday concerns of housewife and motherhood not to be their calling. By the time of Buddhism's brilliant final centuries in India, the nuns' order nonetheless had faded to a pale shadow beside the much more prestigious and better-supported order of Buddhist monks.

The final two chapters of this section record stories with much happier outcomes. The resourceful nuns of the Pütrich convent described in Chapter 17 outwit their bishop again and again as they struggle against the Catholic Counter-Reformation's efforts to shut them away from public contact. Their bones of contention are literally bones—those of a martyr named Dorothea—in this article which shows that stories of women in religion can sometimes also be humorous. Finally, Marian Neudel traces the development of an unusually egalitarian Jewish congregation, the Upstairs Minyan of the University of Chicago Hillel Foundation, during early decades of the women's movement. She shows how women used traditional Jewish values and skills to earn for themselves a place of respect and equality within the congregation.

13

Islam and Tribal Women in a Village in Iran

ERIKA FRIEDL

Religiously sanctioned ideologies and practices are said to be less restrictive for Muslim tribal women than for Muslim urban women.[1] For example, the necessity for mobility and outdoor work in nomadic or transhumant groups makes it unfeasible to seclude women as strictly as is demanded by many interpreters of Islamic scriptures, while it is relatively easy to keep women indoors in towns. Small rural-tribal communities are organized along lines of kinship, and thus the distinctions between strangers and kinsmen as well as between public and private are rarely relevant. Therefore they do not influence the organization of the social environment very much—women are among kinsmen most of the time and can move among them freely. In these communities, colorfully dressed women go about their work openly, often not even wrapped in the veil. They seem to have considerable influence in all affairs and to hold their places next to the man,[2] despite their lack of prominent economic or political positions officially. In urban, religiously conservative circles, tribal women often are considered immodest or improperly taken care of by their menfolk because of their relaxed dress code and relatively free access to

---

ERIKA FRIEDL holds a Ph. D. from the University of Mainz in Germany and currently is the Edwin E. Meader Professor of Anthropology at Western Michigan University. She has lived in a tribal area in Iran for a total of nearly seven years, concentrating her studies on women's issues, the ethnography of children, and philosophy. She is the author of several books and articles on various aspects of this people's culture.

Author's Note: Various stages of the research for this chapter were supported by grants from the Wenner Gren Foundation for Anthropological Research, the Social Science Research Council, the National Endowment for the Humanities, and Western Michigan University.

areas and people outside their homes. Along with the men, they are said to be lax Muslims.

These impressions of tribal women's relatively shallow observance of Muslim propriety and their purported "freedom" have been formed by outsiders, who tend to base their judgments mainly on outward signs of appearance and behavior. On closer look these judgments turn out to be stereotypes. To the best of my knowledge, there is no systematic study of women's religious lives in a tribal or rural Shi'ite Muslim community in the Middle East that would allow us to support the popular stereotypes. In fact there are very few, if any, systematic studies of rural Muslim women's religiosity altogether.

Between 1965 and 1998 I conducted a total of seven years of ethnographic fieldwork in a tribal area in southwest Iran in the southern ranges of the Zagros Mountains, centering on a large village which I call Deh Koh.[3] During my visits I became especially interested in the ways religious knowledge is learned and transmitted, how women participate in religious rituals, the criteria for morally good behavior in men and women, and the relationships between women's self-images and their worldviews. Information for the following analytic description of women's religious lives in the tribal area comes from numerous discussions with women and men, from content analysis of hundreds of local songs, proverbs, tales, and legends, and from observing women's religious activities before and after the revolution of 1979. We have to be careful about drawing generalizations about women's religious lives in Iran based on the few available case studies. As religious beliefs and practices reflect many cultural and economic factors, we can expect to find a variety of religious systems in different Shi'ite communities. We also know that urban women live with different religious frameworks than villagers, and that class differences have an influence on religious belief and practice as well.[4] However, from the first-hand experiences I have of other Iranian villages, I would expect the religious system in which women operate there to be very similar to the one I describe here. Only further research can reveal the exact similarities and differences.

The people of the tribal area traditionally lived on a mixed economy of sheep and goat herding and agriculture. By now, however, most families have settled in villages and are participating in various economic enterprises facilitated by the modern state. Intense and lively relationships with the outside world and educational opportunities (mostly for men) have created a culture gap between men and women and also between generations. Inevitably, men and young people, especially young men, come in contact with various religious trends in the towns, ranging from extremist Islamicist views to those of educated sceptics, from liberal middle-class ideas to the cynical opinions of critics of the kind of Islam many government functionaries propagate. By contrast, in the village even literate women tend to hold less diverse beliefs and rituals, more from lack of alternatives than by choice. But today, especially among younger women, different forms of piety and of religious ideologies can be found, similar to those of men. Thus, in the wake of intense proselytizing by government-supported agencies such as schools and television programs, the rural/urban as well as the gender gap in religious beliefs are diminishing in the Islamic Republic. The following description will draw on the women's traditional religious notions and on "new" ones that are relevant for understanding women's religious lives today.

Islam is a book religion, and reading the Qoran and religious literature is considered indispensable for religious education and knowledge. The literacy rate for women has gone up dramatically over the past twenty-five years (to nearly 100% for able-minded girls under the age of eighteen in Deh Koh, and to about 50% in more remote areas). Nevertheless the postulate that the Qoran has to be read in its original Arabic, the lack of easy access to literature and lack of leisure still make it hard for women to gain literature-based religious knowledge outside of school. The written word, so important in a book religion, does not reach women directly, especially not older women.[5]

The *mullah,* or preacher, sermons and religious education programs on television, and participation in mosque-centered rituals are women's main sources of religious teaching outside the family or school. Deh Koh has both a preacher and a mosque, and even remote corners of the tribal area are visited by itinerant preachers now. The mullah in Deh Koh however, gives relatively few sermons, provides no formal religious education for women, and has little professional contact with the village women. He sees himself more as a theologian than as a teacher and missionary; he also perceives the women as uneducated and therefore not ready to follow his explications. Although women in the Islamic Republic are wooed by the religious establishment, few women attend Friday sermons in the mosque. Traditionally, the mosque was considered to be a public, male domain. Even twenty years of missionary efforts by the government and the clergy to get more women to attend such services has not changed this notion significantly.

Occasionally, itinerant lay preachers give performances in the village. They might handle snakes or use painted canvasses to illustrate dramatic legends about exalted figures from Islam's past. Such preachers are discouraged by the clerical establishment. Most of the spectators are women and children; men usually claim not to have time for such undignified spectacles. The information women get from these shows is of no particular educational value, in contrast to the many television programs on religious themes. Sermons, broadcasts of Friday-prayer services from important mosques, Qoran lessons, recitations of the Qoran and of religious poetry, explanations of religious holidays, and lessons in Islamic history can be seen and heard daily. Women, people say, make little use of them—during the day they are busy with chores, and in any case, the eloquent and highly educated Farsi in which many of the sermons and lessons are delivered, and the talking-head format of the shows make it hard for many relatively uneducated people to keep attention focused on these broadcasts. Nevertheless in Deh Koh, as in a great many similar villages, most households have a television set.

The ceremonial side of Islam is largely closed to rural women. In Deh Koh, ceremonies in the mosque are attended by only a few women. Asked for a reason for the poor attendance, the mullah and the more zealotic men quickly explain that women in general do not pay much attention to religious duties, that they are not "good Muslims." The women, however, say that they cannot go to the mosque when they are ritually impure (during menstruation, for example), when they have urgent duties at home, and when they have to take care of young children—a mother cannot leave her young children at home alone but she cannot take them to the mosque either because the children disturb everybody there with their noise. Thus, women explain the neglect of this religious duty with a moral conflict. In fact, however, women are never an integrated part of mosque rituals. Those who attend sit in a room above the main assembly hail, where they cannot see the preacher and often cannot even hear him well. They are unseen and rarely addressed directly, except when their whispered conversations prompt the preacher to admonish them to be quiet. They are not included in the distribution of tea or food during sacrificial meals in the mosque in memory of important religious events or martyrs. Women draw very little social or religious meaning or satisfaction from participating in mosque services. Thus it is not surprising that they avoid going there—for them, the mosque is a male space.

In rituals that take place outdoors, such as processions mourning the death of the Shi'a martyr Husain, women watch from rooftops and sidelines, well wrapped in their veils. Many more women attend these rituals than mosque services. Although participating in such rituals even if only as a compassionate spectator is considered religiously meritorious, some people question the women's motives for attending, claiming that women watch the young men in the processions lustily and entice them to sinful displays of virility during the ritual flagellation and chest-beating routines.

During a funeral—another open-air ceremony—women function as mourners, crying and singing around the body while a grave is dug. As soon as the body is buried and the prayers begin—in other words, as soon as the ritual takes on a distinctly religious character—the women retreat or leave altogether.

Unlike women in towns and cities, tribal and village women have no regular religious rituals that are exclusively or specifically for them, and no religious gatherings in which they receive instructions or can actively engage in a communal religious activity. Therefore, they have no means to complement the men's rituals from which they are almost completely excluded. Not surprisingly, when women discuss their access to religious knowledge and to rituals, they often declare that religion as practiced around them has been "made for men" and not for women, and that it is easier for women in the cities to follow religious rules, to participate in Friday prayers in mosques, and to attend Qoran-lessons given by women. They see a marked urban-rural difference in the accessibility of religious practices for women. Young women who attend high schools in the area receive regular Qoranic instruction and are encouraged to compete in local and national competitions for Qoran recitations. When they leave school, they are well versed in Islamic doctrine and rituals. But they cannot apply this knowledge easily in the everyday life of the village, where requirements of work, lack of facilities, and traditional customs make it hard to follow all the rules or to take advantage of them. Again, they feel that the discrepancy between their book-knowledge about their religion and restrictive village conditions puts them at a disadvantage. In some instances, their knowledge creates conflicts within the family. For example, recently women successfully have started to challenge tribal inheritance traditions that do not allow them any of their fathers' inheritance, on the ground that, according to Islamic law, daughters should inherit half as much as their brothers. Religious authorities and government agents are quick to point out that Islam, if practiced "correctly," would make life much better for tribal people, especially women.

However, a few religious activities are readily open to local women. These activities relate to the use of extra-human powers thought to be inherent in certain plants and minerals as well as special prayers and rituals said to help avoid or overcome problems such as the sickness of a child or economic hardship. As most of these rituals are private, occur locally, and entail minimal expense, women are relatively free to act according to their own judgment. Because women are more exposed to the nitty-gritty of everyday life than are men, they are more involved than men in the use of religion (or magic) to alleviate domestic hardships. It is mostly women who resort to such devices as fumigating a house against the evil eye,[6] having a powerful prayer written in an amulet to cure a headache, or preparing a string of amulets to protect a baby against malevolent spirits. Such activities are diminishing now that various health-related services are becoming available in the course of the development of rural areas of Iran, and also because religious functionaries as well as "enlightened" young people label many of these traditional beliefs and practices as "superstition." Of all the traditional self-help practices with religious overtones, only prayers and vows have remained unchallenged for women.

For help with everyday problems women may also make vows to saints. These mostly consist of a promise to distribute money or goods (such as a lamb or a meal) among people, especially the poor, in honor of the specific saint who is asked for help. Alternatively, they may promise to pay a visit to the saint's shrine. Most of these powerful personages (which we, for want of a better term, call saints), are taken to be descendants of the Prophet Mohammad; their powers derive from their membership in this exalted lineage. Out of pity, kindness, and compassion, saints, both male and female, can use their privileged position to help people in distress. Although saints can be petitioned anywhere and at any time, people say that it is especially effective to invoke their help at their shrines. Several popular small shrines are scattered throughout the tribal area, but the big, famous shrines of the most powerful saints are in cities and attract pilgrims from all over the country. A visit to one of those shrines requires special effort and major travel expenses. Pilgrimages are especially popular with women, because they provide women with the otherwise rare opportunity to travel to interesting places.

Women say that they can make vows to saints without consulting their husbands and that a husband must honor the vow of his wife eventually by giving her the means to fulfill it. Actually, however, most women are very careful not to overstep their husband's means when they make vows and not to pledge something to which they know their husbands would not agree. For example, a woman in Deh Koh wanted her husband to sacrifice a goat to a saint to strengthen her plea for better healing of a fractured leg. The husband was reluctant to give up a goat after heavy losses of animals during a bad winter and spring. When her leg got worse, the woman complained bitterly about her husband's reluctance but he would not change his mind and she did not dare to dispose of the goat herself. Another woman, setting out on a pilgrimage with her family, pointed to her son: "We are going for him; I made a vow for his health when he was born thirteen years ago!"

When making vows and pilgrimages to a saint's shrine, a woman feels equal to a man. Her ability to communicate with the saints, to evoke their pity, and to elicit their help is the same as a man's. Among the saints, certain female saints are considered to be especially open to women's problems because they have insights into women's difficulties that no man, no matter how saintly and sympathetic, could have. Many women have a deep emotional attachment to these saints. They invoke their names in times of distress such as during childbirth, make vows to them, promise pilgrimages to their shrines in return for help, and tell legends about them.

Until the early 1980s, most religious education for local men and women was informal, unspecific, and casual. Children learned about religion just as they learned songs and proverbs. Even today, early religious education is by imitation: children copy their elders' prayer gestures and ablutions long before they know the text of a prayer; they invoke saints' names long before they know what they mean; they flagellate themselves playfully as they see their elder brothers do. This way, children learn some basic religious concepts. They learn that God will punish them if they are disobedient or lazy; that certain acts are sinful and therefore "bad," while others have religious merit and thus will help one be admitted to paradise eventually. They learn about judgment after death and that one has to guard against *djenn,* beings that are potentially dangerous and usually invisible. The information children get in this way is sketchy and often contradictory, as they see many successful people behaving contrary to pious expectations.

While the differences between the indigenous (tribal)-Islamic, and formal-religious value systems are the same for both sexes, the religious messages in the moral code are quite different for boys and girls. For men, good conduct is defined rather generally, and moral commands are few and dramatic: above all, a man has to care well for his dependents; he must avoid murder, theft, lies, and adultery; he has to be hospitable and charitable; and he must pray and fast punctually. Some commandments are taken to be more important than others, and offenses against a lesser one can be justified if they are deemed necessary to fulfill a more important one. Thus, it may be argued that lying to safeguard one's family's interests will be pardoned as necessary. An urgent agricultural task is sufficient reason for not saying the prayers on time. The sin of stinginess is balanced by a man's saving for his son's education. For rare major crimes like robbery or murder, the claim of coercion may be used to justify oneself. Adultery, which is rare too, is not pardonable by any of these arguments. However, it usually is blamed on the permissive or provocative behavior of the woman involved and is therefore considered much more of a sin for her than for the man. After the revolution, the more formal aspects of Islam (such as prayer, fasting, religious taxes, and the pilgrimage to Mecca) implicitly are put above the more social aspects such as truthfulness and generosity by the clerical establishment and its loyal followers. This created a conflict with traditional Islamic values as understood and honored by local people. "I have heard a hundred times on television how to wash myself correctly before prayer, but only rarely did I hear a sermon about kindness and truthfulness," said a woman.

For women the boundaries of good behavior are narrower, and the moral code is more specific than for men. Obedience to her father or husband and submission to the legitimate authority of men are absolutely essential. Taking care of husband and children competently and industriously, behaving modestly, peacefully, and kindly, minding her own business and not giving cause for gossip are the next most important commandments for women. Theft and murder are not considered typical crimes of women and are of little relevance in the women's moral code. Saying her prayers and performing the ritual ablutions and fasts are, like for men, high on the official list of a Muslim's duties now, and are much talked about in sermons, but are less urgent in the traditional code. Unlike men, women are rarely allowed excuses for failure. There is no valid excuse for disobeying a husband, for fighting with a neighbor, for neglecting a child, or for gossiping. Thus, women generally regard themselves as "more sinful" than men.

The following legend told locally dramatically illustrates the next to impossibly high standards for a wife's correct attitude toward her husband.

One day the Prophet Mohammad sent his daughter Fateme to visit a woman who, he said, was the best wife in town. Fateme went to her house but was not admitted by the woman because her husband was not at home and thus she could not ask him for permission to receive a visitor. The next day Fateme went there again, this time accompanied by her little son. The woman meanwhile had gotten permission to admit Fateme but not her son, and turned Fateme away again. This happened again on the third day, when Fateme came with both her sons. On the fourth day, finally, Fateme was let into the house. She found her hostess sitting in the courtyard near the door, a cup of water standing in the sun, some pieces of hard, dry bread in her lap, a stick leaning against the wall, and her skirts gathered to be lifted easily. Asked for an explanation, the woman said that she drank only tepid water and ate only hard bread because her husband, a shepherd, had nothing better to eat either; she kept a stick ready in case her husband found fault with her and wanted to beat her; and she gathered her skirts to be ready in case her husband was overcome with desire when he came home.

Obedience, compassion, and total submission, the legend suggests, are a wife's most noble virtues. Measured against these standards, women in the village find themselves sadly inadequate. Although women actually do attend to their husbands like servants in their homes, they nevertheless often act on their own judgment, speak their minds, and disagree with their husbands to the point of open quarrel. They are, in short, "bad wives" compared to the ideal, and they resent this label. Especially young, educated women even go so far as to question the wisdom and theological legitimacy of such wifely ideals, and point out that with such behavior women cannot really contribute to the development of either their families or the country, as they are exhorted to do by the government.

Men and women are told to expect the same worldly results from good and bad behavior—punishments for sins, rewards for goodness—although they know that this doesn't happen often in real life. Men's and women's traditional expectations about the afterlife, however, are substantially different. For men, promises of rewards are specific and detailed. From the fragrance of heavenly flowers to the shining faces of the houris, the paradisical virgins; from the refreshing gurgling of cool springs to the taste of delicious fruits and the sweet sounds of music, men can describe eternal pleasures very concretely. For women, the same paradise is rather vague and general. Women will "see the angels" and "never be hungry" or simply "have no more worries," although paradisical fruits and fragrances should be the same for men and women. Women expect no counterpart for the beautiful virgins men will enjoy. They don't even expect to be together with their husbands. "What would a man want his wife for in paradise," a woman declared, "with all the virgins to play with?" People are not at all sure what women can expect from paradise beyond leisure and general bliss, and even modern religious education and the ongoing reinterpretation of religious scriptures have not been able to fill this gap.

Yet, while rewards are specific for men and general for women, punishment in the afterlife for sins on earth is described in general terms for men ("He will go to hell; he will burn in the fire; he will have great pain") but is very specific for women: a woman who nursed another woman's baby without her husband's consent will be hung from a hook by her breasts; a woman who spoke ill of others will have her tongue pierced with a red-hot spit; her ears will be cut to tiny pieces for eavesdropping, her feet shackled for leaving the house without permission.[7]

As we have seen already, legends as well as other stories are important sources of religious and moral knowledge, especially for illiterate people. Although they might be told simply to entertain, they always convey information about the prevailing moral code and what is expected of people. Most of them present a negative image of women: women appear as bad wives, evil forces, antagonists of the hero, or just ridiculous figures.[8] Through these stories women learn that they are unimportant, foolish, or threatening to men. The following legend about Adam and Eve, told by an elderly man in Deh Koh to a largely female audience, is a good example.

One day Eve was sulking and not speaking to Adam—as women always do if they want something. God had pity on the lonely and neglected Adam and opened the door to paradise a crack, just enough for Adam to take a good look at the beautiful houris inside. Eve—nosy like all women—peeked too. What she saw made her run back to Adam in a hurry, falling all over herself to be at his service. With this little trick God had shown Adam how to make a stubborn wife pliable.

Women as well as men hear these stories and accept the implications that women are weak in a physical, intellectual, and moral sense and that they are more prone than men to commit sins. When asked, for example, how many women there might be in paradise in relation to men, one woman in Deh Koh went so far as to say that she thought there were only very few women in heaven other than the saints. This, she said, was God's will because otherwise God would have arranged things so that women wouldn't be ritually impure so often and wouldn't have weak, sinful characters. "When we are young," another woman said, "we cannot help being unclean all the time from menstruation, childbirth, and the babies who soil us. When we are old, it is easier to keep ritually clean, but the older a woman gets, the worse her character becomes. So what can we do?"

For most tribal people, being a "true Muslim" is largely a matter of satisfactory behavior as demanded by God—of taking care, getting along, being responsible, not harming anybody. Knowledge of Islamic dogma and scriptures, and the meticulous performance of rituals without behaving well means, in the critical eyes of the local people, that one is a Muslim only in name and outward signs—not a true Muslim but a kind of infidel. People use the charge of being a heathen generously in their judgments of others around them. Given the strictures of the women's moral code and the demands of everyday interaction with family and neighbors, women are especially open to these charges. A man irrigating his fields alone all day long hardly will meet with opportunities to sin; his wife at home meanwhile will be challenged to gossip, to curse a misbehaving child, quarrel with a neighbor, neglect a crying baby, forget to feed the chickens, or do something against the husband's will or without his permission, such as visiting her own father. These are all sinful acts, committed all the more easily in as much as women think of themselves as weaker than men in moral fiber anyway. Thus, women regard themselves, and are regarded by others, as weak Muslims.

Just as the women's purportedly weak nature makes them prone to sinful quarrel and disobedience, it also makes them prone to commit the major sin of suicide. But just as the label "sin" is not a deterrent to bitchiness or shrewdness, so it is not a deterrent to suicide attempts either. Suicide attempts are so frequent in the area that in 1998 the province's agent for women's affairs named suicide as a top problem for women.[9] Reasons for this are complex. For our purposes, it is enough to state that women who attempt or commit suicide are not irreligious, nor do they deny that suicide is a sin. Rather, local people assume that women's general weakness and ignorance make them prone to do foolish things like commit suicide: women don't known any better; they give in to the devil's persuasion; they are disobedient. Although they seem not to be fully accountable for this weakness, nevertheless such behavior is regarded sinful. Women who attempt suicide are scolded by everybody, including the physician who saves them. They get no sympathy, and even may be cursed for leaving young children behind, although in the same breath their critics may well concede that given her circumstances, the woman who committed suicide had "no choice."

Women's weaknesses are taken to be a key problem in this world. One man declared that a woman's weak character is as unalterable as a man's inability to fly. But like other problematic conditions in this world, a woman's disposition has to be accepted as God-given. For women, then, free will and choice are impaired severely, and even religion cannot provide an effective incentive for choosing certain morally good behavior because religion also supports the notion that these behaviors contradict women's God-given nature. Despite this predicament, however, no form of a woman's bad behavior ever is excused by the generally inferior stuff women are said to be made of. It is only explained by it. How has it come about that women are made of such inferior moral material? The legend of Noah's daughter has an answer.

When Noah got the order to build the ark, he could not find anybody to help him with this crazy task. So he promised his only daughter to three different craftsmen in exchange for their help. After the ark was built, each of the three men wanted the promised bride, and Noah was in serious trouble. In his despair he implored God to help him—after all, His command had caused the predicament. God told him to lock the girl in a room overnight together with a dog and a donkey. This was a strange request indeed, because both animals are looked down upon, and a dog is considered ritually impure. Ordinarily neither animal would be let into a house. Nevertheless Noah obeyed. In the morning the dog and donkey had turned into exact copies of his daughter and Noah could keep his promise to the craftsmen. But the girl who had been a dog was very bitchy and the one who had been a donkey was a stupid ass; only Noah's own daughter was a good, understanding woman. The moral of this story is that all women are descendants of these three and retain the basic characters of their respective ancestress. This explains why today most women are either loose and bitchy or stupid and stubborn, and only a few are decent.

Here, then, lie obvious cognitive and practical conflicts for every woman. A woman is largely excluded from religious rituals, although participating in them is meritorious if not obligatory. She is considered weak by nature and prone to sin, yet she is also held fully responsible for the offenses she inevitably will commit. She is part of a religious universe that is said to include her, yet in practice centers around men.

Every woman I talked with found it hard to come to terms with these conflicts, even if she could not articulate the problem in abstract terms. In their attempts to deal with such dilemmas, women construct an astounding variety of individual philosophies and worldviews. Through these personal views they try to clarify for themselves, with more or less satisfactory results, their own position within their religion. These views range from simple resignation to their alleged inadequacies, usually coupled with hopes for the mercy of God, to forthright denial of the validity of the present order and demands for a "true" interpretation of the holy scriptures.

This denial was expressed, for example, by an illiterate, deeply religious older woman exceptionally knowledgeable in religious matters and with an amazingly assertive personality, who declared firmly that she thought religion as preached and practiced was not made by God, but by men in order to suppress women. God had meant men and women to be equal, she said, but, if taken seriously, this would mean the end of male superiority. This sentiment is now echoed by many women and men in Iran, especially educated people who demand reevaluation of beliefs and practices not rooted in the Qoran and of misogynist Qoranic interpretations.[10] A kind of Islamic feminism has developed in the Islamic Republic that slowly is extending even to backwoods rural communities. However, the opposite view is also frequently heard, which, in its extreme, zealotic form, holds that women are more or less weak if not evil, and only tight control can keep them from harm and sin. Others look at the world in quasi-existentialist terms: people's basic situation is senseless and often cruel but unavoidable, given by God for reasons only known to Him. Every person must carry his or her own burden as best as he or she can, without assurance that these efforts ever will be adequately compensated for in this or any other life. The most common attitude is a helpless and at the same time sceptical and grudging resignation to the status quo. Women doubt the validity of all the claims about themselves but are in no position to decide what is true and what is false. For this reason and because they have little authority, women say they must go along with the rules they are given.

I have not met an atheistic woman in the tribal area. God, although generally perceived as far away and rather aloof, is recognized by all as the provider and ultimate giver of life as well as the final judge of one's conduct. Therein lies many women's ultimate hope: that despite of all hardships in this life, including hardships placed on them in the name of their religion, and all the moral failures they hardly can avoid, God the merciful and generous will be a just judge who will take into account a woman's total situation and will pardon her sins precisely because she is a weak woman. Until then, the established order in the world as they know it rests on women upholding their end of the bargain.

Notes

1. See, for example, Raphael Patai, *Golden River to Golden Road: Society, Culture, and Change in the Middle East* (Philadelphia: University of Pennsylvania Press, 1962), p. 120.

2. See, for example, Lois Beck, "Theoretical Perspectives on the Position of Women in Iran," paper presented at the seventh annual meeting of the Middle East Association, 1974; Lois Beck, *Nomad: A Year in the Life of a Qashqa'i Tribesman in Iran* (Berkeley: University of California Press, 1991); Erika Friedl, "The Dynamics of Women's Spheres of Action in Rural Iran," in *Women in Middle Eastern History,* Nikki R. Keddie and Beth Baron, eds. (New Haven and London: Yale University Press, 1991), pp. 195–214; Nancy Tapper, "The Women's Subsociety among the Shahsevan Nomads of Iran," in *Women in the Muslim World,* Lois Beck and Nikki R. Keddie, eds. (Cambridge, Mass.: Harvard University Press, 1978), pp. 374–98; Susan Wright, "Prattle and Politics: The Position of Women in Doshman-Ziari," *Journal of the Anthropological Society of Oxford,* 9, no. 2, (1978).

3. The tribal people under consideration are Luri-speaking Shi'a Muslims, organized in several subtribes within the province of Kohgiluye-Boir Ahmad. Most of the approximately 500,000 people have settled over the past twenty years. Fast population growth and heavy influx of outsiders have swelled towns and villages. In the course of the integration of the whole area into the infrastructures of Iran since about 1965, and especially since the revolution of 1979, the area has lost many of its tribal cultural characteristics and has been subjected to intense religious education via mosques, sermons and lectures on television, newspapers, slogans on billboards, state propaganda, and schools. For a description of the early integration process see Reinhold Loeffler, "Recent Economic Changes in Boir Ahmad: Regional Growth without Development," *Iranian Studies,* 9, no. 4 (1976): pp. 266–87. For descriptions of life in Deh Koh, see Erika Friedl, *Women of Deh Koh: Life in an Iranian Village* (New York: Penguin Publishers, 1991); Erika Friedl, *Children of Deh Koh: Young Life in an Iranian Village* (Syracuse, N.Y.: Syracuse University Press, 1997); Reinhold Loeffler, *Islam in Practice* (Albany, N.Y.: State University of New York Press, 1988).

4. See Anne H. Betteridge, "The Controversial Vows of Urban Women in Iran," in this volume; Zahra Kamalkhani, *Women's Islam: Religious Practice Among Women in Today's Iran* (Ph.D. Dissertation, University of Bergen, Norway, 1996); Mary Elaine Hegland, "Aliabad Women: Revolution as Religious Activity," in *Women and the Revolution in Iran,* Guity Nashat. ed. (Boulder: Westview Press, 1983), pp. 171–94.

5. Yet another reason for older women's lack of ready access to literature is the fact that reading glasses—any spectacles, for that matter—are considered inappropriate for women and thus either not available or used only surreptitiously.

6. The so-called evil eye is said to be a destructive force inherent in certain people's glances. It cannot be controlled by the person who has the evil eye other than by avoiding to look at things or people admiringly, but everybody can guard against the effects of the evil eye by wearing, for example, a blue bead.

7. See also Jane Smith and Yvonne Y. Haddad, "Women in the Afterlife: The Islamic View as Seen from the Qur'an and Tradition," *Journal of the American Academy of Religion,* 43, no. 1 (1975): pp. 39–50; Fatna Ait Sabbah, *Woman in the Muslim Unconscious* (New York: Pergamon, 1984); Adele K. Ferdows and Amir H. Ferdows, "Woman in Shi'i Figh: Images through the Hadith," in Nashat, *Women* (1983), pp. 55–68; Wiebke Walther, *Women in Islam* (Princeton and New York: Markus Wiener, 1993).

8. Erika Friedl, "Women in Contemporary Persian Folktales," in Beck and Keddie, *Women* (1978), pp. 629–50.

9. Suicides by women are estimated by Iranian authorities to be very high in Iran generally, but no figures are available. The topic warrants special investigation, but figures are hard to come by, especially for outside investigators.

10. See Mahnaz Afkhami and Haleh Vaziri, *Claiming Our Rights: A Manual for Women's Human Rights Education in Muslim Societies* (Bethesda, Maryland: Sisterhood is Global Institute, 1996). This popular manual, written by two Muslim scholars, is used for consciousness raising among Muslim women. It is based on the notion that Islam, if "read" and practiced free of androcentric biases, liberates women from oppressive traditional local practices and helps women to gain self-worth and self-confidence.

Further Readings

Afshar, Haleh. *Islam and Feminism.* New York: St. Martin's Press, 1998

Afkhami, Mahnaz, and Erika Friedl, eds. *In the Eye of the Storm. Women in Postrevolutionary Iran.* Syracuse and London: Syracuse University Press and I.B. Tauris, 1994.

Ahmed, Leila. *Women and Gender in Islam.* New Haven: Yale University Press, 1992.

Ait Sabbah, Fatna A. *Woman in the Muslim Unconscious.* New York: Pergamon Press, 1984.

Asayesh, Gelareh. *Saffron Sky: A Life between Iran and America.* Boston: Beacon Press, 1999.

Betteridge, Ann. *Ziärat: Pilgrimage to the Shrines of Shiraz.* Ph.D. dissertation, University of Chicago, 1985.

Friedl, Erika. *Women of Deh Koh.* New York: Penguin, 1991.

———. *Children of Deh Koh.* Syracuse: Syracuse University Press, 1997.

———. "Ideal Womanhood in Postrevolutionary Iran." *Mixed Blessings: Gender and Religious Fundamentalism Cross Culturally,* ed. by Judy Brink and Joan Mencher. New York: Routledge, 1997, pp. 143–57.

———. "Notes from the Village: On the Ethnographic Construction of Women in Iran." *Reconstructing Gender in the Middle East,* ed. by Fatme Muge Gocek and Shiva Balaghi. New York: Columbia University Press, 1994, pp. 85–99.

———. "Sources of Female Power in Iran." *In the Eye of the Storm. Women in Postrevolutionary Iran,* ed. by Mahnaz Afkhami and Erika Friedl. Syracuse and London: Syracuse University Press and I.B. Tauris, 1994, pp. 151–67.

———. "Women in Contemporary Persian Folk Tales." *Women in the Muslim World,* ed. by Lois Beck and Nikkie Keddie. Cambridge, Mass.: Harvard University Press, 1978, pp. 629–650.

Hegland, Mary Elaine. "Political Roles of Iranian Village Women." *MERIP, Middle East Report,* no. 138, vol. 16, no. 1 (January-February 1986): 14–19, 46.

Keddie, Nikki, and Beth Baron, eds., *Women in Middle Eastern History.* New Haven: Yale University Press, 1991.

Tabari, Azar, and Nahid Yeganeh, eds. *In the Shadow of Islam: The Women's Movement in Iran.* London: Zed Press, 1983.

14

No Women's Liberation: The Heritage of a Woman Prophet in Modern Japan

KYOKO MOTOMOCHI NAKAMURA

One striking feature of nineteenth- and twentieth-century Japan has been the emergence of many so-called new religions.[1] Crystallizing around the revelatory experiences of a central prophetic figure, they usually reinterpret and recombine older elements of the Japanese religious heritage. Much research has been done on various aspects of these movements, but little attention has thus far been paid to one of the movements' most remarkable features–namely, the very prominent role of women within them. Women have founded many of the new religions, and, according to Japanese tradition, it is generally expected that the founder's offspring, daughters as well as sons, will inherit the sect's leadership. This pattern might seem to suggest some sort of female dominance in the Japanese new religions.[2] However, the situation is much more complex, and, while it is indeed true that the new movements are often founded by women, the pattern of strong female leadership does not continue once the movements have been established. Nor do the new religions advocate dramatic changes in sex roles or power relationships between women and men.

In this chapter I will discuss the life and teachings of Sayo Kitamura, founder of the

KYOKO MOTOMOCHI NAKAMURA is Professor of History of Religions and currently heads the department of Japanese Culture at Kawamura Gakuen Woman's University in Japan. She holds M.A. degrees from both the University of Chicago (1962) and the University of Tokyo (1964) and has been a teaching assistant at Harvard and a Radcliffe Institute Fellow (1968–1970). She has published books, articles, and translations in Japanese, has authored one book in English, *Miraculous Stories from the Japanese Buddhist Tradition* (Harvard University Press in 1973, reprinted by Curzon Press in 1997), and has also co-authored books and written articles in English.

movement known as Tensho-kotai-jingu-kyo, as well as important problems that her successor faces.[3] I hope to show some of the circumstances that have shaped women founders like Sayo and also some of the reasons why movements like hers revert so swiftly to patterns of male dominance.

SAYO KITAMURA, PROPHET OF TABUSE

Sayo was born on New Year's Day of the year 1900, exactly at the turn of the twentieth century, in the Ekimoto family of the village of Hizumi, in the Yamaguchi prefecture of western Japan. She had six years of education at a local primary school and took three years of lessons in sewing and handicrafts, as was the custom with most country girls of her day.

In 1920 Sayo married Seinoshin Kitamura (1884–1969), who lived with his mother in the village of Tabuse, not far from Sayo's home village. Seinoshin, with ten years' experience as an expatriate laborer in Hawaii, was an obedient son to his mother. The mother was notorious as a harsh taskmaster; she had already turned out five of her son's brides on the grounds that they were not good enough to be her daughter-in-law. In those days a bride had few legal rights; she was at the mercy of her husband and mother-in-law, and, once married, she had to obey them in any situation. Sayo, who was treated like a laborer, farmed many acres of land. She was given neither adequate food nor enough sleep. However, she survived the trial and served her mother-in-law until her death twenty years later. In the meantime Sayo gave birth to her only son, named Yoshito, and became a devoted mother. When her mother-in-law died in 1940, it was not her husband but Sayo who assumed financial responsibility for the family and began to manage the household.

The turning point in Sayo's life came when she experienced a catastrophe. The Kitamuras' barn was destroyed by fire on the night of July 22, 1942. This fire weighed heavily on Sayo's conscience; she viewed it not merely as a loss of personal property but as her personal failure in managing the household. She felt sorry for both the family ancestors and her son, who had been serving in Manchuria as an army veterinarian. She severely accused herself of losing a part of the family fortune during wartime when everything was so scarce and precious, for she had felt responsible for transmitting all the Kitamura household property to her son without any loss.

At that time she became acquainted with an ascetic diviner in a nearby village, who received an oracle that attributed the fire to an arsonist. He urged Sayo to pay a monthly visit to the local Hachiman shrine for a year, but, instead of following his suggestion, Sayo vowed that she would make an ox-hour (2 A.M.) prayer for twenty-one days in succession. Each night she underwent the austerity of cold-water ablutions,[4] rode a bicycle to the shrine to pray, and stopped at the diviner's shrine on her way back. Because she began to feel an indescribable joy in these midnight devotions, she extended her disciplinary practices for thirty more days after the original vow had been fulfilled. Then she extended them again, disciplining herself in this way until the first anniversary of the fire. She had still, however, failed to discover the fire's real cause. After the diviner told her that her prayers had not fully reached God, she observed a continuous vigil for two weeks at the shrine.

From this time on, Sayo had a series of religious experiences that culminated on May 4, 1944, with her first experience of direct revelation. Now a strange One possessed her body and began to speak with her. Because she initially thought that it was an evil spirit, she sought the diviner's help to free herself. But she never succeeded. The possessing spirit first identified itself as "Tobyo" (a snake spirit in Japanese folk belief), then as "Controller of the Mouth," then as "Guardian Deity," and finally as "Tensho-kotai-jingu,"[5] whom she finally identified as the universal God. According to Sayo, Tensho-kotai-jingu had revealed himself through her as the God of the whole universe who demands complete surrender to his will; before her birth he had chosen Sayo as his temporary abode.

Under this influence, Sayo was transformed from a polite, modest, humble woman into a severe, critical, daring person. She began to offend old friends and relatives, as well as strangers, by reproaching them for injustice, dishonesty, and lack of faith. Sayo delivered her first sermon on July 22, 1944, exactly two years after the fire at her home. She declared herself to be the savior and redeemer of humanity and announced that the Kingdom of God was being established here and now. According to her, World War II was God's punishment inflicted on the corrupt Japanese; she condemned her countrymen for their lack of faith and for the corrupt morality that was especially conspicuous during the last stages of the war. Her words indicated that she saw herself as the chief actress in a divine drama whose curtain had already risen.

Tensho-kotai-jingu had descended into her body on November 27, 1944. On the night of August 11, 1945, at the end of the war, after atomic bombs were dropped in Hiroshima and Nagasaki, she experienced her adoption as heir to the Divine Couple of Tensho-kotai-jingu and Amaterasu-omikami, the female divinity of the sun and ancestress and guardian of the Impperial Family, who had already lost the aura as the national guardian of Japan.

Seinoshin Kitamura had been a respectful son to his mother and a rather fastidious husband to his wife. Seventeen years older than his wife, he worked diligently, neither drinking nor smoking. But Sayo excelled him, even in farming or driving a cow. The Kitamuras had traditionally been Shin Buddhists. Every morning Seinoshin recited Shinto prayers in front of a family sanctuary, while Sayo recited the Shin Buddhist formula *Namu-Amida-butsu* ("I take refuge in Amida Buddha") to Amida Buddha and the Kitamura family ancestors. She reported all family affairs to the ancestors, including her own whereabouts. When the fire broke out in the Kitamura barn, she carried the ancestors' tablets outdoors to protect them in case the house, too, should catch fire.

On the morning of May 4, 1944, after Sayo heard the Inner One speak, her family life was dramatically altered. While praying, she was led to her husband's bedside. She kicked away his pillow, saying, "Listen, Seinoshin. Osayo's prayers have reached heaven as a result of her devotional sincerity. . . . How dare you sleep comfortably without praying? Get up and pray!"[6]

The good-hearted husband was greatly shocked at this sudden change in the wife who had served him so obediently all those years. From this time on, Sayo treated her husband as her follower. She addressed him by his first name, "Seinoshin" (which is not customary for a Japanese wife), instead of the more familiar "Daddy" that she had used for many years. However, although she no longer seemed to be a wife to her husband, she never abandoned her maternal love for their only son. She explained this apparent contradiction by saying that, when her son returned home from Manchuria, God had told her to say, "I have no parents nor any family ties," but he never asked her to say, "I have no son."[7]

Sayo herself had a great deal to say about appropriate family roles, both in her teaching and by the example of her life. Answering a question about the essence of her teaching, she once said, "Practical application of my teaching in your daily life is the way of advancing along the road to heaven. Home and society are the places where you should put my teaching into practice."[8] In other words, people come closer to God by fulfilling traditional human roles. The founder herself had tried her best to be a trustworthy wife and daughter-in-law, an affectionate mother, and later a mother-in-law and grandmother. At the same time, Sayo considered herself to be a prophet in the line of Sakyamuni Buddha and Jesus Christ. However, Sakyamuni and Jesus had left their families to fulfill their missions, while Sayo continued as head of the Kitamura family–a difference that was important to her whole message. Furthermore, since she refused to accept any remuneration for her teaching, she had to make a living by farming. She thus combined the roles of prophet and matriarch in her daily life. In the beginning this fact confused her family not a little, particularly her son, Yoshito, who had joined her followers and helped her manage the organization.

Sayo once prophesied that her teachings would be transmitted without much distortion as long as her son and grandchildren lived with cherished memories of her. Just as she believed that the home was the place where her teachings must be applied first, so, with this remark, she identified her own descendants as the best-qualified transmitters of her teachings.

As was the case with all of Sayo's words and actions, the choice of Sayo's successor was dictated by God. When her son's first child was about to be born, God told her that it would be a boyish girl or a girlish boy. They must name it Kiyokazu ("Pure and Peaceful"), which in Japan would ordinarily be a boy's name. Thus the baby was destined to become her successor before its birth. As the child's birth was being celebrated, Sayo publicly proclaimed that the little girl Kiyokazu would be her spiritual heir. She also asked for her congregation's help: "I shall raise this child myself, and it is God's will that she be my successor. I shall appreciate it very much if you, comrades, will help me bring her up properly. Please bear it in mind that she must not be spoiled, because she is to be my successor." Reportedly, the whole congregation was struck with a sense of joy and responsibility for the child. After the baby was forty-seven days old, Sayo began taking Kiyokazu with her to the prayer hall three times a day. When the child began to toddle, the founder would make her perform an "ego-free" dance in the hall following the afternoon prayer ("ego-free" dances will be discussed later in this chapter). Sayo took her granddaughter wherever she went, so that she could use every opportunity to prepare the child for her divine mission.

In a sermon on Kiyokazu's seventh birthday, Sayo said that she had trained her daughter-in-law and her granddaughter harder than anyone else, for the former was to be mother to the latter, who was to be God's instrument. Sayo contended that children of God are needed to establish the Kingdom of God and that worthy parents are needed to raise such children. Accordingly, she taught that the mother's responsibility is heavier than the father's, for the mother's influence on children is often stronger than the father's. The founder impressed not only her daughter-in-law and Kiyokazu but also her other grandchildren with her strict and yet loving discipline.

As the child matured, Sayo continued to supervise her training, even sending Kiyokazu for four years of study in England and the United States.[9] When Sayo felt that her last days were approaching, she also sent her son and daughter-in-law on a world tour to visit the foreign branches she had founded, in order to deepen mutual understanding. In this way the transition from the founder to her successor would not be a sudden change but an anticipated procedure in which Sayo's followers had participated. However, no matter how carefully Sayo had prepared for the change, the loss of her charisma was to be deeply felt. After becoming Sayo's successor, Kiyokazu has courageously led the movement herself, supported by her father, who manages the organization with its many spiritual, economic, political, administrative, and artistic functions. The two have so far tried to keep the founder's spirit alive in their community. Even younger members who have joined the movement after the founder's death are familiar with Sayo's taped sermons, played daily during prayer meetings at the headquarters and branches. Sayo's biography and teachings have also been edited and printed for circulation.

However, in spite of her successor's efforts and her faithful followers, the movement is confronted with the problem of trying to convert people without recourse to Sayo's striking psychic powers. Sayo herself placed little emphasis on healing or on the promise of worldly benefits; she stressed primarily the need for spiritual revolution to realize the Kingdom of God. But her followers' accounts of their conversion experiences reveal other sources of attraction, such as awe at her prophetic powers and experiences of healing as a result of her ardent prayers. Theoretically, her followers, too, can attain such powers through praying. But her powers seem to have had a different quality, for she was God's heir.

DOCTRINAL TEACHINGS OF SAYO'S MOVEMENT

Sayo insisted on the imminent need to establish the Kingdom of God on earth, a spiritual community of the faithful. By establishing such a Kingdom of God on earth, people would become free of all evil and would be able to achieve world peace through individual purification. Only those who were converted and lived a God-centered life might join the community as comrades. Those who did not were called "beggars" and "maggots," strong pejoratives that Sayo liked to use.

Several themes predominate in Sayo's sermons on the nature of the Kingdom of God and the means for establishing it on earth. One of the more important seems to be a new interpretation of traditional Japanese beliefs and rituals regarding the souls of the dead. In Japanese folk belief the souls of the dead are transformed into benevolent ancestral spirits through a series of rites–funeral and memorial services–mostly performed by Buddhist priests and bereaved families.[10] According to Sayo, today's world is afflicted with untransformed spirits who instigate quarrels among individuals, cause nations to war, inflict sickness on people, and arouse anxieties. By praying, she and her followers sought to redeem these destructive spirits. In effect, she taught an internalization of traditional practice. She rejected all the old rites as degenerate and ineffective, because she felt that both Buddhist and Shinto priests were incapable of communicating with the psychic world. Instead, she insisted that faith in God, prayer to God, and a God-centered everyday life were the only means of gaining the power to communicate with the psychic world and thus to redeem the malevolent spirits of the dead.[11]

However, prayer to God and a God-centered life had, in Sayo's teachings, a far broader purpose than the transformation of the dead, for they were also seen as instruments of self-transformation. Like the Buddhist tradition from which she often drew, Sayo consistently emphasized the importance of overcoming egotism. The achievement of such a state was the reason for the ecstatic "ego-free" dancing revealed to Sayo through a vision, which had initially led mass media to label her movement "The Dancing Religion." As another avenue to the conquest of egotism, she enjoined her followers to "polish their souls." This central disciplinary practice combined resolute will, sincere prayer, constant self-reflection, and confession. Sayo stressed that her followers' loud and energetic prayers required faith, for without faith such prayers were just egotistic supplications. And, Sayo insisted, resolute prayer based on faith would bring the followers–as it had brought herself–to union with God.

At first glance, Sayo's movement appears to be new and unique among Japanese religions for its radical theocentrism and its rejection of all other beliefs and practices. On February 5, 1946, the first day of Sayo's new "Age of God," the founder burned Buddhist *sutras,* religious amulets, and the Kitamura family's ancestral records to symbolize her break with the past and its corruption. She ordered her followers to throw away their ancestors' tablets, to break off with the Buddhist temples whose cemeteries held their family tombs, and to refuse to join Shinto rites. It is not hard to imagine how much this iconoclastic action disturbed the local Buddhist monks and Shinto priests. As a consequence, Sayo's followers had a hard time living in local communities, where close human relationships governed all spheres of social and economic life.

Despite their emphasis on radical change, Sayo's teachings also preserve much traditional content. First of all, both her understanding of history and her own historical role are based on traditional Japanese ideas, especially the concept that time passes in repetitive cycles, returning again to the same point. A cycle of world history consists of four world ages; the present cycle (as well as the first age) began when the mythological first emperor of Japan, Jimmu, was enthroned. The age begun by Jimmu, which she called the "Age of Man," lasted for 2,605 years, until 1945, when World War II ended. We are now in the second age, the Age of God, or the Age of the Sun, which began on New Year's Day in 1946 and, Sayo has predicted, will last for 2,300 years. At the end of the Age of God there will be an Age of the Moon, which is to last for 1,999 years; then will come the Age of the Stars, which will last for another 1,526 years. The cycle ends in a phase that she called the "Waters." Each age is ushered in by the descent of God's heir–either male, as in the case of the Emperor Jimmu, or female, as in the case of Sayo–and ends in destruction and calamity. Just as Sayo was adopted by God to establish his Kingdom and save the nation, so, when the Age of God ends, she will be reborn as a fisherman's daughter to save the nation again.

As one can see from the preceding summary, much of Sayo's teaching was grounded in traditional and familiar Japanese Shinto mythology, and her view of history did not go beyond Japan and the Japanese nation. Also, she dwelt frequently on the well-known theme of the golden age of the Kami that starts at the beginning of Japanese mythical history. Apparently she identified the Age of God she was proclaiming with that first golden age.

Even the striking theocentrism and universalism of her teachings are more similar to traditional Japanese ideas than they at first seem to be. This can be seen quite clearly in the following literal translation of her most significant prayer.

> Tensho-kotai-jingu and eight million kami,
> May there be peace in the whole world.
> When all the nation complies with God's will,
> Give us a Heavenly Kingdom which is pleasant to live in.
> May the six functional elements in my soul be purified.
> The six functional elements in my soul are now purified;
> Since the six functional elements have been purified,
> It cannot be that this prayer will not be fulfilled.

This is my own translation, which differs from the English version authorized for use by the branches of her movement in the West. The authorized version begins with the line "Almighty God of the Universe and host of angels. . ." In this authorized translation we are impressed by Sayo's cosmopolitanism–an inclusive emphasis on which the founder herself insisted. However, in the Japanese original, both the opening phrase and Sayo's use of the term "nation" (*kokumin*) also communicate some nationalistic Shinto overtones. According to her successor's interpretation of Sayo's teachings, Japanese myths have nothing to do with modern nationalism; they are simply the ancestors' gift to the people.

But Sayo herself preserved a kind of balance between universalism and nationalism. She once asserted that the Japanese national polity (*kokutai*)[12] had never been changed after the end of the war. She interpreted this polity as a trinitarian unity of the Japanese land, the deity Tensho-kotai-jingu, and the emperor, who watches the country. The deity Tensho-kotai-jingu had revealed himself through her, Sayo, as the Universal God; she also calls him "Heavenly Father," a title rather unfamiliar to the Japanese religious tradition. But concepts of this same deity are imbedded in traditional Japanese mythology. He was revealed to Sayo as consort to Amaterasu, the Sun Goddess and ancestress of the imperial family as well as the Japanese nation. Furthermore, in Sayo's teachings the universal God was not really viewed as fully transcendent; instead, Sayo perpetuated the traditional Japanese view of an immanent and personified God, thus retaining striking continuity with traditional Japanese mythology.

WOMANHOOD IN SAYO'S EXPERIENCE AND TEACHINGS

Different facets of Sayo's experiences and actions show different responses to her own femininity. When the goddess Amaterasu descended into Sayo's body to join her consort Tensho-kotai-jingu, the "Inner One," the two united as one God, making Sayo's body a temple for both male and female divinity. Thus, in a sense, she transcended her old female human nature and became androgynous. Sometimes she seemed to cultivate and emphasize deliberately a new, more "masculine" style, in contradiction to Japanese norms of "feminine" virtue. For example, Sayo sometimes sat cross-legged, a position few Japanese women dare to assume but that men often take when relaxed. After reversing her relationship with her husband in the pillow-kicking incident described earlier, Sayo began to wear masculine clothing, and a black pantsuit became her standard uniform several years later. Her speech and behavior became more aggressive. She started to call people "maggots" and "beggars," two strong epithets that not even men dared to utter; and she shocked her audiences with her fiery speeches, in a country where men and women ordinarily speak quite differently and where women are expected to avoid impolite expressions.

At the same time, some of Sayo's statements and experiences show that her femininity remained part of her consciousness both during and after her transformative experiences. Between the descent of Tensho-kotai-jingu, her "Inner One," and the later descent of Amaterasu, Sayo underwent a rapid process of spiritual rebirth and maturation. This process was accompanied by physical symptoms. One was diarrhea, which, it was said, God inflicted on her to cleanse her dirty human stomach when she was about to become God's baby. Within about a month she developed into an "angel" with the mannerisms of a seventeen-year-old girl, and then into a young woman of twenty-five. God told her to sew a snow-white dress and to prepare a set of white bedding. When these were ready, she was told to wear the dress and to use the bedding to sleep before the altar on the night of August 11. On this night, by her own account, the Divine Couple adopted her as their only daughter and heir. In this respect, she continued to think of herself as a woman. It is interesting to note that, on her deathbed, she said that she was going to wed soon.

Sayo's advice to her women followers also reveals some ambiguity toward womanhood. It is clear that Sayo held high expectations for women. She taught that women who, like herself, have known many trials are very close to the Kingdom of God. In the coming Age of God, women would play a role more significant than the role they had played in the preceding era. This, she said, is a man-centered age in which power rules the world, while the coming age will be a wholesome one in which women will march in the vanguard on the road to the Kingdom of God. Her teachings to women, based as they were upon her own experiences, were realistic and substantial and contained detailed individual instructions; they also seem more strict than her teachings to men, for women must "polish their souls" more than men to meet the future's challenge.

Sayo taught all her followers, including the women, to speak frankly and directly like herself. When her followers put this teaching into practice, they ran into not a little trouble, as had Sayo herself. Her women followers especially had problems, since, traditionally, they had not been allowed to express themselves freely or to talk back to elders, husbands, or men in general. Their new boldness often seriously upset domestic harmony. However, Sayo tempered the impact of this new freedom by stressing the importance of traditional family responsibilities as *gyo*, disciplinary exercise. Thus she also taught her female followers to obey their husbands and elders, even if the women were right nine times out of ten. Emphasizing the different roles of the sexes, she used to say, "A husband has his own duty, a woman has her own, and parents have their own. After you perform your own duty, then you can demand your rights."[13]

The extent to which Sayo perpetuated conventional ideas about women's role can readily be seen throughout her references to women. In her teachings, women are never separated from the family; they remain dependent upon, and subordinate to, the family's traditional masters–father, husband, parents-in-law, and other male relatives; their role is to help men by carrying out miscellaneous tasks with divinely sanctioned motherly devotion. Sayo listed the human desire to love and be loved among the "six functional elements of the soul" that she challenged her followers to purify, and she taught that egocentric love should be abandoned. Maternal love, which traditionally has been valued in Japan, was highly valued also by Sayo because in her view it is the least egoistic love of all. Furthermore, maternal love was considered essential to the prosperity of the household and family line, which Sayo saw as important.

Thus, on the whole, Sayo's teachings about women follow the traditional, rather than the innovative, side of her message. It would be misleading to call Sayo a feminist. It is true that she taught women to speak out, and perhaps it is also true that she brought them a new sense of importance and mission. But she did not challenge the old patterns of authority that had been so oppressive for women like herself. Nor did she address herself at all to the new situation of women in a changing postwar society in which women's activities are no longer limited to the household.

CONCLUSIONS: FEMALE LEADERSHIP AND WOMEN'S LIBERATION

Like Sayo, several women have been important leaders in many new religious movements in Japan. They are regarded as human deities, or they act as mediums who deliver a divine message. Some work alone in the beginning, as Sayo did in her movement's earliest days. If the organization is small, and hence easy to manage, women may continue as sole leaders for a much longer time. More often they come to be assisted by some man, who is sometimes a husband, a son, or other relative, or just a spiritual friend, such as a teacher, a disciple, or other comrade. Many new movements have been jointly founded by a male and a female, with the woman serving as source of revelatory experiences.

Generally speaking, most women founders undergo their first transforming experiences in their later years. Thus they have experienced the whole life cycle of a woman, having lived as a girl, a wife, a mother, and sometimes a divorcee or widow. To put it another way, women begin to preach after they have raised their children or have parted with their husbands either physically or spiritually. By this time they are their own masters, free from family bondages. Because lay leadership has always been a prominent feature of the Japanese religious tradition, women rarely leave their families, who eventually come to assist them. Thus they also become the real heads of their families, even if their husbands are still alive. For female leaders the new position is a powerful personal liberation, won after the numerous hardships that result from living in a society in which women tend to be dependent on, and subordinate to, men and are traditionally discriminated against.

Many women founders have proved that women can be amazingly strong as charismatic religious leaders. They fight fiercely against the establishment, in which they have had no place from the beginning. They attack the government and willingly go to prison; having little to lose, they endure hardships without flinching. At the same time, they are able to guide their followers with down-to-earth individual advice from the accumulated wisdom, revelatory or otherwise, that they have accquired during a life full of hardships and trials. We must admit, however, that they tend to be poor in systematic thinking and self-expression.

Despite the founders' personal strength, the new traditions have thus far failed to realize their potential for women. Why? Four important problems, most of which are exemplified in Sayo's movement, seem to provide the answer.

The first two are byproducts of the standard mode of succession within the movements. In Japan callings and professions of all kinds, including religious ones, have traditionally been handed down through family lines. Thus it is natural for a woman founder like Sayo to name a family member as her successor–and also natural that the successor's family will continue to lead the organization. The successor may or may not be another woman. But even if a woman is chosen and trained very carefully, it is very unlikely that she can duplicate her predecessor's achievements, for the life experiences of the founder are very different from those of her successor. Nine times out of ten, the women founders have lived dramatic lives of material as well as spiritual oppression; their own sufferings allow them to attain a most penetrating insight into the sufferings of others. Can the disciplined education of a successor substitute for such hard realities and the psychic powers achieved through them? Doubtless the successor, like Kiyokazu, will faithfully follow her predecessor's path. But it may be extremely difficult for her to have genuine revelatory experiences without having experienced the human boundary situation. Thus the pattern of strong female leadership is sporadic and is generally limited to the founder's own lifetime.

In addition, the young woman successor faces the problem of marriage. She must marry and bear children to secure the line of succession and the transmission of leadership. But how can she serve God and be a wife at the same time? In Japan, where the tradition of lay leadership is prevalent–and the leader is, therefore, likely to be married–this conflict in roles is never a problem for male religious leaders, but it is often a problem for female leaders. Ideally, of course, a woman leader's husband should be her follower, content with a supporting role. Such a man is hard to find in the male-dominated Japanese society. The most common compromise is a husband with managerial talents or theological training, who then himself assumes a major role in running the organization. Thus the husband may come to overshadow the wife up to the point that she becomes a mere figurehead. In Kiyokazu's case, this problem has not yet been encountered. At the time of this writing, she is still single–a condition that causes her family not a little worry. It seems that she has not received a proposal from a suitable man.

The ease with which the husbands of religious leaders rise to power points to another important reason why women's initial prominence is often blunted or lost. As an organization expands, the founder or her heir can no longer manage it alone. She needs expert assistants–administrative, financial, theological, and secretarial. Because most Japanese women have less education and less training for public activity than men, more men than women move into key positions on the full-time staff as the movement grows. They build magnificent buildings, introduce high levels of efficiency, and give the founder's teachings much-needed systematization; but they often dilute the movement's initial radicalism and tend to make concessions to the prevailing social norms.

But perhaps the most serious obstacle to sustained female leadership is the new movements' own inherent conservatism. Most new movements are still based on traditional world views and are concerned with preserving the traditional family as an essential condition for maintaining society. Hence women's maternal function and family responsibilities are still considered of paramount importance, while their role in society as individual human beings is not. Historically, Japanese religions have offered only pacifiers to the frustrated women who have been boxed in by traditional family structures; this remains true, unfortunately, of the new religions as well. Furthermore, these religions' repeated sermons on the essential differences between the sexes and their respective roles have by now become too static for a society in transition. Looking back on her long, strenuous life, a woman leader like Sayo is likely to say that women who aspire to paradise should follow the model provided by the leader's own early life. But the society out of which such leaders have come is itself changing, and the traditional ideal of service to family is no longer adequate to meet women's changing roles and needs. This is why no constructive contribution to women's liberation has yet been made by the new movements in Japan, despite the fact that women members usually outnumber the men, and women's missionary zeal has most often been responsible for the movements' success.

Notes

1. A comprehensive bibliography of Western-language materials on the new religions is found in H. Byron Earhart, *The New Religions of Japan* (Tokyo: Sophia University, 1970).

2. See Ichiro Hori, *Folk Religion in Japan* (Chicago and London: University of Chicago Press, 1968); Garmen Blacker, *The Catalpa Bow* (London: George Allen & Unwin, 1975).

3. For her life, see *The Prophet of Tabuse* (Tabuse: Tensho-kotai-jingu-kyo, 1954), an abridged English-language version of the still incomplete *Seisho* (vol. 1, 1951; vol. 2, 1967, vols. 3–6, forthcoming).

4. She got up about 1:30 A.M. and went out to the well in the yard to pour pails of cold water on herself there in the open before getting dressed for a visit to the shrine.

5. "Tensho" is another name for Amaterasu, the mythical ancestress of the Japanese imperial family, and "Kotai-jingu" is the inner sanctuary of the Ise Shrine where Amaterasu is enshrined. One tradition says that Amaterasu is a priestess in service of God and that Sayo made her consort to the universal deity (many deities are coupled in Japanese mythology).

6. *The Prophet of Tabuse,* pp. 30–31. "Osayo" is a politer form of "Sayo" with an honorific "o."

7. *The Prophet of Tabuse,* p. 71.

8. Sayo Kitamura, "Tensho Kotai Jingu-kyo" (The Dancing Religion), *Contemporary Religions in Japan,* 2, no. 3 (September 1961): p. 37.

9. Kiyokazu studied at Pitzer College, California from 1969 to 1971 and at Vassar College, New York in 1971–1972. Then she went to England for further education as well as to establish the London Branch.

10. See William H. Newell, ed., *Ancestors* (The Hague: Mouton, 1976); Robert J. Smith, *Ancestor Worship in Contemporary Japan* (Stanford, Calif.: Stanford University Press, 1974).

11. It is probably unwise to use Western analogies in trying to understand what Sayo meant by "praying to redeem the dead." She apparently did not pray *to* them, or seek to assuage them, although sometimes she spoke of "converting" them. Nor did she intercede for them with the God who possessed her. Her prayers were viewed as a vehicle of spiritual power which worked directly to effect a transformation.

12. "National polity" was a favorite term of the nationalists before and during World War II and was explicated by State Shinto scholars. For its detailed discussion see D. C. Holtom, *Modern Japan and Shinto Nationalism* (Chicago: University of Chicago Press, 1943); David Magarey Earl, *Emperor and Nation in Japan: Political Thinkers of the Tokugawa Period* (Seattle: University of Washington Press, 1964), Appendix D: Kokutai.

13. *Ogamisama Says . . .* (Tabuse: Tensho-kotai-jingu-kyo, 1963), p. 29.

Further Readings

Davis, Winston. *Dojo; Magic and Exorcism in Modern Japan.* Stanford, Calif.: Stanford University Press, 1980. See especially chapter titled "Women and their Sexual Karma," pp. 161–200.

Hardacre, Helen. *Kurozumikyo and the New Religions of Japan.* Princeton, NJ.: Princeton University Press, 1986.

———. *Lay Buddhism in Contemporary Japan: Reiyukai Kyodan.* Princeton, N.J.: Princeton University Press, 1984.

———. "The Shaman and Her Transformations. The Construction of Gender in Motifs of Religious Action." Wakita, Bouchy, and Ueno, eds., *Gender and Japanese History,* Vol. 1 (Osaka University Press, 1999), pp. 87–120.

Kawamura, Kunimitsu, "Deities and the Female Shaman: Gender and the Careers of Possessing Spirits." Wakita, Bouchy, and Ueno, eds., *Gender and Japanese History,* Vol. 1 (Osaka University Press, 1999), pp. 121–44.

Lebra, Takie Sugiyama. *Japanese Women: Constraint and Fulfillment.* Honolulu: University of Hawaii Press, 1984.

———. "Self-Reconstruction in Japanese Religious Psychotherapy." *Cultural Conceptions of Mental Health and Therapy,* ed. by Anthony J. Marsella and Geoffrey M. White. The Hague: D. Reidel, 1982, pp. 269–83.

Nakamura, Kyoko. "Women and Religion in Japan: Introductory Remarks." *Japanese Journal of Religious Studies;* special number on Women and Religion, X, nos. 2–3 (1983): pp. 115–21.

———. "Religious Consciousness and Practices of Contemporary Japanese Women." Wakita, Bouchy, and Ueno, eds., *Gender and Japanese History,* Vol. 1 (Osaka University Press, 1999), pp. 145–84.

———. "Revelatory Experiences in the Female Life Cycle: A Bibliographical Study of Women Religionists in Japan." *Japanese Journal of Religious Studies,* VIII, nos. 3–4 (September–December 1981): pp. 187–206.

15

Alinesitoué: A Diola Woman Prophet in West Africa

ROBERT M. BAUM

When I first started traveling to Senegal, in 1973, Alinesitoué Diatta was remembered in Diola communities of southern Senegal, the Gambia, and Guinea-Bissau as a powerful prophet of the supreme being, Emitai. During the difficult years of the Second World War, she had introduced a series of important new rituals and teachings into Diola traditional (*awasena*) religion. In January of 1943, the Vichy French seized Alinesitoué and exiled her to the French Soudan. Her ultimate fate remained a secret. Even her family did not know what had happened to her. In 1978, Teté Diadhiou, the interpreter who guided the French to her home and subsequent arrest, told me that he had met with the French officials who arrested and tried her and that they had all taken a vow of silence about what had happened. He told me that it would take an order of the Supreme Court of Senegal for him to be able to reveal what had ultimately happened to Alinesitoué.[1]

Since 1987, when a Senegalese government commission determined that Alinesitoué had died of starvation in 1944 while in a detention camp, considerable discussion has

---

ROBERT M. BAUM received his PH.D. in History from Yale University in 1986, after living in southern Senegal for approximately three years. A former Resident Fellow at the W.E.B. Du Bios Institute for Afro-American Studies at Harvard University, he is currently an associate professor of Religious Studies at Iowa State University. His major research interests are in the history of West African religions, religious responses to imperialism, and the religious constructions of genders.

Author's Note: This article is excerpted from a longer work on the history of Diola prophetism, a work in progress, tentatively entitled *Messengers of God: Alinesitoué and the History of a Diola Prophetic Tradition in West Africa.*

occurred in Senegal about Alinesitoué as a prophet, martyr, and nationalist figure. Senegalese television documentaries and plays have portrayed her life and the Casamance secessionist movement has claimed her as its Joan of Arc. While memories of Alinesitoué are firmly planted in the public discourse of Senegal, a variety of groups contest her legacy, calling her the inspiration for whatever political program or social agenda they wish to advance. The vast majority of Diola venerate her as one whom "Emitai commissioned" (*Emitai dabognol*), that is, as one who introduced a new series of shrines and new religious teachings based on revelations from Emitia, the Diola supreme being.

Alinesitoué was born around 1920 in the township of Kabrousse, a Diola community of approximately 2,000 people on the Atlantic coast of West Africa, just north of the border between Senegal and the Portuguese colony of Guinea. The Diola communities of the region supported themselves by farming rice, fishing, and herding cattle. Anthropologists have described them as the best wet rice farmers in West Africa. Before colonization, Diola political systems were usually described as "stateless": political authority was vested in local councils of elders rather than in political specialists, and both men and women participated in local decision making.[2] Men controlled powerful spirit shrines (*ukine*) associated with iron-working, rain, and male circumcision, while women controlled shrines associated with women's fertility and the fertility of the land. While Alinesitoué's birthplace Kabrousse had intermittent contact with European traders before the twentieth century, Christian missionary work in the area did not begin until the 1880s. Contact with Islam before colonization come only through occasional visiting traders.

Although Alinesitoué was neither the first nor the last person to claim direct revelation from the supreme being within Diola traditional religion, she has been the most influential. Before the colonial conquest eleven men claimed such revelations from Emitai.[3] Since the colonial conquest, there have been more than forty others, most of whom have been women. Before the 1980s, Alinesitoué alone was able to inspire religious movements throughout Diola areas of Senegambia; those who came before her and most who came after had only local followings. Such traditions of prophetic revelation, involving over fifty different individuals, are extremely rare within African religious history. Not surprisingly, the Diola also include the largest number of people retaining allegiance to their traditional religion within the Senegambia region.

Little is known of Alinesitoué's childhood, except that she grew up at a time when the French were determined to establish their authority in the southern portion of Senegal. The French created a system of canton and village chiefs, all of whom were men, to serve as local agents of French colonial rule. Benjamin Diatta, one of Alinesitoué's cousins and an early convert to Christianity, was appointed as the head of the canton chiefs in an area known as the Subdivision of Oussouye. This Diola area was the one least affected by Islam or Christianity.

Alinesitoué Diatta was one of the first women from her township of Kabrousse to make the long and arduous journey to Dakar, the capital of French West Africa. She had gone there to find work as a maid. Shortly after her arrival she suffered a serious illness that temporarily paralyzed her. Her recovery from this disease, probably polio, was later regarded by many Diola as a sign of Emitai's goodwill toward her.[4] The event that transformed her life occurred early in 1941, after she had recovered and returned to work. While walking through the Sandaga market in the heart of Dakar, Alinesitoué received a vision of Emitai amidst the crowds of buyers and sellers. Compelled by her vision, Alinesitoué left the market and walked down to the sea. There, "she dug a hole in the sand and water entered the bottom. Thus, the object of her mission was revealed to her, to obtain rain."[5] She was told she would receive a spirit shrine that would help the Diola get rain, hence ending the drought that had plagued southern Senegal for several years. She was also told that "Emitai had sent her work"; she was to teach people to perform the "charity" of *Kasila.*[6]

The intensity of her vision and the enormity of her task frightened the young woman into inactivity. Again she received visions commanding her to start teaching. She finally accepted the task because she feared that Emitai would kill her if she continued to refuse.[7] Despite such threats, however, she did not tell people of her visions, even after she returned to her home community of Kabrousse. Her continued ecstatic experiences there convinced her family that she was deeply troubled, perhaps even insane. One of her maternal kin, Goolai Diatta, claimed that before she began preaching: "If you saw her you would say she was crazy. . . if you let her go, she would flee."[8] During one of her visions, Alinesitoué went to a spring near the ocean. There she took some palm leaves, some white sand, and a large conch shell, and made a place for prayer. She prayed to Emitai and it began to rain.[9]

Early in 1942, Alinesitoué summoned the elders of her quarter of Kabrousse and revealed the cause of her strange behavior; Emitai had visited her and had ordered her to teach of the "charity" of *Kasila.*[10] She told them that Emitai had shown her the spirit shrine of *Kasila* and that Emitai continued to speak to her directly through dreams and visions and, indirectly, through her personal spirit shrine of *Houssahara.* She told the elders about the nature of her dreams and visions and began to instruct them as she had been ordered. She taught them how to perform the rituals of *Kasila* and the "charity" associated with it, the sacrifice of a black bull. She also said they should revive the southern Diola's market and religious day, *Huyaye,* a Diola sabbath held every sixth day. Renewing this sabbath and instituting the practice of the "charity" of *Kasila* would end the severe drought, she told the elders.

Her visions explained that the drought had been caused by her community's neglect of charity and by pollution of the rice paddies caused by working on the day dedicated to the major rain priest, the *oeyi,* or priest-king. However, they also went beyond this, demanding renewed commitment to community, stripping away social and religious hierarchies, and reaffirming many customs that had fallen into disuse. Alinesitoué taught of Emitai's role in the world, reaffirming Emitai's involvement with the Diola and Its insistence on the fulfillment of community obligations. She also rejected the French claim of sovereignty by insisting that the people must first fulfill their duties as Diola before undertaking any other tasks.

Through her visions and dreams, Alinesitoué received two spirit shrines, called *Houssahara* and *Kasila.* Her command of the shrine of *Houssahara* depended on two spiritual gifts: an ability to "see" the *ammahl,* a spirit associated with water, and to communicate with it. This ability depended on innate faculties or spiritual election. However, people could observe her while she communicated with *Houssahara.* Goolai Diatta has described her method of ritual supplication at the shrine. The shrine consisted of some pots, three cups, a conch shell, a knife, and a spear. When asking for rain, Alinesitoué would draw a circle on the ground and place the knife between two of the pots. Twice she would pour libations of fresh water on the ground. Then she turned one of the pots upside down, drank some of the water, and turned the three cups face side up. Then she took the spear and began to twirl it in her hand. She took the knife and the shell in her left hand. Then she performed the libations for a third time and plunged the knife into the ground. Finally, she made a motion toward Emitai and rain began to fall. As it rained, she placed her spear on the pots, took the knife, and sacrificed a chicken whose blood she poured in the same place where the water libations were made.[11] People who knew her have claimed that she could also bring rain without recourse to *Houssahara,* depending only on the assistance of *Emitai.* Some people have claimed that she could cause rain to fall in one area and to pass over another section of paddy land.[12]

While her powers to receive visions and to "see" spirits at *Houssahara* were not something she could teach others, Alinesitoué did teach the rites associated with the charity of *Kasila* to the people of Kabrousse and to others who heard about her work. She told them "If you kill cattle, Emitai will send rain. *Husila* (*Kasila*) is of Emitai. Emitai created it.[13] Alinesitoué provided detailed instructions about the prayers, sacrifices, and communal meals that were central to the ritual. Only black bulls could be sacrificed, because they were linked to the black clouds that carried rain. The cattle had to be killed in such a way that all their blood flowed into holes at the base of shrine.[14] Citing one of his informants, Jean Girard has described the creation of a *Kasila* shrine: "Above the steer's hole will be planted two stakes: one made of lath of the fan palm tree, thick and short. . . the fan palm is the symbol of power. The other stake will be a long stick carved from the wood of that tree that grows in the river and the rice paddies and that one calls *emank* in Diola. One chooses this type because it is always filled with water."[15] Every neighborhood (subquarter) of every township had to sacrifice a black bull to create the shrine and then had to share the meat of the sacrifice for six days and nights in communal meals taken in a public area by the shrine. No one was to eat in their own homes. "People ate at the site of the shrine and there was no work for six days."[16]

In sharp contrast to most Diola rituals, at *Kasila* no distinction was made between elders and children, or men and women; all had to be present for the ritual and for the communal feasts that followed. The priest of *Kasila* was chosen by divination: a chicken had its head cut off and it ran around until it dropped dead in front of the new priest.[17] Once again, no distinctions of age or gender were drawn. Anyone could become the priest of *Kasila,* wielder of the community charity to bring rain, the basis of all well-being.

Alinesitoué also told people that in order to ensure a bountiful harvest, they must continue to grow the various Diola varieties of rice and not just the Asiatic varieties (*oryza sativa*) introduced by the French. The new varieties offered higher yields, but were more susceptible to drought and the depredations of insects and birds. However, despite administrative claims to the contrary, Alinesitoué did not prohibit the planting of the new varieties. She merely insisted that the Diola varieties (*oryza giaberrima*) continue to be planted and used in the rites of *Kasila.* She prohibited foreign rice only for ritual use.[18] This prohibition was part of a broader ban on the use of all products of foreign origin at the shrine of *Kasila* and at a few other shrines. In the *Kasila* ritual, Diola rice had to be used in the making of rice cakes, and honey had to be used to flavor these, rather than sugar, which was considered foreign. Foreign rice and sugar could be used on a daily basis, but not in ritual supplications for rain.[19]

Alinesitoué did prohibit growing peanuts, a cash crop that the French had introduced. The southern Diola had shown little desire to grow peanuts, but under Vichy rule government agricultural officials forced local farmers to accept a sack of peanuts and to repay it with two sacks the following year. Some people ate the peanuts and fulfilled their obligation by buying other peanuts with palm wine. Peanut cultivation required clearing away large areas of forest and diverted men's labor from their work in the rice paddies, leaving women with the full responsibility for cultivating rice, the staple crop. Alinesitoué was well aware of diminishing attention given to rice cultivation in Muslim Diola areas to the north, where peanuts were grown and where women's workloads in agriculture were increasing dramatically. Peanuts were a disruptive crop; their value in hard currency lured men into abandoning rice cultivation and overloading wives and daughters with total responsibility for growing the food that people ate daily.[20]

News of Alinesitoué's prophetic powers and of her new spirit shrines that could ensure adequate rainfall spread quickly throughout the Casamance, the Gambia, and Portuguese Guinea. Teachings about the drought's cause and the way to end it could not have been voiced at a better time. The harvest of 1941–1942 had been the worst since the drought began. So little rain fell that the cattle had to be given water from the wells; the usual grazing areas had all gone dry.[21] Pilgrims from neighboring Diola communities, Muslim Diola from the north, even non-Diola from Senegal and neighboring countries came to hear Alinesitoué's teachings and to take back with them the knowledge of *Kasila.*[22] Delegations from each neighborhood of each township came to see her, including men and women of all age. Each delegation brought gifts of small baskets of rice and fruit.[23] Alinesitoué greeted the delegations, assigned them a place to stay, and provided them with food. Then they met with her formally and presented their needs. Alinesitoué took the chicken and palm wine that each delegation brought and performed a ritual with these at the shrine of *Houssahara.* Then she told her visitors that "the rains will come to your village and they [the rains] would come."[24] Her prayers on behalf of the visiting groups were followed by performances of *nyakul,* the men's funeral dance, and of *djigum,* a social dance of men and women that is also used in women's fertility and healing rituals.[25] Then she performed a second ritual in which she directly invoked the power of Emitai. After rituals and feasting were completed, the delegations remained for a few days of instruction concerning her teachings and performance of the rituals.

As delegations returned to their homes, they carried with them news of Alinesitoué's teachings. They also carried a cow's horn filled with soil from Alinesitoué's shrine, which they used to create a *Kasila* shrine in their home villages. In the meeting place of each neighborhood, they killed a black bull according to Alinesitoué's instructions. The entire community watched the sacrifice and the shrine's creation. Then they ate together beside the shrine for six days: "When they do *Kasila,* the meat must not enter a house." After the rite and communal meal, the neighborhood performed the funeral dance and sang songs composed by Alinesitoué, such as the following.[26]

> *Kasila* ho!
> Ata-Emit ho! [Emitai]
> We are tired.
> Emitai will send rain.[27]

Abundant rainfall did come; by September of 1942, people knew that the drought had ended.[28]

Soon the constant stream of pilgrims to visit Alinesitoué began to alarm the local French administrators. Under-staffed and already confronting Diola hostility over requisitions of Diola rice, cattle, and men, they worried about the growing influence of Alinesitoué. Although she was primarily concerned with religious questions, they feared she had the potential to become an effective leader of Diola resistance to the French. In June 1942, the governor of Senegal ordered the *Commandant de Cercle* at Ziguinchor to follow the activities of Alinesitoué closely. He urged Colonel Sajous to increase the number of patrols through the affected area. At the first sign of trouble, Sajous was ordered to use all necessary force to arrest Alinesitoué and to remove her from the region.[29] French fear of Alinesitoué's activities was heightened by the colonial authorities' keen awareness that their control over her region was extremely fragile. As Colonel Sajous noted: "If the public tranquility of the region is not properly speaking 'troubled,' it is a fact that, taking into account the unquestionable authority taken by Ansioutouée [Alinesitoué], it risks suddenly becoming the object of new fantasies that the visionary could invent from one day to the next."[30] Evident in Colonel Sajous' remarks is a deep suspicion of Alinesitoué's claims to spiritual authority and a presupposition that her visions and teachings were irrational or deliberately manufactured. Such assumptions were reinforced by longstanding French convictions that Diola religious authorities were the major obstacle to French rule within Senegal. As the Senegalese governor noted:

> . . .this visionary is not the first woman who has created or tried to create an independent religious sect in Basse Casamance. . . These rudimentary populations of the Basse Casamance are very sensitive to such movements; the influence of this visionary could disappear quite rapidly; that is the opinion of Monsignor Faye, with whom I have discussed this question for a long time and who knows the country because he is from here. But in the troubled times in which we live, it could come to pass that to the contrary, the influence of the visionary wings on the increase, and because we could not tolerate a threat to our authority, I was led to give the necessary orders to Colonel Sajous.[31]

That is to say, to the French, Diola claims to religious authority were, by implication, also calls to resistance.

In Senegal, the main center of rural unrest had been the Subdivision of Oussouye, in the extreme southwestern portion of the Casamance. This same Subdivision was also the region of Senegal that had been least receptive to Islam and Christianity. French officials regarded Christian and Muslim residents of the area as less troublesome and more loyal to French authority than those who upheld Diola traditions. Hence the French began to consult with Bishop Faye and other local Christians on such issues as the prophetic movement. Practitioners of Diola religion frequently refer to the Christian Diola as the people who betrayed Alinesitoué to the French. Paponah Diata clamed that: "They told the Europeans. . . the Christians did. They said that the elders of the community were killing cattle" and that Alinesitoué was a quarrelsome person.[32]

While it is unlikely that local Christians complained directly to French administrators, they did complain to their catechists and priests about growing hostility toward them on the part of the Diola majority who still practiced traditional religion. Christian priests had ready access to local administrators. Father Doutrémepuich, who headed the Oussouye mission during the time of Alinesitoué, firmly believed he should confront the *awasena* majority while conducting his mission work. As the situation worsened, French Catholic priests were warned against touring rural areas.[33] For more overt assistance, the French authorities turned to the Muslim minority in the Subdivision. Colonel Sajous summoned many Muslim traders working in the Subdivision and asked them to report on incidents in the region. Many were hired as informants and guides without being given an option of refusing.[34] French administrators also appointed Muslims to local positions such as head of the Subdivision of Oussouye and canton chief in Esulalu, thereby adopting a style of local chieftaincy much like that in northern Diola areas that had been converting to Islam.[35]

While the French were appointing more Muslim local chiefs in southern Casamance, they also renewed demands on local residents for tax levies of cattle, rice, and men. In the towns of Siganar, Efok, and Youtou, many people refused, telling government officials that during the drought the French had not provided them with rice. They told the French: "Before we pay taxes, we will pay Alinesitoué; she has made it so that there is rain."[36] Although Alinesitoué never urged tax resistance or withholding grain, such statements reinforced French perceptions of threat from her movement. Increasingly, French officials viewed practice of *awasena* rituals as a challenge to colonial rule. ". . .The innumerable sacrifices to the fetishes, ordinarily for material motives, too often involve recourse against administrative action."[37]

Alinesitoué had requested that every neighborhood sacrifice a bull at the shrine of *Kasila,* but this was done to bring rain, not to thwart colonial rule. Each neighborhood sacrificed one bull for its *Kasila* shrine and ate the meat of the sacrifice in communal feasts. Although people in Esulalu willingly gave cattle for the rituals, they told the French they had no spare cattle for government requisitions.[38] French administrators believed that Alinesitoué arbitrarily determined the number of cattle to be sacrificed and that she received part of the meat, although neither belief was accurate.[39] The large number of cattle being sacrificed while Diola were refusing cattle to the French signified to the latter that Alinesitoué commanded greater loyalty than the officials. In an effort to block cattle sacrifices, local administrators levied fines in cattle on communities that had performed the charity of *Kasila.*[40]

However, it does not appear that the French were Alinesitoué's main concern. Several months after Alinesitoué began to teach, Colonel Sajous and his assistants met their quota of men for military recruitment from her home village of Kabrousse, despite lesser success among most southern Diola. Had she been preaching actively against the French, as they insisted, her own village would not have responded to the recruitment drive so favorably.[41]

Although the threat she posed to French authority was the main objection to Alinesitoué, she was also alarming the slowly growing Christian communities in the Casamance region. Bishop Faye believed that her influence would eventually decline and advised the administration against arresting her. But her success was nonetheless a serious challenge to the Church. In 1942 Father Joffroy, a veteran missionary in the region, complained that "there are virtually no more catechumens and so many Christians abandon the Religion!"[42] It is unclear whether Alinesitoué forbade Christian participation in the rites of *Kasila* or whether Christians declined to participate. Whatever the reason, they did not join in the rites, thus clearly separating themselves from the *awasena* majority. Several elders noted that Alinesitoué spoke out against the Christians, claiming that their neglect of *awasena* obligations had helped cause the drought: "Christians broke the country. . . The Christians came and it stopped raining."[43]

Local missionaries likewise spoke out against *Kasila.* "They said that the ritual was nothing but the deceptions of Satan."[44] A man named Sirkimagne Diedhiou described how he stopped going to catechism because of *Kasila.* He had seen the power of Alinesitoué proved by the recent rains. Because he could not attend both catechism and *Kasila,* he stopped attending catechism.[45] Alinesitoué's reintroduction of the Diola day of rest on every sixth day also precipitated arguments over whose day of rest was proper. Alinesitoué taught that no one should work in the rice paddies on *Huyaye.* Christians preferred to rest on Sunday and defied her prohibition, despite threats from *awasena* Diola. Christian violations of *Huyaye* and their refusal to participate in Alinesitoué's rituals were seen as polluting the land and endangering the efficacy of rain rituals. One song attributed to Alinesitoué expressed the growing *awasena* hostility toward the Christian minority, who they claimed, always spoke of God, but disobeyed God's orders:

> Oh, God!
> Each person speaks of God, of you the creator.
> Really. What a pity that all these people do not want to respect your words,
> And nevertheless each day I hear spoken,
> I see some people who by their mouths proclaim the power of God.
> That those who do not respect Its order, they should beware.[46]

In the waning months of 1942, tensions began to escalate, both between the French and Diola, and between the various local religious communities. When the harvest began in late November, several southern Diola communities refused to pay their taxes in rice, as was usual. Angry crowds prevented French patrols from collecting rice taxes and from conscripting young men into the military. By January, several villages along the border with Portuguese Guinea were in open revolt.[47] Entire villages fled across the border into Portuguese territory rather than pay a fine and submit to French authority. Such vigorous resistance to the isolated and under-staffed Vichy administration caused it to abandon monitoring of Alinesitoué's activities and to consider removing her from the region. In every village where disturbances had occurred, Alinesitoué's teachings had become important. Often, when villagers refused to pay French requisitions, they invoked the name of Alinesitoué, even though she herself had not called for direct resistance. Resisting villages reminded the French that, while the government had done nothing for the Diola and nonetheless asked for taxes, Alinesitoué prayed for them and provided rain, but asked for nothing. One of the court interpreters for the Casamance described the villagers' responses to the French: "What you want to do, you must ask Alinesitoué. . . Perhaps one would ask about work:. . . no, we cannot say a word, ask Alinesitoué, she knows. Emitai sent her to us. . . to work on the road, we cannot say."[48]

Even before armed conflict began, Grimaldi, the French commandant at Oussouye, went to Kabrousse to meet Alinesitoué. A Diola elder, Paponah Diatta, described how Alinesitoué terrified the commandant with her power: "After it started to rain for a while, the white man went. . . Alinesitoué, he said, was lying." He asked her: "What do you do to make it rain?" She said she would show him. She did the ritual, picked up the sand and there was thunder and lightning. "The white man fled and entered the house."[49] Teté Diadhiou, a Diola interpreter who had accompanied Grimaldi, warned her of the dangers of her activities and told her that only he could protect her: "I am there. . . I am between the Diola and the whites. . . you are between men and God." He suggested that they work together, but she refused. Again, he warned her of the dangers that she was creating for herself. Then he and Grimaldi returned to Oussouye.[50]

Within a week after open hostilities began in Oussouye, Colonel Sajous decided to arrest Alinesitoué. He and a small column of men set out for Kabrousse. One of the guides, Ibu Konté, thought he saw her trying to escape. He fired and killed the woman he had seen, but that woman was not Alinesitoué. Then Alinesitoué appeared and told them that she had been in seclusion because of menstruation. Colonel Sajous struck her, knocking her to the ground. Then he arrested her, her entire family, and many of the movements' leaders. No one offered resistance, although many of her followers fled across the border into Portuguese Guinea. Alinesitoué and the other prisoners were taken to Ziguinchor, the administrative center of the Casamance region. She and twenty others were held there for trial.[51]

Alinesitoué was tried under the *Indigènat,* a legal code applying only to people of "subject" status within French West Africa. She was charged with "having incited the people of the province of Oussouye to systematic disobedience," that is, with inciting the series of disturbances in the region. Her defense was a simple assertion that she had a mission among her people: "In response, she satisfied herself by affirming that she was an envoy of God, who had appeared to her several times; and that all she did was 'transmit the directives that He had dictated.'" In the same fashion she denied taking part in the revolt and denied all responsibility for its instigation.[52]

Only a year and a half had passed since Alinesitoué summoned the elders of Kabrousse to reveal her mission as Emitai's messenger. In that short time, she had introduced two new spirit shrines and had reemphasized the Diola day of rest. To a people burdened with troubles, she offered plausible explanations for their problems and taught them how to regain control over their communities and lives by reaffirming their traditions. She taught them to stop neglecting the commmunity obligations that Emitai and the ancestors had laid upon them. At the same time, she challenged customs that undermined once-strong communal institutions. The steady stream of pilgrims that visited her at Kabrousse carried back to their townships not only the rain ritual of *Kasila,* but also the conviction that Emitai had not abandoned them. Throughout the Casamance, in Gambia, and in Portuguese Guinea, people gathered together to sacrifice a black bull and to create *Kasila* shrines. Together, without distinctions of age or gender, they prayed, feasted and renewed their sense of solidarity as Diola communities. The plentiful rains of 1942 strengthened their conviction that Alinesitoué was leading them along a proper path.

Early in 1943, as Diola throughout the region harvested the best rice crop they had had in years, Colonel Sajous arrested Alinesitoué, tried her in a local French court, and exiled her from Senegal for ten years. Her accomplices received lesser sentences of from three to five years of prison or exile at various places in the Western Soudan. Many of them died in prison. As for Alinesitoué, neither her family nor the Senegalese public were permitted to know that she had died of starvation at Timbuctou in 1944. Not until 1987, did this enter the public record after an official Senegalese government investigation.

Assessments of the significance of Alinesitoué's life and teachings have varied considerably, according to the assessors' religious and intellectual positions. Father Diamacoune Senghor, a Catholic priest from the region, historian of Diola culture, and leader of the Casamance nationalist movement, claimed that Alinesitoué was an archetypal woman, who symbolized for the Diola all that was excellent in Diola women, just as Mary had done for Christians.[53] This was a less than accurate assessment. In many ways, Alinesitoué was an outsider who failed to meet most of her culture's criteria for judging a woman's excellence. In a society that valued highly both men's and women's ability to work hard in the rice paddies, Aliensitoué was lame, or at least slower in her work. Moreover, while working in the town of Ziguinchor before her visionary experiences, she gave birth to a child out of wedlock, thereby violating a series of community norms. When she began to teach of *Kasila,* she had not yet reached the age or social status normally attained by a woman who could claim to have spiritual gifts. Alinesitoué was unmarried and hence still a girl by Diola standards. She could not even participate in the rites of the most important of the women's shrines, *Ehugna,* which were restricted to married women who had given birth to a child. She did marry and bore a second child shortly after she began to teach. But even then, because her marriage was new and she was still less than twenty-five years old, Diola would not have expected her to display spiritual powers, or even to gain full initiation into the rites of the women's fertility shrine.

She was neither a model of Diola womanhood nor a likely source of religious learning.

However, in many ways, Alinesitoué's unusual life strengthened her claim to be Emitai's emissay. While many Diola women had gone to Dakar to seek work, few women from Kabrousse had done so. This heightened her image as an independent and determined woman. Her unmarried status did the same. Furthermore, her recovery from a life-threatening illness was widely interpreted as a sign of divine favor.[54] As we have seen, her visions and trances were initially interpreted as a sign of madness, not spiritual power. However, as she began to take up her calling, the same traits that had been atypical for Diola women served to set her apart for the distinctive role that she had assumed. In sharp contrast to the Diola norm, Emitai had ordered Alinesitoué not to marry and to remain in the home of her maternal kin. Because she finally disobeyed this directive, some traditionalists blamed her arrest and exile on this transgression. One, Paponah Diatta, explained her downfall as follows: "Emitai had told Alinesitoué not to marry. . . If she had not married, they [the French] would not have been able to take her. Emitai would have refused. But since she disobeyed, Emitai allowed her to be seized."[55]

A prohibition of marriage, common for male priests of major rain shrines (*Cavyinte*) during the nineteenth century, meant that the priest who did not marry sacrificed his fertility in an effort to obtain fertility for the community. In many other ways, rites performed by Alinesitoué and songs sung about her were more characteristic of men than of women in Diola culture. In the course of her prayers at *Houssahara,* Alinesitoué twirled a spear, a weapon normally carried by men and used in men's funeral rituals. Spears were associated with male ancestors, courage, and wisdom. In most women's rituals, priestesses carried wooden staffs, not spears. At the shrine of *Houssahara,* when the young Alinesitoué assumed the task of intervening before Emitai, she took on not only the authority and wisdom of the elders, but also the courage of men. One song sung about Alinesitoué describes her as a "strong woman, courageous, brave like an elephant."[56] In Diola culture, descriptions of people who act like elephants are usually reserved for men.

Alinesitoué was set apart in many ways which could be interpreted as evidence of her charismatic authority and divine election. For example, someone with the power to "see" spirits and to receive visions from Emitai was often said to have special mental powers, a power of the "head." The same was said of Alinesitoué: "Alinesitoué had a head. Emitai spoke to her."[57] From the first day when Alinesitoué revealed her mission to the elders of Kabrousse, she claimed that Emitai had taught her what to preach and had ordered her to spread these teachings among the Diola. She had been afraid to teach, but Emitai returned and threatened to punish her if she continued to refuse.[58]

Alinesitoué's claims that Emitai had approached her were not altogether new to Diolas. As already noted, Diola tradition retained memories of eleven divine revelations to men before the time of European occupation.[59] After the colonial conquest, four women before Alinesitoué had also claimed that Emitai spoke to them.[60] The new factor was that her communications kept on coming. Emitai did not simply give her the spirit shrine and then leave her alone; It continued to summon and teach her. Thus, Alinesitoué was more than just the recipient of a new shrine; she became an ongoing link between her people and their supreme being. Paponah Diatta described how Emitai visited Alinesitoué: "*Ata-Emit* was as white as a white cloth. It came. It came and spoke to her. It discussed things seriously with her. It came at noon, but no one [else] could see It." Others said that she had dreams of Emitai or that her soul left her body and went up into the heavens.[61] These communications occurred so that Alinesitoué could guide the Diola back to their proper path, as the following song attests:

> Let us sing, give us courage and joy
> Because God invites every person living in this world
> To ask Him for the reasonable satisfaction of his needs,
> Even the most secret.
> Oh! God! We believe and are sure that
> Our guide Alinesitoué has received this chance from you.[62]

Alinesitoué's message introduced a series of innovations into Diola religious practice. Central to the Diola's task in the world, according to her revelations, were obligations to observe *Huyaye* and to perform the charity of *Kasila*. While *Huyaye* was not new to the Diola, Alinesitoué gave it new importance and a new meaning. She explained that failure to observe the Diola day of rest was a primary cause of the drought that plagued the Diola. On one day in six, the rice paddies needed to rest in order to retain their fertility. (*Huyaye* was a day of rest for the land, not for the farmers who worked it. They were free to perform other types of work). Violations of *Huyaye* had polluted the land and had alienated Emitai, the source of all rain.

Alinesitoué introduced *Kasila* as a new rain shrine which differed from other rain shrines in its emphasis on Emitai and on the community of supplicants. Alinesitoué emphasized the importance of Emitai as the source of the power of all the spirit shrines. This is illustrated in a song attributed to Alinesitoué:

> Oh my people, I ask you in the name of God, the brave *Jibasor*
> Who has given his power to my fetish, to do your "charities" in His name.
> Sing, sing, do your "charities," sing for God and not for any other
> Because it is God alone who is your recourse
> And it is He who has given the force and His blessings to the power of my fetish.[63]

It was important that the entire neighborhood participate in the rituals, abstain from working in the rice paddies for the six days of ritual activity, and join in the communal feast. The people of the neighborhood had to join together to strengthen the power of community prayer. For Alinesitoué, it was not enough to come together and pray for rain. People had to have a tangible experience of their community, partaking of food in common for six days, singing and dancing and praying for rain together, all without distinctions of wealth, age, or gender. They had to sing the songs of the ancestors and of Alinesitoué. Singing the former linked the new rituals to the first ancestors and integrated the new rites into ongoing Diola tradition, while the songs of Alinesitoué praised Emitai for sending them a new spirit shrine and a prophet. Some of these songs, offered in prayer, sought forgiveness from Emitai for the sins of the community.

> To you God, we ask that you pardon us
> And to let us pass our errors near to You,
> Oh! God! Forgive us.
> Sing! Sing!
> God will pardon us before we disperse from here.
> And we can say farewell in peace,
> A peace that will fill the heart of each one with peace.
> That God grant all our wishes,
> That our charities be agreed to by God
> By the intermediary of our stake [*Kasila*] to which He has given power.
> Good bye, good bye.
> That each one with peace.[64]

In sharp contrast with most Diola spirit shrines, Alinesitoué's *Kasila* was profoundly public. In most spirit cults, people were not taught about the rituals until after they had been "seized" by those cults' spirits or had sought out knowledge through extensive sacrifices. At *Kasila,* the rites were explained in front of whole neighborhoods: men, women, and children. No restrictions on ritual knowledge were placed on a community and anyone could watch the shrine's preparation. Everyone knew what was placed in the holes beneath the shrines, the bones of sacrificed cattle and other livestock, and everyone watched the entire ritual of consecrating the shrine. As pilgrims came to see Alinesitoué, she informed them that women and children should take part in their delegations and should have full access to ritual knowledge.[65]

Furthermore, at the *Kasila* shrine, radically new rules were put into practice for selecting priests and granting access to ritual knowledge. In sharp contrast to most Diola rituals, those who supplied animals for sacrifice gained no special privileges in the *Kasila* ritual. Wealthy donors of these cattle merely fulfilled the obligations that any wealthier member owed to a community. In Diola, the word for wealthy means literally, "give me some." In the "charity" of *Kasila*, the wealthy were reminded that they must help take care of those with fewer resources. At *Kasila*, too, rich and poor alike were supplicants, and sometimes the poorest among them received the power to lead the rituals at the shrine.[66]

As a further sign of her commitment to equality of age and gender and her opposition to hierarchy, Alinesitoué insisted that priests of *Kasila* be chosen by divination. Those who made the pilgrimage and those who gave cattle for sacrifice had no special rights to be chosen as priests. To choose a priest, an elder slit the throat of a chicken and let it run around until it died.[67] The person in front of whom it died was the chosen candidate. This process of choosing priests was intended to demonstrate that *Emitai*, not humans, made the selection. In a song composed by Alinesitoué, people expressed their confidence that even the most unlikely priest could carry their prayers to Emitai:

> All the women of the family have heard said
> That an idiot has taken charge of the fetish
> There it is, very happy.
> All of a sudden, we hear the thunder high in the sky.
> We are all in a great hurry to take our canoe.
> The French are approaching
> There it is that the rice is thrown all over the place.
> There is the bird that flew high up between the clouds and the sky.
> Oh! God! Pardon us.
> Give us water, thanks to our "charity"
> Because the French have plunged us into famine.[68]

(Birds are of regarded as emissaries of Emitai.)

In addition to her teachings about *Huyaye* and *Kasila*, Alinesitoué promoted a sense of the Diola's duties toward Emitai as a people. She encouraged a "spiritual renaissance" in which the Diola would retain "all the positive heritage of the past. . . be it of religion, . . . of customs. . . or of material life."[69] She taught that they should continue to cultivate the red rice, also known as Diola rice (*oryza glaberrima*), that their ancestors had grown because Emitai gave it to them and because it had a special relationship to their own soil. The latter assertion reflected an awareness of Diola agricultural knowledge as well as a religious concern. The Diola grew several varieties of rice, some of best suited to the deepest, best-watered rice paddies, some more salt resistant, and others better suited to drier, more marginal land. Historically, women had controlled the selection of rice seed and a typical woman might use as many as twenty different varieties. By insisting that only Diola rice could be used in ritual meals, Alinesitoué insured that the tougher and better adapted local varieties would survive. Furthermore, she forbade using products of European origin at the *Kasila* shrine because Emitai had not given them. Alinesitoué stressed the idea that Emitai had given the Diola their land and their knowledge of rice farming. Anything threatening their central duty to grow rice was a threat to Diola religion and traditions, and could lead to loss of their autonomy.[70]

Alinesitoué therefore also banned the French's newly introduced peanut. She was well aware that less and less attention was being paid to rice cultivation in Muslim Diola communities where peanuts were grown, and she also knew that women were being forced to bear the entire burden of rice cultivation. Peanut cultivation struck at the heart of a family mode of production in which husband and wife shared the burden of rice cultivation, which is extremely labor-intensive. Men and their sons increasingly spent their time growing peanuts and left the harsh tasks of plowing paddies and building irrigation dams and dikes to already overworked wives and daughters. Peanut farming also required clearing forest and grassland areas not formerly suited for growing rice. Thus the women lost the thatch for their houses that had grown there, as well as a variety of medicinal herbs. Furthermore, peanut farming disrupted a ritual calendar that was based on rice production, for rice had been the staple crop not only of the Diola diet but also of the Diola imagination. In criticizing French agricultural policies, Alinesitoué also became a powerful spokesperson for a Diola moral economy. She reaffirmed a central Diola idea that rice farming is a sacred task and must not be neglected for less central forms of agricultural production.

In general, although European technical knowledge attracted the Diola, the colonial presence also threatened the religious and material basis of Diola life. One of Alinesitoué's songs recognizes this dilemma:

It rains.
I who was always skillful in my farming.
Everyone cites my name.
The Europeans bring some cloths that they give to the inhabitants.
Really we regret that we cannot like the European.
Leave them in peace, because God has shown them knowledge of all things.[71]

In little more than a year, Alinesitoué imparted her knowledge of *Kasila* and *Huyaye* to the Diola people. Through these practices, she sought to reestablish a commitment to Diola traditions and a new realization of the centrality of Emitai's role in the community. But her arrest and subsequent exile brought an abrupt end to her teachings. Her arrest was seen as a bitter blow: "When the Europeans seized her, they broke the country."[72] After her arrest, the drought returned; the harvest of 1943–1944 was as bad as it had been in the years before Alinesitoué began to teach. As they watched their rice shrivel in the paddies, the Diola had strong reasons to believe that the French had broken the country.

As happens in many prophetic movements, once the leader was removed, the message of her movement began to change. Alinesitoué and many of her followers died in prison. Her township of Kabrousse was forced to pay a large fine to the colonial administration. The French authorities moreover destroyed many spirit shrines throughout the subdivision of Oussouye.[73] All of these events made the movement become more self-consciously anti-French and anti-Christian. Many of the songs of Alinesitoué collected by Jean Girard reflect this more recent period. One song suggests that a day of reckoning is coming for the French who tyrannized the Diola.

I am very happy to show you how you must take it,
To cut the neck of a steer
Because I regret to see the Europeans kill people with their long rifles.
A day will come when God will inflict upon them a harsh punishment,
Because that which they do is not good
And God does not like evil-doers.[74]

Other changes were also made that blunted the reformist quality of Alinesitoué's teachings. The practice of having children direct rituals at important shrines and of having women direct rituals at an important community-wide shrine made many male elders uncomfortable. They began to insist that the priests of *Kasila* be chosen from the group of married men with children, who also controlled most other important Diola shrines. The resulting shift in control seems to have been completed by the 1970s. Furthermore, a more modest sacrifice of chickens replaced the sacrifice of cattle and a more modest single-day celebration replaced the original six-day *Kasila* feast. Nevertheless, despite these changes in the rites, many teachings of Alinesitoué have survived.

Moreover, Alinesitoué's mission was carried forward by other prophets who claimed, as she had, that Emitai had sent them. These began almost immediately after her arrest. In 1944, two other women became active among the southern Diola. That same year, in the predominantly Muslim northern area, Kuweetaw Diatta of Tendouk began to teach and was arrested, but not taken to trial. The rites she started are still performed among the northern Diola, just as Alinesitoué's are still kept up in the south. Since Alinesitoué's arrest, roughly thirty prophets, mostly women, have claimed that Emitai sent them to teach the people. Some, like Todjai Diatta, of Djivent, gained an extensive following in the 1980s. Others attracted less attention, but all of them claim to be in the tradition of Alinesitoué. Two women prophets active in the late 1980s and 1990s had earlier been part of a troupe that performed improvisational theater about the life of Alinesitoué, in the late 1960s. One of these women, from the village of Boukitingor, claimed that her soul traveled back to Kabrousse to receive the blessing of Alinesitoué's family and she herself took on the name of Alinesitoué (Berthe Alinesitoué Diatta). Sixteen women and men are currently claiming that Emitai has sent them on a prophetic mission. New forms of *Kasila* are regularly performed, not only among the southern Diola where Muslim and Christian influence is limited, but also among the northern Diola in areas that have been mostly Muslim for over fifty years.

Today, the Senegalese government calls Alinesitoué a national martyr, and has commissioned plays about her and named schools and an athletic stadium in her memory. Nonetheless, Alinesitoué's most important legacy seems to be the more than thirty people following in her tradition, who claim that Emitai speaks through them to those who seek to preserve their autonomy and heritage by following the Diola religious path. Many women elsewhere in Africa have claimed to receive revelations from lesser spirits or have been mediums for supreme beings of other African traditional religions. A number of African Christian women have also become prophets. But the lineage of female prophets launched by Alinesitoué Diatta is unique. I know of no other ongoing, predominantly female, prophetic tradition within indigenous African religious experience.

Notes

1. Field research was conducted in 1974–1975, 1977–1979, 1987, 1988, 1994, 1996, and 1997. Research on Diola prophets was supported by research grants from the national endowment for the Humanities, the American Philosophical Society, and the American Academy of Religion. Prior research was supported by fellowships and grants from the Thomas J. Watson Foundation, Fulbright Hays Doctoral Dissertation Fellowship, Social Science Research Council, and the Institute for Advanced Studies in the African Humanities at Northwestern University.

Interview with Teté Diadhiou, Ziguinchor, 1/25/79 and 7/7/78.

2. For a detailed discussion of precolonial Diola prophetic movements, see Robert M. Baum, *Shrines of the Slave Trade: Diola Religion and Society in Precolonial Senegambia* (New York: Oxford University Press, 1999), passim.

3. Louis Vincent Thomas, *Les Diola: Essai d'analyse fonctionelle sur un population de Basse-Casamance* (Dakar: IFAN, 1959), passim. Olga

Linares, *Power, Prayer, and Production: the Jola of Casamance, Senegal* (Cambridge, 1992), passim.

4. Jean Girard, *Genèse du Pouvoir Charismatique en Basse Casamance (Senegal)* (Dakar: IFAN, 1969), p. 240.

5. Ibid, p. 251.

6. Interview with Paponah Diatta, Mlomp-Etebemaye, 3/21/78.

7. Interview with Sambouway Assin, Kagnout-Bruhinban, 1/8/79.

8. Interview with Goolai Diatta, Kabrousse-Mossor, 4/29/78.

9. Interview with Alouise Diedhiou, Kabrousse-Mossor, 4/29/78.

10. Interview with Goolai Diatta, Kabrousse-Mossor, 4/29/78. Girard, *Genèse,* p. 240.

11. Interview with Goolai Diatta, Kabrousse-Mossor, 4/29/78/. Jean-Baptiste Diatta claimed that she used an indigo blue cloth that is used in Diola funerals. Both the spear and the cloth are used in funeral rituals to invoke the power of the ancestors. Interview with Jean-Baptiste Diatta, Mlomp-Kadjifolong, 9/16/78.

12. Interviews with Silebeh Diatta, Kabrousse-Mossor, 4/30/78; Siopama Diedhiou, Kadjinol-Kafone, 11/12/77; and Sikakucele Diatta, 11/12/77.

13. Interview with Paponah Diatta, Mlomp-Etebemaye, 7/1/76.

14. Interview with Wuuli Assin, Samatit, 6/20/78. Girard, *Genèse,* p. 247.

15. Girard, *Genèse,* p. 248.

16. Interview with Etienne Manga, Kadjinol-Kandianka, 7/30/76.

17. Ibid and Girard, *Genèse,* p. 247.

18. Paul Pelissier, *Les Paysans du Sénégal* (St Yrieix: Imprimerie Fabrèque, 1966). Girard, *Genèse,* p. 264. Interview with L'Abbé Diamacoune Senghor, Senghalene, 11/24/78. "Lieutenant Colonel Sajous, Commandant de Cercle de Ziguinchor à Monsieur le Gouverneur du Sénégal," Archives Nationales du Sénégal, September 17, 1942. ANS 108, 13G13 Versement 17.

19. Interview with Ramon Sambou, Kadjinol-Ebankine, 7/28/76.

20. Interview with Father Diamacoune Senghor, Senghalene, 11/24/78. Peter Mark, "Economic and Religious Change among the Diola of Boulouf (Casamance) 1890–1940; Trade, Cash-Cropping and Islam in Southwestern Senegal," Ph. D. Dissertation, Yale University, 1976, Chapters Four and Five, passim.

21. Interview with Jean-Baptiste Diatta, Mlomp-Kadjifolong, 9/16/77.

22. Interviews with Paponah Diatta, Mlomp-Etebemaye, 3/21/78; Wuuli Assin, Samatit, 6/20/78; Henri Diedhiou, Kadjinol-Kafone, 7/5/76. Commandant Sajous, op. cit.

23. Interviews with Asenkahan Diedhiou, Kadjinol-Kafone, 5/13/78; Paponah Diatta, Mlomp-Etebemaye, 3/21/78; Henri Diedhiou, Kadjinol-Kafone, 7/5/76.

24. Interviews with Ramon Sambou, Kadjinol-Ebankine, 7/28/76; Sidionbaw Diatta, Kadjinol-Kafone, 6/9/75; Emehow Diedhiou, Kadjinol-Kafone, 8/10/76.

25. Interview with Etienne Manga, Kadjinol-Kandianka, 7/30/76.

26. Interview with Hilaire Djibune, Kagnout-Ebrouwaye, 12/17/78.

27. Song of Alinesitoué. Interview with Paponah Diatta, Mlomp-Etebemaye, 3/21/78.

28. Interviews with Sinyendikaw Diedhiou, Kadjinol-Kafone, 4/7/78; Emehow Diedhiou, Kadjinol-Kafone, 8/10/76; Terence Galandiou Diouf Sambou, Kadjinol-Ebankine, 11/7/78; André Bankuul Senghor, Kadjinol-Hassouka, 4/78.

29. Governor of Senegal, Orders to Colonel Sajous cited in "Le Gouverneur du Sénégal à Monsieur le Gouverneur Général: Haut Commisaire de l'Afrique Française, Direction des Affaires Politiques et Administratives," #551/APA. October 30, 1942. 13G12 versement 17. "Affaire Alinsitoué Diatta," ANS.

30. Colonel Sajous, "Commandant de Cercle de Ziguinchor à Monsieur le Gouverneur du Sénégal," Ziguinchor, September 17, 1942. ANS 13G13, versement 17.

31. "Gouverneur du Sénégal à Monsieur le Gouverneur-Général," op. cit.

32. Interviews with Paponah Diatta, Mlomp-Etebemaye, 3/21/78; Sihendoo Manga, Kadjinol-Kafone, 7/15/78.

33. Archives des Pères du Saint-Esprit. Interview with Teté Diadhiou, Ziguinchor, 1/29/79.

34. Father Diamacoune Senghor, Senghalene, citing the Journal of the PreSeminary at Carabanc, in his radio broadcast of November 12, 1978. Ziguinchor, Radio, Channel 4.

35. Interviews with Mahlan Cambai, Oussouye, 12/12/77 and 8/12/76; Boolai Cissoko, Loudia-Ouloff, 12/11/78; Teté Diadhiou, Ziguinchor, 1/29/79.

36. Interview with Terence Galandiou Diouf Sambou, Kadjinol-Ebankine, 11/26/78.

37. Sénégal: Cercle de Ziguinchor et d'Oussouye: Rapport Annuel politique annuel d'ensemble, 1943. ANS 2G 43:73.

38. Interview with Antoine Djemelene Sambou, Kadjinol-Kagnao, 10/29/78.

39. Colonel Sajous, September 17, 1942, op. cit.

40. Interview with Sihendoo Manga, Kadjinol-Ebankine, 7/15/78. "Sénégal: Cercle de Ziguinchor: Subdivision d'Oussouye: Rapport Mensuel d'ensemble, 1944, aout-septembere."

41. Interview with Teté Diadhiou, Ziguinchor, 7/7/78.

42. Father Henri Joffroy, "Lettre à Monseigneur LeHunsec," July 24, 1942, Archives des Pères de Saint-Esprit, Correspondence, Boite 264, B-VI.

43. Interview with Ramon Sambou, Kadjinol-Ebankine, 7/26/76; Terence Galandiou Diouf Sambou, Kadjinol-Ebankine, 3/30/78.

44. Terence Sambou, op. cit.

45. Interview with Sirkimagne Diedhiou, Kadjinol-Kafone, 3/15/78.

46. Song of Alinesitoué cited in Girard, *Genèse,* p. 364. Interviews with Georgette Bassin, Kadjinol-Kafone, 2/28/78; Antoine Djemelene Sambou, Kadjinol-Kagnao, 6/5/76; Paponah Diatta, Mlomp-Etebemaye, 7/6/76; Grégoire Diatta, Mlomp-Kadjifolong, 10/23/78.

47. Interview with Teté Diadhiou, Ziguinchor, 11/25/78. Girard, *Genèse,* p. 221–22.

48. Interview with Lamine Diedhiou, Ziguinchor, 2/1/79.

49. Interview with Paponah Diatta, Mlomp-Etebemaye, 3/21/78. This is quite reminiscient of Belgian fear of Simon Kimbangu in their initial encounters. See Paul Raymaekers, *Histoire de Simon Kimbangu: Prophèt d'après les Ecrivains Nfinangani et Nzungu, 1921.*

50. Interview with Teté Diadhiou, Ziguinchor, 7/7/78.

51. Girard, *Genèse,* pp. 226–28. Interviews with Teté Diadhiou, Ziguinchor, 1/25/79; Fulgence Sagna, 6/94.

52. "Rélation de l'interrogatoire d'Alinsitoué par le Colonel Sajous," April 1, 1943, cited in Girard, *Genèse,* p. 225.

53. Father Diamacoune Senghor, Senghalene, in a radio broadcast, Ziguinchor, November 12, 1978. Chaine #4.

54. Girard, *Genèse,* p. 240.

55. Interview with Paponah Diatta, Mlomp-Etebemaye, 3/21/78. Girard, *Genèse,* p. 261.

56. Song of Alinesitoué cited in Girard, op. cit., p. 241.

57. Interview with Sikakucele Diatta, Kadjinol-Kafone, 7/11/76; Paponah Diatta, Mlomp-Etebemaye, 7/1/76.

58. Interview with Sambouway Assin, Kagnout-Bruhinban. Girard, *Genèse,* p. 240.

59. Baum, *Shrines,* passim.

60. Robert M. Baum, "Alinesitoué's Predecessors: Diola Prophets in Precolonial and Early Colonial Senegal." Paper presented at the West African Research Association, First Annual Conference, Dakar, Senegal, 1997.

61. Interviews with Paponah Diatta, Mlomp-Etebemaye, 3/21/78; Goolai Diatta, Kabrousse, Mossor, 4/29/78; Sambouway Assin, Kagnout-Bruhinban, 12/17/78; Siopama Diedhiou, Kadjinol-Kafone, 2/16/78.

62. Song of Alinesitoué, cited in Girard, *Genèse,* p. 241.

63. Ibid, p. 347.

64. Song of Alinesitoué.

65. Interview with Casimir Sambou, Kadjinol-Hassouka, 5/28/78.

66. Interviews with Antoine Djemelene Sambou, Kadjinol-Kagnao, 10/29/78; Boolai Senghor, Kadjinol-Sergerh, 7/12/78.

67. Interviews with Boolai Senghor, Kadjinol-Sergerh, 7/12/78. Interview with Koolimagne Diedhiou, cited in Girard, *Genèse,* p. 247.

68. Song of Alinesitoué cited in Girard, *Genèse,* p. 353.

69. Father Diamacoune Senghor, Radio Broadcast, 11/12/78, Ziguinchor, Chaine 4.

70. Interview with Father Diamacoune Senghor, Senghalene, 11/24/78.

71. Song of Alinesitoué, cited in *Genèse,* p. 355.

72. Interview with Ramon Sambou, Kadjinol-Ebankine, 7/28/76. Interviews with Casimir Sambou, Kadjinol-Hassouka, 7/28/78; Assinway Sambou, Kadjinol-Kafone, 5/25/78.

73. Calendrier des Evenements Historiques, Archives de la Sous-Préfecture de Loudia-Ouloff.

74. Song of Alinesitoué, cited in Girard, *Genèse,* p. 355.

Further Reading

Baum, Robert M. *Shrines of the Slave Trade: Diola Religion and Society in Precolonial Senegambia.* New York: Oxford University Press, 1999.

Girard, Jean. *Genèse du Pouvoir Charismatique en Basse Casamance (Sénégal)*. Dakar: IFAN, 1967.

Linares, Olga F. *Power, Prayer and Production: The Jola of Casamance, Senegal.* Cambridge: Cambridge University Press, 1992.

Waldman, Marilyn R. and Baum, Robert M. "Innovation as Renovation: The 'Prophet' as an Agent of Change," in Michael A. Williams, Collet Cox, and Martin S. Jaffee, ed., *Innovation in Religious Traditions: Essays in the Interpretation of Religious Change.* Berlin: Mouton de Gruyter, 1992, pp. 241–84.

16

The Case of the Vanishing Nuns: The Fruits of Ambivalence in Ancient Indian Buddhism

NANCY AUER FALK

For a number of years I have been fascinated by a puzzling aspect of the history of ancient Indian Buddhism. The Indian order of Buddhist monks was still flourishing in 1198 A.D., when Afghan invaders began the series of raids that would destroy its greatest monasteries within the next two hundred and forty years. Many centuries earlier, however, the parallel order of Buddhist nuns had virtually disappeared from the historian's view. Yet the order of *bhikshunis,* "female beggars," as these women were called—flourished in China and Japan until modern times. The very similar order of Jain nuns that probably even antedated the *bhikshunis'* venture still prospers in Jain regions of modern India. Furthermore, even as the nuns themselves became less prominent, other women remained important to the Buddhism of India. The generous gifts of great laywomen-

NANCY AUER FALK is Professor of Comparative Religion and Women's Studies at Western Michigan University. She was trained initially in History of Religions at the University of Chicago (M.A. 1963; Ph.D. 1972), with specialization in the religions of South Asia. Her principal research interest is the study of women's religious roles and lives, both in South Asia and cross-culturally, and she has written scholarly articles on aspects of women's lives and practice in both the Buddhist and Hindu traditions of South Asia. Besides co-editing the several editions of *Unspoken Worlds,* she has published *Women and Religion in India: An Annotated Bibliography of Sources in English 1975–92* (Kalamazoo, Mich.: New Issues Press, 1994).

Author's Note: Portions of the research for this chapter were supported by the National Endowment for the Humanities (Summer Stipend, 1976) and by Western Michigan University's sabbatical leave program (1977–1978). An early version of this study was presented during the 1978 W.Y. Evans-Wentz Lecture Series at Stanford University.

donors are on record until the tradition's final days. And the same centuries that were so silent for the nuns produced the Vajrayana path with its women *siddhas,* who are described in Chapter 19 of this volume.

Materials on the nuns are very sketchy, and we will probably never know in detail what caused their decline. The most likely cause was a general decline in the Buddhist community's economic fortunes that had a long-term impact on the men's order as well. But bad luck hit the nuns first and disproportionately; thus we must look further to explain the reasons for the different fates of monks and nuns.

At the root, the major problem of the women's order probably rested in the Buddhist tradition's inability to affirm completely the idea of women pursuing the renunciant's role. This led to an institutional structure that offered women admirable opportunities for spiritual and intellectual growth, but not for the institutional and scholarly leadership that such growth should have fitted them to assume. The nuns' troubles were compounded by an ambivalent image created in a tradition of Buddhist stories that sometimes praised their achievements but just as often undercut and attacked them.

NOW YOU SEE THEM; NOW YOU DON'T

To appreciate the puzzle of the nuns' disappearance, one must have some minimal acquaintance with the sources and facts of the order's history in India. Overall, the history of the nuns, like that of the larger Buddhist community in India, can be divided into three phases.

The first, so-called primitive, period extends from the Buddha's first conversions (ca. later sixth century B.C.) and the early spread and consolidation of the tradition's teachings and institutions to the time when the great emperor Ashoka (ca. 272–236 B.C.) became a patron of Buddhism and facilitated its spread throughout and beyond the Indian subcontinent. Sources for this period are exclusively oral traditions; these were preserved by means of memorization and were recorded in writing only at later times. According to these traditions, the Master himself founded the women's order during the early years of his teaching career. The inspiration for its founding is said to have come from the Buddha's maternal aunt, Mahaprajapati by name, who had raised him from birth after the death of his mother. The order was founded on the premise, affirmed in the Buddha's own teachings, that women were as capable as men of reaching *arhat*ship, the state of spiritual liberation characterized by total victory over desire. Memories of the early days testify to the order's thriving existence. It drew women from all walks and conditions of life, especially the mercantile and aristocratic classes that provided the entire tradition with its major bases of support. Many were matrons, turning to the order's rest after a full and exhausting life; others were young, moved by disgust for marriage or saddened by the death of children or other kin. Through the path of renunciation many of these women achieved the *nirvana* (coolness) that they sought. An extraordinary testimony to their accomplishment is a collection of stanzas preserved in Buddhism's southern, or Theravada, tradition, in which their most distinguished members celebrate their new spiritual freedom.[1]

The second period extends from the time of Ashoka through two later great empires, the one ruled by the Satavahanas in the south (ca. 55 B.C.–250 A.D.) and the other by Kushanas in the northwest (ca. 20 A.D.–240 A.D.) During this period, the Buddhist order became a significant religious force throughout India. Although the nuns' presence is still attested in some works of literature that originated during this period, the most important historical testimonies to their existence are the numerous inscriptions left by donors to Buddhist building projects and monuments. These provide evidence of a thriving nuns' community in virtually all areas where the men's order is also present. Especially in the south, the nuns seem to have been both numerous and wealthy. Their names are found in inscriptions in numbers almost equal to the monks' and they were able to offer generous gifts themselves as well as to receive donations.[2]

During the third period of Buddhist history in India, after the third century A.D., the nuns' fortunes deteriorated; the few traces of the women's order suggest that the order became much smaller. This was a time of general diminution for the Buddhist community as a whole, although it remained strong in some regions and kingdoms. It was also the best-recorded period in Buddhist history. One would expect, therefore, to find abundant materials on nuns. Instead, they become almost invisible. I have found a few inscriptions: the last gift from a nun was recorded in 550 A.D. in the city of Mathura,[3] and a few donations reveal a small cluster of convents near the famous Buddhist "university" at Valabhi (last on record, 629 A.D.).[4] None of the famous philosophical treatises and commentaries that made the period so illustrious are attributed to nuns. Moreover, nuns rarely appear in the brief sketches of eminent figures' lives that are found so often in literary sources of the times. Once in a while we catch the nuns' shadow in the background: thus we learn that the Buddhist nun-mother of Kumarajiva, a famous scholar of northwest India who later made his home in China (ca. 344–413 A.D.), was an important influence in his life;[5] that another eminent monk, Vasubandhu, used part of the many gifts offered to him to build housing for nuns in the northern capital city of Patna, where he tutored members of a royal household (ca. 455–467 A.D.);[6] and that the widowed sister of the Buddhist emperor Harshavardhana *may* have taken the vows with her brother at the end of his rule (ca. 605–647 A.D.).[7]

Even the Chinese pilgrims who have otherwise provided such rich records of later Buddhist life in India have surprisingly little to say about nuns. Fa Hsien, who traveled across northern India in 399–400 A.D., mentions the *bhikshunis* only once, in describing a rite at Mathura. Hsüan Tsang, who lived in India for more than twenty years (629–643 A.D.) and visited virtually all of its major centers, refers to nuns only in connection with the same rite described by Fa Hsien.[8] He must have seen nuns, however, for twenty-eight years later another voyager, I Ching, encountered them during his stay at Tamralipti in east India. I Ching noted how strictly they were supervised; they had to walk two by two outside the monastery grounds and traveled in fours if they visited a lay household. But he was most impressed by their poverty:

> Nuns in India are very different from those of China. They support themselves by begging food, and live a poor and simple life. . . . The benefit and supply to the female members of the Order are very small, and monasteries of many a place have no special supply of food for them.[9]

I Ching might have mentioned also that in India the nuns lived very differently from the monks. The monks he saw lived in richly endowed monasteries, and their lives could hardly be called poor or simple. Clearly the nuns had seen better days.

AN ECONOMIC MATTER

As brief as it is, I Ching's note on the nuns provides an important clue to the crisis in the women's order. Their singularly poorer state, as compared to the monks', indicates that they had problems in finding economic support.

The record of Vasubandhu's contribution to the nuns in Patna probably means that the Patna community faced the same problem.

It is important at this point to examine the economic structure of the Buddhist monastic community.[10] The community had begun as a loosely knit group of mendicant wanderers. As early monks and nuns moved from town to town, they lived on handouts provided largely by lay members who had also taken refuge in the Buddha's doctrine. The beggar's life was essential to the community's discipline, for it helped the renunciants to sever their ties to all worldly things. Hence it was retained as an important part of the monastic rule even after the wanderers began to settle down in fixed and permanent monastic settlements. Thus monks and nuns remained dependent on donations. Lay persons built their monasteries, provided their robes and other modest possessions, and fed them, either as they went on daily begging rounds or by supplying food to monastery kitchens. Some of the wealthy made large endowments; a king, for example, might donate tax revenue from a village to ensure a favored monastery a continuing supply of basic requisites. Still, as in the Buddhism of Southeast Asia today, many of the renunciants' needs were cared for on a day-to-day or year-to-year basis. During times when Buddhism experienced a broad base of popular support, the whole monastic community flourished. This was especially true when the supporting community enjoyed an abundant surplus of wealth, as was the case, for example, in the southern empire of the Satavahana (or Andhra) dynasty, where the most successful nuns' community appears to have been located. When the economic bottom dropped out or popular support was eroded by competition from other religious teachings, the renunciants were in a less comfortable position. Both these negative forces were operating in the third century A.D., when the fortune of the nuns began to turn. The merchants and members of the Satavahana court, who had been the principal supporters of the Buddhist community, saw their profitable trade with ancient Rome decline and their empire fall to pieces. Furthermore, in many regions where Buddhism had been strong, devotional movements that honored Hindu gods were gaining new converts.

As Buddhism's popular base declined, a different source of support became preeminent. Kings and royal families had been conspicuous donors since the community's earliest days. Perhaps the most famous example of all was Ashoka, ruler of ancient India's largest empire. In those early days royal donors like Ashoka were motivated at least in part by personal commitment to Buddhism. Later, however, the records of royal grants show that many of the generous donors had taken Hindu names. Apparently, their donations had less to do with personal piety than with prestige. The Buddhist community was by now winning a high reputation for its scholarship. Learned stars like the brilliant Chinese visitor Hsüan Tsang were paraded by kings in public debates; famous philosophers like Vasubandhu were sought out to tutor royal families. Royal dynasties built up piece by piece the massive monastery-universities of these latter days, whose reputations shone throughout the Indian subcontinent. In this league, however, the nuns were at a decided disadvantage, for they were not stars, and their community had never enjoyed the lion's share of prestige. If the men's and women's communities had to compete for donations, there was no doubt that the men would capture the greater share of support.

ALMOST EQUAL

The reasons for the nuns' lower profile and lesser fame seem once again to lie partly in the institutional structure of the monastic orders. To find them, we must widen our circle of understanding. Our focus this time is on the Buddhist monastic Rule. According to the claims of the legendary histories that frame it, the Rule was the creation of the Buddha himself, who formulated its two-hundred-plus precepts in response to specific situations arising in his community. According to Western historians, the Rule probably developed slowly over a period of perhaps two centuries, becoming essentially complete around 350 B.C. The monastic Rule became one of the most stable features of the Buddhist tradition; although Buddhism developed many different sects and sometimes very different interpretations of the Buddha's teaching, the provisions of the Rule remained basically constant.[11]

The Rule provided a total framework for Buddhist monastic life. Many of its provisions expand and interpret the Buddhist renunciant's four major moral precepts: not to destroy life, not to take what was not given, not to have sexual relations, and not to speak wrongly. Other provisions spell out the prohibitions against luxury that were also an integral part of Buddhist practice. Still other portions of the Rule stipulate the fine organizational details that allowed the community to run smoothly and furthered its members' opportunity to pursue spiritual liberation.

In most respects the Rule approached monks and nuns with admirable equity. Before the monastic settlements were established, monks and nuns led the same wandering life, free of the domestic ties and labor that left neither men nor women in ancient India much chance for serious pursuit of spiritual discipline. Both monks and nuns went on the daily begging rounds; both held the important biweekly assembly in which the Rule's provisions were recited. Monks and nuns even looked alike; both shaved their heads bare, and both wore the same patchcloth robes dyed to earth color and draped identically over the left shoulder.

At times the Rule made special provisions to protect and help the nuns. Monks could not call upon the women's skills, for example, to sew or to dye and weave the small rugs on which they sat. Nor could the monks divert to themselves any food or robes that the nuns acquired as donations. For, it was said, "women come by things with difficulty"[12]—thus suggesting, incidentally, that economic problems were not new to the women of the order's later days.

It was important that nuns receive adequate instruction. To facilitate the observance of the rule on celibacy, monks and nuns usually led strictly separate lives; thus, for the most part, nuns served as their own teachers. Those of early times sometimes gained brilliant reputations, such as the brahman Bhadda Kapilani, whom the Buddha himself praised for her knowledge of his teachings, or Patacara, whose insight into the meaning of suffering was deepened by a personal history of former rebellion and staggering loss. Nevertheless, the transmission of the teaching was for the most part in the hands of the men's community that had originally traveled with the Buddha; so the Rule allowed women to receive instruction from men as well as from other nuns. Ironically, this provision, so conspicuously designed to benefit the nuns, was probably one of the factors that worked ultimately to undo them, for the corresponding allowance was not given: monks could instruct nuns, but nuns could not instruct monks. Perhaps they did so anyway, informally; some early accounts seem to suggest that this happened at times. But no record of later times ever shows a man citing a woman as his *acharya,* or principal spiritual mentor. Thus the men owed nothing to the women, while that same provision justified their keeping the community's main educational apparatus in their own hands.

Other features of the Rule also played a part in the eventual decline of the nuns' order. In addition to the Rule they shared with the men, the nuns observed another, smaller Rule of their own.[13] Some of its precepts dealt with minor problems special to women—for example, how to cope with menstruation or how to handle the situation if a nun became pregnant. Many others elaborated the eight special rules that, according to legend, the Buddha had imposed on the women as a price for allowing them to found their order. These provided that the women would be permanently subordinated to the men:

1. Any nun, no matter how long she had been in the order, must treat any monk, even the rudest novice, as if he were her senior.
2. Nuns should not take up residence during the annual rainy-season retreat in any place where monks were not available to supervise them.
3. Monks would set the dates for the biweekly assemblies.
4. During the ceremony at the end of the rainy-season retreat, when monks and nuns invited criticisms from their own communities, the nuns must also invite criticism from the monks.
5. Monks must share in setting and supervising penances for the nuns.
6. Monks must share in the ordination of nuns.
7. Nuns must never revile or abuse monks.
8. Nuns must not reprimand monks directly (although they could and did report one monk's offensive behavior to another, who then might take the appropriate actions to correct it.)[14]

We must avoid jumping to conclusions about the effects of these rules. Women of ancient India had always been subordinated to men. For the most part the nuns apparently did not find these rules oppressive, although one protest is on record against the rule of seniority. Nor, apparently, did they consider themselves inferior; what little record we have of their thoughts suggests that they either regarded themselves as equals or simply did not think to compare themselves with the men at all.

The extra rules did not hinder women in what was considered to be their most important pursuit—practicing the discipline that led to liberation. Nor did the special rules deny the nuns the opportunity, if they sought this out, to develop their minds and their insight into the tradition's teachings. In these respects, especially when one considers the time and cultural context, the Rule's approach to women was extraordinarily open.

The damage inflicted by the special rules was of a subtler and worldlier nature. The discriminatory provisions meant that women would never be leaders in the life of the whole community or have any decisive voice in shaping its direction. They meant that the men would never be beholden to any of the nuns, in the way that students are beholden to the teachers whose efforts have helped them find meaning and direction. These negative effects became most pronounced in the days of the great universities and the royal patrons who built their own fame though these foundations. They communicated a damaging image to the greater world that picked up the monastic community's tab, because they affirmed that the monks were the more significant and worthier part of such a community. In other words, the discriminatory rules implied that the men deserved the richer offerings, the more elaborate buildings, and the greater opportunity to shine in court and in public confrontations.

ONE HAND GIVES; THE OTHER TAKES AWAY

Unfortunately this image of male superiority was reinforced from another direction as well, for the Buddhist literary tradition conveyed an ambivalence about the nuns that must have further eroded the order's standing. I am concerned here not so much with the sophisticated philosophical literature that was studied and taught primarily in monastic circles as with the many stories that once circulated, and still circulate, in the wider community. Ancient Buddhism, like all the traditions native to India, communicated its fundamental values and much of its understanding of human life and destiny through a rich storytelling tradition. We shall never know, of course, just exactly what form was given to these stories in the different times and regions of India where Buddhism was a living tradition, for the storytelling tradition was largely an oral one, with new versions constantly being shaped as the stories were told and retold. But some versions have been preserved, scattered in many places throughout Buddhist literature.

References to nuns appear in a number of Buddhist stories, especially those that tell about Buddhism's formative period. Such references come in two forms: (a) explicit evaluations of the nuns' spiritual capacities and of their role within the community, and (b) portrayals of their activities and spiritual accomplishments. The ambivalence that I have referred to pervades both types.

For example, one current in the Buddhist storytelling tradition unquestionably carries a strong positive image of the nun. The motif of the women's capacity for *arhat*ship is frequently iterated and is backed up by portrayals of *arhat*-nuns, such as biographical legends about many of the *theri*s, famous *arhat*-nuns whose stanzas were mentioned earlier in this chapter. Some of the names and accomplishments of these nuns appear again in stories about the Buddha and his community that accompany accounts of the Buddha's sermons and dialogues with his followers. For example, in one old account the Buddha cites the most distinguished members of each of his community's four segments—the monks, the nuns, the laymen, and the laywomen.[15] Among the nuns we learn of Khema, most eminent in wisdom; of Nanda, first in meditation; of Sona, greatest in energetic effort; and of Sigala's mother, preeminent in faith. This list of distinguished members also includes the nun Dhammadinna, who is cited as the most skilled teacher of the Buddha's insights; Patacara, who knows best the rules of the discipline; and Kisha Gotami, who is first in the ascetic practice of wearing coarse robes. Uppalavanna is chief among those of supernormal powers; Sahula is first in clairvoyance; and Bhadda Kapilani is best at remembering past lives. These are no second-rate achievements. Other narratives scattered throughout the literature recall further details of these women's careers. Mahaprajapati, the nuns' founder, had a modest legendary cycle of her own, beginning, as most accounts of great Buddhists do, with stories of the deeds in former lives that brought her to her exalted role as the Buddha's aunt and the nuns' founder and ending with an account of her *parinirvana,* or final liberation.

Perhaps the strongest affirmation of the nuns' role is found in a little collection of stories that was apparently very widely known, inasmuch as a number of versions have been found from quite different Buddhist times and regions. This collection contains the stories of ten nuns who, through wit, discipline, and purity of thought, managed to overcome the tempter Mara. All of them speak out strongly as Mara approaches and tries to awaken the lustful thoughts, painful memories, and past fears that would make a weaker person abandon the path of spiritual attainment. The message is clearest and strongest in the words that one of the sisters, Soma, speaks in answer to Mara's remark that she has merely a woman's "two-finger intelligence" (enough to use a common and simple way of measuring rice). Soma's answer rings like a credo for all the nuns:

What does the woman's nature do to us if the mind is well-composed
If our knowledge progresses rightly, giving insight in the Teaching?
Pleasure is completely destroyed for me; dark ignorance has been pierced.
Thus know, Evil Death, you are destroyed!
If a person still thinks to ask: "Am I a woman in these things? Or am I a man?"
This is the one to whom Mara can talk.[16]

Offsetting the impact of such stories as those of Mahaprajapati and Soma, however, is another series of accounts which denigrate the nuns and their accomplishments. Many of these are clearly just tales of human foibles and failings and are not directed specifically at the nuns as such; similar stories are also told about the monks. A few have a gently humorous touch, such as the Vinaya tale of a country bumpkin nun who tosses the contents of her chamberpot over her convent's wall and hits a stuffy brahman on the head.[17] My own favorite is the story of Fat Tissa, who noisily celebrates the nuns' monk patron Ananda above the much more distinguished—but also womanhating—Mahakassapa, thus bringing down the latter's wrath on poor Ananda.[18]

Other tales, however, strike quite a different and ominous note. Some accounts seem defaced, as though stories initially intended to celebrate the nuns' achievements had been altered to play down their accomplishments. Thus a very old story telling of the efforts of the founder, Mahaprajapati, and her initial group of followers states that they very nearly attained insight on their first day of instruction. However, the story continues, unlike many of their male brethren they didn't quite make it; thus they had to return for more teaching on the morrow.[19] The implication is that they were a little on the slow side. This didn't-quite-make-it theme appears several times. I know at least one instance in which both the celebratory and the denigrating versions of the same story have been preserved. This apparently popular story tells of a nun who wanted to be first in greeting the Buddha after he had spent a three-month rainy-season retreat in heaven. Not knowing quite how to accomplish this in the glorious company that was assembling for the occasion, she transformed herself into a universal emperor. One of my sources simply reports that she was, indeed, first—thus implying that hers was a great accomplishment. Another source states instead that, when she met the Buddha, he informed her that a male meditation master had in fact seen him first with his spiritual eye. And yet a third source reports that the Master censured her for abandoning her proper business of meditation.[20]

Certainly the most damaging of all must have been the story concerning the eight special rules that subordinated the nuns to the monks. It purports to tell how the nuns' order was founded over the Buddha's own objection to letting women renounce the world. To the Buddha's credit, the story may be a fraud, for it does not belong to the oldest stratum of Buddhist literature. But it was widely circulated as the authentic founding narrative; hence its charges must have cast a very long shadow on the nuns' endeavor. It is said that, when Mahaprajapati and her retinue of five-hundred Sakya women first approached the Buddha to ask for ordination, he refused brusquely and sent them away in tears. They went home, shaved their heads, put on the renunciant's robes and then, with bare feet, followed the Master and his male disciples to a distant town to show their determination. The Buddha refused again; but this time Fat Tissa's hero Ananda intervened on the women's behalf. The Master finally relented, but he extracted the women's promise to observe the eight rules as a condition for their admission. Many versions of this story include a particularly vicious coda: because the women had been admitted as renunciants, the Master announced afterward, his teaching would last only five hundred years instead of the thousand that the had originally anticipated.[21]

Once upon a time I attributed these kinds of stories to simple misogyny among the celibate monks' community. Today, after many years of study, I believe that the explanation is probably not so simple. Another group of women—the Buddhist laywomen—comes off very well in Buddhist stories, in spite of the fact that the Buddhist lay community in general was considered spiritually inferior to the monastic community. Buddhist laywomen tend to be presented in much more positive terms than the nuns, and their deeds and virtue are almost invariably praised. The stories that relate to laywomen are far more numerous and more lavishly and enthusiastically developed than those that relate to nuns. The grand heroine of Buddhist storytelling is not the nuns' founder Mahaprajapati, as one might expect, but Vishakha, a prominent merchant's daughter and wife who belonged to the early community and who never took the nuns' vows. Moreover, in the stories of outstanding nuns the focus is often on the deeds that they performed before, not after, taking the renunciant's vows. This is not true for the monks, for there are many, many Buddhist stories whose hero is a monk. Thus one cannot escape the impression that the community was more comfortable with its laywomen than with its nuns and that it probably found the latters' presence to be an embarrassment.

WHEN MODELS CONFLICT

As perplexing as the relative strength of the laywomen's position may seem, it offers an important clue to the ambivalence surrounding the nuns' role. Such ambivalence, I believe, is linked to Buddhism's attempts to reconcile two separate and somewhat contradictory understandings of sexual difference, each with its own implications for the respective roles of nuns and laywomen. The first is the more authentically Buddhist of the two and by far the more consistent with the greater body of Buddhist teachings. It perceives the difference between male and female, like other varieties of human difference, as products of humans' essentially fallen state; this is in accordance with the workings of *karma*—Buddhism's basic premise that different kinds of beings are the products of their own past desires. As one works toward spiritual perfection—essentially by learning to break the hold of desires—the consequences of fallenness, including sexual differentiation, tend to drop away. This means essentially that the process of spiritual development, in which the renunciant's vocation represents a relatively advanced step, tends to nullify sexual identifications and limitations.[22] This ideal of convergence of the sexes is reflected in the renunciants' identical clothes, as well as in their virtually identical spiritual paths and disciplines. It is certainly the basis as well for the triumphant song of Soma cited in the last section.

The nuns' subordination to the monks, however, as well as their uneasy status vis-à-vis the laywomen appear to draw on another model of sexual difference, which comes not from the Buddhist tradition itself but from the norms of the surrounding culture. This is the model provided by the Hindu conception of *dharma*—the vision of an all-embracing order in which everything and everyone has a place. This "place" is simultaneously a "nature" and a "role", for being born in a particular slot means that one is at least ideally endowed with the natural capacity to fulfill that slot and has the duty to see that such a capacity is properly channeled. Failure to honor one's *dharma* invites disaster—for oneself, one's family, and ultimately the whole order. The *dharma*'s central image is that of an organism in which the various "slots" are, in effect, the equivalents of bodily members.

Now, a woman's "slot" is that of child-bearer. This is also her natural capacity; hence she is the repository of a powerful generative force that seeks, above all, to put babies in the womb. Marriage and motherhood represent the proper and effective means of channeling a woman's generative drive. Her subordination to men further ensures its control—hence, the *dharma* teaching that a woman must always be subordinate to some man: in childhood, to her father; in maturity, to her husband; in old age, to her sons. In her proper place, with a living husband and surrounded by her children, a woman may achieve great honor. Out of place, she is suspect. The Hindu tradition's distrust of female ascetics is well documented, and so is its unease with other women who fail to fill their ideal role, such as the unmarried, childless, and widowed women who so often took refuge in the Buddhist community.

Buddhism was a path of enlightenment, not a revolutionary vision of renewed social order. It made peace with the Hindu *dharma*'s precepts wherever it could, often incorporating them into its own prescriptions for ordinary human behavior and social relationships. Thus the subordination of nuns to monks can probably best be traced historically to the early community's efforts to stay at least somewhat in line with the conventional practice of the day. More important for the nuns, the Hindu *dharma*'s values percolated through into popular Buddhist expectations as well. Buddhists, like Hindus, honored fecund housewives, especially if they were also pious laywomen. We can therefore suspect that many Buddhists, like Hindus, also preferred to see women at the hearth rather than on the road or within a monastery's walls. Such preferences could easily compromise early Buddhism's rather remarkable tolerance for renunciant women.

ACCENTUATE THE POSITIVE

Given the powerful currents pulling against the nuns, I have come to wonder whether, in fact, I have not been puzzled by the wrong mystery. For it is less strange that the nuns finally came in second to the monks (and laywomen) than that they survived so well for so long. When I Ching described the poor and simple nuns of North India, their order had existed for over a thousand years. Furthermore, it continued to survive for at least two full centuries longer. Once upon a time I believed that I Ching had spoken the last word on the nuns and that they must have faded and died out shortly after his visit. Yet I continue to discover traces of later nuns. A few days before completing this chapter, for example, I found another record of the nuns in a grant to a monastery of eastern India. Among the allocations for this very large establishment were ten servants for the community of nuns that was housed within the monastery's precinct. The grant is dated at 885 A.D.[23] Thus it becomes more likely that the nuns lived on until the monks' traces also vanished from Indian history.

Notes

1. Therigatha, translated with the traditional commentary by C.A.F. Rhys Davids in *Psalms of the Early Buddhists* (London: Luzac, 1964). For an excellent summary of these and other sources on the earliest nuns, see I. B. Horner, *Women under Primitive Buddhism* (London: Routledge, 1930).

2. It may seem somewhat puzzling that nuns and monks who had supposedly rejected most material possessions nonetheless had the economic resources to make donations to Buddhist building projects and monuments. In some cases relatives remaining within the lay community seem to have offered donations on the monks' or nuns' behalf. In some cases, like that of the distinguished monk-scholar Vasubandhu, the monks or nuns redirected a surplus of gifts that had been offered by laypersons for their own personal use.

3. J. J. Fleet, *Gupta Inscriptions* (Calcutta, 1988), no. 70.

4. K. J. Virji, *Ancient History of Saurashtra* (Bombay, 1955), pp. 263 and 287, no. 49.

5. As described by Richard Robinson, *Early Mādhyamika in India and China* (Madison, Wis.: University of Wisconsin Press, 1967), pp. 72–73.

6. J. Takakusu, "The Life of Vasubandhu by Paramārtha," *T'oung Pao,* ser. 2. Vol. 5 (1904): p. 286.

7. This is suggested in the romantic epic on Harsha's life, Harshacarita (8. 288), but not in historical accounts of Harsha. His sister's knowledge of Buddhist philosophy and enthusiasm for Buddhist teachings are, however, attested independently.

8. For both pilgrims' accounts, see S. Beal, *Buddhist Records of the Western World,* Vol. 1 (London: Kegan, Paul, Trench, Trübner, 1884), pp. xxxix, 181.

9. J. Takakusu, trans., *A Record of the Buddhist Religion* (London: Clarendon Press, 1896), p. 81.

10. Probably the best available source on the monastic community's structure and history is S. Dutt, *Buddhist Monks and Monasteries of India* (London: Allen & Unwin, 1962).

11. I have followed the most accessible version, the Vinayapitakam of the Southern Buddhists' Pali Canon. For a readily available translation, see I. B. Horner, *Book of the Discipline,* Sacred Books of the Buddhists, Vols. 9–14, 20 (London: Luzac, 1949–1963).

12. Vinayapitakam, Suttavibhanga, Pātidesaniya 1.

13. See Vinayapitakam, Bhikkunīvibhanga.

14. Vinayapitakam, Cullavagga 10. 3.

15. Anguttaranikāya 1, 14. 4.

16. Sanyuttanikāya 1. 5. 2.

17. Sanyuttanikāya 16. 10.

18. Vinayapitakam, Bhikkunīvibhanga, Pācittiya 8.

19. Nandakovādasutta of the Majjhimanikāya.

20. The first version was heard and repeated by the Chinese pilgrim Fa Hsien; the second, by the later pilgrim Hsuan Tsang. For both, see Beal, *Buddhist Records,* Vol. 1, pp. xl, 204–205. The third version is translated in S. Levi, *Mahākarmavibhanga et Karmavibhangopadesa* (Paris: E. Leroux, 1932), p. 174.

21. This story has been retold many times throughout Buddhist literature. The most readily accessible version is in the Pali Vinayapitakam, Cullavagga 10. 1–3.

22. I am indebted to Diana Paul for helping me to understand this model. See her book, *Women in Buddhism: Images of the Feminine in the Mahayana Tradition* (Berkeley, Ca.: Asian Humanities Press, 1979).

23. Reported in D. K. Barua, *Vihāras in Ancient India* (Calcutta: Indian Publications, 1969), p. 191.

Further Readings

Bartholomeusz, Tessa J. *Women under the Bo Tree: Buddhist Nuns in Sri Lanka.* New York: Cambridge University Press, 1994.

Blackstone, Kathryn R. *Women in the Footsteps of the Buddha: Struggle for Liberation in the Therigatha.* Surrey, England: Curzon Press, 1998.

Davids, Caroline A. F. Rhys. *Psalms of the Early Buddhists I: Psalms of the Sisters.* London: Henry Frowde, 1909.

Dutt, Sukumar. *Buddhist Monks and Monasteries of India: Their History and Contributions to Indian Culture.* London: George Allen and Unwin, Ltd., 1962. (For background information on Indian monasticism; little attention is paid to nuns.)

Gross, Rita M. *Buddhism under Patriarchy: A Feminist History, Analysis, and Reconstruction of Buddhism.* Albany: State University of New York Press, 1993.

Horner, Ivy Baker. *Women under Primitive Buddhism: Laywomen and Almswomen.* London: G. Routledge and Sons, 1930.

Kabilsingh, Chatsumarn. *A Comparative Study of Bhikkuni Patimokkha.* Varanasi: Chaukhambha Orientalia, 1984.

Paul, Diana Y. *Women in Buddhism: Images of the Feminine in Mahayana Tradition.* Berkeley, CA: Asian Humanities Press, 1979.

Tsai, Katherine Ann. *Lives of the Nuns: Biographies of Chinese Nuns from the Fourth to Sixth Centuries.* Honolulu: University of Hawaii Press, 1994.

17

Bones of Contention: Catholic Nuns Resist Their Enclosure

ULRIKE STRASSER

FEMALE CLOISTER AFTER TRENT: PRISON OR SANCTUARY?

In 1662 a group of cloistered Franciscan nuns in Munich accomplished an unusual feat. From afar and without the knowledge of their male superior, the so-called Pütrich sisters managed to acquire the entire skeleton of the early Christian martyr St. Dorothea from Italy. Confined but uninhibited by cloister walls, the nuns orchestrated the purchase of St. Dorothea's corpse in Rome and its shipment to Munich. The clandestine operation was driven by a single vision: the

---

ULRIKE STRASSER received her Ph.D. in History from the University of Minnesota in 1997. She currently holds an assistant professorship in the History Department at the University of California at Irvine where she is also an Affiliate in the Women's Studies Program and Core Faculty in the Religious Studies Program. During the academic year of 1999–2000 she was a Research Associate and Visiting Lecturer in the Women's Studies in Religion Program of the Harvard Divinity School. Ulrike Strasser has published a number of articles on religion, sexuality, and gender in medieval and early modern Europe. She is also a co-editor of "Kinship, Gender and Power: A Comparative and Interdisciplinary History" (Routledge, 1996).

Author's Note: A more detailed version of this article entitled "Bones of Contention: Cloistered Nuns, Decorated Relics, and the Contest Over Women's Place in the Public Sphere of Counter-Reformation Munich" was published in the Archiv for Reformationsgeschichte/Archive for Reformation History (1999). I would like to thank the journal for permission to reprint parts of the piece. My thanks also go to the University of Minnesota and to the municipal government of Munich for their generous support of the research involved. Finally, I would like to express my gratitude to the sisters of the Kloster Reutberg, in particular to the convent archivist, Sister Petra, and to the convent's mother superior, Sister Notburga, for the use of their archival records and for providing a glimpse of life behind closed doors.

sisters hoped to decorate the body of Dorothea and exhibit it for public veneration in their convent church. After they had lost access to the urban public earlier in the seventeenth century when the convent became subject to strict cloistering, the nuns strove to have a different kind of public presence through the exhibition of holy bones. Before their plan came to fruition, however, Provincial Modestus Reichart, the man in charge of the sisters, became aware of their secret actions. Reichart's discovery marked the beginning of a prolonged conflict between the nuns and the male hierarchy over the procurement and display of the relic.

In the following article I will present an analysis of this conflict, of its context, course, and meaning. A particularly revealing tale, the story of St. Dorothea and the Pütrich nuns offers us a glimpse of the largely unknown world of women's cloister in the wake of a major church council held at Trent in Italy between 1545–1565. For the first time in the history of the Catholic Church, the Council of Trent mandated strict enclosure (so-called claustration) for all women religious and called for an end to the open, socially engaged female monastic communities characteristic of the Middle Ages. Even though this unprecedented norm affected Catholic nuns everywhere, the enforcement of Trent-inspired cloistering and its implications for convent life have only recently received scholarly attention. We know little about the ways in which enclosure changed piety and work inside female convents or the nuns' social relations with the world beyond walls. What we do know suggests that the imposition of claustration came slowly and that it met with great practical and political difficulties.[1] Female communities apparently tried to ignore the church ruling as long as possible. When they could not longer avoid facing enclosure, religious women seem to have joined together with their families and local elites in an effort to resist such institutional change. Some of the reasons for the women's resistance come into view once we consider the cases of female communities that indeed became subject to strict cloister after Trent. Nuns who suffered enclosure generally experienced a severe reduction of their female networks and a dramatic curbing of their religious autonomy; as a result, already existing dependencies on male authorities in church and society became more pronounced.[2] Female liberty appears to have been the price of enclosure.

The history of Munich's Pütrich sisters is illustrative since it throws many of these general themes into sharp relief. More important still, these nuns also left us a unique record of their ability to maintain their independence despite, and at times even because of, enclosure: the story of the conflict over St. Dorothea's remains.[3] Recorded by a Pütrich nun, who does not reveal her name but was herself involved in the affair, this story sheds light on less visible aspects of female enclosure after Trent. It shows the cloister not merely as an institutional tool for controlling women but also as a place for female agency where women could and did create religious and social meaning. Closed doors may have locked women in, but they also locked men out. After the abolition of urban brothels in the sixteenth century, nunneries were in fact the only all-female institutions in early modern Germany, leaving women to their own devices in an unparalleled space of their own. What then happened after the doors closed? What use did nuns make of the separate sphere of the cloister? And did the violent imposition of cloister really put an end to women's resistance to involuntary enclosure?

In order to answer these questions, it is necessary first of all to begin at the beginning and to say a few things about the Pütrich sisters' way of life in the days leading up to their sequestration.

PERMEABLE WALLS AND CIVIC ENGAGEMENT

Founded in the thirteenth century, the original Pütrich convent was among those medieval female religious communities whose inhabitants, unlike the inhabitants of more contemplative and enclosed convents, lived a life of close contact with the surrounding urban community. An activist, self-directed piety marked the first centuries of the convent's existence.[4] First as medieval beguines—laywomen who did not take formal vows and followed only a very basic set of rules—and later on in loose affiliation with the Franciscan order—as so-called tertiaries who took vows and accepted more elaborate precepts—the Pütrich sisters played a conspicuous role in Munich's civic society.

While still uncloistered, the community offered a place of residence to women in need, such as unemployed maidservants, old widows, or impoverished single women, thus accommodating a steady stream of temporary guests and visitors. The sisters also took care of Munich's sick and dying. Although most of this work was done inside their convent, the religious women also ventured into burgher homes and tended the ill there if needed. The sisters' care of bodies moreover extended far beyond the deathbed. Their most noticeable public function was as mourners who performed rituals of grief during funerals and commemorative prayers for the salvation of the deceased's soul at each anniversary of death. This pious practice entailed regular forays into the larger urban environment, into various parish churches and to the private altars in the homes of Munich's wealthy. Earning them the title of soul-nuns ("Seelnonnen"), this spiritual labor represented an important source of income, for the prayers and rituals were performed for benefactors in return for economic support. The religious women on occasion supplemented these returns with proceeds from the labor of their hands by producing and trading textiles. Textile trade represents yet another example of the many people and services that traversed in and out of this religious community: female kin and friends took supplies to the sisters and picked up finished products for sale on the local market.

The Pütrich community thus carried out a multiplicity of religious and social functions in Munich and was deeply woven into the fabric of civic life in Munich. Because the religious women met important social needs in the city, the burghers by and large appreciated the sisters' public presence. Over time, however, clergymen and the Bavarian Court, for their own respective reasons, began to interfere with the sisters' unregulated access to urban society and the flexible form of religious life inside their convent. The church's male hierarchy found unstructured and unsupervised female religious communities in general to be increasingly problematic. From the fifteenth century onward male church officials, sometimes in collaboration with especially zealous sisters, sought to institutionalize stricter rules of conduct and closer male supervision in women's religious houses. At the same time, Bavaria's territorial rulers were gradually consolidating and expanding their power over various urban institutions in the state capital. As state authorities strove to establish themselves as the central power and eminent moral authority in a profoundly religious society, they also developed a vested interest in imposing what they considered higher spiritual standards upon religious communities. In this manner, these authorities hoped to be able to harness the sacred power associated with monastic communities to the state's own ends.

It was only a matter of time before these two developments in church and society came together, dramatically transforming Munich's open Pütrich convent into a strictly cloistered nunnery. A brief discussion of the circumstances surrounding the convent's final sequestration in 1621 will help set the stage for the story of St. Dorothea.

CAUGHT BETWEEN CHURCH AND STATE: THE ENCLOSURE OF 1621

The vicious religious conflicts connected with the Protestant Reformation provide the larger context for the cloistering of the Pütrich sisters in the Bavarian capital. During the sixteenth and seventeenth century theological rivalries between Protestants and Catholics became a catalyst for social, cultural, and political change. Those in power usually saw religious dissent as a threat to law and order, and were therefore unwilling to tolerate diversity of beliefs in the territories under their control. Rulers took sides and, with the advice of theologians, they proceeded to try to prove the superiority of their respective faiths by creating a more godly society. According to an imperial law of 1555 Germany's territorial rulers had the right to dictate the religious faith of those living under their rule. This particular legal provision gave sovereigns a powerful justification for regulating numerous aspects of their subjects' lives and for tightening their grip on various institutions that had enjoyed greater independence in the past. In the course of the Protestant Reformation and the Catholic Counter-Reformation, rulers all over Germany thus discovered that by promoting religious reform they could also expand the reach of their own governments.

In Catholic Bavaria, as in many other territories, the mixture of religious reform, state formation, and social disciplining led to a strengthening of patriarchal rule in society.[5] Secular and ecclesiastical authorities in this stronghold of the old faith found common ground in a vision of religio-political order built on three pillars of male authority: first of all, God the Father should exercise authority over humanity; second, the "Landesvater" (the Father of the land or ruler) should exercise authority over his subjects; finally, the "Hausvater" (the Father of the house or male head of a household) should exercise authority over his dependents, including the women in his charge. In this scheme of things, patriarchal authority guaranteed order on all levels, with the household as the smallest building block of society and a part of the public sphere.

At this stage of state building, however, Bavaria's rulers still lacked direct means to exercise social control over households. To compensate for this lack, they made legal changes that aimed at strengthening the position of the *Hausvater* and deploying him as an agent of state authority. For men this meant that more and more the state held male heads of households publicly accountable for the behavior of their female dependents. For women, on the other hand, the greater social and cultural import of male-headed households created a situation in which female respectability became inextricably tied to being under the supervision of a man at the helm of a household community. "Masterless" women, as they were called in the language of the time, became ever more suspect at the same time as female-headed households were defined out of a respectable existence altogether.

Female convents could not remain unaffected by these trends since they were not just religious houses but also female-headed households of sorts. The changing meaning of the term "Frauenhaus"—literally a house of women—captures the larger developments very well.[6] In the Middle Ages, any house without male supervision—be it a religious house, like the initial Pütrich convent, a female-headed household, or one of Germany's many urban brothels—was simply called a Frauenhaus. The term was encompassing and value-free. In the early modern age, however, authorities tried to draw a distinction between brothels and other houses of unmarried women based on the dwelling's accessibility to men. By the time of the Protestant Reformation, the only socially sanctioned Frauenhaus that was open to men was the civic brothel. It is no accident that the German term "oeffentlich"—public—derives from "offen"—open. This etymology reflects the emergence of a particular kind of public sphere reserved for men. Women who ventured into *this* public sphere risked being labeled *not* respectable. Similarly, women who lived in open households without a male head were in danger of being associated with houses of prostitution. The term Frauenhaus, especially in conjunction with "open," became unequivocally linked to immorality. To the extent that religious houses of women were open, they moved close to brothels in terms of cultural signification.

Protestants and Catholics alike saw a connection between convents and brothels and they shared a profound distrust of unsupervised women, although they disagreed on the theological points behind the sentiments. Protestants believed that sexuality was a natural human need but should be confined within the safe haven of marriage alone; they rejected celibacy, celebrated marriage as the condition most pleasing to God, and condemned every form of extra-marital sexuality. The amoral state of affairs in many monastic houses, Protestants argued, was living proof for the accuracy of their doctrines. The "wanton nun" was a stock character in Protestant sermons and pamphlets. It is telling that when Protestants took over an area one of their first moves, in addition to setting up new marriage laws, was to abolish monastic houses and disband urban brothels.

Catholics, on the other hand, clung to the notion that celibacy and virginity were superior to the married life. Yet in the end this belief brought about convent reforms that were clearly influenced by the Protestant critique of nunneries as camouflaged brothels. These changes began with several new regulations passed by the Council of Trent, which inaugurated the Catholic Counter-Reformation. Significantly, the council fathers abolished brothels in the territories under Catholic rule, as part of an intensified campaign against extra-marital sexuality that rivaled the Protestant efforts. In addition, Trent decreed convent reforms that were designed to re-establish monastic houses as unambiguously sacred spaces, thus lending credibility to the doctrinal claim that the chaste life was most pleasing to God. This agenda had distinct consequences for male and female religious communities.

Following a long tradition of clerical misgivings about women's moral capacities, the council fathers of Trent issued more explicit reform measures for female religious houses than for male monasteries. Specifically, they installed a double safeguard against women's allegedly greater proneness to sin: strict male supervision and spatial control through enclosure. After Trent every female religious house "should be ruled" by a clergyman, either a bishop or a male superior of the women's order of affiliation. These men should also see to the women's obedience toward the claustration norm. Issued at the council's conclusion in 1563, this unprecedented norm implied a tightening of discipline in already somewhat enclosed communities and the imposition of physical segregation on open convents.[7] By 1566, the norms of cloister and guardianship were moreover extended to female tertiaries such as the Pütrich sisters, overriding retroactively the more liberal conditions under which current members had entered religious life.[8] In other words, the Council of Trent lay the groundwork for re-creating nunneries in the image of male-headed households with the added component of confinement, which would clearly differentiate these female religious houses from the offensive open houses of public women.

It comes as no great surprise, given the Pütrich community's traditional openness and engagement with the larger world, that the sisters resisted this Trent-inspired drive for enclosure. In the 1580s the religious women succeeded in fending off a first claustration attempt on the grounds that it was fundamentally at odds with their customary ways. This clash between female monastic practice and the Trent regulations recurred in 1621, when the religious women were once again confronted with enclosure. This time, however, the nuns had to surrender to the combined clout of church and state authorities, both of whom were bent on reform.

In the charged atmosphere of the beginning decade of the Thirty Years' War between Catholics and Protestants, Maximilian I, Bavaria's most zealous ruler and fervent advocate of patriarchal power, at last initiated the process by which the religious women in the Pütrich convent were put under lock and key. Convinced that the only way of securing God's ongoing support for the Catholics was to make sure that his subjects led moral lives, Maximilian made moral and social reform the order of the day. In Munich, his state capital and designated showcase of the new order, there was a wave of legislative efforts to combat human vice, as well as numerous other interventions in local affairs.[9] Among other things, Bavaria's territorial ruler called upon a particularly strict group of Franciscan monks from Italy, the so-called Reformati, to clean house in Bavaria's Franciscan religious communities and to subject their inmates to the reforms outlined at Trent. He asked them to begin their work in Munich.[10]

When the Reformati were finished with their task, the women's community in the Pütrich convent had become a radically different place.[11] First, the physical structure was altered. The sisters' living quarters and their devotional spaces now formed a compact area of confinement to which the mother superior and the newly appointed gatekeeper alone held a key. The cloister interfaced with the world at only two points. A chamber adjacent to the cloistered sphere, the so-called "parlatorium," served as an area for the reception of outsiders who could speak to the nuns through the barred windows separating the chamber from the cloister itself. There was also a convent church where the nuns fulfilled their liturgical duties in the choir while Munich's faithful gathered for prayers and masses in the nave.

Second, as decreed at Trent, cloistering went hand in hand with close supervision by male Franciscans. The only men allowed to set foot in the convent after its enclosure,[12] the Reformati, conducted repeated visitations in the community. During the first decade after enclosure these visitations regularly resulted in the ousting of convent officials and their replacement with nuns who were more amenable to the new regime. Needless to say, the cloistered female tertiaries could also no longer seek out spiritual guides of their own preference among Munich's religious. Confined to their own community, they instead were required to confess their sins to a confessor whom the Reformati appointed.

Third, claustration resulted in a profound restructuring of convent piety and a reconfiguration of social relations with the outside world. The nuns were suddenly cut off from urban life and from their kin, who were restricted to a few visits to the convent's parlatorium per year. The religious women could no longer take care of the sick and dying, nor could they carry out their traditional textile work or participate in funeral services. All they could do was pray behind walls. We can imagine that this externally imposed complete segregation must have put a serious strain on the psyches of the convent's female inmates, most of whom were only in their twenties, thirties, and forties. Because leaving was not an option, they would have to live for many years with the new restrictions.

Finally, the life of isolation spelled greater dependence on the Bavarian Court for the nuns. Maximilian founded a daily mass for his own and his wife's salvation to be celebrated within the cloistered area. The Pütrich women were required to attend and recite prayers in return for the Court's financial support. The measure might have eased the economic burden of cloistering, but it also tied the sisters more closely to the ruling dynasty. Having been mourners for the public in the days before Trent, the sisters were now designated to become, above all, cloistered guardians of the spiritual welfare of Bavaria's rulers. Or so the reforming men hoped.

BEHIND CLOSED DOORS AND CRANNIED WALLS

The internal convent document chronicling how St. Dorothea's remains were obtained contains ample evidence that the Pütrich nuns had managed to poke gaps into their cloister walls at least by 1662, if not earlier. By summer of that year the sisters, under the leadership of Mother Superior Maria Geroldin, had begun negotiations with a Capuchin brother and friend named Gregorius. Like other members of the Capuchin order, Gregorius was known for his skillful trading in relics. Even though they did not have their Franciscan superior's official permission, the cloistered women could not pass up the opportunity to take advantage of the Capuchin's expertise and mobility. When a meeting of his order's General Chapter took him to Rome, the women asked Gregorius to pick up a precious relic for their convent church during his visit there, a favor for which they would compensate him financially.

Once in Rome, Gregorius chanced upon a special opportunity. He could purchase for the sisters the entire corpse of an early Christian martyr from the catacombs! Since the accidental rediscovery of these subterranean tombs in 1578 and their subsequent exploration by archaeologists and clerics, such holy bones had become much easier to acquire.[13] Gregorius knew that the Pütrich sisters had coveted an entire saint's body for a long time. As soon as he had found one in good shape, the corpse of a virgin martyr named Dorothea, Gregorius wrote to the religious women in Munich to tell them that this great treasure was available.

Delighted at the prospect of acquiring St. Dorothea, the sisters began the process of moving the sacred virgin's corpse across Europe's map, despite the fact that they themselves were stuck behind cloister walls. They corresponded with Gregorius and made arrangements with him for purchasing St. Dorothea and transporting her from Rome to Munich via Bologna, Venice, and Bozen. The corpse travelled in a trunk, which also contained a carafe with the martyr's thickened blood and Roman attestations identifying the body as that of St. Dorothea. It was agreed that the Capuchin order's network of religious houses crisscrossing Italy and Germany would provide secure way stations for the corpse. Gregorius's task also entailed keeping the sisters up to date on the progress of the precious trunk and making sure that the body would not be put on a merchant carriage lest "the holy bones. . . will come out less than whole." Such a fate would reduce the body's value as a sacred object.

Cloister walls also did not prevent the nuns from organizing payment for the shipment and for Gregorius's efforts in Italy. To do this, kin connections were invaluable; these could be cultivated through letters and conversation in the parlatorium. Several nuns had grown up in merchant families and were therefore familiar with long-distance trade. Given this family background, it is no accident that the convent paid for their saint's remains via a bill of exchange, the means of payment used by most merchants. A local merchant named Gugler, a relative of a Pütrich nun, agreed to forward the bill directly to Gregorius in Italy.

Although the plan was simple, execution proved to be difficult. Gregorius obtained the body of St. Dorothea, but due to an idle courier the corpse did not leave Rome for about a month. And worse was yet to come. Somewhere between Rome and Bologna, Gregorius lost track of the travelling martyr. In the frenzied correspondence that ensued between Gregorius and the convent, the Capuchin assured the sisters that he was doing his best to find St. Dorothea. Again, enclosure did not deter the sisters from carrying out what they considered to be their share of the recovery mission: the convent immediately launched an involved program of daily prayers and masses, appealing above all to St. Anthony of Padua, the celestial helper in cases of loss.

At last St. Dorothea's body surfaced in Bologna, just in time. Anxieties over the corpse's whereabouts had been rising, and a faction of nuns had indeed begun to question the wisdom of the purchase as well as the good judgment of their mother superior. As soon as Gregorius's letter with the good news appeared, Mother Maria assembled her convent, hoping to soothe tempers of mutinous members. Undoubtedly with relief, she read out loud the Capuchin's letter, which also contained a rather enticing and diplomatic reminder of the benefits of acquiring and housing a saint. Gregorius reported a recent Capuchin success in transferring three sacred bodies to Linz in Austria. His account stressed that a large crowd of people had watched the solemn procession through the city's street and later on visited the saints in their final resting place.

This success story went to the heart of the matter: Europe's Catholic faithful imputed to holy bones and bodies of saints a sacred power that also translated into the social and cultural capital of admiration and respect for those who housed them.[14] During the sixteenth and seventeenth centuries the cult of the saints rose to new prominence among Catholics, partly because relic veneration was receiving so much criticism from Protestants. The Council of Trent endorsed heavily this uniquely Catholic practice, praising the invocation of the saints as "good and beneficial" and calling believers to the veneration of "the holy corpses of the holy martyrs" and other "relics of the saints."[15] With this dictum, the same church council that had launched the campaign for the enclosure of nuns ironically also staked out a field of pious activity which would allow cloistered women to cultivate ties with the world beyond the cloister. Providing a home for a saint was a potent and highly legitimate means of attracting visitors. Counter-Reformation Bavaria itself witnessed both a revival of traditional pilgrimage sites and the founding of many new ones, often with the support of the ruling dynasty. Ordinary people as well as clergy streamed to these local shrines in large numbers.[16] Gregorius' account of the events in Linz was intended to remind the Pütrich sisters of this potential to attract crowds, their reason for acquiring St. Dorothea in the first place.

But apparently not all the nuns were mollified; somehow word spread to the male Franciscans about the occurrences in the Pütrich cloister. Provincial Modestus Reichart, head of Bavaria's Reformati and the man in charge the Pütrich sisters, was incensed. Reichart was most horrified by two reports. First, it was a Capuchin, not a Franciscan, who had obtained the body of the saint. Second, the sisters seemed to be planning to duplicate the public spectacle around the holy bodies in Linz. From Reichart's point-of-view, these two acts violated the fundamental rules of Counter-Reformation nunneries: supervision through male superiors and the constraints of enclosure.

What linked these two issues and gave them their particular sting was the notion of the public presence of nuns. The term "Oeffentlich"—public—reverberated through the subsequent debate between Reichart and the sisters. Yet, the meaning of this term was far from unequivocal. A closer look at the debate between the clergymen and the nuns reveals that their disagreement was part of a much larger contest over gender roles in early modern European society which pitted male state and church authorities, on the one hand, against secular and ecclesiastical women, on the other. Reichart essentially argued from the male-headed household model outlined earlier when he scolded the nuns for conspiring with the Capuchins. Like any other male head of a household or Hausvater, Reichart knew that his honor was at stake if his women openly circumvented their male superior authority. As the chronicling nun summed it up:

> It was going to be to the disadvantage and disrespect of them (the male Franciscans) that we obtained the holy corpse in Rome through the Capuchins . . . and not through the Reformati, under whose obedience we live.

It was not without irony but entirely in line with the logic of a society organized around male-headed households that Reichart threatened to turn the nuns over to the Capuchins if they further refused to obey him.

The Pütrich sisters, in a shrewd application of the same logic, defended their decision to have a Capuchin mediator on the grounds that the order had a reputation for the successful and inexpensive procuring of relics. The Capuchins had proven this ability many times, the women stressed, unlike their Franciscan superiors who "up to this point . . . had not once brought a single body out of Rome." The underlying message was clear: governance was predicated on competence. The inability of one male authority could legitimate the women's resort to another.

Reichart also accused the sisters of plotting with the Capuchins to sponsor a public procession of Dorothea through Munich's streets. Such a procession would have demonstrated even more sharply his inability to control the women in his care. But not only his authority was at stake here. Reichart had a very strict understanding of female cloister. To his mind, the boundaries of enclosure would be violated not only by a public procession, but also by exhibition of the saint in the convent church. At most, he was willing to let the nuns keep Dorothea inside the cloistered area for personal veneration.

The Pütrich sisters, on the other hand, argued from a different understanding of their place in public. They contended that they had never even considered a public procession, but they did feel entitled to exhibit Dorothea's body to the public in their convent church. They treated their church as an extension of the cloister, while Reichart treated it as an extension of the "Öffentlichkeit"—the public—which was barred to religious women. Interestingly, the nuns' defense of their access to the cloister church parallels the rhetorical strategies of secular women in defending their access to the newly emerging public sphere. Women of all ages and social strata seem to have been aware of the sociopolitical changes occurring in the age of confessional conflict. Moreover, they knew what these developments meant for them: they were being relegated to the sphere of the household. Many secular women fought the new restrictions, often justifying their presence in the world of men by claiming a continuum from their households to urban life. They, like the early modern state, regarded the household as part of the public realm; yet, in contrast to state authorities, they conceptualized their role in the household as public and therefore radiating outward into other social domains. Because they already had a recognized public role as wives, women argued they could also speak on other matters of public concern.[17] There were clear parallels between secular and cloistered women's modes of resistance, just like there were clear parallels between church and state strategies of establishing patriarchal order.

When Reichart failed to intimidate the sisters through debate and moral pressure, he resorted to a different strategy. He retreated from his initial order to have the corpse of Dorothea delivered directly to his convent. Instead he told the sisters that although they "had begun this work without his knowledge and approval, he had resolved to help them see it through." Reichart gave the sisters permission to receive St. Dorothea and to initiate the procedure for authenticating the relic after it had arrived in Munich. All the while, however, the Franciscan monk was plotting an insidious course. He proposed that he would open the sealed trunk himself, ostensibly to verify Dorothea's identity. According to the Council of Trent, any newly acquired relic had to be approved by the bishop before it could be displayed and venerated.[18] The procedure entailed several steps, none of which were easily taken from a cloister. Most relevant in this instance, the shipped martyr had to be unpacked with a license from the bishop, who resided in Freising, an eight-hour walk away from Munich. Furthermore, the unpacking had to be done in the presence of witnesses and a notary. The strict observance of the regulations was especially important because the temporary disappearance of Dorothea's body was bound to raise doubts about the relic's authenticity. Reichart planned to open the trunk without an episcopal license, to violate proper procedure for authentication and thus to strip the body of any claim to sanctity.

The strategy, however, did not go unnoticed by the nuns, who had done some information gathering of their own. At this juncture, their tight connections to the Bavarian Court proved to be fortunate, even though these connections had been formed under less than freely chosen circumstances. The nuns had consulted a knowledgeable secular friend, a court official named Höcken, about the exact nature of the ecclesiastical guidelines. When Reichart made his well-calculated offer to open the trunk and verify the identity of the saint, the nuns were aware of his subterfuge. They were also ready to approach an even more powerful ally at the center of power:

> in order to preempt this, we turned to Herrn Zeller, the servant of our widowed duchess, and asked him to intercede with her on our behalf whether she might not be willing to remind and ask the pater provincial [Reichart] whether he had already obtained an order and a license from the bishop to open the holy corpse, and also that the opening . . . needed to happen according to the procedure of other relics . . . in the presence of a notary and other witnesses.

Even though she was the widow of Maximilian I, who had initially subjected the convent to enclosure, Duchess Anna in this case knowingly or unknowingly helped the sisters contest the confines of the cloister. She put pressure on Reichart to observe the rules, which bought the sisters time to develop a defense tactic.

When Dorothea at last arrived in Munich in December of 1662, the religious women were prepared. They sent Reichart Christmas greetings, told him about Dorothea's arrival and gently reminded him to request the episcopal license if he had not already done so. Alarmed by the nuns' apparent knowledge of protocol, Reichart paid a visit to the cloister "that very same evening." Speaking to the mother superior and the convent's administrator through the barred windows of the parlatorium, the provincial requested that they bring the corpse before him immediately. He claimed that he had received orders from the bishop to open the trunk right there, despite the absence of a notary or secular witnesses. The nuns knew better, and simply kept the doors shut. Ironically, the same cloister walls that Reichart had designated as boundaries for the sisters' radius of action now stood in the way of his realizing his scheme. "It was too late," said the mother superior and administrator, excusing the nuns' refusal. She proposed that Reichart come back the next day.

The night passed in turbulent debate over future action. So determined were most sisters to thwart Reichart's plan to strip the corpse of any claim to public veneration that they decided to return the locked trunk with the bones to the Capuchins if they themselves could not give the relic due respect. They also contacted Court Offical Höcken again for advice, informing Duchess Anna about the latest developments so that she would continue to throw her moral weight behind the sisters' cause. Determined to stop Reichart from opening the trunk improperly, the sisters then began mustering witnesses and a notary among their uncloistered kin. Unfortunately Reichart returned before they could round up a notary.

This time the provincial, accompanied by two other Franciscans, had his mind set on getting his way. He demanded that "the honorable mother should either open up enclosure or have the trunk with the holy body carried down into the parlatorium." The nuns did neither. Rather, they engaged in a very well-timed, tactical embrace of Counter-Reformation ideals. Instead of letting Reichart in or bringing Dorothea out, the sisters rushed into the parlatorium. They fell on their knees and began pleading with Reichart to rethink his decision. The gesture signaled submission while in fact it amounted to a refusal of obedience. The women then invoked in their own defense various norms backed by the authority of Trent. They pointed first to the need of obtaining approval from ecclesiastical superiors, in this case clearly the bishop and not Reichart. Second, they appealed to the duty of venerating the saints in a proper manner. And finally, the nuns did not hesitate to use their trump card: cloistering. They insisted that Reichart really needed to get an episcopal order to obtain the body and told him they were resolved to hold St. Dorothea in the meantime: "we will keep the holy body locked in our cloister and venerate it." Even when Reichart threatened to report the sisters to the Roman General of the Franciscan order, the nuns did not back down. In the end, Reichart was forced to accept that neither the door nor the package was going to be opened that day. He left, the anonymous chronicler tell us, "with great indignation and a bitter temperament."

There is no record of the subsequent settlement, but official approval must have been obtained because nine months later Dorothea was the center of a public procession in the Bavarian capital.[19] Next to the saint, however, Franciscan men were the focus of attention as they carried the holy body through Munich's streets and into the Pütrich cloister church before a crowd of onlookers. All the sisters could do was to catch a glimpse of the festivities from up high in the choir, after the procession had entered the convent church. Yet what the nuns saw from above was the result of the labor of their own hands. Prior to the procession, the women had spent no less than seven months preparing the corpse of Dorothea, tailoring and embroidering a radiant garment for the saint. The sisters themselves had provided the labor and raw materials and had donated precious stones and other valuables for the occasion. Some gave the rings they had received upon entering the convent, while others sold pillows and beds from their cells to be able to afford a proper contribution. In this way, the women behind walls essentially had secured some presence for themselves in the public spectacle. Moreover, this procession was only one of several ways in which the holy bones became thresholds for nuns to interact with the world beyond the cloister.

HOLY CORPSES AND THE CREATIVITY OF CLOISTERED WOMEN

In theorizing about the relationship between space and social practices, Michel de Certeau has drawn an intriguing distinction between strategy and tactics based on control over space. De Certeau uses this distinction to capture the essentially asymmetrical power relations between ruler and ruled without depriving the ruled of their agency. While the powerful can devise long-term strategies from their own "proper place," de Certeau suggests, the weak can at best resort to short-term tactics. Quasi-exiles in the social territory of the powerful, they have to make creative use of the spaces assigned to them, seizing the opportunities for the pursuit of their own interests as they arise, and, if necessary, appropriating the norms of the powerful.[20]

De Certeau's reflections offer a useful tool for thinking about the space of the Pütrich convent after Trent-inspired claustration. When the space of the cloister became important to male secular and ecclesiastical authorities, these men decreed enclosure, and the religious women had little say in the matter. Yet, even though new boundaries were effectively imposed upon nuns, the women proved themselves to be resourceful tacticians who made the best of circumstances they did not choose and even devised ingenious ways of countering new controls. The nuns' appropriation of the cult of the saints represents a particularly striking example of their creativity in contesting enclosure. St. Dorothea was only the first of a number of holy corpses and other relics that the Pütrich nuns acquired, decorated and displayed "for public veneration." The prominence of these sacred bones suggests a profound connection between the symbolic, the sacred and the somatic, straddling the physical boundaries of the cloister.

First, the practice of handling and outfitting sacred bones enabled the sisters to draw lines of continuity between the cloistered present and the uncloistered past of textile production and care for the dying. Instead of taking care of Munich's dead, the sisters took care of the remains of Christian saints. Rather than producing for the local market, the nuns produced textiles for relics. In this way, the women pieced together a world of their own from old traditions, such as care of bodies and production of cloth, on the one hand, and more recent Counter-Reformation dictates, such as the veneration of saints through their relics, on the other.

Caring for the bodies of others was also a social role that was reserved for women in early modern society. At least on the symbolic plane, care for the bodies of dead saints therefore connected cloistered women to women in the secular world. Beyond the symbolic, the bones of St. Dorothea, and perhaps also other relics, offered opportunities of direct connection and exchange with those living in the world. Once she was on exhibition in the church, St. Dorothea is reported to have worked a series of miracles whose beneficiaries were mainly women and their children, among them a number of the nuns' kin. Out of gratitude to the saint, these family members donated precious materials of the kind the sisters coveted and collected for decorating martyrs. The body of St. Dorothea thus became a medium of exchange for spiritual and material goods, as well as for gifts of affection between the female saint, the cloistered women and their secular female kin.

In addition, sacred remains were a forceful vehicle through which the nuns represented themselves to Munich's pious public. The nuns could no longer be in public, but they could draw the public into their own home, as it were, all the while engaging in a pious practice sanctioned by the Counter-Reformation Church. It was for good reasons that the convent published a pamphlet advertising the treasures in the cloister church and encouraging visitors to worship and see for themselves. These holy bones, lovingly decorated, signaled to the visiting public both the virtues and the riches of the Pütrich nuns, women who were bound by vows of poverty and enclosure. Signifying their virtues and carrying the nuns' intimate objects, these sacred remains became an extension of self. They served, in effect, as prosthetic bodies for the women whose own bodies were barred from public view.

There is yet another intriguing possibility for thinking about holy bones as a means of transcending the physical limits of the cloister. The Catholic cult of the saints deemed dead martyrs intermediaries between this world and the next and endowed their physical remains with a potency analogous to the possibilities with which contemporary sorcery credited bodily parts.[21] The vitae of cloistered nuns contain many tales of relics being alive and of nuns having experiences of corporeal transcendence while around holy bones. To us, bones signify death, and talk of out-of-body experiences has a ring of New Age philosophies that makes scholars uncomfortable. Hence academic instinct tells us to ascribe these tales to either psychological or hagiographic invention because they deal with a realm with which scholarly discourse does not deal easily: the realm of the spirit. Unless it is done in an "exotic" context, such as spirit possession in Africa or Asia, scholars generally have difficulties suspending Western ways of knowing. But perhaps we should at least consider grounding these seventeenth-century European tales of spirituality in the anthropological context of post-Trent cloistering. Thus we might begin to probe Counter-Reformation spirituality for the way it allowed cloistered women to move beyond convent walls and to counter exclusion from public life by entering into another world altogether. The invisibility or outright incredibility of some means of female resistance should not blind us to their power.

Notes

1. For examples from Catalonia, see H. Kamen, *The Phoenix and the Flame: Catalonia and the Counter Reformation* (New Haven, London, 1993).

2. For a general overview, see Gabriella Zarri "Gender, Religious Institutions and Social Discipline: The Reform of the Regulars," in *Gender and Society in Renaissance Italy,* Judith Brown and Robert C. Davis, eds. (London: Longman, 1998) 193–212, esp. 210–11.

3. This story is contained in a manuscript at the Franziskannerinnenkloster Reutberg (Landkreis Bad Tölz—Wolfratshausen), Klosterarchiv, Schublade 63/3: The text is entitled *Ordentliche Beschreibung Des gantzen verlauffs, wie die H.H. Reliquien und Cörper S. Hyacinthj Martyrers und S. Dorothea Martyrin wie auch vier benandten Stuek Heilthumber Der H.H. Martyrer Si. Calisti, Si. Elpistij, und Si: Demetrj mit Authentischen Brieffen und Sigill von Rom herauss in Diss würdige Gottshaus and Closster Si. Christophori gebracht: Dernach von dem Durchleuchtigisten hochwürdigisten Fürsten und Herrn Herrn [sic] Alberto Sigismundo Bischoffen zu Freysingen, als ordinario Loci, approbiert und mit dessen genedigisten Consens zu oeffentlicher verehrung, und allgemainen Trost Der Christglaubigen In unnser Clossterkürchen transfferiert und beygesetztworden.* Reutberg (Landkreis Bad Tölz—Wolfratshausen), Franziskannerinenkloster, Archiv, Schublade 63/3: The unpaginated manuscript is written in a single seventeenth-century hand and ends abruptly, suggesting that this was a copy of an original text. All details and quotes pertaining to the story of the corpse of St. Dorothea are taken from this source unless otherwise noted.

4. For an overview of the history prior to claustration, see Ulrike Strasser, "*'Aut Murus Aut Maritus?' Women's Lives in Counter-Reformation Munich* (Ph. D. Diss., University of Minnesota, 1997), pp. 156–90.

5. On this development in the German territories, see Joel Harrington, *Reordering Marriage and Society in Reformation Germany* (Cambridge: Cambridge University Press, 1995).

6. Beate Schuster, *Die freien Frauen: Dirnen und Frauenhäuser im 15. und 16. Jahrhundert* (Frankfurt a. M.: Campus, 1995).

7. Wilhelm Smets, ed., *Des hochheiligen, Ökumenischen und allgemeinen Concils von Trient Canones und Beschlòsse* (Sinzing, 1989 [Fotomechanischer Nachdruck der 1. Auflage, Bielefeld, 1869], pp. 167–79.

8. Ruth P. Liebowitz, "Virgins in the Service of Christ: The Dispute over an Active Apostolate for Women During the Counter-Reformation," in *Women of Spirit: Female Leadership in the Jewish and Christian Tradition,* Rosemary Ruether and Eleanor McLaughlin, eds. (New York: Simon and Schuster 1979), p. 150, n. 27.

9. Reinhard Heydenreuter, "The Magistrat als Befehlsempfäger: Die Disziplinierung der Stadtobrigkeit 1579–1651," in *Geschichte der Stadt München,* Richard Bauer, ed. (München, 1994), pp. 189–210.

10. Benno Hubensteiner, *Vom Geist des Barock: Kultur und Frömmigkeit im alten Bavern* (München, 1978), p. 90.

11. A fascinating record of these changes can be found in the journal of a nun who lived through the reforms: *Abschrifft die ander grosse Reformation und Clausur betr. so von einer Schwester die zur selben Zeit gelebt mit Vleis beschriben worden.* Munich, Bayerisches Hauptstaatsarchiv, Klosterliteralien, Fasz. 423, Nr. 3.

12. In emergencies, doctors could also enter.

13. See, for example, Hansjakob Achermann, *Die Katakombenheiligen und ihre Translationen in der schweizerischen Quart des Bistums Konstanz.* (Stans: Verlag Historischer Verein Nidwalden, 1979).

14. The beginnings of this phenomenon are traced in Peter Brown, *Cult of the Saints: Its Rise and Function in Latin Christianity* (Chicago: University of Chicago Press, 1981).

15. Smets, *Canones,* p. 166.

16. Philip Soergel, *Wondrous in His Saints: Counter-Reformation Propaganda in Bavaria* (Berkeley University of California Press, 1993).

17. Merry Wiesner, "Women's Defense of Their Public Role," in *Women in the Middle Ages and the Renaissance,* Mary Beth Rose, ed. (Syracuse: Syracuse University Press, 1986), pp. 1–27, esp. 21.

18. Smets, *Canones,* p. 167.

19. For a detailed discussion of this procession see Sabine John, "Mit Behutsamkeit und Reverentz zu tractieren': Die Katakombenheiligen im Münchner Pütrichkloster—Arbeit und Frömmigkeit," in *Bayersiches Jahrbuch für Volkskunde* (1995).

20. Michel de Certeau, *The Practice of Everyday Life* (Berkeley: University of California Press, 1984), pp. xviii–xix.

21. Lyndal Roper, *Oedipus and the Devil: Witchcraft, Sexuality and Religion in Early Modern Europe* (London Routledge, 1994), pp. 171–98.

Further Readings

Bilinkoff, Jodi. *The Avila of St. Theresa: Religious Reform in a Sixteenth-Century City.* Ithaca, N.Y.: Cornell University Press, 1989.

Liebowitz, Ruth. "Virgins in the Service of Christ: The Dispute over an Active Apostolate for Women During the Counter-Reformation," in *Women of Spirit: Female Leadership in the Jewish and Christian Tradition,* ed. by Rosemary Ruether and Eleanor McLaughlin. New York: Simon and Schuster, 1979, pp. 132–52.

Monson, Craig, ed. *The Crannied Wall: Women, Religion and the Arts in Early Modern Europe.* Ann Arbor, Mich.: University of Michigan Press, 1992.

Monson, Craig. *Disembodied Voices: Music and Culture in an Early Modern Italian Convent.* Berkeley: University of California Press, 1995.

Rapley, Elizabeth. *The Devotes: Women and Church in Seventeenth-Century France.* Montreal: McGill-Queen's University Press, 1990.

Roper, Lyndal. *Oedipus and the Devil: Witchcraft, Sexuality and Religion in Early Modern Europe.* New York: Routledge, 1994.

Strasser, Ulrike. "Brides of Christ, Daughters of Men: Nuremberg Poor Clares in Defense of Their Identity (1524–1529)," in *Magistra: A Journal of Women's Spirituality in History.* 1995, pp. 193–248.

Zarri, Gabriella. "Gender, Religious Institutions and Social Discipline: The Reform of the Regulars," in *Gender and Society in Renaissance Italy,* ed. by Judith C. Brown and Robert C. Davis. London: Longman, 1998, pp. 193–212.

Idem. "Ursula and Catherine: the Marriage of the Virgins in the Sixteenth Century," *Creative Women in Medieval and Early Modern Italy,* ed. by Ann Matter and John Coakley. Philadelphia: University of Pennsylvania Press, 1994, pp. 237–78.

18

Innovation and Tradition in a Contemporary Midwestern Jewish Congregation

MARIAN HENRIQUEZ NEUDEL

The Upstairs Minyan is a small Jewish congregation founded in 1965 at the University of Chicago Hillel Foundation. The two rabbis who have belonged to it are officially affiliated with the Conservative denomination (midway in traditional observance between Reform and Orthodox). The Minyan uses the Conservative prayerbook and regards itself, somewhat loosely, as a Conservative congregation. Its membership varies from twenty-five to fifty active members; a regular Saturday morning service may be attended by as few as five (especially in the summer) or as many as fifty (for bar mitzvahs and other special occasions). The membership is drawn from the university (especially graduate students and junior faculty), the neighborhood surrounding it, and, to a lesser extent, the rest of the city and its suburbs.

As a Conservative Jewish congregation, the Upstairs Minyan has operated in the context of a Jewish tradition that historically placed women on the periphery of religious ritual and organization. In the strictest practices of orthodox Judaism, women cannot be counted toward the quorum of 10 people required for public prayer, must not even be visible or audible to the male congregants in the synagogue, and are not permitted any role in public worship. They may not wear the prayer shawl and phylacteries required for men at prayer. And they may take no part in the enterprise of study, interpretation, and teaching by which Jewish religious tradition continually

MARIAN HENRIQUEZ NEUDEL, A. B. Harvard 1963, M.A. (English Lit.) Roosevelt 1973, J. D. DePaul 1977, has also done extensive graduate work in sociology and history of religions at Brandeis and the University of Chicago. She is now a practicing attorney and a member of the National Association of Women Cantors.

shapes, reshapes, and transmits itself through the centuries.[1]

For the past 100 years, this definition of the position of women in Jewish ritual and religious life has been under attack from many directions, and has been eroded among the majority of Jews in the United States. Reform Judaism at its outset abolished most of the ritual functions unique to men, including the quorum for prayer, the prayer shawl and phylacteries, and the authority of traditional jurisprudence. It abolished separate seating for the sexes, abolished the *bar mitzvah* (which marked a young man's accession to the age at which ritual obligations become binding upon him), and instituted confirmation as a coming-of-age ritual for boys and girls. At least two women were ordained as rabbis in the early years of Reform (before 1940), one in Germany and one in the United States. Another woman rose to an outstanding public position in Liberal Judaism in England.[2]

Conservative Judaism adopted mixed seating, but rejected virtually all the other Reform innovations which affected the position of women. Unlike the Reform rabbinical seminaries, the Conservative seminary admitted women only for its graduate program in religious education.

When the Upstairs Minyan was founded, the current wave of feminism was just beginning, and had had virtually no impact on any major religious body in the United States. Nevertheless, the Upstairs Minyan self-consciously organized itself on the basis of six principles that, while not directly inspired by feminist thought, helped women become influential early members of the group. These six principles also made the Minyan different from any other Conservative congregation at the time. A member of the Minyan who wrote a history of the group during this era lists the six principles. First is intellectual openness on religious questions and second is respect for tradition. Affirming the legitimacy of pluralistic religious and Jewish experience is third, while respect for the resources of nonprofessional group members is the fourth organizing principle. Concluding the list are belief that maximum self-involvement is beneficial for both individual and group, and a preference for informality and flexibility.[3] Clearly, such principles, reflecting commitment to using skills and meeting needs of members, combined with the fact that some of the Minyan's most influential early members were women, resulted in definite influence from women and increased participation by women.

The influence from and increased participation of women in the Minyan can be clearly documented in three important areas. First, one can trace women's increasing participation in liturgy. At the outset, women were confined mainly to doing English readings in the mainly-Hebrew service. Initially they began to do Hebrew readings and to be counted in the quorum required for worship; services were still led by men, however. Next, they began to lead regular Saturday morning services, to recite the blessings for reading the Torah, and to read from the Hebrew Torah scroll. Finally, women began to lead services and to read from the Torah scroll for the High Holiday services, which involved a much larger congregation composed mainly of people not familiar with the Upstairs Minyan and its innovations. A second area in which women were innovative deals with ritual accessories important to formal Jewish worship but not usually used by women. Relatively early in the Minyan's history, women began to wear the prayer shawls and skull caps typically worn by men for Sabbath worship. Thirdly, the liturgical text of the Jewish prayerbook was sometimes changed to reflect the Minyan's increased sensitivity to the exclusion of women from traditional forms and a need to include them. Less radical was the earlier inclusion of female ancestral heroes (Sarah, Rebecca, Rachel, and Leah) alongside the usual male ancestral heroes (Abraham, Isaac, and Jacob) and general references to "our Mothers" as well as to "our Fathers." More radically and less frequently, female language has also been used to describe and address the deity.

These innovations took place over a fifteen-year period; like the most recently hypothesized path for biological evolution, they happened in intermittent jumps rather than a slow, steady progress. The participation of women in English readings happened almost at the outset, perhaps because, by their very nature, English readings were not perceived as part of the traditional ritual, and were therefore not off-limits to women. Women had been similarly involved in Reform services for many years, and some of the Upstairs Minyan's members have always come from the Reform tradition. At about the same time, women were also being called on to take peripheral ceremonial roles in the service for the reading of the Torah, such as calling people up to the reading and helping cover the scroll after reading.

Parallel to these developments, women were extremely prominent in another, nonritual but very important, area. The rabbis who founded the Minyan encouraged substitution of a discussion, prepared and led by various Minyan members, for the traditional sermon. Women became very active in preparing, leading, and participating in these discussions. As a result, many of those discussions focussed on the role of women in Judaism, and raised questions that the rest of the Jewish community would not be considering for at least another five years.

Almost from the outset, women were counted toward the "*minyan*" or quorum of ten, required for public prayers. This was partly a matter of logistics; it would have been impossible to hold services at all on many Saturdays if the group had had to wait for ten *men*. The Conservative movement as a whole finally accepted the practice about ten years later.[4]

The use of English readings in the early years of the Minyan met several needs. It was a medium of "experimental" and "interpretive" approaches to the liturgy. Many of the readings were drawn from contemporary poetry and music, but some were written by Minyan members themselves. They also served the needs of a large proportion of early Minyan members, slightly more women than men, who knew very little Hebrew. Thus the use of English readings encouraged the participation of women readers, who might otherwise have dropped out.

As time went on, the level of Hebrew knowledge in the Minyan increased considerably, for several reasons. Many of the original members, through their participation in the Minyan, learned Hebrew and other ritual skills. Some took courses at local colleges to speed up the process. The Hillel house in which the Minyan met also offered courses in Hebrew and related fields. Concurrently, the use of English readings diminished, and an increasing number of members, both female and male, took at least occasional responsibility for Hebrew readings and for leading services. In addition, typically, *incoming* members had a higher level of Jewish education since the quality of education provided by the Reform and Conservative movements had improved. At about this same time, women began to read the blessings for the reading of the Torah—again, about ten years ahead of the Conservative movement as a whole.

As more women became comfortable with the Hebrew and developed a real sensitivity for its meaning, they—and several men in the Minyan as well—found some of the Hebrew unnecessarily exclusive of women and their experiences. The role of women in Jewish history became a particular focus of attention. Jewish history originates in a series of covenants between God and the sacred ancestors, usually listed as "Abraham, Isaac, and Jacob." The *text* of that history, in Genesis, gives much more prominence to the *female* ancestors ("Sarah, Rebecca, Leah, and Rachel") than does the language of the prayerbook.[5] A tradition is defined and laid out by its remembered beginnings; this element of Jewish origins had been lost, tragically and unnecessarily. And it could be recaptured easily enough. The numerous places in the traditional liturgy referring to the "fathers" were rewritten to include the "fathers and the mothers." References to "Abraham, Isaac, and Jacob" were paralleled by references to "Sarah, Rebecca, Leah, and Rachel." The first blessing in the central daily prayer, which ends "Blessed are You, Lord our God, Shield of Abraham" was revised to "Shield of Abraham and Sarah." After a few months, printed inserts were placed in the prayerbook at that blessing for the use of new members and nonmembers.

The reading of the Torah scroll, in more traditional congregations, is both an honored liturgical function and an occasional logistical problem. The Torah scroll, unlike most religious Hebrew texts outside of Israel, is written without vowels (rather like speedwriting). It is generally chanted to a particular set of cantillations. Learning to read the correct vocalizations in an unvoweled text and to follow the traditional musical line requires considerable skill and study. Well-educated orthodox boys learn it as the necessary preparation for their Bar Mitzvah ceremony. But Conservative religious education was, at the time, somewhat less reliable and many Reform religious schools considered such skills minimally important. Until recently, the religious education of women in *all* Jewish denominations paid virtually no attention to these skills. Therefore, most Conservative congregations tend to rely on the rabbi, the cantor, and a few male congregants or occasional paid readers to read from the scroll. Since the Minyan had already deemphasized the role of the rabbi, had no cantor, and lacked the funds to pay outside readers, it relied for many years on the better-educated men for Torah reading. But as women members improved their Hebrew skills, Torah reading seemed to many of them a reasonable next step. They attended classes, arranged for private tutoring, or had knowledgeable men make tapes for them. Many of these concerted efforts to produce more readers were directed at *all* members, including the men who lacked childhood training. But as a practical matter, most of the new readers were women. The Minyan's response involved no ideological shock but only considerable practical relief that a logistical problem had been solved.

At about the same time, women also began to wear the prayer shawl for services—sometimes just while reading the Torah, sometimes for the whole service. Some people—men and women—found this "jarring." It never became a universal practice, though it is universally accepted as something women can do if they choose.

Over the last eight years, a few women have been exploring the use of female language to describe and address the divinity. Experimental services have been done on several occasions; rewritten versions of the blessings have been provided as optional inserts in the prayerbook. The issue has been raised on numerous occasions and is likely to be important in many further discussions.

Usually, two or three years elapse between what the Minyan has accepted as common practice in its own Saturday morning services, and what Minyan members will do in High Holiday services for the larger community. All forms of ritual participation by women as well as liturgical changes reflecting the role of the biblical matriarchs have followed this pattern. Some of these changes are explained by the rabbi at the beginning of the holiday services in which they were introduced. Others, such as calling women to read the blessings for the Torah or to read the scroll itself, were simply left to speak for themselves. The reason for this timelag has never been made explicit but is probably a combination of two factors: the need of Minyan members, especially those who lead the holiday services, to feel completely at ease with the innovation, so they do not make an error or omission due to nervousness or unfamiliarity, and the sense that the outside world was moving in the same direction on many of these issues and should be given a chance to catch up.

A few innovations have been tried, and often retried, without ever becoming the norm. The wearing of *kipot* (skullcaps) by women is one such example. Though it is commonly done in some Reform and Conservative congregations, and though married orthodox women are required to cover their hair, even the women in the Minyan who regularly wear prayer shawls rarely wear skullcaps. This may be a residue of feminist reaction against the orthodox custom, which is based on a concept of *z'niut* (modesty) offensive to some feminists.

The most significant innovation which has not so far become generally accepted is the use of "female god-language." Despite numerous efforts by members, both male and female, with respected skills, knowledge, and status, the Minyan still predominantly uses traditional male images such as "father," "king," and "lord," and masculine pronouns when talking to or about the divinity. Gender is much more intrusive in Hebrew than in English or many other languages: there is no neuter gender, verbs have gender, gender persists even in the plural forms of nouns and pronouns and in the second person. The author suspects that female god-language has not yet conquered the barrier of the sheer grammatical difficulty pursuant to changing the masculine to the feminine gender.

Jewish knowledge and its place in the system of values and relationships common to the Jewish culture in general is crucial to the success and acceptance of all these innovations, including the grammatical changes from masculine to feminine gender. That knowledge can be characterized as having three components. First is the ability to read, speak, and understand biblical and liturgical Hebrew. Knowledge of Jewish history and literature, including biblical, talmudic, and medieval writings, along with the ability to convey that knowledge to others is also important. Finally the ability to sing and chant in traditional melodies is highly valued. Because the Minyan has always valued all of these forms of knowledge, status derives largely from such knowledge and the willingness and ability to share it with others. Because the Minyan is small and because it respects people with such knowledge, considerable attention is paid to their opinions and wishes. Members are strongly encouraged to acquire knowledge and are rewarded with status and deference for doing so.

This emphasis on skills has been important in determining women's position in the Minyan over the years. Although at the outset most of the women in the Minyan did not have the requisite knowledge and training, they all shared the Minyan's perception of itself as a place where such skills could be taught and learned. Most of them felt an obligation to acquire what learning they could. Once they acquired it, they felt both the obligation and the right to use it communally. Moreover, once they had these skills, they were in a position such that other members (of both sexes) took their opinions—including their feminism—seriously.

The Minyan thereby encouraged a self-reinforcing process in two ways. First, the emphasis on authentic liturgical skills moved the group quickly toward doing services entirely or primarily in Hebrew. This put pressure on members to acquire or improve their skills in Hebrew and discouraged new members who felt unwilling or unable to do so from remaining with the group. Thus the felt need for English readings diminished even further and even greater Hebrew and liturgical skills were demanded from even the less active members who remained. Second, as the women who remained with the Minyan acquired greater liturgical and linguistic skills, their participation became more important to the group as a whole, and their beliefs and commitments—including feminism—became more accepted by the group. As they became more central to the group, they were in a position to press for even greater openness to female participation, thereby bringing even more women into positions of status. And so on.

Let me clarify what is—and, more important, what is *not*—meant by "status" in this context. The Minyan is a voluntary organization; it owns no property, pays no salaries, and has an annual budget in three digits, raised by assessing dues and spent primarily for charity and refreshments. There is a treasurer, whose duty is to sign checks and keep the books for these purposes. There is a coordinator, whose duty is to see to it that the responsibilities for leading services, reading from the Torah scroll, bringing refreshments, and leading discussions are covered every week. Both these positions are considered obligatory burdens rather than honors. The rabbi is a member of the Minyan; at most his status may be that of *primus inter pares;* his opinions carry weight because of his learning and because as an individual he is firm in his opinions. When the Minyan is acting on behalf of Hillel, or of the local Jewish community as a whole, his position gives him more weight.

Consider a recent example: Among the responsibilities of the Minyan in planning the High Holiday services is the selection of extra, nonliturgical, readings added to the service at various points for reflection and meditation. For the past four years, the committees in charge of these selections have brought in poems by German holocaust survivors, such as Nelly Sachs, both in the original German and in English translation. Although the Minyan normally reads all non-English readings in both the original and in English, the Sachs poems and other German selections have so far been read only in English. The rabbi and a few other members feel strongly that the German language—even when used by German Jews to write about the Holocaust—cannot properly be used in a Jewish liturgy. There is strong opinion on the other side, both on the literary principle that, when available, the original—especially for poetry—should always be read along with the translation and on the political principle that no language should be abandoned to the enemies of its Jewish writers. But so far the rabbi's opinion has been the last word, primarily because the High Holiday services are not merely a Minyan function, but represent the Minyan and Hillel to the larger Jewish community. Presumably, if a member leading a Saturday morning service chose to insert a Nelly Sachs poem in the original German, that choice might lead to some heated discussion, but it would not be vetoed.

Status clearly does not derive from holding administrative office in the Minyan. Nor does it determine who holds office, except perhaps in a negative sense. A member whose skills are valued and who regularly puts those skills at the disposal of the Minyan can avoid group pressure to volunteer as coordinator or treasurer. Conversely, a person who feels ill at ease leading a service may choose to volunteer as coordinator instead, thereby fulfilling a sense of obligation to the group. Status inheres in the rabbi's position for reasons extrinsic to the Minyan and rooted in its relationship to outside groups.

Status within the group derives almost entirely from ability and willingness to lead services, read Torah, teach skills, and share Jewish knowledge. It should also be noted that while people with strong singing voices are likely to be perceived as having a high level of liturgical skills, several members are deeply involved in liturgical functions and respected for their abilities, despite a somewhat limited ability to carry a tune.

In conclusion, it is appropriate to turn from internal analyses of the Minyan to analysis of the Minyan as innovative precursor in American Judaism in general. During the twenty years of the Minyan's existence, the role of women in the Conservative movement to which the Minyan is linked has changed drastically. The pattern of change somewhat parallels the changes within the Minyan; in the Conservative movement women have progressed from being counted toward a quorum, to being called to read the blessings, to being ordained as rabbis and cantors. But in every instance, the Minyan was at least five years ahead of the Conservative movement. Furthermore, many of the changes common within the Minyan have not yet happened in the Conservative movement as a whole and may never happen. Most notably, the new Conservative prayerbook,[6] published in 1985, still includes no mention of the biblical matriarchs, much less any female god-language.

Why has the Minyan been able to transform the role of women in a way that the Conservative movement as a whole has not yet achieved? The Minyan, and especially the feminists and pro-feminists within it, have succeeded primarily by taking advantage of two elements deeply rooted in Jewish tradition.

One is the heavy emphasis on congregational autonomy, local custom, and lay leadership of the congregation.[7] Although in the last hundred years American Jewish religious organization has often sought to mimic the centralized denominational authority of American mainstream Protestant church organizations,[8] the imitations are more apparent than real. In all three Jewish denominations, the rabbi, if there is one, is hired and fired by the congregation, usually on the basis of whether the more active and prestigious members of the congregation agree with his views on ritual and on relations between the congregation and the larger community. Especially among the orthodox, it is entirely feasible for a congregation to maintain itself with no rabbi at all or to import one only for the High Holidays, leaving the liturgical functions for the rest of the year to the most learned members of the congregation.

Among the orthodox, some control is exerted over the ritual and doctrinal vagaries of local congregations by other rabbis' responses and especially by responses of the more prominent rabbinical authorities. They may say, for instance, "It is forbidden to eat in the houses of the members of such-and-such a congregation because one cannot rely on their kitchens to be *kosher*" (to serve ritually proper food). Reform congregations have a fairly strong central organization and depend on it for logistic and sometimes financial support. Furthermore, the position of a Reform rabbi often parallels that of the Protestant minister in terms of his centrality to congregational and liturgical function. Reform congregations usually do not function without a rabbi on any permanent basis.

The Conservative denomination, however, lacks both sets of denominational controls. Neither rabbis speaking for the authority of traditional Jewish law nor rabbis central to congregational existence characterize the Conservative movement. Such relatively uncontrolled congregational autonomy has enabled feminism to flourish in the Upstairs Minyan and in many congregations like it, long before the Conservative movement confronted feminism on any organized basis.

The other element of Jewish tradition which has enabled women to become so central to the Minyan is, of course, the emphasis on skills and knowledge. A group as small as the Minyan simply cannot afford to reject the skills and commitment of any member. Because of its unique orientations and its geographical distance from New York City, the Minyan cannot increase its membership significantly by drawing from the major source of learned male congregants for the Conservative movement—the disaffected orthodox. Instead, the Minyan had to develop these skills of its own members—*all* of its members who were willing and able to acquire such skills—and then had to give them the status that almost any Jewish congregation gives its most learned members. Arguably, the role of women in the Minyan was to some extent the rather common one of "reserve troops" brought in when the usual sources of man-power [sic] had failed.[9]

It is fair to ask, as Riv-Ellen Prell-Foldes does in her article on a similar group, the Westwood Free Minyan,[10] whether such groups merely allow women to take on roles traditionally appropriated by men in a system which is still fundamentally male-defined, male-oriented, and male-dominated. The failure of female god-language to become a regular part of the liturgy certainly raises that question. Two alternative explanations of that phenomenon present themselves. One, already alluded to, is the Minyan's commitment to high standards of liturgical practice, including grammatical Hebrew. The difficulty of producing a grammatically correct and literarily graceful redrafting of the liturgy using the feminine gender has so far deterred any attempts in that direction; no one wants to risk a superficial or hasty solution to such problems.

A more philosophical reason is perhaps more important. The fact that the liturgy has been revised to include references to the biblical matriarchs wherever their male counterparts are alluded to but not to include female images of deity whenever male images are used, suggests preference for historical rather than theological concerns. As one member has put it, "We know *Jews* are male and female, and always have been. We aren't willing to make such drastic statements about God, because most of us are a lot more literate historically than theologically." Furthermore, Jewish tradition, at least in this century, has strongly encouraged that orientation.

These explanations are further supported by the fact that the Minyan has used many feminist poems as readings, not only in its own Saturday morning services but in High Holiday services as well. This development, as we have seen, normally indicates complete and long-standing acceptance of the practice in question by the Minyan. Thus lack of female God-language is not the result of a rejection of feminist values, especially since for the past two years, the High Holiday readings have included an exploration of God's maternal traits in the books of the Prophets and other biblical sources. Rather these developments indicate that feminist language and thinking are introduced into the liturgy when they are consistent with the biblical and historical roots of the liturgy, and when they can be done either in literate English, when appropriate, or in grammatical Hebrew. Only if one argues that lack of female god-language radically excludes women could one argue that women are merely taking on male roles in the Minyan with its current liturgy.

The participation of women in all phases of liturgical activity has affected male participation very differently from what might have been expected. When the Conservative movement was debating whether to count women toward a *minyan,* and again when they were debating the ordination of women as rabbis, one of the more popular arguments against both innovations was that if women took on more active liturgical roles, men would drop out of them.[11] This approach ignored the fact that the dependency of many Conservative congregations on a few Jewishly well-educated men for liturgical and organizational leadership excluded less-educated *men* as much as it discriminated against women. The Minyan's emphasis on acquisition and exercise of skills by *all* members has drawn many men into more active roles than would otherwise have been possible for them. Essentially, perhaps without so intending, the Minyan has provided a new model for Jewish education for both sexes—education as part of an ongoing adult involvement, in a group with a high tolerance for errors, slipups, and awkwardness among beginners.

Again, well within the models provided by Jewish tradition, the Minyan has always placed more emphasis on practice and practical skills than on doctrine. Like many Jewish groups, it has often changed its practice first and theologized about it later, if at all. The female god-language problem has remained unresolved, in part because many perceive it to be more theological than practical. A resolution of that problem will probably have to await the highly practical remedy of a grammatically thorough-going revision of the prayerbook.

An informal study of sixty two current and former Minyan members[12] indicates that many of them have affiliated with other Conservative congregations since leaving the Minyan's locality. Almost all who have done so characterize their current congregations as "egalitarian," though not necessarily as egalitarian as the Minyan. Many others who do not now belong to any congregation have stated that they have been unable to find any group like the Minyan in their current location. This suggests that the egalitarian values promoted by the Minyan are not a mere ephemeral "trend" among its alumni.

If this is the case, Minyan alumni may be in a position to help propel the Conservative movement in the direction of equal participation in liturgy, organization, and study. They will do it by the same quintessentially Jewish methods which have moved the Minyan in its basic direction—the slow, often irksome methods of learning, using, and sharing liturgical and linguistic skills to achieve lay leadership within individual congregations.

Because this is a slow process, it is almost certainly still incomplete, even within the Minyan. The next step may be a solution to the problem of female god-language—or it may be the beginning of a system of religious education for the children of Minyan members. But it will happen as all the previous developments have happened, by trial and error, on the most practical level possible.

In sum, to the extent that women have achieved equal involvement in the liturgical and organizational leadership of the Minyan and in other such egalitarian congregations, they have done so by using Jewish values and traditions. They have seen themselves not as imprisoned inside a web of strictures trying to get out, but as walled out of a garden of possibilities and trying to get in. And they have gained entry using a key procured from within.

Notes

1. Adler, Rachel, "The Jew Who Wasn't There," *Response*, summer 1973.

2. Umansky, Ellen, *Lily Montague and the Advancement of Liberal Judaism,* Mellen Press, 1983.

3. Ticktin, Esther, "Exchange of Resources and the Process of Change in a Jewish Worship Group," unpubl. dissertation, Department of Education, Univ. of Chicago, 1971.

4. For the Conservative movement's own characterization of the history of women's increasing ritual involvement, see pp. 105–11 of *Conservative Judaism,* by Herbert Rosenblum, United Synagogues of America, 1983.

5. See, for instance, Linda Kuzmack, "Agadic Approaches to Biblical Women" in *The Jewish Woman: New Perspectives,* ed. Elizabeth Koltun, Schocken, 1976, pp. 248–56.

6. *Siddur Sim Shalom,* Rabbi Jules Harlow, United Synagogues of America/Rabbinical Assembly of America, 1985.

7. *American Judaism,* Nathan Glazer, Univ. of Chicago Press, 1957, p. 35.

8. Jerome Carlin and Saul Mendlovitz, "The American Rabbi" in *The Jews: Social Patterns of an American Group,* ed. Marshall Sklare, Free Press, 1958, pp. 377–414.

9. Obviously, other Jewish congregations faced with the same choice in the past—to admit women to its cadre of central personnel, or to wither and disband for lack of such personnel—have chosen the latter alternative rather than the former. The Midwest in particular is littered with the remains of Jewish congregations where today no living Jew resides.

10. Prell-Foldes, "Coming of Age in Kelton," in *Women in Ritual and Symbolic Roles,* ed. Judith Hoch-Smith and Anita Spring, Plenum Press, 1978, pp. 81–82.

11. See, for instance, Lucy Dawidowicz, "On Being a Woman in Shul," in *The Jewish Presence,* Holt, Rinehart and Winston, 1977, pp. 46–57.

12. *The Minyan Report,* Marian Neudel, unpublished but circulated to former and current Minyan members, 1985.

Further Readings

Adler, Rachel. "The Jew Who Wasn't There." *Response,* summer, 1973.

Dawidowicz, Lucy S. *The Jewish Presence: Essays on Identity and History.* New York: Holt, Rinehart and Winston, 1977.

Glazer, Nathan. *Amercan Judaism.* Chicago: University of Chicago Press, 1957.

Greenberg, Blu. *On Women and Judaism: A View from Tradition.* Philadelphia: Jewish Publication Society of America, 1981.

Heschel, Susannah, ed. *On Being a Jewish Feminist.* New York: Schocken, 1983.

Koltun, Elizabeth, ed. *The Jewish Woman: New Perspectives.* New York: Schocken, 1976.

Meiselman, Moshe. *Jewish Women in Jewish Law.* New York: Ktav, 1978.

Reisman, Bernard. *The Chavurah: Contemporary Jewish Experience.* New York: Union of American Hebrew Congregations, 1977.

Rosenblum, Herbert. *Conservative Judaism: A Contemporary History.* New York: United Synagogue of America, 1983.

Sklare, Marshall, ed. *The Jews; Social Patterns of an American Group.* New York: Free Press, 1958.

Umansky, Ellen. *Lily Montague and the Advancement of Liberal Judaism: From Vision to Vocation.* Lewiston, N.Y.: Edwin Mellen Press, 1983.

V

SUCCESS STORIES

Women And Men in Balance or Equality

In this section we offer a different kind of success story—different because here are examples of women who achive eminence and satisfaction not despite their defined options but, at least in part, because of them. Each chapter describes an aspect of women's religious activity within a system that incorporates some principle of male and female balance or equality and in which, theoretically, neither sex predominates. Three possible variants of this theme are explored.

The first is exemplified in a tradition of Tantric Buddhism that developed in the final days of Buddhist history in India and then flourished for many centuries in Tibet. Here women and men who became *siddhas,* or "accomplished ones," found equal achievement and recognition in large part because gender was considered irrelevant to attaining their tradition's goals.

In the second variant, men and women are not equal in the sense that all the tradition's options are available to both; men must fit the male norm, and women, the female norm. But the men's realm and the women's realm exhibit balance and complementarity rather than hierarchy. In such situations of gender complementarity, women ritual specialists achieve prominence specifically as *women* who take on important ritual tasks that, in some cases at least, can only be done by a woman. Two examples of this pattern are explored here. The first follows Rosinta, a woman diviner of Bolivian highlands, as she weaves a ritual designed to banish misfortune. The second describes the popular women healers of *curanderas* recorded in Mexico since pre-Columbian times. Both examples have their roots in a dualistic, gender-based, cosmological system assuming that men and women both have powers special to them that link them to other male and female components of their universe. It is no accident that both these examples come from the Americas; such systems were not uncommon among native American peoples, especially from Mexico southward through the Andean regions.

The third variant is perhaps least common among examples of men and women in balance and equality. The Shakers, a millenarian Christian group, had inherited Christianity's common notions of sexual hierarchy. However, they proclaimed a radically new message of salvation that stood those inherited norms on end. Christ the savior had come again in the person of a woman, Ann Lee. Her appearance abolished the old social order and required a transformed relationship between women and men. The Shakers created utopian communities in which they lived out their vision of a heavenly society activated upon earth. By abolishing marriage and private property, and requiring dual male and female leadership, they came at least very close to achieving both balance and equality between the sexes.

Certain aspects of some of these "success stories" will, however, seem ironic to the Western reader. Tantric Buddhism itself may have been very open to women practitioners, but the surrounding milieu made it far more difficult for women than for men to take up the Tantric path. Furthermore, both men and women on this path attracted public scandal and persecution. In the Andean tradition described in the next chapter, male and female ritual specialists guard and use their respective powers, and both sets of powers are vital to community survival. However, in this division of labor and symbolism the power of men is connected with the good luck and the power of women with the bad. Finally, although the Shakers in the concluding chapter self-consciously balanced women's and men's roles and authority in their communities, this balance was not the result of their belief in either the intrinsic equality of the sexes or the irrelevance of gender to achieving the final goal. Women's subordination could be ended only because Shakers had entered the millennium, the time when "all things are made new." According to Shaker teachings, women had been even more vulnerable to evil than were men in pre-millennial times and settings. Furthermore, unlike men, who gained access to perfection after the life of Jesus, women had no access to perfection until the appearance of Christ as a woman brought a redemption specific to them.

19

Accomplished Women in Tantric Buddhism of Medieval India and Tibet

REGINALD A. RAY

Vajrayana, or Tantric, Buddhism is a late development both historically and in terms of a practitioner's progress in spiritual discipline. Historically, Vajrayana Buddhism emerged in North India probably some time after 400 A.D., and it spread to Tibet after 600 A.D. Although Vajrayana Buddhism, as well as Buddhism in general, became largely extinct in India after 1200 A.D., the Vajrayana was the main form of Buddhism in Tibet until the Communist take-over in 1959. Although Tantric Buddhism may now be extinct in Tibet as well, Tibetan teachers are transmitting this form of Buddhism to Western students. These students, like Tantric practitioners of every culture and historical period, begin the practice of Vajrayana Buddhism only after thorough grounding in more preliminary forms of Buddhist discipline.

The Vajrayana is unique among Buddhist traditions in the prominence it gives both to feminine symbolism and to women practitioners. The role of women in the Vajrayana is nowhere seen more clearly than in the Tantric "biographies" of the *siddhas* ("accomplished ones" or "enlightened ones"), who lived in India roughly between the eighth and the twelfth centuries A.D. These legendary biographies[1] present a vivid and moving picture of women as Tantric students and teachers journeying on their spiritual paths and transmitting the Vajrayana from one generation to another.

However, it is also important to recognize that there were always far fewer women Tantric practitioners than men and that only occasionally were major teachers female. No doubt the woman's essential role of wife and

DR. REGINALD A. RAY is Professor of Buddhist Studies at Naropa Institute, Boulder, Colorado, and Adjunct Professor of Religion at the University of Colorado, Boulder, Colorado.

mother in ancient India and Tibet made spiritual practice only a remote option for most women. It is also likely that people of the time, influenced by prevailing cultural mores, had more difficulty accepting women than accepting men as ascetics, yogis, and Tantric practitioners. Certainly, contemporay Buddhist monastic systems were predominantly male oriented and provided more options and encouragement to men than to women. In such a situation, women probably found it much more difficult to undertake Tantric practice than did men.

Nevertheless, many "accomplished women" did exist. If the women managed to step onto the Tantric path, two elements of Tantric tradition aided them in their journey. First of all, spiritual accomplishment in the Vajrayana does not depend on monastic withdrawal as it did in earlier Buddhist traditions. The householder yogi (feminine *yogini*) who is married and has a family is as apt to become a *siddha,* or accomplished one, as the monk or nun. The extra restrictions placed on Buddhist nuns that helped precipitate the decline of the nuns' order do not apply to the householder *yogini,* nor are householders who have their own sources of income as vulnerable economically as the nuns' communities were in India.[2] Second, basic teachings of the Vajrayana insist that women and men share equally in the same fundamental human nature, including the potential for enlightenment. People have different psychological traits, which are conventionally labeled "male" and "female," but these traits can be part of both men's and women's psychological makeup.[3] In an enlightened person, whether male or female, these traits are ideally balanced.

In this chapter I will discuss some of the most important themes found in traditional life stories of female *siddhas,* particularly from the Indian period of the Vajrayana. The material to be analyzed falls naturally into four major categories: the situations of women when they first undertake Tantric practice; women as Tantric practitioners; women and men as companions on the Tantric path; and women as accomplished teachers or *siddhas.*

WOMEN AT THE BEGINNING OF THEIR TRAINING

Marriage looms at the beginning of the stories of most women *siddhas.* Parents, friends, and suitors expect that the woman will follow what they consider her destiny. Some women, confronted with the prospect of marriage, refuse to cooperate because of their spiritual aspirations. Princess Mandarava, who later became one of the main disciples of Padmasambhava (founder of a major Tantric lineage), was pressured by her father to marry. She resisted him, because she wanted to devote her life to spiritual goals. Her father, angry and unyielding, placed a heavy guard around the palace to prevent her from fulfilling her desire. She escaped from her confinement and discarded her royal clothes; she pulled her hair out and scratched her face with her fingernails, so that no suitors would want her, and began her meditation practice. Only then did her father finally relent and accept her aspirations. There is a striking parallel between this story and the story of how the Buddha abandoned his royal station and undertook an ascetic life; however, this story places far more emphasis on the woman's determination.

Other women *siddhas* are impelled into spiritual practice by the failure of a marriage or by the death of their husband. For example, we know of Ni.gu.ma, who entered into Vajrayana practice after her husband Naropa (another major Tantric teacher) announced to her that he intended to leave her and enter into religious practice. She readily agreed with his decision and, after some discussion, both of them decided to present the matter to their families as if Ni.gu.ma's inadequacies were causing insurmountable problems for the couple. After it was finally agreed that the marriage should be dissolved, both Ni.gu.ma and Naropa entered religious practice and finally became ardent and famous Tantric *siddhas.*

Yet other women marry, only to find that the marriage is incompatible with their Tantric aspirations and practice. Laksminkara was married as a young child to the son of a neighboring king. As was the custom, she continued to live with her own family until she reached puberty. During this time she was a devout student of the Tantra. When she was finally sent to her husband's palace, she immediately perceived that her new environment was incompatible with her Tantric practice. She distributed her dowry to the poor, sent her retinue of servants home, and feigned insanity. She removed her clothes, smeared her body with ashes, and refused the attentions of the doctors sent to treat her. Her husband finally abandoned her, and she subsequently became an ascetic, living off refuse and sleeping in cremation grounds.

Several themes run through these and similar stories. All the women are depicted as spiritually precocious children who, at a tender age, hear and understand the *Tantras* and are accepted by some *siddhas* as disciples. Common to all the stories is also the theme of opposition from fathers, husbands, and in-laws, who do not understand the women's callings. These biographies present an interesting evaluation of the impact of marriage and men on women's spiritual aspirations. One often finds vividly negative depictions of both. Marriage is frequently portrayed as spiritually unproductive, and men as hostile and dangerous to spiritual aspirations and completely lacking in spirituality themselves. These stories describe men in such unflattering terms not because men as a whole were regarded as anti-spiritual but because the particular men who occupied important roles in these women's lives happened to represent and advocate an unenlightened view. This perspective may shed some interesting light on the negative attitudes toward women often expressed in early Buddhist literature. Do these attitudes indicate a blanket judgment of the limitations inherent in all women, or do they reflect experiences with particular women who were hostile to spiritual discipline?

Marriage, however, is not always depicted in the biographies as a spiritually neutral or negative situation for women. As we shall see, it can be a spiritually productive state, although this is generally true only if the woman's mate is another Tantric practitioner. The legends indicate that marriages with men who lack some positive relationship to Tantrism only rarely succeed.

It should also be noted that not all the women *siddhas* were involved in marriage during the early stages of their careers. Some were professional women with occupations of one sort or another, who may or may not have been married. Tilopa (founder of a major lineage) had a woman disciple who ran a liquor shop in Shravasti. She was highly successful in her trade, and her liquor was famous for its high quality and commanded a high price. Tilopa met her while drinking in her shop and accepted her as a disciple after some severe tests. Another student operated a liquor distillery for a king in Uddiyana. She is depicted as an able and perceptive woman, who knew not only her business but also the particular psychology of her employer, the king, who happened to be a non-Buddhist. Her Tantric teaching began when she told a Tantric teacher who was passing through the area exactly how to convert the king to Buddhism. The teacher was so impressed with her that he immediately gave her initiation and oral instruction.

WOMEN AS TANTRIC PRACTITIONERS

The stories about the women *siddhas* also cover the time between the women's formative experiences and their final success as fully enlightened *siddhas.* This intervening period of Tantric training and practice was usually very long; in one case, it lasted forty years. As one might expect, the largest proportion of biographical information on the women deals with this training period. However, most details of this training period are virtually the same for men and women and the accounts are technical and repetitive, filled with endless lists of names of teachers, initiations granted, meditation practiced, places visited, and Tantric deities of particular importance to the individual. For this reason, I will briefly summarize this period and only briefly describe what I consider to be some of its more important themes.

For most of the women *siddhas,* entry into the Vajrayana marked a radical change in their external situations. Often this change was a complete break with what had formerly been most important in their lives—their social roles as actual or potential wives. From this point of view, the women's stories are quite different from the men's, who usually did not experience such a radical and total break with their pre-Tantric life, since their primary roles were occupational, not social, and they could continue in their occupations while undergoing Tantric training.

Because of the women's complete break with their pasts, the accounts of their early periods of training stress social rejection and isolation, solitude and desolation. The story of Laksminkara, who had feigned madness to escape her marriage, is typical. Her life of royal comfort and status completely behind her, she roamed alone through the back alleys, scavenging garbage heaps, sleeping in cremation grounds, and practicing in isolated caves. The motif of feigned madness as a way of extricating oneself from an impossible situations recurs frequently in these stories and further underscores the women's social isolation and solitude.

Another major theme in materials about the women's training period is that of their relationships with their gurus, both female and male. These relationships are as difficult, painful, and costly for the women as they are for the men. The highly successful and wealthy liquor saleswoman from Shravasti had her entire business destroyed by Tilopa before he accepted her as a pupil. Another woman was accepted as a pupil only after she remained fearless and resolute in the face of a horrifying spectacle. Much is asked by the teachers, and apparently little or nothing is given in return. In many of the stories the students, whether female or male, are shown practicing under a teacher's guidance for many years, without receiving so much as a nod of the head. Even after important initiations and attainments, the trainees' trials and difficulties are by no means over, as the following vivid story about an important Tibetan teacher, Ma.gcig, illustrates.

After her separation from her husband, Ma.gcig was accepted as a student by a lama. She became his Tantric consort and received from him valuable teaching and guidance. After eleven years, when she was twenty-eight, her guru consort died. During the next three years, Ma.gcig experienced intense confusion, hardship, and pain. She developed incurable infections, and her body was covered with abscesses and pustules. Her mind became so completely disoriented and ridden with passion that the Tantric deities stood aloof from her, and even animals refused her offerings. Finally she met a teacher who showed her that she had brought her sad condition on herself through her own lack of awareness, her immaturity, and her attachment. He showed her the way to overcome her confusion, and later she became one of the most renowned and accomplished teachers, male or female, in Tibet at that time.

The qualities shown by the women students are the same as those shown by the men. They are persevering and often fiercely determined. They show openness, receptivity, and intelligence. They possess courage and fortitude, and their characters are independent and uncompromising. These traits are especially interesting, because many of them do not conform to the classical Indian views of what a woman is or should be. It is important to repeat that, within the framework of Tantric Buddhism, such qualities are not regarded as the province of one sex or the other but as human traits that can be found in both women and men.

One final aspect of the *siddhas*' training deserves mention. In the course of their initiation, Tantric practitioners are confronted with deities, the Yidams, that embody the practitioners' own enlightened nature in its pure form. In the Vajrayana such deities are both masculine and feminine. Significantly, just as men and women may have either male or female gurus, so they may be especially associated with male or female deities. Such personal deities are not mentioned in the stories very often, but, when they are, we note that women have special connections with male deities as often as with female, just as men may have special connections with female deities as well as with male deities.

WOMEN AND MEN AS COMPANIONS ON THE TANTRIC PATH

In the biographies women frequently appear as solitary *siddhas.* But just as often we find them in the company of men who are also Tantric practitioners. Also, when wife and husband are interested in Tantric teachings, both partners receive instruction together from a teacher and practice together. Many stories demonstrate that the female/male relationship can be an important part of the Tantric path for both men and women. For example, at a certain point in his career, Saraha, an important Tantric teacher, felt a need to do his practice with a female companion who was also a Vajrayana practitioner. The need was brought about by Saraha's realization that he was blocked from further attainment—a realization that seems to have motivated him to search for a companion. He journeyed to the south, where he met a woman Tantric practitioner who was an arrowsmith's daughter. Saraha worked with her, making arrows as part of his *sadhana* (the spiritual discipline assigned by one's guru). With and through her, whom he eventually married, and through his work, he gained valuable insights and attainments.

Such relationships between men and women, although they went against conventional Indian practice, were an important dimension of Tantric practice. In traditional India most intimate male/female relationships existed within the limits of caste restrictions. In the Vajrayana, however, other considerations were the basis for intimate relationships. Great importance was assigned to the capacity for insight, to the ability to see the relativity of caste structures, and to the willingness to step beyond them. Intimate associations with people from different castes would severely challenge one's own identity, both personal and social. Such associations were therefore encouraged because they would promote a breakdown of personal and social identity. Thus in the Vajrayana one often finds relationships between people of widely separated castes. For example, Princess Laksminkara worked closely with a latrine cleaner, and Princess Sankajati married a merchant. Similarly, many high-caste men were associated with women of low caste.

As one might expect, such relationships were considered as an outrage to Indian society, and stories of misunderstanding and even persecution of Tantric couples by their social environment abound. For example, one of these stories tells us that, after a certain king had received instruction from a *siddha,* he carried out his practice with a low-caste girl for twelve years. When he was finally found out, public outrage against him forced him to leave his throne in favor of his son. He and his consort went into the jungle and continued their practice there for many years. In the end, the two were put to death for their illicit relationship. Padmasambhava and Mandarava, two very important teachers, were also persecuted on account of their relationship. In one biography, their persecutors try to burn Padmasambhava to death, and Mandarava is thrown into a pit of thorns. Later both are wrapped in oil-soaked rags and burned at the stake, although once again they are able to survive because of their Tantric powers.

Some of the biographies, in spite of the opposition they describe, have a happy ending. Saraha was both a brahmin (a member of the highest caste) and an ordained monk. And yet, as we have seen, he married the daughter of a low-caste arrowsmith. Enraged at what they considered intolerable lack of propriety, a great crowd of people and the king of the region himself gathered to deride and criticize the couple. Saraha stood in front of them and said, "I am indeed a brahmin, and I live with the daughter of an arrowsmith, caste or no caste: there I do not see any distinction. I have taken the sworn vows of a monk and I wander about with a wife: there I do not see any distinction. Some may have doubts and say, 'Here is an impurity!' but they do not know . . ." At the heart of Saraha's message is the idea that social and religious distinctions have no ultimate foundation or substance and, therefore, no value. The story tells us that the king and the people accepted Saraha's view and left him and his wife alone.

One of the more interesting motifs of the male/female relationships depicted in these biographies is the degree of communication between the partners. In Tantrism communication is essential for spiritual growth, and transformed passion (total appreciation and love that expects nothing in return) is the driving force of communication. The fact that communication, which can result only from transformed passion, is considered so important in Tantrism helps us understand why relationships between women and men often play a very significant role in the ultimate success of both.

More specifically, communication between women and men is frequently used to improve each other's practice. A typical example is that of a male student who had been deeply immersed in meditation practice for many years. One day his consort interrupted his meditation because, having had an important insight into his practice, she wanted to share it with him. The interruption and her insight turned out to be decisive for his practice, and he subsequently experienced extremely high attainments. Another vivid example of the importance of communication is found in another legend about Saraha and his wife. At one point, the two went to a new locality and settled down. One day Saraha told his wife that he would like to eat radish curry. She prepared it, but when she brought it to him, she found him deeply immersed in *samadhi* (a meditative state), and she left him alone. The story tells us that Saraha stayed in that *samadhi* for twelve years without interruption and without getting up once. When he finally stirred from his meditation, he turned to his wife and asked for his radish curry. His wife replied, "You sit in *samadhi* for twelve years without getting up. And now you want your radish curry, as if it still existed. Besides, there are no radishes at this time of year." Saraha replied, "Then I will go into the mountains to meditate." And his wife said, "Simply removing your body from the world is not true renunciation. Real renunciation takes place when your mind abandons frivolous and absorbing thoughts. If you sit in meditation for twelve years and cannot even give up your desire for radish curry, what is the point of going into the mountains?" Saraha realized that his wife was right. He succeeded in his efforts to overcome unproductive thoughts and doubts and attained the highest state of self-realization.

The lively communication between men and women illustrated in these and similar Vajrayana accounts is not based on sex roles or other fixed identities, but rather on insights. One of the two practitioners has seen something significant about the other and confronts him or her with it. In both of these examples, the woman's observation challenges the man's conception of himself and his practice. Such a communication presupposes and demonstrates a point stressed above: according to the *Tantras,* men and women share the same psychological and spiritual world; they understand the workings of the mind and experience enlightenment in the same way. In these sketches, drawn not without tenderness, the women are depicted as highly insightful and intelligent, and their message is courageous and decisive. It cuts through the men's conceptual illusions about who they are and where they are, and confronts them with the reality of their situations. Here the women act as midwives to the men's own insight and to their spiritual ripening. Since these stories are told from the male practitioner's viewpoint, they stress the importance of the women's insights. But, needless to say, communication in a relationship is a two-way process that requires openness on both sides. No doubt the women would have had similar stories to tell.

Another important Tantric teacher whose story is told in the legendary biographies owes not only his accomplishments but also his initial exposure to Tantric practice to encounters with a mysterious female stranger. Abhayakaragupta, a famous scholar who came from a high-caste family in Orissa, one day was immersed in the recitation of a text when a beautiful maiden came up to him and said, "I am a Candala [a very low-caste] girl, and I would like to stay with you." Abhayakaragupta drew back and replied, "How can that be? I am from a higher caste, and I would be disgraced." The girl disappeared. A friend reprimanded him: "That was Vajrayogini (a Tantric goddess). It is too bad that you did not receive teaching from her."

Abhayakaragupta studied in Bengal, where his scholarship became more and more vast and illustrious. He knew all the *sutras* and the *Tantras* and received initiations from many masters. One day he was in the courtyard of a monastery when a young maiden came up to him dragging a chunk of raw beef dripping with blood and shoved it at him. Once again she said, "I am a Candala girl. Eat this beef that has been slaughtered for you." But Abhayakaragupta replied, "I am a pure monk. How can I eat meat that has been so blatantly prepared for me?" Again she withdrew.

Still not satisified with his learning, Abhayakaragupta wandered everywhere to receive different teachings. For a while he stayed at Nalanda (the greatest university of his time) and became even more famous. One night a girl who looked exactly like the servant girl who drew his guru's water came to him. She carried the ritual implements for a *ganacakra* (a Tantric ceremony involving drinking, singing and dancing together) in a small basket. "I have been sent by your teacher to perform with you a *ganacakra,* which, up to now, you have not been willing to enter into. Now is the time to do so!" When his misgivings won out and he refused her, she said, "You know three hundred *Tantras,* and you have intellectually mastered all of their teachings, right up to the end. How can you possibly justify these reservations about the actual practice of the *Tantras?*" Then she picked up her basket of *ganacakra* implements and went away. Next morning Abhayakaragupta's guru said, "You have excessive scruples. You had the opportunity to receive 'accomplishment' (*siddha*) from Vajrayogini, and you refused!"

Abhayakaragupta fell into deep despair and for seven days spent his time in prayer and refused all food. In the night of the seventh day, he saw an old woman in a dream. He recognized her as Vajrayogini and confessed and prayed to her. Although he finally recognized her and, letting go of his hesitation, opened himself up to her, she reminded him of his constant unwillingness to communicate with her and implied that his refusals had injured their relationship. In spite of the goddess' reproaches, the dream was the turning point of Abhayakaragupta's quest for knowledge. He had finally seen Vajrayogini, she had accepted him, and he had received valuable teaching from her. So he went on to become accomplished in practice as well as in scholarship.

This story illustrates the pitfalls of dwelling on one's own conceptions of oneself rather than being open to communication. The story also contains another, and even more important, theme. Constant ambiguity about the maidens' identity is obvious. When they appear to Abhayakaragupta, one does not know whether they are ordinary women or Tantric deities. Although they appear as human beings, there is something special about them that leaves Abhayakaragupta constantly in doubt. In fact, the ambiguity cannot be resolved. They appear as human women, but as women who represent enlightened and unusual points of view. They speak with the voice of insight and, in expressing pure intelligence, they assume a transcendent form, which is the form of the Tantric deities. It should be remembered that in Tantrism the deities are the forms humans take on when they have shed the impurities of an ego-centered mind. The question about whether women and men, when they communicate purely and truly with each other, transcend their human natures underlies much of the interaction of men and women in the Vajrayana.

WOMEN AS FULLY ENLIGHTENED SIDDHAS

When the women's training period comes to an end, they are called *siddhas* and they become teachers themselves, with their own disciples. Much can be said about the images of enlightened teachers in Tantric literature—images that are remarkably consistent for both men and women. Two characteristics stand out as typical of the fully accomplished *siddha:* personal wisdom and effectiveness in working with others.

Female *siddhas* are often regarded as the foremost, or among the foremost, disciples of their teachers. Many of them became specialists in their traditions, and Tantric practitioners, both male and female, would travel great distances to receive teaching from these women. These *siddhas* were renowned for their attainments in both the scholarly and the yogic (meditative or practicing) aspects of their discipline. A typical, if unusually detailed, example is provided by the story of the *siddha* Dinakara. Her biography credits her with a remarkably sharp and penetrating intellect and tells us that she mastered much of the scholarly literature of the day, both secular and religious. In addition to her intellectual achievements, she was a renowned *yogini,* who understood the innermost essence of the *Tantras,* possessed extraordinary vision, and was unequaled in the *siddhis* (extraordinary powers).

Perhaps the women *siddhas*' greatest accomplishment was their role as teachers—a role that is emphasized in many of the stories about them. For countless other *siddhas,* the encounter with these women marked a decisive turning point in their careers, as illustrated by the following story. One day Luhipa knocked at the door of a house of prostitution, begging for food. The head of the house, an unnamed but obviously "enlightened" woman, filled his bowl with rotten food. When Luhipa threw the offering away in disgust, she angrily asked him how it was that he, a *yogi,* still saw distinctions in the food he ate. Thanks to this observation, Luhipa realized the impurity of his conceptual mind, which still discriminated and made judgments. Thereafter, in order to purify and transcend his mind, he lived for twelve years on the banks of the Ganges eating only the innards of fish discarded by the fishermen.

A particularly interesting story concerns the *siddha* Khambhala, who received his Tantric training from his mother. The son of a king, Khambhala inherited the throne when his father died. When his mother expressed grief because his involvement in government detracted from his spiritual development, the young king took her words to heart and suggested that he might become a Buddhist monk. His mother assented. Later, after he was ordained as a monk, his mother expressed sorrow because his life of wealth and status in the monastery distracted him from higher spiritual development. Again he took her words to heart and left his monastic setting to live as an ascetic in the jungle. Once again his mother expressed sadness at the way he was living; this time she observed that he lived in one place, comfortable with his few possessions, at the expense of higher development. And once again her son listened to her and adopted the life of a wandering *yogi* practicing Tantrism. Then his mother gave him important secret initiations and teachings. After he had become a *siddha* endowed with magical powers, she appeared to him once more to convince him to stay on earth to help others.

Another story concerns a woman *siddha* who taught the Vajrayana in her town after a somewhat unusual training period. Manibhadra was married at the age of thirteen to a man of corresponding caste but still lived with her parents. During this period she received Tantric teachings from a *siddha.* One day she disappeared from her house and spent a week meditating with the *siddha* in the town's cremation ground, receiving initiations and oral instruction. When she returned to her house, her parents were extremely angry and beat her, because her behavior would, if known, bring disgrace to the family and be grounds for the dissolution of the marriage. Yet for the next year she did nothing but practice her assigned spiritual discipline. Then she went to live with her husband's family. Apparently he did not know about, or was not particularly interested in, her special connection with the Vajrayana. She was the ideal Indian housewife, performing her duties competently, showing proper respect toward her husband, and giving birth to a son and two daughters. Eleven years passed, and apparently during this time she continued with her Tantric meditation. One day, as she returned in the early morning from the village well carrying the water for the day's needs, she tripped over a root, and fell down. Her water pot was smashed to pieces, and Manibhadra attained enlightenment. From that time on, she devoted herself to the teaching of the Vajrayana in her town.

CONCLUSIONS

The preceding discussion permits us to draw several generalizations about women in the Vajrayana. First of all, the Vajrayana very strongly defines itself as a tradition for both women and men, even though, in sheer numbers, men practitioners and *siddhas* always outnumbered female practitioners and *siddhas.* Much of the Vajrayana's openness to women may be due to its complex and sophisticated psychology, which sees the human traits defined by other traditions and cultures as "masculine" or "feminine" as part of both men's and women's psychological makeup. Therefore, women and men have the same inherent obstacles to overcome and the same inherent potential for spiritual discipline and enlightenment. All in all, the image of women *siddhas* presented in the traditional literature is highly positive; they are depicted as insightful, dignified, courageous, independent, powerful, and creative—the same qualities that are displayed by male *siddhas.* In brief, Tantrism is a tradition that ennobles both women and men who can overcome great obstacles and regards them as capable of the same accomplishments.

Notes

1. The main texts referred to are the "Lives of the 84 Siddhas" (ca. eleventh century) by Abhayadatta and the "Seven Revelations" (ca. fourteenth century) by Taranatha. We also draw on some other Tibetan histories, mainly Gos.lo.tsa.ba's *Blue Annals,* Buston's *History of Buddhism,* and Padmakarpo's *History of Buddhism.*

2. See Nancy Auer Falk, "The Case of The Vanishing Nuns," in this volume.

3. These are summarized in the so-called five buddha families. The *Vajra* family (Diamond family) is intellectual sharpness and precision and critical clarity. The *Ratna* family (Jewel family) embodies personal color, warmth and richness, and the ability to fully appreciate and enjoy life. The *Padma* family (Lotus family) expresses concern for love, communication, and interpersonal relationships. The *Karma* family (Action family) manifests efficiency, directness of action, and creativity—all combined to produce concrete results. The *Buddha* family (Awake family) embodies a basic openness, accommodation, and nonjudgmental acceptance of what occurs in one's life. Although cultures characteristically divide these types of intelligence into "male" and "female," the Vajrayana sees them as available to both men and women.

Further Readings

Dowman, Keith, tr. *Sky Dancer: The Secret Life of the Lady Yeshe Tsogyel.* London: Routledge and Kegan Paul, 1984.

Gross, Rita M. "Yeshe Tsogyel: Enlightened Consort, Great Teacher, Female Role Model." *Feminine Ground: Essays on Women and Tibet,* ed. Janice Dean Willis. Ithaca, NY: Snow Lion, 1989, pp. 11–32.

Ray, Reginald A. "Mahasiddhas." *The Encyclopedia of Religion.* New York: Macmillan, 1987.

———. "Marpa:" *The Encyclopedia of Religion.* New York: Macmillan, 1987.

———. "Milaraspa." *The Encyclopedia of Religion.* New York: Macmillan, 1987.

———. "Naropa." *The Encyclopedia of Religion.* New York: Macmillan, 1987.

———. "Some Aspects of Tulka Tradition in Tibet." *Tibet Journal,* Winter 1986.

———. "Tilopa." *The Encyclopedia of Religion.* New York: Macmillan, 1987.

———. *Buddhist Saints in India.* Oxford: Oxford University Press, 1994.

20

Rosinta, Rats, and the River: Bad Luck Is Banished in Andean Bolivia

JOSEPH W. BASTIEN

A distinctive mark of Andean religion is its highly specialized rituals and ritual experts. In Andean regions, the state, the territory, the community, the lineage, and the family all have separate and distinctive shrines, rituals, and ritualists. Each territory, for example, has its own pattern of place shrines, with territorial ritualists who know their names and locations. The various economic activities connected with different ecological zones also have their own rites and ritual specialists. Thus highland herders have rites for alpacas, llamas, and sheep; people of the mountain's central slopes have potato rituals; and people of the lowlands perform rites for corn. Because the rites are so specialized, there are many ritualists and a great variety of ritual roles.

This system of ritual specialization is itself quite old, being evidenced as far back as the Spanish Conquest. One feature of the system that is prominent now, however, seems to

---

JOSEPH W. BASTIEN received a Ph.D. in Cultural Anthropology from Cornell University in 1973. As Professor of Anthropology at the University of Texas at Arlington, Dr. Bastien has studied among Bolivian natives since 1963 and as recently as August 1998. His most famous publications, *Mountain of the Condor: Metaphor and Ritual in an Andean Allyu* and *Healers of the Andes: Kallawaya Herbalists and Their Medicinal Plants,* deal with diviners and herbalists of the Kallawaya Andeans. The University of Texas awarded him Outstanding Research Awards for these publications. His most recent work, published in 1998, is titled *The Kiss of Death: Chagas' Disease in the Americas.*

Author's Note: I spent the 1976–1977 academic year as a National Endowment of the Humanities Postdoctoral Fellow at Tulane University. I would like to thank the N.E.H. for providing me with the opportunity to study with Professors Arden King and Donald Robertson of Tulane University, who assisted me with this article.

have been less sharply defined in ancient times. This is the distinction of rituals by sex, with the belief that only men or women can perform certain crucial functions. This chapter will investigate one such sex-specific ritual and the woman diviner who performed it. My wife Judy and I were both subjects and observers of this ritual in 1972, during a year of fieldwork in the Bolivian Andes.

MEN AND WOMEN, MOUNTAIN AND RIVER

In midwestern Bolivia, northeast of Lake Titicaca, stands Kaata, a sacred mountain. On its central slopes is a community, also called Kaata, that is renowned throughout the central Andes for its diviners. Among its approximately one thousand inhabitants, forty-six men are diviners *(qari yachaj),* while no less than sixty-one women are *warmi yachaj,* women diviners. Together, these make up a full 25 percent of the adult population.

One reason for the Kaatan diviners' special fame is their linkage to an ancient Andean religious tradition handed down by the Kallawaya Indians. These renowned ritualists of the Andes, who travel from Columbia to Chile, are a special cultural subgroup of the Aymara. Purveyors of a tradition of curing and divination, the Kallawaya of Mount Kaata performed brain surgery as early as 700 A.D. and carried the Inca emperor's chair in the fifteenth century (the emperor was considered a descendant of the sun, and we can assume that only very sacred people could carry him). An early ethnographer in South America, Bandelier, described the Kallawaya as "Wizards of the Andes."[1] He thought that an analysis of their rituals would provide the key to understanding Andean religion. Because Kaatan diviners draw on symbols of the Kallawaya heritage, the rites that they perform today still offer a unique mode of entry into the traditional Andean religious world.

The special import of women diviners in Kaata is due in large part to their role in a complex of rituals concerned with good and bad fortune. Men diviners perform good-fortune rituals to set in motion a series of favorable events, such as a good harvest or the renewed health of a sick person. Women diviners perform misfortune rituals to remove bodily or social disintegration. This contrast between male and female ritualists is in turn part of a very complex local symbolic system. This system clusters together men, stability, and the mountain and contrasts them to women, the river, and a natural and social cycle of dissolution and renewal.

Let us examine these important sets of associations more closely. Kaatans equate their mountain symbolically to a human body and draw fairly detailed parallels between areas of the mountain and parts of the body. Thus Apacheta, the highland community of herders, is the mountain's head; Kaata, the central community of potato growers, is its heart and bowels; and Niñokorin, the lowland community of corn producers, is its legs. Men seem best fitted to preserve this mountain body because of their inherent stability, for, just as the mountain is stable within the Bolivian landscape, so the men are stable within the Kaatan social system. Kaatans practice virilocality and exogamy; that is, sons always remain at the place on the mountain where their fathers and mothers lived and worked the land, and their wives come to join them there. Daughters, instead, must always move away to marry and live with a husband from one of the adjacent levels.

Thus men diviners, fixing good fortune, offer highland symbols of llama fat and foetuses to all thirteen earth shrines of Mount Kaata in a yearly cycle of ritual performances. They feed all the levels of the mountain in a meal that symbolizes both the community's unity and its bodily integrity. Women diviners, instead, offer lowland symbols of pig fat and dead rats to wind, river, and landslide—the mountain's erosive elements. These women work especially with the river, which flows down the mountain, linking its different levels but also causing destruction through erosion, floods, and landslides. The latter often bring death, especially to people who live in the lowlands. Hence Kaatans associate the river with personal calamity—not only the death that the landslides bring, but also the sickness that destroys the human body as the river dissolves the mountainside.

Women belong with the river in part because they flow like it and experience losses from their body through the menstrual cycle. Because of menstruation, it is said, women are better able than men to get rid of bad things. The flow of blood cleanses women of misfortune, such as infertility. It also helps to prepare the woman for conception.

But women also flow in other ways—through the marriage system, passing from level to level, just as the river passes down the mountainside. Furthermore, like the flow of the river and that of the menstrual blood, the flow of women in marriage also carries a promise of cleansing and renewal. Kaatan legend says that, after flowing down the mountain, the river circles underground to return to its source. This is the *uma pacha,* the mountain's summit and, according to Kaatan myth, the original source of llamas and people. The dead return with the river to the highland lakes, and so do the organs destroyed by sickness and the land lost through theft; therefore the river can restore them. Permanent misfortune occurs only when such bad luck is not given to the river so that it can complete its restorative cycle. Similarly, the Kaatan social cycle finally restores the women to their families. For Kaatans also practice bilateral inheritance, which means that women as well as their brothers inherit access to their parents' land. Of course, women themselves cannot work it when they move away to marry. But women come back in the next generation. Land rights passed on to the daughters entice the daughters to return to and marry men from the level of their mothers' birthplace.

Thus ultimately both women and river have the power to transform bad luck into good fortune. Note, incidentally, that despite the difference between symbols and practice, both men and women protect the mountain. Men feed the entire mountain body and thereby protect its future wholeness. Women divine and remove misfortune and thereby help the person, society, and community to become whole once again.

ROSINTA

Sex not only distinguishes the Kaatan diviners' functions but also determines how the diviners' roles will be inherited. Male and female diviner roles are passed along, respectively, through the father's and mother's lineage. Thus the renowned male diviner Sarito Quispe learned to set up good fortune tables from his father's father, whereas the equally famous Rosinta Garcia learned her ritual role by serving as apprentice to her mother's sister, who was a very powerful ritualist. Aspiring diviners master all the rituals' intricacies only after years of apprenticeship. One day, after some natural manifestation—such as lightning for the male diviner or a landslide for the female—they announce to the community, "The ancestors have chosen me to divine. I know!"

Like diviners of many other cultures, Kaatan diviners may make use of a trance induced by chewing coca (cocaine), to help them see into the future. Her clairvoyance has made Rosinta Garcia especially successful.

Many Andeans, who are quite poor, travel from afar to the Kallawaya region where Rosinta lives and offer her a month's supply of food in return for divination. They seek out Rosinta because she is powerful; and, indeed, many of Rosinta's predictions have been fulfilled. Andeans believe Rosinta's evil eye has caused the death of seven people, and they may solicit her to send bad luck as well as to remove it. Rosinta bewitches Andeans by sticking pig fat and the victim's hair (called a *chije,* or misfortune) inside a cat's and a dog's skull, putting them together as if they were fighting with each other. If the victim discovers the *chije,* he or she can either throw it in the river or retaliate by soliciting another sorceress, who then engages in a mystical war with Rosinta. If either sorceress is caught in the act, she is taken to the sheriff, who fines her a month's salary and makes her promise on the cross never to bewitch again. The sheriff, however, fears Rosinta, so she is never arrested.

BAD LUCK

Rosinta was called upon when a string of misfortunes fell upon the Yanahuaya family, with whom Judy and I were living. The first misfortune was a long-standing complaint. Carmen's husband, Marcelino Yanahuaya, blamed Carmen for her failure to give him a living son. Carmen had borne two sons, but they both died shortly after birth. Consequently, Marcelino had no male heir to help him work his land and take it over as he grew old. Instead, Carmen's five daughters—Elsa, Celia, Gloria, Sophia, and Valentina—had survived, and now they were marrying away from his extensive landholdings in the central hamlet of Kallawaya. Furthermore, Marcelino was upset with his oldest daughter, Elsa. Because Elsa had been herding when a landslide killed two of her father's sheep, he thought she had lost her competence as a herder. He blamed this loss on the fact that she had lived for two years as a bread seller in La Paz, where her maternal uncle had mistreated her badly. She returned in ill health.

The next disaster occurred when the couple's beloved granddaughter Erminia got sick with chronic diarrhea and vomiting. Erminia's parents were Carmen's daughter Celia and her husband Martín Mejía, who lived in Chaqahuaya, a lowland hamlet. When Erminia could not retain the pills I gave her, a male diviner was called in to restore her health, a function within the sphere of male ritualists. The diviner assured the parents that Erminia would soon be cured. The child showed some temporary signs of recovery. But a month after his divination, she was dead. Soon after, Marcelino's sister died of the same disease, now diagnosed as typhoid. Erminia's death increased the already existing hostility between Celia and her husband Martín's lineage. When her mother-in-law accused Celia of causing Erminia's death, Celia struck her in the eye and blackened it. On behalf of the mother-in-law, I reprimanded Celia, who then avoided me for three weeks.

The final misfortune struck when Martín's collarbone was fractured soon after Erminia's funeral. A woman smashed his collarbone with a rock and broke it while Martín was fighting with her husband in a drunken brawl. If it was not cured, a crippled collarbone would permanently prevent Martín from using his hand plow.

The broken collarbone stopped the feuding between the Mejías and the Yanahuayas, for both families realized that another person would be lost if they did not help each other. In a gesture of reconciliation, Marcelino called another male diviner to cure his son-in-law. The diviner applied a compress of dried frog skins and herbs to the front and back of the broken bone. Several elders also visited Martín, and they recalled that someone had died the year before, after his broken bone had protruded and became infected from the herb medicine. This time the herbs failed, and Marcelino asked me to cure Martín. Martín, bedridden with pain, cried as he showed me his deformed collarbone; it was setting in its broken position. Celia begged me to do something, so I sent Martín, accompanied by Marcelino, to La Paz to have the bone set. When Marcelino and Martín returned, they were very happy, not so much because Martín was on his way to recovery, but because they had the legal papers to sue the woman who had hit Martín. A common enemy had united two families. I was glad that I had been able to help Martín recover; my good feelings, however, suffered a blow when one morning I saw him cross the patio carrying a one-hundred-pound sack, wearing no cast. It turned out that he had chipped the cast off because it bothered him. Carmen and Marcelino were disgusted with Martín for removing the cast, and they called him an ass.

Then Judy and I became ill with typhoid. The Yanahuayas thought that their bad luck would never end. Marcelino, representing "male" interests, blamed his bad luck on the women and his wife's relatives. He contended that the misfortunes had begun when his daughters had left home to live in other communities, where they were mistreated. If his daughters had been able to stay with him, this ill treatment would not have occurred. Incidentally, this would have been, of course, impossible, since in Kaata it is women's lot to move away when they marry.

Carmen had her own "female" set of interpretations. She said that the landslide, which had killed the two sheep, had been caused by Marcelino's disrespect toward her people. She also had an explanation for Martín's injury; she complained that Martín had not set up a table for Erminia, their dead granddaughter, during the Feast of the Dead and that he had avoided her gravesite. During the feast, Celia had sat alone in front of Erminia's grave and had given bread, bananas, and oranges to those who prayed for her daughter. Carmen was certain the ancestral spirits were punishing Martín for his blatant disrespect toward the dead.

One evening, as the two were arguing again, Carmen insisted in a high-pitched, whining voice that women were not the only causes of misfortune and that men were also to blame. Carmen then invited Rosinta Garcia to divine the "masculine" causes of their bad luck.

BAD LUCK IS BANISHED

Rosinta performed her ritual on Tuesday, December 12. (She had previously discovered during a trance that I was the target of sorcery and the cause of bad luck.) Eight people participated: myself and Judy, Carmen and Marcelino, and their daughters Celia, Elsa, Sophia, and Valentina. The absent daughter, Gloria, and the dead sons, Sabino and Roberto, were represented by symbols.

It was dark when Rosinta arrived through the back gate of Marcelino's house. Her wrinkled and leathery face reflected her supernatural powers. She quickly unpacked her ritual paraphernalia inside the supply house; Carmen was thrilled to see the dead rat that Rosinta had strangled for the occasion. Marcelino nervously prodded Rosinta to move more quickly, but from the start she set her own pace. Methodically and confidently, she began removing the misfortunes. Cupping a bowl in front of her mouth, Rosinta blew puffs of incense around our heads and feet; then she balanced a cup of alcohol on our heads and then threw it to our earthshrines. She explained that the aspersions were to ask permission of the spirits of the patio and kitchen, as well as of the spirits of the various levels of the mountain. She needed their approval to perform this ritual for the river.

After Rosinta had purified the participants, she asked for the wind's permission as well, by throwing alcohol into the air so that the wind could carry it "where the wind blows." That same wind had also brought the present misfortunes to the Yanahuayas. In retaliation, Rosinta poured another cup of alcohol for the wind; she passed this cup over our heads and went into the patio to throw it more directly into the wind. This gesture was meant to ensure that the wind would parch the land of those who had cursed the Yanahuayas.

In these opening rites, the wind's significance and function parallel those of the river that would later in the ceremony become paramount, for the wind, too, both destroys and restores. On the one hand, the wind parches the earth, and Kaatans use it as an instrument for cursing people. But, on the other hand, the wind brings the rain clouds and blows away misfortune. Furthermore, both wind and river, through their natural changeability, prefigure the change in luck that the ritualist hopes to achieve. Thus both wind and river are fed the symbols of misfortune: rats, moss, and cacti. Rats eat valuable supplies, moss cracks the foundations of homes and fences, and cacti are harmful to animals and difficult to remove from the fields.

Sharing the meal with the wind and the river in our ritual performance were the dead ancestors of Marcelino's patrilineage, the patron spirit of the patio, the matron spirit of Carmen's kitchen, and Mount Kaata. For these guests, Rosinta served six cotton wads of coca, llama fat, carnations, and incense into the shrine alongside the supply house. The wads were thrown in the fire that burned within the shrine. Rosinta set aside another six wads to be burned and fed into the river. We were admiring Rosinta's skill, when she asked each of us to name two of our enemies, so she could send them a calamity. I could not hear whom the others specified as their enemies, but, when Rosinta asked me, they all listened intently as I named Lionel Alvarez of Charazani. Alvarez was the owner of a truck. Over and over again, after my wife and I had reserved the cabin of his truck for our twenty-hour trip to La Paz, he would inform us that the cabin was no longer available. We knew that he had sold the seats to someone else for more money. When I named Alvarez as my enemy, Carmen and Marcelino smiled; they, too, disliked the mestizo, because he exploited the Indians, crowding them into the back of his truck and charging them high rates.

Midnight marked a shift in both the sites and the ritual foods of our misfortune ritual. Before midnight our spiritual "guests" were fed llama fat and cotton in Marcelino's patio. After midnight, they ate pig fat and black llama wool at the Kunochayuh River. The pig traditionally comes from the lower mountain levels, and its fat symbolizes negative power from that area. The llama is native to the highlands, but its dark wool symbolizes death. Both symbols together suggest that the negative forces of death and decay from the lower levels are restored by the highlands' positive forces. Although land and people erode and die on their journey down the levels toward the lowlands, they will return to the highlands and regenerate when they die.

After midnight Tuesday morning, Rosinta began preparing the meal for the river by divining with a gray guinea pig, which she had first touched to everyone's forehead. She opened its viscera with her fingernails and poured its blood into a cup with wine, eggs, and corn. After removing the ribcage, she examined the protrusion in the front, which formed a small half-moon. She said it looked fine. On the guinea pig's pancreas she spotted two incisions, which she said were two mouths. They represented enemies who were bewitching us, she explained. Marcelino identified one mouth as that of Dominga Ari. Dominga had become impoverished after the death of her husband, who, twenty years earlier, had usurped Marcelino's land. Marcelino said that Dominga's blindness and poverty were punishments from Marcelino's ancestors, but Dominga accused Marcelino of soliciting a sorceress to send these misfortunes. When two hostile Andean families suffer calamities, an exchange of sorcery is invariably suspected.

Josefa Waque, identified as the second mouth, was suspected of cursing me. This tough seventy-year-old woman had been trampled by horses, severely damaging her skull. She was dying when they brought her to me to be cured. After I shaved her head, I cleansed and bound the bone together with a bandage. She recovered in a month and came to me asking for her hair. When I explained that I had burned it, she suspected me of using her hair in witchcraft against her. At the same time, Dominga and Josefa became close friends, further arousing Carmen's suspicions about them.

At 2:30 A.M., Rosinta began to prepare servings for the river. She laid the rat at the head of the ritual cloth and sorted out twenty wads of dark llama wool. Earlier Carmen had secretly snatched some coca leaves from various shrines in the community, and Rosinta placed twelve of these leaves on each wad. She put slivers of pig fat on the coca, and then daisies, seeds, herb clumps, and moss. Once Rosinta had laid the food out, she wrapped the dark wool tightly around it. She tied one wad to the rat's back and gave two to each participant, setting one beneath a man's hat or woman's headband, and the other between the left big toe and sandal. She then stuffed two wads into the corners of each main room in the house as well as in the sheep, horse, and burro corrals. While the wads were drawing evil forces from these areas, we rested and ate to prepare for our journey to the river.

Then Rosinta gathered the wads from their different places, each time passing a llama thread from a spindle across the threshold of the room's door or around the legs of the animals in the corrals and then breaking the string. Marcelino hurried everyone along, fearing that Josefa or Dominga would hear us if they were awake when we passed their homes. Rosinta finally collected all the wads, and we were ready to go; but then she could not find her coca cloth. Carmen raced around looking for it, and finally gave her another one. We filed out the front gate into the mud and rain. Each of us carried a large bag of dirty clothes, which we would wash in the river just as we washed our bodies. We stumbled along in the dark, Marcelino leading, and Rosinta in the rear. The trail cut across the side of the mountain and over a landslide, where the going was very dangerous because of the rocks and slippery clay. Several times Marcelino told me to help the elderly Rosinta, who hobbled along loaded with a large sack of dried food, which had been the payment for her night's work. However, in spite of her seventy years and the heavy load she was carrying, she needed little help and kept pace with everyone.

Somewhere I lost the misfortune wad that was stuck between my foot and my sandal. I dreaded what Carmen and Marcelino would say if they found out that it had been left behind, so I removed the wad from my hat and divided it into two. It was a very dark night, and no one noticed. Two hours later, we arrived at the bridge crossing the Kunochayuh River and climbed another steep path three hundred yards up the mountain. Then we entered a cave alongside the river. We crouched inside the grotto, the women deep within and Marcelino and I by the entrance. Rosinta threw an offering of coca to the Lord of the River, and prayed that our sorrows and misfortunes would go away. Carmen served us hot potatoes and coca, and we talked about the river.

The Kunochayuh flowed rapidly in front of the grotto, descending twenty feet in about twenty-five yards. The river was about fifteen feet across, winding in and out of the gorges cut into the mountainside and flowing around and over large rocks pushed down by its swift current. Owing to the steep slope, the river descended in a series of stepped waterfalls that resembled the terraces of the land. Marcelino told us how he had played on the rocks of the river when he was a boy. He pointed out places where he used to sit and which were now washed away, and ponds, now filled with boulders, where he once swam.

Marcelino gathered dry straw and wood to build a small fire inside the grotto. Rosinta placed one cotton wad in each of our hands. We presented the offerings to the lords of the mountain and the river, and prayed that our enemies would let us alone. Rosinta burned all the wads and threw the ashes into the river. Then Carmen gave Rosinta a large black-and-white guinea pig, which she dissected to examine its viscera. The still-beating heart predicted good health. Everyone crowded around as she showed us the two pancreases, dark red with white tips. She said that this sign indicated lack of life in the Yanahuaya household and that the household had not been feeding the ancestral shrines for its lineage. If the family wanted life to grow, they should begin to offer more rituals. Marcelino and Carmen immediately promised to do so.

We knelt facing the river's descent. Rosinta threw the yolk and white from a chicken egg into the waters, and then she removed the black wads from our hats, headbands, and sandals. As she had done when she took them from the house and the animals, she once again passed a llama wool thread, this time around our hands and feet, and then broke it. She put the black wads into an old coca cloth with the guinea pigs, rat, coca quids, cigarette butts, and ashes. Everyone looked away as Rosinta flung the cloth into the river, saying, "Begone, misfortunes!"

Rosinta was anxious to return home. She bade everyone good-bye as she crossed the river; for an instant she entered its icy waters, holding her skirt in her right hand and her sandals in her left. The water rushed around the woman diviner as she took one final step into the whirling pool and then stepped out again. She rapidly ascended the zigzag path, rising into a cloud, and disappeared into the darkness just as she had come out of it earlier that evening when she came to our house.

Our physical bodies also needed cleansing; so Marcelino and Carmen began brewing a concoction of cacti, thorny weeds, and water. Carmen and her daughters took the spiny water to the shores of the river. After gargling with it, they stripped naked and thoroughly washed each other with the spiny water, making sure that they didn't miss any part of the body. Marcelino and I stayed out of sight in the cave, as Kaatan women are very shy, even during rituals. After they had finished, Marcelino and I also washed. The earthen pot and washbasin were then floated down the river.

Carmen and Marcelino removed every trace of our presence; even the ashes were thrown into the waters, and the place appeared as if no one had ever been there. We returned to Kaata by a higher path. I had been warned by Marcelino and Elsa, "Once we have left the river, you may look only in front of you—not to the right, nor to the left, nor behind you." Carmen and Elsa were always more careful to observe the ritual's details, but Marcelino soon forgot the taboo as we climbed up the steep incline and began to talk about the river and the old irrigation canal whose route our path was following. After an hour's journey we could see Kaata. Marcelino and Elsa told me not to look down at the path over which we had traveled to the river earlier that morning. I didn't. Eventually we arrived behind Marcelino's house and climbed over the fence just as a traveler came around the side of the house. Marcelino said that we had been very lucky not to meet anyone while we were going or returning. Our travels had made a large circle. We had taken a low route when we were going to remove our misfortunes by the river; by taking the upper road across the highlands on our way back, we had compensated for our losses. In short, like the river and the women in their marriage cycle, our route had joined together the mountain's different levels.

Once inside the patio we passed our hands and feet through the smoke of a fire to dispel, Carmen said, any of the grief remaining from the misfortunes. Celia brought us large plates of pig-head soup, which we ate heartily after eleven hours of ritual activity. I found the black wad that I had carelessly left behind. Marcelino was startled when I showed it to him; he quickly told me to burn it without letting Carmen see it.

Shortly before noon, Josefa Waque came into the patio to beg for food. Carmen angrily chased her away, disturbed that one of the bewitchers had arrived so soon after we had got rid of the misfortunes. Carmen and Marcelino began to question the efficacy of the misfortune ritual, until they saw visible effects of Rosinta's powers that same afternoon. Dominga Ari and her son, Julian, began screaming at each other toward suppertime, and at one point Dominga struck Julian. Marcelino smiled, and Carmen was smug with glee. Later Carmen explained that Rosinta's sorcery had been effective against Dominga. Dominga had collected strands of her son's hair with the intent of bewitching him. When Julian heard about it, he took his mother to the sheriff, who severely reprimanded her. Carmen complimented Rosinta's powers by saying, "*Yachan.* She's a prophet!"

CONCLUSION

In this chapter I have tried to show how a female ritualist exercises her distinctively female powers to end misfortune by using symbols intimately associated with femaleness. Rosinta effectively divined the sources of misfortune. Using the power and the associations evoked by the river, she was able to symbolically remove our misfortune. But, in doing so, she also answered Marcelino's original complaint, for she had pointed to the river, which, like the Kaatan women, flows away only to return once again to its source. Although Marcelino's daughters must marry away from his land, his granddaughters will return again. Thus she had successfully protected on all levels the interests of Carmen, who hired her to do so.

Perhaps this is ultimately the key to understanding the distinct importance of the Kaatan woman ritualist. By evoking women's fluid mode of existence through their rituals and symbols, the ritualist recalls and affirms the significance of women's role. Men and women together are needed to make a complete and successful world, just as both the mountain and the river, and both the ability to attract good luck and the ability to control misfortune are necessary to the Kaatan universe.

EPILOGUE

Bad luck revisited the Yanahuaya family in the 1990s when Sophia, the second youngest of Carmen's daughters, was considered the cause of a bus accident. Sophia was talking to the bus driver, her boyfriend, when he lost control, and the bus swerved off the slippery road and down a mountainous embankment. The chauffeur and numerous people were killed. The Kallawayas banished Sophia from Kaata, and they blamed Carmen for the *sajrakuna* (misfortunes). A medical student from UCSF visited Carmen in 1992, and she brought me a letter that Carmen had dictated to her, and related the above incident. Carmen wrote, "I am now blind and live alone. Sophia, Elsa, and Valentina live in the cities. Celia remains on Mount Kaata. You are my son. Uqhamaphan (And Forever, Amen)."

The mountain and the body are tied together by the rivers that connect them.

Notes

1. Adolph F. Bandelier, *The Islands of Titicaca and Kaati* (New York: The Hispanic Society of America, 1910), p. 13.

Further Reading

Abercrombie, Thomas. *Pathways of Memory and Power: Ethnography and History among an Andean People*. Madison: University of Wisconsin Press, 1998.

Allen, Catherine J. *The Hold Life Has: Coca and Cultural Identity in an Andean Community.* Washington, D.C.: Smithsonian Institution Press, 1988.

Arguedas, José Maria. *Deep Rivers,* tr. Frances Horning Barraclough. Austin: University of Texas Press, 1978.

Bastien, Joseph W. *Mountain of the Condor: Metaphor and Ritual in an Andean Ayllu.* Prospect Heights, Ill.: Waveland Press, 1985.

———. *Healers of the Andes: Kallawaya Herbalists and Their Medicinal Plants.* Salt Lake City: University of Utah Press, 1987.

———. *The Drum and the Stethoscope: Integrating Ethnomedicine and Biomedicine in Bolivia.* Salt Lake City: University of Utah Press, 1992.

———. *Kiss of Death: Chagas' Disease in the Americas.* Salt Lake City: University of Utah Press, 1998. Website: UTA. EDU/chagas

Classen, Constance. *Inca Cosmology and the Human Body.* Salt Lake City: University of Utah Press, 1993.

Columbus, Claudette Kemper. "Immortal Eggs: A Peruvian Geocracy; Pariaqaqa of Huarochiri." *Journal of Latin American Lore* 16(2): pp. 175–98.

MacCormack, Sabine. *Religion in the Andes: Vision and Imagination in Early Colonial Peru.* Princeton: Princeton University Press, 1991.

Reinhard, Johan, Peru's Ice Maidens: Unwrapping the Secrets. *National Geographic,* June, 1996.

Silverblatt, Irene. *Moon, Sun, and Witches: Gender Ideologies and Class in Inca and Colonial Peru.* Princeton: Princeton University Press, 1987.

21

Women's Religious Space in Mexico

SYLVIA MARCOS

After Mariana, age 60, completed these activities (preparing the temple), which were routine on healing days, she put on her long, spotless white robe. The other three women, ranging in age from 30 to 60, removed their white robes from shopping bags and followed Mariana's example. As they were putting them on, I saw ordinary-looking women being transformed into repositories of power, capable of summoning spirits, and into experts for whose ministrations many people waited to entrust themselves.[1]

INTRODUCTION

Healing in ancient Mexico always took place surrounded by prayer, invocations, and sacred objects in a context that was explicitly religious. Today, healing rituals are most often carried out in the context of contemporary popular religion. There they reflect a relationship with the cosmos that is strongly marked by ancient beliefs and by a dominant presence

DR. SYLVIA MARCOS is the Director of the Center for Psychoethnological Research in Cuernavaca, Mexico, and Visiting Professor of Mesoamerican Religions and Gender at Claremont Graduate University, California. She has recently been awarded the H. W. Luce Visiting Professorship at Union Theological Seminary, New York City. A member of the Permanent Seminar on Gender in Anthropology with the Institute for Anthropological Research at the National Autonomous University in Mexico City, Dr. Marcos is the author and editor of many books and articles on the history of psychiatry, medicine, and gender issues in ancient and contemporary Mexico.

Author's Note: An earlier version of this article was published under the title "Women, Healing Rituals, and Popular Medicine in Mexico" in *Concilium: International Review of Theology* 2 (1991): pp. 110–21.

of women. Current forms of healing may primarily recall tradition or may emerge from the fusion of cultures brought about by the Spanish conquest and subsequent colonization. Either way, popular medicine partakes of the cosmology that dominated Mesoamerican[2] cultures for millennia and still provides the implicit knowledge system for many present-day healing procedures.[3]

Underlying that cosmology was a pervasive concept of duality, of a world divided into feminine and masculine components. There were many important goddesses, and most deities had a feminine and masculine aspect. The cosmic force identified with the feminine was complemented by its male-identified counterpart. Women and men, too, were profoundly influenced to view themselves, their interactions, and their functions in society as different but complementary on all levels and in all areas of life. The prominent role of women healers reflected a worldview in which feminine powers and the female aspect of life were integral to society. Furthermore, accounts from the sixteenth and seventeenth centuries suggest that women outnumbered men as practitioners of the healing arts in pre-Columbian times. Even today within popular medicine we see women healers acting in ways that take them beyond the roles normally imposed on women by their social context. The historical and ethnographic material reviewed later in this chapter indicates the range of healing activities performed by women and suggests the importance of their participation as religious ritual specialists.

Women's role in healing in Mexico is directly related to the nature of popular religion. When we look at current popular healing practices, we see a deeply complex and many-layered whole that is outside of but concurrent with mainstream medicine. As both a living, self-renewing tradition and a repository of pre-Columbian healing methods, values and religious views, "popular medicine" covers all curing actions outside of formal, institutional, mainstream medicine. It includes most of the healing methods of the grassroots people. Its practitioners are almost exclusively of urban poor, peasant and indigenous origin, but those who seek healing, while most often of the same origin, may come from any social background. People resort to *curanderismo,* or popular medicine, both as a first choice and after mainstream medicine has failed them.

"*Curanderismo*" is a Spanish term for a variety of healing practices and rituals sometimes termed "shamanistic." It defines a privileged realm where indigenous ethnicity entrenched itself and managed not only to survive the Spanish conquest, but became a focus for continuing, autonomous invention.[4] Elements from different historical periods fuse, are reorganized and resignified by the agents of this process: the large disadvantaged majorities who live in Mexico's urban centers and peasant communities.

In these communities, it is often the *curandera* rather than the modern medical doctor who reestablishes the multidimensional equilibrium upset by "sickness." ("*Curandera/curandero*" is the term used for these popular healers. Since the majority are women, "*curandera*" will be used.) The *curandera* is, literally, a "*med-dicus*" in the classic sense of one who knows how to pronounce (*dicere*) the measure (Indo-European root: *med*) suitable to restore balance. To understand the deeper meaning of healing in these communities requires submersion in the largely Mesoamerican cosmology which is its source. For example, currently, among the Otomis of the Sierra Madre Oriental, there exists an

> homology between the vision of the body and that of the universe. . . . The Otomi concept of sickness reveals a series of concepts that are shown to be identical to those that orient their vision of the world, . . . the sickness localized in the body can-

not be separated in certain form from disorder at a cosmic level.[5]

The integration of body and universe means that healing can only be conceived of in cosmological-religious terms. To mend the body, that is to say, one must also in some sense mend the world, and set straight one's relationship to it and its pervading powers. Let us see how those powers have been understood in Mexico.

COSMOLOGY AND THE PRESENCE OF THE FEMININE IN THE MESOAMERICAN PANTHEON

Popular medicine as practiced in Mesoamerica is fed both by the deep and powerful streams of ancient cosmology and by concepts of European origin introduced by Spanish colonizers. These elements live an underground yet impressively vital existence nourishing, especially, healing practices and the religious forms associated with them. However, there are no purely Aztec or purely Spanish elements making up these perceptions, images, influences, and ideas which form the conceptual framework within which the majority of people in Mesoamerica face life and death. What is instructive and surprising is how they have meshed and persisted through the centuries despite ideas of progress and modern means of communication.

Basic to the cosmology that survived and continues to shape its participants is the feminine-masculine duality which is responsible for the creation of the cosmos, its regeneration and its maintenance. "What these Indians understood as Divine Nature . . . [was] divided into two gods [known as] Man and Woman . . ."[6]

A recurring feature of Mesoamerican thinking was the fusion of feminine and masculine into a singular, but polarized principle which was reflected in a pantheon where the divinities were conceptualized in pairs. Manuscripts from the sixteenth century testify to these concepts[7]: the Mother and Father, Tonacatecuhtli-Tonacacihautl and their creation; Uxumuco and Cipactonal, the gods of water; Tlaltecuhtli and his wife Chalchiuhtlicue, etc. Primary sources show the divine principle divided into numerous pairs: for example, Ometeotl-Omecihuatl, the god who is two, demonstrates the principle of complementarity. This double deity lived at Omeyocan, the place of duality. In the lower regions of the earth lived Mictlantecuhtli-Mictecacihuatl, the pair of gods who permitted access to the nine cosmic levels of the underworld.[8]

The feminine as a cosmic force was not a presence that imposed itself on its opposite, nor did it invalidate the masculine, try to negate it or make it appear secondary and subordinate to it. Rather the central concern was to keep the two forces in balance, to establish an equilibrium. The feminine presence complemented the masculine, flowed into or encompassed its masculine opposite, or the two fluctuated in an eternal alternation. On the level of iconography, images of goddesses at times incorporated masculine or androgynous attributes. The concept of dual unity was found throughout all cultures of Mesoamerica. Thus, historian of Maya religion Eric Thompson spoke of Itzam Na and his partner Ix Chebel Yax in the Maya region.[9] Bartolome de Las Casas mentions Izona and his wife,[10] and Diego de Landa refers also to Itzam Na and Ixchel as the gods of medicine.[11]

Feminine deities were assigned many special and crucial functions: Chantico was fire goddess of the earth; Chalchihuitlicue was the female principle of fertility and a goddess of lakes, rivers, and springs. The four Izcuiname supported the cosmos at its four angles. Tlazolteotl was goddess of that which is cast off and of confession (an important ritual for pre-Columbian societies). The Cihuateteo goddesses helped the sun descend from the zenith to sunset. Coatlicue, "serpent skirt," was giver of life and mother of the gods; Xochiquetzal was mother goddess of flowers; Xilonen was mother goddess of corn, and so on.

A MULTIPLE, FLUID, AND SACRED UNIVERSE

Goddesses, however, were not personified as discrete entities, eternally separate from one another and from their masculine counterparts. Given that the divine reality was multiple, fluid, and encompassing of everything, their aspects also were ceaselessly changing and their images dynamic, never fixed but continuously re-created and redefined. During brief moments in the constant shifting and flow, a goddess or god could be conceptualized.[12] But such conceptualizations could not be understood as static.

In that dual, fluid universe, the domain of the sacred was all-pervasive. Hence continuity existed between the natural and supernatural world. Sacred beings were closely interconnected with humans, and each was dependent upon the other. Humans who failed to fulfill religious obligations could provoke divine anger and punishment. But the deities also needed worshipers, sacrifice, ritual, and food.[13] This mutual interdependence was a matter of life and death both for the divine beings and for the humans who adored them. Such a construction of the sacred is quite different from that of the great European and Middle Eastern theistic traditions. The human relationship is not with an all powerful being who is eternally benevolent, beyond the good or bad deeds of devotees and independent of their rituals. In the same vein, the divine included the earth, sky, clouds, rain, seeds, plants. Its images were so ever-changing, unfixed and dynamic, precisely because the divine reality encompassed life's whole, itself so multiple and fluid.

In addition, because God was not thought of as a transcendent person separate from the world, Pre-Columbian peoples did not individuate personhood in the same way as did Christians or other Western traditions, nor did they locate responsibility for human actions in individuals in the same way as did, for example, Christian conceptions of sin.[14] Collectives—community, town, *Calpulli* (neighborhood), extended family and ritual networks—were the main sources of identity for Mesoamericans, and also the main loci of responsibility. I have analyzed in another work the difficulties the Indians had in understanding the concept of sin within the Church's framework of free will and individual responsibility.[15]

Nor did pre-colonial Mexicans separate and solidify good and evil in the same way as Christians. The concept of the devil shocked the Aztec mind. Personifications of pure evil and pure good were alien to Mexican Indians. Aztec moral thought, like cosmological thought, was fluid and characterized by changing rather than rigid or fixed dualities. The supernatural forces represented as gods and goddesses shifted continuously between the two poles of good and evil. They could protect and help or they could harm and destroy. The concept of a separate, all-beneficent entity was as unfamiliar as that of an all-evil one.

The merging and overlapping of divine images, which sometimes discourages linear-thinking researchers from making sense out of the primary sources and materials from Aztec cosmology, does not reflect an "unfinished" pantheon. Rather, merger and overlap was the pantheon's very nature. The Aztecs and other Mesoamerican societies were neither monotheistic nor polytheistic. In their view, reality, nature, and experience were nothing but multiple manifestations of a single unity of being.[16]

It was within this cosmology with its duality and fluidity, with its divinized feminine presences and all-pervasive deity, and its human-divine homologies and reciprocities, that the *curanderas* and other Mexican healers of the past moved and worked. The following accounts, one undertaken to record and the other to eradicate traditional beliefs, show how *curanderas* functioned in their social setting during times when the pre-colonial cosmology still retained a powerful influence on the minds of native Mexicans.

CURANDERAS OF THE PAST

The *Florentine Codex.* Born in Spain around 1500, Fray Bernardino de Sahagún, a Franciscan, came to Mexico in 1529. Some ten years later he began traveling to gather material for a massive study he was compiling on indigenous Mexican culture, the *General History of Things in New Spain,* also known as the *Florentine Codex.* Called the father of modern ethnology, Sahagun drew up a questionnaire that enabled him to inventory much of the culture systematically. Despite his critical comments about native religious beliefs, his extremely comprehensive accounts are regarded as one of the most reliable sources on them.

Female images in the Mesoamerican pantheon, as portrayed by Sahagún, offer reflections of both women's medical and social functions. Sahagún speaks of Temazcaltoci, calling her the goddess of medicine. Also the patron of the *temazcal,* the healing vapor bath, she was the "heart of the earth and our grandmother; . . . doctors, surgeons and bleeders venerate her as well as the diviners who foretell the good or bad fortune that children will have according to their birth."[17]

In his first encounter with this female healing power, Sahagun recorded the activities of what he called female doctors or *Titici* (*Ticitl* in singular):

> The female doctor knows well the properties of herbs, roots, trees and rocks. She has a great deal of experience with them and likewise knows many medical secrets. She who is a good doctor knows how to cure the sick, and, for the good which she does them, practically brings the dead back to life, making them get better or recover with the cures she uses. She knows how to bleed, to give purges, administer medicine and apply ointments to the body, to soften lumps in the body by massage, to set bones, lance and cure wounds and the gout, cut away bad flesh and cure the evil eye. . . .
>
> [By] blowing on the sick, subtly tying and untying cords, looking into water, throwing the large grains of corn customarily used in divination . . . she learns about and understands illnesses.[18]

Sahagun also described the practice of midewifery. Throughout the world, midwifery has traditionally been women's specialty, but additionally, in the Aztec world, midwives presided as priestesses at the rituals surrounding birth. Birth was conceived as a battlefield, and on this battlefield, these midwife-priestesses provided women with encouragement and support. Midwives directed the birth process, gave massages, prayed, administered herbs, and took the women to the *temazcal* bath of healing vapors. Their duties included preparing pregnant women to become "Cihuateteo," the goddesses that accompanied the sun from its height to its setting. If a mother were to die in her first childbirth, she would then become one of these goddesses. She was regarded the same as a warrior who dies on the battlefield.

> And when the baby arrived on earth, the midwife shouted; she gave war cries, which meant that the woman had fought a good battle, had become a brave warrior, had taken a captive, had captured a baby.[19]

In the *Treatise on the Heathen Superstitions.* After nearly 100 years of catechization, church authorities in colonial Mexico saw that native religious practices still persisted and even flourished. The church's official position when confronted with the complex, highly evolved religious system and beliefs of the New World's inhabitants was to attribute them to the devil. For Christians, there was only one God, so the native deities—perceived by the catechizers as real and effective—had to be defined as evil spirits. Religious customs and acts that superficially recalled church practices were regarded as attempts by the devil to lead souls astray by imitating Christian practices. These included ritual bathing and naming four days after birth, confessing (to the goddess Tlazolteotl), eating figures of the gods fashioned from amaranth, as well as other rituals.

The effort to eliminate native religious customs focused on bringing to judgment their practitioners—the healers—especially those who used incantations, since these were regarded as prayers to the devil. Due to his zeal in persecuting those presumed guilty of practicing native beliefs, Hernando Ruiz de Alarcon, a local priest born in Taxco, Guerrero (and brother of the famous playwright Juan Ruiz de Alarcon), was appointed an ecclesiastical judge and assigned the task of surveying the persistence of these old customs and beliefs. The result was his *Treatise on the Heathen Superstitions That Today Live among the Indians Native to This New Spain*, published in 1629.[20]

The *Treatise* is one of the most important sources dealing with native religion, beliefs, and medicine for early colonial Mexico and has attracted the attention of many scholars. Although Ruiz de Alarcon is regarded as a flawed ethnographer due to his obvious biases against native traditions, the accounts and invocations recorded in the document nonetheless provide valuable information about cosmology, concepts of deities and their interactions with humans, and ideas about health and sickness. Between Sahagun's *Florentine Codex* and the *Treatise* we can note a shift in the indigenous rituals due to the adoption of Christian images and symbols. However, the underlying structure revealed in this document continues to be that of the indigenous religion.[21]

> I have arrested and punished many Indian men and women for this crime (healing with invocations to Mesoamerican deities and fortune telling) although, having made a calculation, there have been more women than men . . . [They] are found in many provinces, because, on account of the name of seers, they are highly respected and regarded and very well provided with necessities.[22]

Of the thirty or so healers mentioned specifically by Ruiz de Alarcon, around twenty were women. The portrait that emerges is of women with authority who were staunch, resolute, and wise. It suggests that, just as the old religious beliefs persisted, the presence of powerful women healers may have likewise been a continuation of women's role in healing before the conquest. The scholar Gruzinski comments:

> One would hardly exaggerate these women's importance, who participate on equal footing with men, in the transmission of ancient cultures. Besides, it is not the first time that we see them intervene so manifestly in the process of acculturation and counter acculturation.[23]

Analyzing the social context of those women healers, he adds: "It seems that their function has little to do with social origin, age (some are old but not all) or condition (widows, married women) and only one knows how to read and write."[24]

Some healers achieved great prestige and notoriety and even outwitted the clergy's efforts to find them. Ruiz de Alarcon tells of the case of the

> old woman Isabel Maria, an inhabitant of Temimilzinco who uses spells and incantations, I took measures to get my hands on her. And she was so careful that for more than one year I was not able to discover her. . . . This old woman was so pleased with the strength of this false incantation, that she said she had unburdened her conscience with having made it known and not hiding any of the things that God had communicated to her for the benefit of man.[25]

Ruiz de Alarcon also speaks of a woman with a considerable reputation among the indigenous populations of Guerrero and Morelos:

> In the village of Iguala [in Guerrero] . . . I arrested an Indian woman called Mariana, a seer, a liar, a healer, of the type called "Ticitl." This Mariana declared that what she knew and used in her sorcery and frauds she had learned from another Indian woman, Mariana's sister, and that the sister had not learned it from another person, but that it had been revealed to her, because when the sister was consulting the *ololiuhqui** about the cure of an old wound, having become intoxicated with the strength of the drink she summoned the sick person and blew upon the wound some embers, where upon the wound healed immediately.

The account goes on to relate how "a youth whom she judged to be an angel" appeared to her and consoled her, telling her that God was granting her a favor. She would be able to cure wounds and diseases and thereby support herself even though she lived in "poverty and much misery." The youth put her on a cross and taught her the ways she knew for curing "which were seven or more exorcisms and invocations."[26]

*The seeds of this plant are used to prepare a drink that produces an altered state of consciousness.

CURANDERAS OF THE PRESENT

Apparently the efforts of Ruiz de Alarcon and others like him to stamp out the women healers and their curing methods were less than successful, for, as we have seen, *curanderas* are still an important presence in the popular medicine of Mexico today. Moreover, as in the past, calling on divine forces by means of prayer and ritual is as important a part of the healing process as administering a plant or its products to heal a disease. Almost all the women herbalists, bone-setters, and other healers whom I have come across carry out rituals. These may be simple prayers or invocations, or they may be long and complex, but they involve the *curandera* in an encounter with divine power. For them, illness cannot be reduced to a simple imbalance susceptible of being restored by taking the correct chemical substance. It is in this dimension that the power of women healers is most evident. The ability to drive out bad airs (spirits) from their patients, to neutralize the evil eye, to go in search of a lost *tonalli* (life force), to free patients from mischievous or evil spirit entities depends on the *curanderas'* capacity to act in the realm of the spirit. As Jacinto Arias, an indigenous anthropologist, points out:

> Traditional doctors, those which we call "iloletik," have as the center of their healing action the spirit, the soul, and not the plants or other kind of material medicine. This is why they read pulses and use other methods to diagnose social causes of sickness rather than physical or physiological causes. . . . [C]ertain medicinal plants are used as a support but these are not the core of their actions.[27]

Elena Islas speaks of the method used by her mother Dona Rufina to heal in San Miguel Tzinacapan, in the sierra of Puebla:

> My mother cured everything: fright, bad airs, evil eye. . . . She cured everything

> but she never did any evil, even though she knew how to do it. She had to pray all day. Only if she went out or if people came to visit her did she stop. . . . she prayed till midnight.[28]

Observations made by myself and others who study popular healing today show, however, that its combination of rite and technique can take many different forms. I shall end by offering a sample of just a few healing practices with which I have become familiar. Let us start with a description from my notes on a healing session conducted by a woman of Mexico City.

> It is just after dawn in the simple house of a peasant woman, Dona Lucia, who stands before a Mexican woman from the city. On the floor a black pottery incense burner of pre-Columbian design sends up a steady stream of incense. Both patient and healer are fasting. She has previously diagnosed her patient as suffering from an illness brought on by the jealousy and harmful thoughts of her co-workers. Dona Lucia looks toward her altar with its many holy pictures and statues of Jesus, Mary and the saints. After lighting several candles, she invokes the divine presence asking God to take away the perturbances that afflict the woman. Picking up the burner, she fans the incense to every part of the woman's body. Then she gives her a packet of finely chopped plant root and tells her how to take it. It will purge her, Dona Lucia explains, but after that she will begin to get better. Before setting out for home, the woman leaves a donation on the altar.

Several elements of clearly pre-Columbian influence can be seen in Dona Lucia's actions, some echoing the descriptions of Sahagun and Ruiz de Alarcon. Note the design of the pot, the mutual fasting, and the diagnosis: the illness has been caused by a world put out of balance by the wrongful thought of co-workers. Another common feature of pre-Columbian healing method was the use of agreeable smells, to attract healing presences to the patient—as well as the use of disagreeable odors to drive away presences that might be destructive.[29] We have already noted that the combination of herbal treatment—the plant root—with divine invocation is itself a classic remnant of pre-Columbian method. The deities addressed in the invocation, however—"Jesus, Mary, and the saints"—reflect Mexico's many centuries of strong Christian presence. Healing ceremonies such as this one have been carried out for centuries in Mexico by women, most of whom have no formal medical or ritual training. They begin practice within their own families, and when they gain a reputation for effectiveness, requests for aid come from their neighbors and other community members. At times the knowledge of a special healer's abilities can extend even beyond the boundaries of her state and country.[30]

Dona Lucia's actions, of course, do not exhaust the roster of techniques available to popular healers. Another style of healing involves establishing an altered state of consciousness in order to diagnose and cure. Hallucinogen researcher Gordon Wasson, for example, has observed and described the use of the *ololiuhqui* seed by the healer Paula Jimenez in San Baratolo Yautepec, a Zapotec village in the state of Oaxaca.[31] (See also Ruiz de Alarcon's example of this practice, p. 259.) A drink is prepared in a ritual that requires precise handling of the seeds, chanting, invocations, and awareness of proper time and place. The potion, in different quantities, is drunk by the *curandera* and patient. The healer now has access to divine knowledge and power, and hence can facilitate the cure.

Moreover, when Christian powers are invoked within healing rituals, the healers do not always address them in classically Christian ways. Ethnobotanist Bernard Baytelman has described the ritual healing of a scorpion bite by a woman called "Sister" Julia by the residents of her poor urban neighborhood in Cuernavaca.[32] Throughout a ceremony to cure a small girl of this potentially fatal bite, Sister Julia talks to an image of Jesus. Her speech indicates her expectation that Jesus is there healing through her as she gives an injection to the girl. She speaks informally to the image, even harshly when the girl at first does not improve. The divinity she calls on is clearly not a transcendent being but an immanent one. The image she addresses is the crucified Christ. Both she and the witnesses to her ceremony assume that the cure is accomplished through her power to call on divine aid.

One of the most interesting examples of pre- and post-colonial fusion of healing approaches that I have found is a movement known as Marian Spiritualism. Marian Trinity Spiritualism is a popular—mainly urban—religion which is expanding rapidly throughout Mexico and into Central and South America. According to some researchers, ex-seminarian Roque Rojas founded the movement in 1866 in the town of Contreras outside of Mexico City.[33] Within its beliefs and rituals can be found traces of pre-Hispanic, Christian, Hindu, and Judaic elements. Followers refer to themselves as the Lost Tribes of Israel; they believe in reincarnation; in their chants they address a divinity that is present in oceans, rivers, stones, light, insects, and earth. An image of the Trinity, a triangle with an eye at the center, is the central piece of their altars.

In spiritualism, curing is accomplished through "spiritual" techniques. Healers sometimes administer herbs (this varies from chapter to chapter) and use massage, but healing takes place for the most part by means of the action of spirit protectors working through the healer, while she or he is in a trance state. Spiritualism encourages direct relationship with the world of spirit protectors. In spiritualist temples, both men and women have access to all levels of the hierarchy. Often women hold the highest positions, both in practice and in myths.[34] One prominent example is Dona Lola, founder of the spiritualist temple in Cuernavaca, Morelos, and for many years an important leader of the movement. She selected and trained members who had "faculties." Through her trances and spirit possession, a woman of the movement becomes a bearer of knowledge and acquires special dignity. Transformed into a receptacle of the divine, she becomes a guide, a curer, and a teacher.

Currently, the spiritualists have seven chapters or "seals," each with its own characteristics. The Sixth Seal was founded by Damiana Oveido whose biography was converted into a founding myth and begins as follows: "The first woman who descended to the planet earth in order to make the light of the Lord known was Damiana Oviedo. Since her birth she predicted many things that the Lord had indicated." According to this biography, she only lived three days after birth, then died and

> was brought back to life twenty-four hours later and led a normal life. . . . At thirteen years of age, she went to Manzanillo and there founded the first temple. . . and the Lord spoke with her and told her that she should plant the light in Mexico and she went there and founded a temple and many followed her.[35]

Accounts such as this show that, even in today's patriarchal Mexican culture, a woman can still attract great esteem and authority when she shines in the old women's calling of spiritual healing.

CONCLUSION

It would doubtless be a mistake to conclude from this article that ritualized healing was the only context in which women of ancient

Mexico could achieve prominence. From time to time still today in native Mexican practice, one finds tantalizing customs that are very likely survivals of important functions women may have exercised in pre-colonial times. One such example is found among a special type of *curanderos* known as *graniceros* found in the volcano region near Mexico City, whose special function is the control of rain, hail, and lightning. Although many *graniceros* are men, their highest authority is a woman, and this position is handed down through a female lineage.[36]

However, I have chosen to focus on women healers in this chapter both because the evidence for their pre-colonial importance is so strong and because they remain so prevalent in today's Mexico. Mythological and ethnographic records show that ritual healing has been practiced in Mexico since pre-Hispanic times. As healers, women were—and are—religious and community leaders. Ethnographic evidence indicates also that pre-colonial Mexican healers were in the majority female, just as they are today among the spiritualists, where they predominate in the temple hierarchy. Moreover, not only was there a high number of women healers, but they seem to have achieved positions of great authority.

In the ancient Mesoamerican cosmos and in contemporary healing practices where its influence still pervades, medicine has been an art of exchange with the divine. It entails a capacity for immersion in divinity and mastery over revealed knowledge. It requires the skill to illuminate hidden mysteries and the power to intervene in uncertain destinies and to reorder these and bring them into harmony. Women in Mexico lead healing rituals, and, in thus addressing the needs of those around them, they are priestesses who mediate between life and death, sacred and profane.

Notes

1. Kaja Finkler, *Spiritualist Healers in Mexico: Successes and Failures of Alternative Therapies* (South Hadley, MA: Bergin and Garvey, 1985), pp. 1–2.

2. Mesoamerica stretches from about half-way between the central Mexican highlands and the United States border though Mexico and Guatemala, reaching into parts of El Salvador, Honduras, and Nicaragua. The information concerning popular medicine and cosmology applies to this region as well as to northern Mexico and even to Mexican-American populations that retain these influences.

3. Sylvia Marcos, "Cognitive Structures and Medicine: The Challenge of Popular Medicines," *Curare* 2 (1988): 87–96.

4. Guillermo Bonfil Batalla, " Lo proprio y lo ajeno: una aproximación al problema del control cultural," in *La cultura popular,* ed. Adolfo Colombres (México: Jonás Premià Editoria, 1984), pp. 79–86.

5. J. Galinier, "Cosmologia e interpretation de la enfermedad," *México indigeno* 9 (Mar-Apr 1986).

6. Torquamada, as quoted by M. León Portilla, *La filosofia nahuatl: Estudiada en sus fuentes,* 3rd ed., México: Universidad Nacional Autonóma de México [henceforth UNAM], 1963), p. 155.

7. Angel Garibay, "Semejanza de algunos conceptos filosophicos de las culturas hindu y nahuatl," *Cuadernos del Seminario de problemas cientificos y filosophicos* 15, Second Series (1959).

8. F. B. Sahagún, *Historia general de las cosas de Nueva Espania* [*Florentine Codex*], 2nd ed. ed., 13 vols. in 12, ed. and trans. Arthur J. O. Anderson and Charles E. Dibble (Santa Fe, NM: School of American Research and the University of Utah, 1950–82); originally published 1577.

9. John Eric Sidney Thompson, *Historia y religión de los mayos* (México: Siglio Veintiuno, 1975).

10. Bartolomé de las Casas, *Apologetica historia sumaria,* 3rd ed. (México: UNAM, 1967); originally published 1552.

11. Diego Landa, *Relacion de las cosas de Yucatan,* 10th ed. (México: Porrua, 1960); originally published 1560.

12. Eva Hunt, *The Transformation of the Hummingbird: Cultural Roots of a Zinacantecan Mythical Poem* (Ithaca, NY: Cornell University Press, 1977).

13. Portilla, *op. cit.,* and Evon Z. Vogt, *Tortillas for the Gods: A Symbolic Analysis of Zinacanteco Rituals* (Cambridge: Harvard University Press, 1976).

14. See J. Richard Andrews and Ross Hassig, trans. of H. Ruiz de Alarcon, *Treatise on the Heathen Superstitions That Today Live among the Indian Natives to This New Spain* (Norman: University of Oklahoma Press, 1984); also Serge Gruzinski, *La colonisation de l'imaginaire: Sociétés indigènes et occidentalisation dans le Mexique espagnol XVIe–XVIIIe Siècle* (Paris: Gallimard, 1988).

15. "Curas, diosas y erotismo: El catolicismo frente a los Indios," *Mujueres e iglesia: sexualidad v aborto en America Latina,* ed. A. Portugal (México: Fonamara/CFFC Washington, 1989).

16. Hunt, *op. cit.*

17. *Florentine Codex,* Book I, Chapter 8.

18. Ibid., Book X, Chapter 14.

19. Ibid., Book VI, Chapter 13.

20. English translation by Andrews and Hassig, *op. cit.*

21. As argued by Gruzinski, *op., cit.,* and Andrews and Hassig, ibid.

22. Andrews and Hassig, ibid., p. 148.

23. Gruzinski, *op. cit.,* p. 203.

24. Ibid.

25. Andrews and Hassig, *op. cit.,* pp. 192–94.

26. Ibid., pp. 66–67.

27. L. Herrasti and A. Ortiz, "Medicina del alma: entrevista a Jacinto Arias," *México indigeno* 9 (Mar–Apr 1986).

28. E. Almeida et al, "Psicologia auctoctono mexicana: Dona Rufina Manzono Ramirez de San Miguel Tzinacapan, Puebla" (unpublished ms., 1986).

29. See my article "Curing and Cosmology: the Challenge of Popular Medicines," *Development: Seeds of Change* 1 (1987): pp. 22–24.

30. One such is a woman named Marie Sabina, from the Sierra Mazateca in the southern Mexican state of Oaxaco, mentioned in my article "Cognitive Structures and Medicine," *op. cit.* 95.

31. Gordon Wasson, "Ololiuhqui and Other Hallucinogens of Mexico," *Summa anthropologica en homenaje a Roberto J. Weitlaner* (México: Instituto National de Antropologia e Historia [henceforth INAH], 1966), p. 346.

32. Bernard Baytelman, *Etnobotánica en el Estado de Morelos* (México: INAH, 1981).

33. Silvia Ortiz Echaniz, "Origen, desarrollo y characteristicas del espiritualismo en México," *America indigena* 39, 1 (Jan–Mar 1979): 147–70 and "El poder del trance o la participation femina en el espiritualismo trinitario mariano," *Cuadernos de Trabajo DEAS* (México: INAH, 1979).

34. Ortiz, ibid; also Finkler, *op. cit.,* and Attias Isabel Lagarriga, *Medicina traditional y espiritismo: Los espiritualistas triniarios marianos de Jalapa, Veracruz* (México: Sep-Setentas, no. 191, 1975).

35. Lagarriga, ibid.

36. Viesca, Carlos, "El Medico México," *Historia general de la Medicina en México,* Tomo I: *México antiguo* (México: UNAM Academia Nacional de Medicina, 1984).

Further Readings

Marcos, Sylvia. "Embodied Religious Thought: Gender Categories in Mesoamerica." *Religion* 28, 4 (1998): 371–82.

———. "Mesoamerican Religions." *Encyclopedia of Women and World Religion,* 1998.

———. "Sacred Earth: Mesoamerican Perspectives." *Concilium, International Review of Theology* 5 (October 1995): 27–37.

———. "Indigenous Eroticism and Colonial Morality." *Numen, International Review for the History of Religions* 39, no. 2 (1992): 157–74.

———. "Gender and Moral Precepts in Ancient Mexico: Sahagun's Texts." *Concilium: International Review of Theology* 6 (December 1991): 60–74.

———. "Curing and Cosmology: The Challenge of Popular Medicine." *Development: Seeds of Change;* Special Edition on *Culture and Ethnicity,* 1 (1987): 20–25.

22

When Christ Is a Woman: Theology and Practice in the Shaker Tradition

SUSAN M. SETTA

On the eve of the American Revolution, Ann Lee and a small band of followers left England and set sail to establish a heavenly kingdom in the American colonies. They called themselves the United Society of Believers in Christ's Second Appearing. Only a few of the original Shakers accompanied Lee; the rest remained in England with John and Jane Wardley, who had originally founded the group as an offshoot of the Society of Friends. Within 75 years of its journey west, the United Society had 5,000 fully covenanted members, and probably three times as many devotees who, for personal reasons, could not live with their Shaker brothers and sisters. The religious system of the United Society of Believers in Christ's Second Appearing is unique in human history. It proclaimed the Motherhood and Fatherhood of God, asserted that the second coming of Christ had occurred in the woman Ann Lee, fostered a social and political structure of both male and female leadership, and prohibited both marriage and private ownership of property.

By insisting that Ann Lee was the Christ and that God was both male and female, the Shakers undercut the patriarchal bias of eighteenth- and nineteenth-century Christianity. Because both men and women had been created in the image of God, and because the female Christ had explicitly brought redemption for women, Shakers believed that women as well as men should have full access to all forms of religious practice and leadership.

SUSAN M. SETTA, PH.D., is Associate Professor of Philosophy and Religion at Northeastern University, Boston, Massachusetts. She is a former Chair of the Women and Religion Section of the American Academy of Religion.

Living in their own version of the Kingdom of God on Earth, Shaker women and men had a rare opportunity to live in full accordance with this conviction.

ANN LEE AND THE EARLY SHAKER COMMUNITIES

Shaker sources consistently trace Shaker origins to 1747, when Jane and John Wardley formulated a group based loosely on the ideas of the Society of Friends. A group that emphasized ecstatic religious experience, they came to be known as Shakers because they both quaked and shook during their worship services. One striking feature of the Wardleys' teaching was the expectation that Christ would come soon, probably in female form. In 1758, Ann Lee and her husband Abraham Stanley were drawn to the group. At first Ann was merely a follower of the Wardleys. But eventually she would proclaim herself the second Christ and become a source of divisive controversy.

It is as difficult to uncover the life of the historical Ann Lee as it is to find the historical Jesus. Because Lee was illiterate, the reconstruction of her life, work, and ideas depends upon both the writings of those who knew her and later interpretations of the original accounts. Stories and sayings attributed to her often vary according to the prevailing theology of the time period in which they occur. Despite the difficulties in presenting her biography, several facts about Lee's life are clear. Lee was born to indigent parents in Manchester, England in 1736, five years before the Great Awakening was to sweep New England in the American colonies. Lee married Abraham Stanley in 1756. They had four children, all of whom died at birth or in early childhood. Lee and her parents had been members of the Anglican church, but in the year of their marriage, Lee and Stanley joined the Wardley community.

The loss of her children was very painful for Lee, and during the late 1760s she underwent a period of spiritual crisis. She became extremely troubled by day and unable to sleep by night; she prayed constantly for deliverance. Spiritual and physical agonies plagued her until, as her biographers claim, she perspired blood. Meanwhile, the Wardleys' small association was being persecuted by civil and church authorities for such infractions as Sabbath breaking and blasphemy. While Lee was imprisoned for Sabbath breaking in 1770, she claimed to have a revelation informing her that she herself had been chosen to be the final incarnation of Christ. When Lee was released from prison, returned to the group, and related her vision, other Shakers experienced the same revelation and hence accepted the truth of her claim. From that time on, Lee's vision became a central focus of Shaker teachings. However, in addition to her claim to be the Second Appearance of Christ, Lee claimed God had revealed to her that the root of all sin was lust, which in turn prompted all sexual relations. Thus Lee taught her followers to abandon sex and take up celibacy as a central feature of their spiritual practice. This, together with Lee's increasing prominence in the group, ultimately led to a break with the Wardleys.

In 1774, Lee had another revelation, telling her to take her gospel message to America and to create God's kingdom on earth in the colonies. Together with a small group of followers, who were mostly her relatives, Lee set sail for the Shakers' new home. The trip was difficult: a storm threatened the very lives of the Shakers; their vessel was damaged and came perilously close to sinking. Lee, however, was not daunted by the danger and, according to her companions, she controlled the forces of nature so that a wave mended the ship. This action further convinced an already devoted group that Lee shared in the power of God.

Landing in New York City, the American Shakers soon moved to a rural area in upstate

New York. Despite considerable economic difficulty, the small group of believers proselytized actively, caught the attention of many clergy in the area, and began to attract new members. However, at the same time, many of their new neighbors were eying them with considerable suspicion. For one thing, it was the eve of the American revolution and these English women and men were preaching that a new kingdom was about to be established on earth. At one point Lee was even arrested for treason. But she was released after informing the judge that God had told her he was on the colonies' side. The novel, albeit heretical, religious ideas of the Shakers were scorned by many in the surrounding community. This scorn ranged from derogatory sermons to physical persecution. Lee herself died in 1784 from injuries inflicted by an angry mob.

Lee's death precipitated a crisis for her followers. Although Lee had never claimed to be immortal, some of her followers apparently believed that Christ's Second Coming could not die. Before her death, Lee had named as her successor James Whittaker, one of the original English Shakers; Whittaker led the group until his death just three years later, in 1787. As a result of the uncertainties provoked by Lee's death, Whittaker concentrated on clarifying Shaker doctrine, and the group survived its founder's passing. An American convert, Joseph Meacham, replaced Whittaker and led the group until 1796. Prior to her death, Lee had called Meacham her "first born son in America." Under Meacham's leadership, the Shaker community organized a system of spiritual and temporal governance that has continued until the twentieth century. Lee had set a precedent for dual male and female leadership when she appointed Lucy Wright, another Americanborn member, to oversee women's affairs in the community. Meacham formalized Wright's position in the group, and she became known as Mother Lucy. After Meacham's death, Mother Lucy became the Shakers' leader. Under her tenure, the original small group developed into a successful utopian community and began several missionary ventures westward.

The leadership that followed was never as dynamic nor as successful as that of Whittaker, Meacham, and Wright. Those three had been chosen by Lee herself; later individuals rose to leadership roles primarily because of seniority within the group. Times were especially difficult from the mid-1820s until the 1840s. Financial hardship, coupled with a conservative leadership that had never known the foundress, led to low morale and strained relationships.

During the 1840s, the community's fortunes rose again, as the result of an innovative revival called "Mother's Work." At this time, the spirits of Ann Lee and other historical or spiritual figures began appearing regularly through human "instruments," or mediums, who transmitted to the community their messages, paintings, poems, hymns, and new laws. Lasting until about 1847, this interval of dramatic spiritual activity brought renewed financial prosperity, increased membership, and missionary expansion. By the end of the 1860s, however, the Shaker communities again were in decline; individual societies were closed, members began to leave, and new converts became rare. The membership, once almost equally divided between men and women, now became predominantly female.

The decline and transformation of the Shaker communities cannot be attributed to any one factor. Ironically, financial success contributed to the decline because the group's prosperity attracted members seeking an escape from poverty rather than responding to a spiritual calling. In addition, to gain more converts, Shakers accommodated their theology to American Protestantism and hence became less distinctive. The fervent, innovative, and ecstatic worship that had once been a hallmark of the Shaker tradition now also became more restrained and traditional. Today, only a handful of practicing Shakers remain.

SHAKER TEACHINGS: ANN THE CHRIST

One striking example of increasing conservatism in Shaker teachings was a withdrawal from their initial understanding of Ann herself. The earliest Shaker communities, dating from 1770–1830, contended that Lee and Jesus were co-saviors. To support their claim that Lee had been a second savior, early Shakers reinterpreted the traditional Christian view of Christ. They saw Christ not as Jesus, but as a principle—the "Unity of Divine Male and Female."[1] This had first appeared in Jesus and then finally, and necessarily, in Ann Lee. Christ had to come in both male and female forms, they argued, because God was both male and female. Hence they sometimes called Ann Lee their Mother in Christ because she represented the female aspect of God.

The original Shakers had described the second coming of Christ in terms parallel to those that other Christians had used to refer to the first appearance in Jesus. Hence they also called Lee "the Second Eve," "Ann Christ," and "Ann the Daughter." After Lee's death, Mother Sarah Kendall wrote that she knew Lee was

> the Lord's anointed, the Bride, the Lamb's Wife spoken of in ancient days by holy inspiration; for she did the same work and performed miracles in the same spirit that Christ did while on earth.[2]

Despite the danger of making such heretical statements, Kendall affirmed the strength of her conviction by adding:

> As soon would I dispute that Christ made his first appearance in the person of Jesus of Nazareth as I would that he made his second appearance in the person of Ann Lee.[3]

Lee's earliest biographers tell of Lee's powers, her ability to heal the sick, and her capacity to search a soul merely by looking into someone's eyes. One such account comes from Hannah Cogswell:

> I know of a certainty, that Mother Ann had the gift of prophecy and the revelation of God, by which she was able to search the hearts of those who came to see her; for I have myself been an eye and ear witness of it. I have known some to come to her under a cloak of deception, thinking to conceal their sins in her presence; and I have seen her expose them by the searching power of truth, and to acknowledge that the light and revelation of God was in her.[4]

Rebecca Jackson, who founded the predominantly black community of Philadelphia Shakers, spoke of Jesus and Ann in identical terms. Jackson claimed that Jesus and Ann "lived on earth as angels do in heaven, living angel lives in earthly bodies."[5] Speaking of her vision of the new creation, Jackson said that both Lee and Jesus had existed before the world was made. According to Jackson, Lee had restored four spirits in one: the Mother, the Father, the Daughter, and the Son; by completing this divine quartet, Lee had saved the world.[6] Others argued that when Jesus said "I go to prepare a place for you," he was referring to the completion of God's plan of salvation that had occurred through the appearance of Lee. Lee and Jesus together are the saving pair who come to redeem the world; but it is Ann, not Jesus, who completes the purpose of salvation history.

However, early Shaker writers did not simply add the concept of a female savior to Christian teachings; they rather reinterpreted the entire Bible within the context of Lee's revelation. They used for this purpose a special approach to scripture that was common in the eighteenth and nineteenth century. According to this "typological" method of Biblical interpretation, certain figures or actions called "types" anticipate and point to the final act of salvation. But the significance of any such "type" is not apparent until its fulfillment. Using this approach, the Shakers tried to show that all of salvation history had been moving towards completion of the Christ principle in the woman Ann Lee. When Shaker writers looked to the Bible with the idea of a female Christ in mind, they saw the women of the Bible in a new and more important light. Many Biblical women became "types" of Ann, who pointed to God's redemption of the world through her. For example, the mother of Moses became a "type" of Ann, for Ann "is the true figure of the final deliverance of the people of God though the woman."[7] Of course, Jesus himself was also understood to be a "type." As Son of God and Anointing Spirit, he pointed to the divine Daughter, Ann.

Although early Shaker sources portrayed Lee and Jesus as equals, later Shaker theology downplayed the similarity between them. In a 1904 Shaker publication, the Shaker sisters Leila S. Taylor and Anna White claimed that Shakers had never believed that Ann was Christ.[8] Frederick Evans, who became an elder at the end of the nineteenth century, reiterated this claim. A Shaker sister interviewed more recently, in 1974, asserted that Lee demonstrated the light of Christ that lies within every human being, but Lee herself was not the Christ. To these later writers, Lee became an exemplary prophet, a model for the true Christian. Although Lee's spiritual maturity had been without earthly parallel, she was not considered equal to Jesus. Rather than insisting on a female incarnation of Christ, later Shakers turned to the image of God as Mother to develop their concept of a female aspect of divinity.

GOD AS FATHER AND MOTHER

Whereas Shaker views of the nature of Lee changed over time, their vision of God as male and female, father and mother, remained constant. Taking the first chapter of Genesis as their starting point, they contended that God's statement "Let *Us* create man in *Our* image. . . ." must be taken to mean that God was both male and female. Ridiculing the then-standard interpretation of this passage, which claimed that God was speaking to Jesus in this passage, the Shakers asked:

> Was it to the Son, the Father spoke, as the divines have long taught? How then came man to be created male and female? *Father* and *Son* are not male and female; but *father* and *mother* are male and female, as likewise are *son* and *daughter*. . . .
>
> And without this relationship there can exist no order in creation! Without a father and mother we can have no existence.[9]

In the Shakers' opinion, the truth about the motherhood of God had been suppressed by 2,000 years of Christian teaching. In order for humanity to become perfect and to live in a Heaven on Earth, both the motherhood and the fatherhood of God had to be acknowledged.

The period of Shaker history known as "Mother's Work" saw an important development in the concept of the motherhood of God. During this time a figure called Holy Mother Wisdom began to speak through the Shaker mediums; the first to receive her were a group of male and female children, but later she appeared mostly through female instruments. Holy Mother Wisdom was believed to be a manifestation of the female in God. She was not Ann Lee, but was Ann's and everyone else's Mother in Creation. According to one recorded manifestation, Wisdom had come "to set my house in order to complete and fortify the walls of my Zion."[10] Eternal Wisdom stood with the Eternal Father when she proclaimed:

> Bow down, obey, all ye who hear my Word, both ye who dwell on Zion, and ye who dwell in distant lands, say I Eternal Wis-

> dom. . . . In word of solemn warning I sound my trumpet of wisdom unto you. . . .
>
> Know ye that I am Wisdom, Eternal and Unchangeable Wisdom: one with God I am, and always shall be; even as he is your Eternal Father, so do I Eternal Wisdom, stand as your everlasting Mother with Him.
>
> I sound forth mercy, with Him Judgment proclaim; We stand as one, and work but as one alone; . . .[11]

Often, as in the above passage, Mother Wisdom is portrayed as a Warrior working to complete the creation. But at other times, Wisdom seems almost timid. Paulina Bates's long book titled *The Divine Book of Holy and Eternal Wisdom*[12] recorded revelations of Mother Wisdom in which this female aspect of God was often humble and meek and possessed many attributes considered valuable for the nineteenth-century gentlewoman. According to this view, Holy Mother Wisdom had not made herself known in the past because the world was not safe enough for her appearance. But whether her image was fierce or gentle, Mother Wisdom stood on equal footing with God and gave Shakers a complex image of God as female.

WHY WOMEN NEED A SPECIAL SAVIOR

The images of Mother God as Warrior, Gentlewoman, and Wise Woman, together with the belief in Ann Lee as completion of Christ, offered the Shakers a full reflection of woman in the deity. Furthermore, the Shaker conception of the fourfold nature of God profoundly affected Shaker attitudes towards women and Shaker social institutions. Thus, Shaker theology offered to women a means by which many Shaker sisters could become freer than women who were their contemporaries in United States society.

According to the Shaker view, women were equal to men in their original nature because the two genders had been created in the likeness of a God who was both male and female. Nevertheless, Shakers agreed with mainstream Christianity of the time on two important points of biblical interpretation. First, they agreed that men and women had sinned through Adam and Eve and hence had lost the possibilities of this original condition. Second, the Shakers, along with most Christian interpreters, agreed that women had then become subordinated to men because Eve had brought about humanity's fall. Unlike most other Christian interpreters, however, the Shakers claimed that female subordination was not final. Because the Millenium had arrived through the coming of Ann Lee, male domination had been overcome, and the true equality of men and women could be restored.

Moreover, Shaker writers asserted that women could be redeemed *only* through a female savior. An early Shaker theological compendium noted:

> It was therefore indispensably necessary, for the final restoration of man to eternal life, that the spirit should be revealed *in that sex where sin first began;* and there destroy that enchanting influence which the woman received from the serpent, that alluring power by which the natural man is led, and through which the fall of man was first produced. [Emphasis added.][13]

Note this text's presupposition that sin "first began" with the female sex. The writer assumes that women are even more vulnerable to evil than males. He goes on to say that women therefore had to be raised from "the lowest state of the fall" in order to be "made a fit temple for the Holy Spirit to dwell in." Thus, the Shakers' very positive view of women's potentialities was based on an initially negative assessment.

Until the Second Coming of Christ, women and men had not shared a similar capacity for perfection. Instead, since the fall women and men had had a completely different moral makeup. The female nature was most evident in the character of the first woman, Eve. Like most Christian interpreters of the day, Shaker theology located the origin of the world's evil in Eve's inclination towards what they called "animal sensations." While Adam was somewhat responsible for his own actions, Eve was plainly responsible for the downfall of both human ancestors. Instead of rejecting Eve's role, as one might expect, Shaker writers never questioned this notion. Instead they tried to show why it had been necessary for evil to enter the world through a woman. The Shakers argued that since all humanity had entered the world through women, evil must have arisen out of the same source. Eve's communication with the devil had excited her "animal sensations," and lust, which gave rise to sin, had thus been born. Through the interaction of Adam and Eve, the male had also fallen prey to these sensations. Adam and Eve participated "in the act of sexual coition; and thus partook of the forbidden fruit."[14]

Before the Second Coming, women had been weak, and hence were easily led astray. Like all creatures, Eve had the ability to refuse temptation; but she instead gave in to her fleshly nature. Because of this, the animal nature became humanity's reigning principle. Only by intervention of God's Spirit could humanity be restored to its true spiritual nature. Jesus, a male, had brought redemption for men. However, women required a different plan of salvation, because women's moral quality differed from that of men. Before Ann Lee, women had no savior. Thus, in the Shaker view, men had gained access to perfection almost two thousand years before women had done so. Clearly, the sin of the female was grave, for it took two separate appearances of Christ to eradicate women's sinful tendencies. But women had finally been redeemed, and a new, egalitarian "Heaven on Earth" had now become possible.

WOMEN IN GOD'S KINGDOM ON EARTH

Perhaps the most exciting aspect of Shaker practice was the fact that Shakers actually tried to design and live in such an egalitarian "Heaven." From the time of their beginnings in New York, the Shakers were millenarians; they believed that they were living representatives of the Kingdom of God on earth. Their pattern of daily life could therefore not be ordered by the laws and customs of the fallen, secular, imperfect world. Their own rules of governance and day-to-day activity had to mirror the ways of heaven. To live in the way that they felt the redeemed ought to live, the Shakers founded alternative communities. Situated mostly in rural areas that at the time of founding were part of the American frontier, these communities owned their own land, designed and built their own buildings, and produced most of their own food, clothing, furniture, and even machinery. Being self-sufficient and unobtrusive, they were usually left alone by the new U.S. government and by their neighbors. Hence they were also able to shape their own social and political life-style. Three central components of this life-style held important implications for Shaker women: celibacy, communal property, and the Shaker form of community organization and governance.

From the time of Lee's vision to the present, a central Shaker practice has been celibacy—that is to say, total abstinence from sex and marriage. Like other Shaker teachings, Shaker justifications for celibacy changed during the course of Shaker history.

Lee herself set the tone for the early Shaker abhorrence of sexual intercourse when she stated:

> Those who choose to live after the flesh, can do so; but I know, by the revelation of God, that those who live in the gratification of their lusts will suffer in proportion as they have violated the law of God in nature.[15]

Early Shaker sources, following Lee's own teachings, generally charged that sexual relations are the primary cause of sin in the world. Later sources were less likely to stress the evils of sexuality itself. But they still viewed celibacy as an important way to protect the unity of the millenial community. Sexuality leads to marriage, and married persons tend to look to their spouses' and children's needs rather than committing themselves fully to their spiritual families. Most Shaker defences of the celibate life furthermore emphasized that marriage places women in a subordinate role.[16]

The Shaker practice of celibacy is often misunderstood. Although Shakers preferred a celibate lifestyle and required celibacy before a person could take up residence in one of the Shakers' own settlements, not all Shakers lived within the celibate communities. Noncelibate Shakers, sometimes called "householders," often remained with their worldly families. In all probability, most of these "householders" were women. Eighteenth- and nineteenth-century laws invariably granted custody of children to a father if one of the parents left the household. A woman who joined a celibate Shaker community without her husband would lose all claim to her children and be unable to see them. In contrast, a man who left his wife to join would take his children along with him. Mary Dyer, a woman of the early nineteenth century who published scathing attacks on the United Society, published her exposé, *A Portrait of Shakerism,* as part of her efforts to win custody of her children from her Shaker husband.[17]

Moreover, Shakers at times questioned their own celibate practice. Near the close of the nineteenth century, when their population was dwindling, some Shakers even for a time considered starting a "generative order"; this would be for those who found celibacy too difficult a cross to bear. However, other members disputed this idea, and the noncelibate order was never founded.

In contrast, Shakers never challenged their second major departure from mainstream American practice—the abolition of private ownership. The Shaker belief that members should hold all lands and goods in common was based on Lee's revelation that "Christianity did not admit to private property." This practice was closely linked to the celibate ideal, for *any* interest in the material world was considered to be an expression of lust. All carnality—all desire for worldly things—had to be eradicated in the New Kingdom. This included both the desire for sexual union and the desire for material wealth.

The practice of sharing property was already on record in 1782; in that year, Benjamin Barnes gave all of his land to the settlement which survives today as Sabbathday Lake. From these early beginnings it swiftly became the norm for all fully covenanted members to donate all their property to the community. By the 1820s, Lucy Wright was asserting that the Union was the Gift. That is to say, Union, the united effort of the believers, depended on the sharing of Shaker resources. Shakers argued that private ownership was a barrier to spiritual and temporal equality. Property served to divide rather than unite a community. It led to the subjection of women, to slavery, and even to war.

In fact, the ability to give up property, rather than the practice of celibacy, was the ultimate test of commitment to Shaker teachings. A person living at a Shaker settlement could lead a celibate life and still not be considered fully in Union. Union was reserved for those who signed the Covenant, a document that transferred permanent ownership of the signer's property to the community. Shakers did not do this immediately upon joining; in 1799, Mother Lucy Wright created a "Gathering Order"—a kind of novitiate—that lived exactly like other Shakers and practiced celibacy. But these new members retained their right to retrieve their property if they decided to leave the community. In contrast, if fully covenanted members left, their property remained with the Shaker community. Because Shaker property was jointly held, it was considered to be wholly devoted to God. It could not be used to benefit individual members, even in cases where members retained some right to reclaim it. The Shakers adamantly upheld this position even from the time of the first written covenant.

The Shaker practice of sharing property, like the practice of celibacy, had important implications for Shaker women; for both tended to equalize the relationship between men and women. Nineteenth-century thinkers were well aware of the close correlation between private ownership and the subjection of women. At the time when Shaker communities were enjoying their largest membership and prosperity, Friedrich Engels was writing his *Origins of the Family, Private Property, and the State*. Monogamous marriage, Engels contended, was a means of extending property and insuring its transference to male heirs. This kind of relationship was "the first form of the family to be based, not on natural but on economic conditions, on the victory of private property over primitive natural communal property."[18] Engels argued that the male's ownership of property and consequent economic superiority over the female led to male supremacy in the marriage relationship. Therefore the marriage relationship was not mutual. Instead, in his view, "the modern individual family is founded on the open or concealed domestic slavery of the woman."[19]

Comments remarkably similar to those of Engels on the inequality of the marriage relationship and women's dependent status appear frequently in the writings of Shaker sisters. For example, Paulina Bates commented on the status of the married woman:

> Hence ariseth the belief in many that the female is not in possession of a living soul; but [is] merely a machine for the use and benefit of man in his terrestrial state of existence.[20]

Yet another woman echoed Engels's own words when she wrote, in 1882: "Woman's condition is little superior to slave."[21]

Both Engels and the Shaker writers of course presupposed the economic structure of eighteenth- and nineteenth-century marriage. In America of that time, as in Engels's Europe, ownership of property was allotted almost exclusively to men. American women were subjected to the principle of coverature, which the United States had taken over from English common law. In marriage, according to this legal standard, "the husband and wife were one person—the husband."[22] Because of coverature, married women had no rights of ownership; during the eighteenth and early nineteenth centuries women could hold property only if they were single or widowed. The Married Women's Laws, passed during the 1860s, altered this principle slightly, but they protected only the property that a woman brought to her marriage. Anything acquired by the woman during the marriage was still owned by her husband. Hence within a typical family structure, women became totally dependent upon men; for men controlled their means of financial support. When a woman married she ran the risk of becoming yet another possession, because she had no financial autonomy. And yet for most women of the time, marriage was the only viable option for women; they had no other means of making a living.

Both Shaker celibacy and the Shaker system of community property undercut this system at its foundation. Shaker men did not hold property; nor could they use community property for their own benefit; therefore they could not use it to exercise power over women. Women had equal access to the Shaker community property; therefore they were no longer economically dependent on men. Shaker celibacy meant that men and women did not marry; even if a Shaker couple had been previously married, they did not live together, and their marriage was not recognized by the community. Hence even the habit of wives submitting to their husbands could not carry over into the redeemed community.

But perhaps even more importantly, by doing away with households founded on marriage and individual ownership, the Shakers gained an opportunity to create a whole new style of human society. People in the Shaker community were joined by faith, not by marriage or blood relationships. They lived in Spiritual Families as children of Heavenly Parents. "Families," or living groups of from 30 to 100 men and women, made up a "Community." They were designated by location—for example, they were called "South Family" or "North Family." Several "Communities" were in turn gathered into a "Bishopric"; and the "Bishoprics," in turn, comprised the United Society.

Moreover, at each organization level, the Shakers had multiple leaders. They separated "spiritual" from "temporal" office. The Lead Ministry, consisting of Elders and Eldresses, provided spiritual leadership; Deacons, Deaconesses, and Trustees directed temporal matters. Spiritual leadership was patterned after the heavenly rule of the Father/Son and Mother/Daughter; therefore two men and two women directed spiritual affairs in each administrative unit. The four Shakers in the Lead Ministry were referred to as "Mother" and "Father." They headed the United Society from New Lebanon, New York. Each Bishopric was directed by a "Ministry," consisting, again, of two men and two women. Two Elders and two Eldresses led each "Family." Deacons and Deaconesses, as temporal leaders, did not govern, but rather supervised particular tasks. There were, for example, Farm Deacons and Kitchen Deaconesses. Trustees were in charge of financial matters and controlled the Shaker communal property.

Because this complex governmental structure required leaders at each level, women had much greater access to leadership roles than they did in the greater American society. About one in fifty Shaker sisters would fill a leadership position during her life in the United Society.[23] Moreover, the woman leaders were no mere figureheads; especially those in the Lead Ministry held considerable responsibility. Lucy Wright, the most important Eldress in Shaker history, made final decisions concerning construction of new buildings, missionary expansion, and publications. Wright's opinion prevailed even when her views were controversial. Although later Eldresses were somewhat less visible than Wright, they travelled on missionary ventures, visited the Western societies, and directed spiritual matters. Even in cases where male leaders seemed more prominent than the women, the women still held more power than non-Shaker counterparts.

Lesser ministerial roles of men and women within the community were similar. Confession of sins was a requirement for union. Women heard women's confessions; men were confessors to men. In addition, women taught and produced spiritual sayings that were passed down and revered for generations. Work roles had male and female supervisors; Deaconesses supervised women's work; deacons supervised the work of men.

Still the Shakers made some discrimination between the tasks of men and the tasks of women. Early records indicate that Mary Whitcher was a trustee in 1792,[24] but by 1800 women no longer functioned in this capacity. Although Shaker records do not indicate a reason for this change, women trustees would clearly have endangered the community because of existing U.S. property laws. Any Shaker property held in the name of a female would have been subject to these laws. Although married couples lived separately after joining the communities, the states continued to recognize their marriages. If the former husband of a trustee had left the community, he could have claimed all of her property, including any that the United Society held in her name.

Moreover, with few exceptions, the daily tasks of men and women were assigned along conventional gender lines: women worked within the Shaker kitchens and dormitories, while men worked in the fields and outbuildings. Despite these stereotypical roles, the Shaker division of labor held different implications from the standard practice of the nation. For one thing, in the Shaker community, women's work was not considered to be of lesser value than the work of men. All work was equally sacred because it contributed to God's new creation on earth. Furthermore, the women's work was economically vital to the community. Shakers were farmers; the crops they produced had to be processed and preserved so that the community could use them. Food preservation was especially important; preservation kept food through the winter, and sale of surpluses brought income for necessities. Finally, Shaker work was communal; women worked by the side of other women. This meant that women's "inside" tasks never isolated Shaker women as they isolated other American women within their nuclear homes.

One striking final distinction between Shaker male and female activity is harder to account for or justify. Despite the Shakers' commitment to the sharing of spiritual power, men almost totally dominated the development of Shaker theology. With only one exception,[25] the Brothers edited and authored all theological works until the end of the nineteenth century. On the other hand, during the era of "Mother's Work," women were the primary "instruments," the mediums, through whom Holy Mother Wisdom and other spirits spoke. Hence the Shakers seem to have maintained the frequent human division between men as scholars and thinkers and women as vehicles for religious experience. This distinction has no basis in Shaker theology. Moreover, it did correspond to a difference in power. Those who produced the approved theological writings were senior males of the society; and their writing itself was powerful because it told Shakers and others what Shakers thought about themselves. The mediums in "Mother's Work," however, were often people with little seniority; and because they served as instruments only, their roles brought them virtually no power in the group.[26] Ironically, however, the products of these women who channeled "Mother's Work" are now the best-known aspect of Shaker creativity. Most Americans now know Shakers, if at all, primarily through the mediums' spirit drawings, poetry, and hymns.

CONCLUSION

The Shaker vision of Christianity brought to women a degree of equality and control of their lives that is unparalleled elsewhere in Christian history. Responding to an image of God as male and female, a belief in separate but full redemption for men and women, and a conviction that God's Kingdom could be established on earth, the Shakers founded a society in which men and women shared in power and spiritual authority. Although they failed to solve all of the problems created by gender distinctions, they nonetheless provide us today with a vision of what a truly egalitarian society might be like. Their solution was quite radical: doing away with property, sexuality, and marriage is a sacrifice that few contemporary men or women would be willing to make. Nonetheless, their effort still inspires us, while their view of God as female Savior, Wisdom, Warrior, and Mother offers a positive, empowering vision of all that women can be.

Notes

1. Benjamin Youngs, *Christ's Second Appearing* (n.p.: The United Society, 1808), p. 12.

2. Mother Sarah Kendall, quoted in Roxalana Grosvenor, ed., *Sayings*, p. 9, as quoted in Robley Whitson, ed., *The Shakers: Two Centuries of Spiritual Reflection* (New York: Paulist Press, 1983).

3. Ibid.

4. Hannah Cogswell, quoted in Seth Wells, ed., *Testimonies Concerning the Character and Ministry of Mother Ann Lee* (Albany, N.Y.: Packard and Van Benthuysen, 1827), p. 31.

5. Jean McMohan Humez, *Gifts of Power: the Writings of Rebecca Jackson, Black Visionary, Shaker Eldress* (Amherst, Mass.: University of Massachusetts Press, 1981), p. 287.

6. Ibid., p. 282.

7. Youngs, *Christ's Second Appearing,* p. 52.

8. *Shakerism, Its Meaning and Message* (Columbus, Ohio: Fred J. Heer, 1904).

9. Youngs, *Christ's Second Appearing,* pp. 503–4.

10. Philemon Stewart, *A Holy, Sacred and Divine Roll and Book,* vol. 2 (Canterbury, N.H.: The United Society, 1843), p. 262.

11. Ibid.

12. Canterbury, N.H.: The United Society, 1849.

13. Calvin Green, *A Summary View of the Millenial Church* (Albany, N.Y.: Packard and Van Benthuysen, 1823), p. 230.

14. Ibid., p. 130.

15. Whitson, *The Shakers,* p. 163; quoting Daniel Mosely who is quoting Ann Lee.

16. Ibid., p. 158. Contrary to popular opinion, celibacy was not the reason for the Shakers' decline. In fact, the practice of celibacy probably contributed to the Shaker community's success in comparison with other utopian communities, which could not handle the economic or ideological stress of having to raise and indoctrinate a second generation.

17. (Concord, N.H.: For the Author, 1822).

18. Alice Rossi, ed., *The Feminist Papers: From Adams to de Beauvoir* (New York: Bantam Books, 1974), p. 142, quoting Engels, n.p.

19. Ibid., p. 480.

20. Paulina Bates, *The Divine Book of Holy and Eternal Wisdom* (Canterbury, N.H.: The United Society, 1849), p. 505.

21. Ruth Webster, *The Shaker Manifesto,* XII, no. 4 (1882), p. 82.

22. Norma Beach, *In the Eyes of the Law* (Ithaca, N.Y.: Cornell University Press, 1982), p. 17.

23. Marjorie Procter-Smith, *Women in Shaker Community and Worship* (Lewiston, N.Y.: Edwin Mellen Press, 1985).

24. *The Shaker Quarterly,* III, no. 4 (Winter 1963): p. 92.

25. Bates, *Divine Book of Holy and Eternal Wisdom.*

26. See Priscilla Brewer, *Shaker Communities, Shaker Lives* (Hanover, N.H.: University Press of New England, 1986), Chapter 7.

Further Readings

Brewer, Priscilla J. *Shaker Communities, Shaker Lives.* Hanover, N.H.: University Press of New England, 1986.

Humez, Jean M. *Mother's First Born Daughters: Early Shaker Writings on Women and Religion.* Bloomington: Indiana University Press, 1993.

Proctor-Smith, Marjorie. *Women in Shaker Community and Worship.* Lewiston, N.Y.: Edwin Mellen Press, 1985.

Setta, Susan M. *Woman of the Apocalypse: The Second Coming of Christ in Ann Lee.* Ann Arbor. Mich.: University Microfilms, 1979.

———. "The Appropriation of Biblical Hermeneutics to Biographical Criticism." *Historical Methods* 16, no. 3 (summer 1983).

Stein, Stephen J. *The Shaker Experience in America: A History of the United Society of Believers.* New Haven: Yale University Press, 1992.

VI

WOMEN'S POWER

Mythical Models and Sacred Sources

To modern feminists, the women whose lives we have studied in this volume often appear to have little power, despite our attempts to portray them vividly and empathetically. Why? Women's power, in most traditional societies, was not equivalent to legal, economic, political, social, or religious equality. As we understand it in the modern West, the phrase "equality between women and men" really means overcoming, or at least minimizing, traditional gender roles. The dissolving of gender roles is not the basis of women's power in most of the instances explored in this volume. However, women almost always find avenues to affirm self-worth and to take some control over their lives and their worlds. This volume has surveyed many different methods by which women take such power. Sometimes they bond together. Sometimes they ritually control their environment. Sometimes they live in clear patterns of balance and equality with men.

In our final section, we explore another important method by which women may achieve power. When women *have* powerful or provocative myth-models with which they can identify, or when women *are* exemplary sacred sources, they feel powerful and they are powerful. This power of psychological worth may not translate directly into social, political, or even religious equality. Nevertheless, the power women derive from identifying with female myth-models and the power they manifest as sacred sources should not be overlooked as "merely symbolic."

Chapter 23 examines the relationship between two female spirits of Haitian Vodou and a mother and daughter who serve them as priestess and apprentice in New York City. Author Karen McCarthy Brown points to a close "fit" between the spirits' imagery and personality and the lives of the women who serve them—a "fit" that allows the spirits to bring solace and to "pick up dreams and give them shape." Drawing on personal experience, author Inés Talamantez traces in Chapter 24 the complex response of the Mescalero Apache people to an awesome female deity called Isanaklesh. Mescalero women become Isanaklesh during the ceremony that allows a girl to make her passage into womanhood; hence through the ceremony Isanaklesh comes to be ingrained in Mescalero Apache consciousness. This particular article focuses mainly on the implications of Isanaklesh for women; still it is clear that she brings power to all Mescalero—males included.

The concluding article, by co-editor Rita M. Gross, does not focus on the power of female mythical models, but on the power of women themselves to be a sacred source and paradigm. Aboriginal women of Australia experience themselves as reserves of sacred power that is manifested in their own bodies and physiological processes. Women ritualize these sacred processes; men imitate them, utilizing the powerful image of giving birth in their own most potent and elaborate rituals. In fact, it seems almost as though the men manifest a case of "womb envy."

These chapters, particularly the final chapter, also bring us full circle to our opening critique of Western scholarship and its habitual blindness to women's religious lives. Previous scholarship about Australian religions often contended that only men were sacred or had religious lives; women were said to be both profane and without a significant religious life. However, when the scholar attends to women's religious lives and presumes that women are as interesting and as worthy of study as are men, then such interpretations become unlikely. Gross not only demonstrates clearly that Australian women *have* religious lives; she shows that these are important, both in their own right and for the perspective they lend us on the whole of native Australian culture.

23

Mama Lola and the Ezilis: Themes of Mothering and Loving in Haitian Vodou

KAREN McCARTHY BROWN

Mama Lola is a Haitian woman in her mid-fifties who lives in Brooklyn, where she works as a Vodou priestess. This essay concerns her relationship with two female *lwa,* Vodou spirits whom she "serves." By means of trance states, these spirits periodically speak and act through her during community ceremonies and private healing sessions. Mama Lola's story will serve as a case study of how the Vodou spirits closely reflect the lives of those who honor them. While women and men routinely and meaningfully serve both male and female spirits in Vodou, I will focus here on only one strand of the complex web of relations between the "living" and the Vodou spirits, the strand that connects women and female spirits. Specifically I will demonstrate how female spirits, in their iconography and possession-performance, mirror the lives of contemporary Haitian women with remarkable specificity. Some general discussion of Haiti and of Vodou is necessary before moving to the specifics of Mama Lola's story.

Vodou is the religion of 80% of the population of Haiti. It arose during the eighteenth century on the giant sugar plantations of the French colony of Saint Domingue, then known as the Pearl of the Antilles. The latter name was earned through the colony's veneer of French culture, the reknowned beauty of

KAREN McCARTHY BROWN is Professor of the Sociology and Anthropology of Religion in the Graduate and Theological Schools at Drew University. She began research on Vodou in Haiti in 1973 and among Haitian immigrants in New York in 1978, and has written several articles on Vodou as a resource for American feminists, as well as the books *Mama Lola: a Vodou Priestess in Brooklyn* and *Tracing the Spirit: Ethnographic Essays on Haitian Art.* Professor Brown is also director of Drew University's Newark Project, an ethnographic mapping of the religious life of a city. Funded by the Ford Foundation, the Newark Project is designed to combine Ph.D. level research, education, and community advocacy.

its Creole women, and most of all, the productivity of its huge slave plantations. Haiti is now a different place (it is the poorest country in the Western hemisphere) and Vodou, undoubtedly, a different religion from the one or ones practiced by the predominantly Dahomean, Yoruba, and Kongo slaves originally brought there. The only shared language among these different groups of slaves was French Creole, yet they managed before the end of the eighteenth century to band together (most likely through religious means) to launch the only successful slave revolution during this immoral epoch. As contemporary Haitian history has made amply clear, a successful revolution did not lead to a free and humane life for the Haitian people. Slave masters were quickly replaced by a succession of dictators from both the mulatto and black populations.

Haitians started coming to the United States in large numbers after Francois Duvalier took control of the country in the late 1950s. The first wave of immigrants was made up of educated, professional people. These were followed by the urban poor and, most recently, the rural poor. All were fleeing dead-end lives in a society drenched in corruption, violence, poverty, and disease. There are now well over one-half million Haitians living in the U.S.

Alourdes, the name by which I usually address Mama Lola, came to New York in 1963 from Port-au-Prince, the capital of Haiti and a city of squalor and hopelessness where she had at times resorted to prostitution to feed three small children. Today, twenty-five years later,* Alourdes owns her own home, a three-story rowhouse in the Fort Greene section of Brooklyn. There she and her daughter Maggie run a complex and lively household that varies in size from six people (the core family, consisting of Alourdes, Maggie, and both their children) to as many as a dozen. The final tally depends on how many others are living with them at any given time. These may be recent arrivals from Haiti, down-on-their-luck friends and members of the extended family, or clients of Alourdes's Vodou healing practice.

Maggie, now in her thirties, has been in the United States since early adolescence and consequently is much more Americanized than her mother. She is the adult in the family who deals with the outside world. Maggie does the paperwork which life in New York requires and negotiates with teachers, plumbers, electricians, and an array of creditors. She has a degree from a community college and currently works as a nurse's aide at a New York hospital.

Most of the time Alourdes stays at home where she cares for the small children and carries on her practice as a *manbo,* a Vodou priestess. Many Haitians and a few others such as Trinidadians, Jamaicans, and Dominicans come to her with work, health, family, and love problems. For diagnostic purposes, Alourdes first "reads the cards." Then she carries out healing "work" appropriate to the nature and severity of the problem. This may include: counseling the client, a process in which she calls on her own life experience and the shared values of the Haitian community as well as intuitive skills bordering on extrasensory perception; administering baths and other herbal treatments; manufacturing talismans; and summoning the Vodou spirits to "ride" her through trance-possession in order that spiritual insight and wisdom may be brought to bear on the problem.

Vodou spirits (Haitians never call them gods or goddesses) are quite different from deities, or even saints, in the way that we in North America usually use those terms. They are not moral exemplars, nor are their stories characterized by deeds of cosmic or even heroic proportion. Their scale (what makes

*Editors' note: This article has been reprinted as it appears in our 1989 edition.

them larger than life though not other than it) comes, on the one hand, from the key existential paradoxes they contain and, on the other, from the caricature-like clarity with which they portray those pressure points in life. The *lwa* are full-blown personalities who preside over some particular social arena, and the roles they exemplify contain, as they do for the living who must fill them, both positive and negative possibilities.

Trance-possession within Vodou is somewhat like improvisational theater.[1] It is a delicate balancing act between traditional words and gestures which make the spirits recognizable and innovations which make them relevant. In other words, while the character types of the *lwa* are ancient and familiar, the specific things they say or do in a Vodou ritual unfold in response to the people who call them. Because the Vodou spirits are so flexible and responsive, the same spirit will manifest in different ways in the north and in the south of Haiti, in the countryside and in the cities, in Haiti and among the immigrants in New York. There are even significant differences from family to family. Here we are considering two female spirits as they manifest through a heterosexual Haitian woman who has lived in an urban context all her life and who has resided outside of Haiti for a quarter of a century. While most of what is said about these spirits would apply wherever Vodou is practiced, some of the emphases and details are peculiar to this woman and her location.

Vodou is a combination of several distinct African religious traditions. Also, from the beginning, the slaves included Catholicism in the religious blend they used to cope with their difficult lives. Among the most obvious borrowings were the identifications of African spirits with Catholic saints. The reasons why African slaves took on Catholicism are complex. On one level it was a matter of habit. The African cultures from which the slaves were drawn had traditionally been open to the religious systems they encountered through trade and war and had routinely borrowed from them. On another level it was a matter of strategy. A Catholic veneer placed over their own religious practices was a convenient cover for the perpetuation of these frequently outlawed rites. Yet this often cited and too often politicized explanation points to only one level of the strategic value of Catholicism. There was something deep in the slaves' religious traditions that very likely shaped their response to Catholicism. The Africans in Haiti took on the religion of the slave master, brought it into their holy places, incorporated its rites into theirs, adopted the images of Catholic saints as pictures of their own traditional spirits and the Catholic calendar as descriptive of the year's holy rhythms, and in general practiced a kind of cultural judo with Catholicism. They did this because, in the African ethos, imitation is not the sincerest form of flattery but the most efficient and direct way to gain understanding and leverage.

This epistemological style, exercised also on secular colonial culture, was clearly illustrated when I attended Vodou secret society[2] ceremonies in the interior of Haiti during the 1983 Christmas season. A long night of thoroughly African drumming and dancing included a surprising episode in which the drums went silent, home-made fiddles and brass instruments emerged, and a male and female dancer in eighteenth-century costume performed a slow and fastidious *contradans.* So eighteenth-century slaves in well-hidden places on the vast sugar plantations must have incorporated mimicry of their masters into their traditional worship as a way of appropriating the masters' power.

I want to suggest that this impulse toward imitation lies behind the adoption of Catholicism by African slaves. Yet I do not want to reduce sacred imitation to a political maneuver. On a broader canvas this way of getting to know the powers that be by imitating them is a pervasive and general characteristic of all the African-based religions in the New World. Grasping this important aspect of the way Vodou relates to the world will provide a key for understanding the nature of the relationship between Alourdes and her female spirits. When possessed by her woman spirits, Alourdes acts out the social and psychological forces that define, and often confine, the lives of contemporary Haitian women. She appropriates these forces through imitation. In the drama of possession-performance, she clarifies the lives of women and thereby empowers them to make the best of the choices and roles available to them.

Sacred imitation is a technique drawn from the African homeland, but the kinds of powers subject to imitation shifted as a result of the experience of slavery. The African religions that fed into Haitian Vodou addressed a full array of cosmic, natural, and social forces. Among the African spirits were those primarily defined by association with natural phenomena such as wind, lightning, and thunder. As a result of the shock of slavery, the lens of African religious wisdom narrowed to focus in exquisite detail on the crucial arena of social interaction. Thunder and lightning, drought and pestilence became pale, second-order threats compared with those posed by human beings. During the nearly 200 years since their liberation from slavery, circumstances in Haiti have forced Haitians to stay focused on the social arena. As a result, the Vodou spirits have also retained the strong social emphasis gained during the colonial period. Keeping these points in view, I now turn to Alourdes and two female Vodou spirits she serves. They both go by the name Ezili.

The Haitian Ezili's African roots are multiple.[3] Among them is Mammy Water, a powerful mother of the waters whose shrines are found throughout West Africa. Like moving water, Ezili can be sudden, fickle, and violent, but she is also deep, beautiful, moving, creative, nurturing, and powerful. In Haiti Ezili was recognized in images of the Virgin Mary and subsequently conflated with her. The various manifestations of the Virgin pictured in the inexpensive and colorful lithographs available throughout the Catholic world eventually provided receptacles for several different Ezilis as the spirit subdivided in the New World in order to articulate the different directions in which women's power flowed.

Alourdes, like all Vodou priests or priestesses, has a small number of spirits who manifest routinely through her. This spiritual coterie, which differs from person to person, both defines the character of the healer and sets the tone of his or her "temple." Ezili Dantor is Alourdes's major female spirit, and she is conflated with Mater Salvatoris, a black Virgin pictured holding the Christ child. The child that Dantor holds (Haitians usually identify it as a daughter!) is her most important iconographic detail, for Ezili Dantor is above all else the woman who bears children, the mother par excellence.

Haitians say that Ezili Dantor fought fiercely beside her "children" in the slave revolution. She was wounded, they say, and they point to the parallel scars that appear on the right cheek of the Mater Salvatoris image as evidence for this. Details of Ezili Dantor's possession-performance extend the story. Ezili Dantor also lost her tongue during the revolution. Thus Dantor does not speak when she possesses someone. The only sound the spirit can utter is a uniform "de-de-de." In a Vodou ceremony. Dantor's mute "de-de-de" becomes articulate only through her body language and the interpretive efforts of the gathered community. Her appearances are thus reminiscent of a somber game of charades. Ezili Dantor's fighting spirit is reinforced by her identification as a member of the Petro pantheon of Vodou spirits, and as such she is associated with what is hot, fiery, and strong. As a Petro spirit Dantor is handled with care. Fear and caution are always somewhere in the mix of attitudes that people hold toward the various Petro spirits.

Those, such as Alourdes, who serve Ezili Dantor become her children and, like children in the traditional Haitian family, they owe their mother high respect and unfailing loyalty. In return, this spiritual mother, like the ideal human mother, will exhaust her strength and resources to care for her children. It is important to note here that the sacrifice of a mother for her children will never be seen by Haitians in purely sentimental or altruistic terms. For Haitian women, even for those now living in New York, children represent the main hope for an economically viable household and the closest thing there is to a guarantee of care in old age.

The mother-child relationship among Haitians is thus strong, essential, and in a not unrelated way, potentially volatile. In the countryside, children's labor is necessary for family survival. Children begin to work at an early age, and physical punishment is often swift and severe if they are irresponsible or disrespectful. Although in the cities children stay in school longer and begin to contribute to the welfare of the family at a later age, similar attitudes toward childrearing prevail.

In woman-headed households, the bond between mother and daughter is the most charged and the most enduring. Women and their children form three- and sometimes four-generation networks in which gifts and services circulate according to the needs and abilities of each. These tight family relationships create a safety net in a society where hunger is a common experience for the majority of people. The strength of the mother-daughter bond explains why Haitians identify the child in Ezili Dantor's arms as a daughter. And the importance and precariousness of that bond explain Dantor's fighting spirit and fiery temper.

In possession-performance, Ezili Dantor explores the full range of possibilities inherent in the mother-child bond. Should Dantor's "children" betray her or trifle with her dignity, the spirit's anger can be sudden, fierce, and uncompromising. In such situations her characteristic "de-de-de" becomes a powerful rendering of women's mute but devastating rage. A gentle rainfall during the festivities at Saut d'Eau, a mountainous pilgrimage site for Dantor, is readily interpreted as a sign of her presence but so is a sudden deluge resulting in mudslides and traffic accidents. Ezili's African water roots thus flow into the most essential of social bonds, that between mother and child, where they carve out a web of channels through which can flow a mother's rage as well as her love.

Alourdes, like Ezili Dantor, is a proud and hard-working woman who will not tolerate disrespect or indolence in her children. While her anger is never directed at Maggie, who is now an adult and Alourdes' partner in running the household, it can sometimes sweep the smaller children off their feet. I have never seen Alourdes strike a child, but her wrath can be sudden and the punishments meted out severe. Although the suffering is different in kind, there is a good measure of it in both Haiti and New York, and the lessons have carried from one to the other. Once, after Alourdes disciplined her ten-year-old, she turned to me and said: "The world is evil. . . . You got to make them tough!"

Ezili Dantor is not only Alourdes's main female spirit, she is also the spirit who first called Alourdes to her role as priestess. One of the central functions of Vodou in Haiti, and among Haitian emigrants, is that of reinforcing social bonds. Because obligations to the Vodou spirits are inherited within families, Alourdes's decision to take on the heavy responsibility of serving the spirits was also a decision to opt for her extended family (and her Haitian identity) as her main survival strategy.

It was not always clear that this was the decision she would make. Before Alourdes came to the United States, she had shown little interest in her mother's religious practice, even though an appearance by Ezili Dantor at a family ceremony had marked her for the priesthood when she was only five or six years old. By the time Alourdes left Haiti she was in her late twenties and the memory of that message from Dantor had either disappeared or ceased to feel relevant. When Alourdes left Haiti, she felt she was leaving the spirits behind along with a life marked by struggle and suffering. But the spirits sought her out in New York. Messages from Ezili and other spirits came in the form of a debilitating illness that prevented her from working. It was only after she returned to Haiti for initiation into the priesthood and thus acknowledged the spirits' claim on her that Alourdes's life in the U.S. began to run smoothly.

Over the ten years I have known this family, I have watched a similar process at work with her daughter Maggie. Choosing the life of a Vodou priestess in New York is much more difficult for Maggie than it was for her mother. To this day, I have yet to see Maggie move all the way into a trance state. Possession threatens and Maggie struggles mightily; her body falls to the floor as if paralyzed, but she fights off the descending darkness that marks the onset of trance. Afterwards, she is angry and afraid. Yet these feelings finally did not prohibit Maggie from making a commitment to the *manbo's* role. She was initiated to the priesthood in the summer of 1982 in a small temple on the outskirts of Port-au-Prince. Alourdes presided at these rituals. Maggie's commitment to Vodou came after disturbing dreams and a mysterious illness not unlike the one that plagued Alourdes shortly after she came to the United States. The accelerated harassment of the spirits also started around the time when a love affair brought Maggie face to face with the choice of living with someone other than her mother. Within a short period of time, the love affair ended, the illness arrived, and Maggie had a portentous dream in which the spirits threatened to block her life path until she promised to undergo initiation. Now it is widely acknowledged that Maggie is the heir to Alourdes's successful healing practice.

Yet this spiritual bond between Alourdes and Maggie cannot be separated from the social, economic, and emotional forces that hold them together. It is clear that Alourdes and Maggie depend on one another in myriad ways. Without the child care Alourdes provides, Maggie could not work. Without the check Maggie brings in every week, Alourdes would have only the modest and erratic income she brings in from her healing work. These practical issues were also at stake in Maggie's decision about the Vodou priesthood, for a decision to become a *manbo* was also a decision to cast her lot with her mother. This should not be interpreted to mean that Alourdes uses religion to hold Maggie against her will. The affection between them is genuine and strong. Alourdes and Maggie are each other's best friend and most trusted ally. In Maggie's own words: "We have a beautiful relationship . . . it's more than a twin, it's like a Siamese twin. . . . She is my soul." And in Alourdes's: "If she not near me, I feel something inside me disconnected."

Maggie reports that when she has problems, Ezili Dantor often appears to her in dreams. Once, shortly after her arrival in the United States, Maggie had a waking vision of Dantor. The spirit, clearly recognizable in her gold-edged blue veil, drifted into her bedroom window. Her new classmates were cruelly teasing her, and the twelve-year-old Maggie was in despair. Dantor gave her a maternal backrub and drifted out the window, where the spirit's glow was soon lost in that of a corner streetlamp. These days, when she is in trouble and Dantor does not appear of her own accord, Maggie goes seeking the spirit. "She don't have to talk to me in my dream. Sometime I go inside the altar, just look at her statue . . . she says a few things to me." The image with which Maggie converses is, of course, Mater Salvatoris, the black virgin, holding in her arms her favored girl child, Anaise.

It is not only in her relationship with her daughter that Alourdes finds her life mirrored in the image of Ezili Dantor. Ezili Dantor is also the mother raising children on her own, the woman who will take lovers but will not marry. In many ways, it is this aspect of Dantor's story that most clearly mirrors and maps the lives of Haitian women.

In former days (and still in some rural areas) the patriarchal, multigenerational extended family held sway in Haiti. In these families men could form unions with more than one woman. Each woman had her own household in which she bore and raised the children from that union. The men moved from household to household, often continuing to rely on their mothers as well as their women to feed and lodge them. When the big extended families began to break up under the combined pressures of depleted soil, overpopulation, and corrupt politics, large numbers of rural people moved to the cities.

Generally speaking, Haitian women fared better than men in the shift from rural to urban life. In the cities the family shrank to the size of the individual household unit, an arena in which women had traditionally been in charge. Furthermore, their skill at small-scale commerce, an aptitude passed on through generations of rural market women, allowed them to adapt to life in urban Haiti, where the income of a household must often be patched together from several small and sporadic sources. Urban women sell bread, candy, and herbal teas which they make themselves. They also buy and re-sell food, clothing, and household goods. Often their entire inventory is balanced on their heads or spread on outstretched arms as they roam through the streets seeking customers. When desperate enough, women also sell sex. They jokingly refer to their genitals as their "land." The employment situation in urban Haiti, meager though it is, also favors women. Foreign companies tend to prefer them for the piecework that accounts for a large percentage of the jobs available to the poor urban majority.

By contrast, unemployment among young urban males may well be as high as 80%. Many men in the city circulate among the households of their girlfriends and mothers. In this way they are usually fed, enjoy some intimacy, and get their laundry done. But life is hard and resources scarce. With the land gone, it is no longer so clear that men are essential to the survival of women and children. As a result, relationships between urban men and women have become brittle and often violent. And this is so in spite of a romantic ideology not found in the countryside. Men are caught in a double bind. They are still reared to expect to have power and to exercise authority, and yet they have few resources to do so. Consequently, when their expectations run up against a wall of social impossibility, they often veer off in unproductive directions. The least harmful of these is manifest in a national preoccupation with soccer; the most damaging is the military, the domestic police force of Haiti, which provides the one open road toward upward social mobility for poor young men. Somewhere in the middle of this spectrum lie the drinking and gambling engaged in by large numbers of poor men.

Ezili Dantor's lover is Ogou, a soldier spirit sometimes pictured as a hero, a breathtakingly handsome and dedicated soldier. But just as often Ogou is portrayed as vain and swaggering, untrustworthy and self-destructive. In one of his manifestations Ogou is a drunk. This is the man Ezili Dantor will take into her bed but would never depend on. Their relationship thus takes up and comments on much of the actual life experience of poor urban women.

Ezili Dantor also mirrors many of the specifics of Alourdes's own life. Gran Philo, Alourdes's mother, was the first of her family to live in the city. She worked there as a *manbo.* Although she bore four children, she never formed a long-term union with a man. She lived in Santo Domingo, in the Dominican Republic, for the first years of her adult life. There she had her first two babies. But her lover proved irrational, jealous, and possessive. Since she was working as hard or harder than he, Philo soon decided to leave him. Back in Port-au-Prince, she had two more children, but in neither case did the father participate in the rearing of the children. Alourdes, who is the youngest, did not know who her father was until she was grown. And when she found out, it still took time for him to acknowledge paternity.

In her late teens, Alourdes's fine singing voice won her a coveted position with the Troupe Folklorique, a song and dance group that drew much of its repertoire from Vodou. During that period Alourdes attracted the attention of an older man who had a secure job with the Bureau of Taxation. During their brief marriage Alourdes lived a life that was the dream of most poor Haitian women. She had a house and two servants. She did not have to work. But this husband, like the first man in Philo's life, needed to control her every move. His jealousy was so great that Alourdes was not even allowed to visit her mother without supervision. (The man should have known better than to threaten that vital bond!) Alourdes and her husband fought often and, after less than two years, she left. In the years that followed, there were times when Alourdes had no food and times when she could not pay her modest rent but, with pride like Ezili Dantor's, Alourdes never returned to her husband and never asked him for money. During one especially difficult period Alourdes began to operate as a Marie-Jacques, a prostitute, although not the kind who hawk their wares on the street. Each day she would dress up and go from business to business in downtown Port-au-Prince looking for someone who would ask her for a "date." When the date was over she would take what these men offered (everyone knew the rules), but she never asked for money. Alourdes had three children in Haiti, by three different men. She fed them and provided shelter by juggling several income sources. Her mother helped when she could. So did friends when they heard she was in need. For a while, Alourdes held a job as a tobacco inspector for the government. And she also dressed up and went out looking for dates.

Maggie, like Alourdes, was married once. Her husband drank too much and one evening, he hit her. Once was enough. Maggie packed up her infant son and returned to her mother's house. She never looked back. When Maggie talks about this marriage, now over for nearly a decade, she says he was a good man but alcohol changed him. "When he drink, forget it!" She would not take the chance that he might hit her again or, worse, take his anger and frustration out on their son.

Ezili Dantor is the mother—fierce, proud, hard-working, and independent. As a religious figure, Dantor's honest portrayal of the ambivalent emotions a woman can feel toward her lovers and a mother can feel toward her children stands in striking contrast to the idealized attitude of calm, nurture, and acceptance represented by more standard interpretations of the Holy Mother Mary, a woman for whom rage would be unthinkable. Through her iconography and possession-performances, Ezili Dantor works in subtle ways with the concrete life circumstances of Haitian women such as Alourdes and Maggie. She takes up their lives, clarifies the issues at stake in them, and gives them permission to follow the sanest and most humane paths. Both Alourdes and Maggie refer to Ezili Dantor as "my mother."

Vodou is a religion born of slavery, of wrenching change and deep pain. Its genius can be traced to long experience in using the first (change) to deal with the second (pain). Vodou is a religion in motion, one without canon, creed, or pope. In Vodou the ancient African wisdom is preserved by undergoing constant transformation in response to specific life circumstances. One of the things which keeps Vodou agile is its plethora of spirits. Each person who serves the spirits has his or her own coterie of favorites. And no single spirit within that group can take over and lay down the law for the one who serves. There are always other spirits to consult, other spirit energies to take into account. Along with Ezili Dantor, Alourdes also serves her sister, Ezili Freda.

Ezili Freda is a white spirit from the Rada pantheon, a group characterized by sweetness and even tempers. Where Dantor acts out women's sexuality in its childbearing mode, Freda, the flirt, concerns herself with love and romance. Like the famous Creole mistresses who lent charm and glamour to colonial Haiti, Ezili Freda takes her identity and worth from her relationship with men. Like the mulatto elite in contemporary Haiti who are the heirs of those Creole women, Freda loves fine clothes and jewelry. In her possession-performances, Freda is decked out in satin and lace. She is given powder and perfume, sweet smelling soaps and rich creams. The one possessed by her moves through the gathered community, embracing one and then another and then another. Something in her searches and is never satisfied. Her visits often end in tears and frustration.[4]

Different stories are told about Freda and children. Some say she is barren. Others say she has a child but wishes to hide that fact in order to appear fresher, younger, and more desirable to men. Those who hold the latter view are fond of pointing out the portrait of a young boy that is tucked behind the left elbow of the crowned Virgin in the image of Maria Dolorosa with whom Freda is conflated. In this intimate biographical detail, Freda picks up a fragment from Alourdes's life that hints at larger connections between the two. When Alourdes was married she already had two children by two different men. She wanted a church wedding and a respectable life, so she hid the children from her prospective in-laws. It was only at the wedding itself, when they asked about the little boy and girl seated in the front row, that they found out the woman standing before the altar with their son already had children.

Alourdes does not have her life all sewn up in neat packages. She does not have all the questions answered and all the tensions resolved. Most of the time when she tells the story of her marriage, Alourdes says flatly: "He too jealous. That man crazy!" But on at least one occasion she said: "I was too young. If I was with Antoine now, I never going to leave him!" When Alourdes married Antoine Lovinsky she was a poor teenager living in Port-au-Prince, a city where less than 10% of the people are not alarmingly poor. Women of the elite class nevertheless structure the dreams of poor young women. These are the light-skinned women who marry in white dresses in big Catholic churches and return to homes that have bedroom sets and dining room furniture and servants. These are the women who never have to work. They spend their days resting and visiting with friends and emerge at night on the arms of their men dressed like elegant peacocks and affecting an air of haughty boredom. Although Alourdes's tax collector could not be said to be a member of the elite, he provided her with a facsimile of the dream. It stifled her and confined her, but she has still not entirely let go of the fantasy. She still loves jewelry and clothes and, in her home, manages to create the impression, if not the fact, of wealth by piling together satin furniture, velvet paintings, and endless bric-a-brac.

Alourdes also has times when she is very lonely and she longs for male companionship. She gets tired of living at the edge of poverty and being the one in charge of such a big and ungainly household. She feels the pull of the images of domesticity and nuclear family life that she sees everyday on the television in New York. Twice since I have known her, Alourdes has fallen in love. She is a deeply sensual woman and this comes strongly to the fore during these times. She dresses up, becomes coquettish, and caters to her man. Yet when describing his lovable traits, she always says first: "He help me so much. Every month, he pay the electric bill," and so forth. Once again the practical and the emotional issues cannot be separated. In a way, this is just another version of the poor woman selling her "land." And in another way it is not, for here the finances of love are wound round and round with longing and dreams.

Poor Haitian women, Alourdes included, are a delight to listen to when their ironic wit turns on what we would label as the racism, sexism, and colonial pretense of the upper-class women Freda mirrors. Yet these are the values with power behind them both in Haiti and in New York, and poor women are not immune to the attraction of such a vision. Ezili Freda is thus an image poor Haitian women live toward. She picks up their dreams and gives them shape, but these women are mostly too experienced to think they can live on or in dreams. Alourdes is not atypical. She serves Freda but much less frequently than Dantor. Ezili Dantor is the one for whom she lights a candle every day; she is the one Alourdes turns to when there is real trouble. She is, in Alourdes' words, "my mother." Yet I think it is fair to say that it is the tension between Dantor and Freda that keeps both relevant to the lives of Haitian women.

There is a story about conflict between the two Ezilis. Most people, most of the time, will say that the scars on Ezili Dantor's cheek come from war wounds, but there is an alternative explanation. Sometimes it is said that because Dantor was sleeping with her man, Maria Dolorosa took the sword from her heart and slashed the cheek of her rival.

A flesh and blood woman, living in the real world, cannot make a final choice between Ezili Dantor and Ezili Freda. It is only when reality is spiced with dreams, when survival skills are larded with sensuality and play, that life moves forward. Dreams and play alone lead to endless and fruitless searching. And a whole life geared toward survival becomes brittle and threatened by inner rage. Alourdes lives at the nexus of several spirit energies. Freda and Dantor are only two of them, the two who help her most to see herself clearly as a woman.

To summarize the above discussion: The Vodou spirits are not idealized beings removed from the complexity and particularity of life. On the contrary, the responsive and flexible nature of Vodou allows the spirits to change over space and time in order to mirror people's life circumstances in considerable detail. Vodou spirits are transparent to their African origins and yet they are other than African spirits. Ancient nature connections have been buried deep in their iconographies while social domains have risen to the top, where they have developed in direct response to the history and social circumstances of the Haitian people. The Vodou spirits make sense of the powers that shape and control life by imitating them. They act out both the dangers and the possibilities inherent in problematic life situations. Thus, the moral pull of Vodou comes from clarification. The Vodou spirits do not tell the people what should be; they illustrate what is.

Perhaps Vodou has these qualities because it is a religion of an oppressed people. Whether or not that is true, it seems to be a type of spirituality with some advantages for women. The openness and flexibility of the religion, the multiplicity of its spirits, and the detail in which those spirits mirror the lives of the faithful makes women's lives visible in ways they are not in the so-called great religious traditions. This visibility can give women a way of working realistically and creatively with the forces that define and confine them.

Notes

1. I use terms such as possession-performance and theater analogies in order to point to certain aspects of the spirits' self-presentation and interaction with devotees. The terms should not be taken as indicating that priestesses and priests simply

pretend to be spirits during Vodou ceremonies. The trance states they enter are genuine, and they themselves will condemn the occasional imposter among them.

2. In an otherwise flawed book, E. Wade Davis does a very good job of uncovering and describing the nature and function of the Vodou secret societies. See *The Serpent and the Rainbow* (New York: Simon and Schuster, 1985).

3. Robert Farris Thompson traces Ezili to a Dahomean "goddess of lovers." *Flash of the Spirit: African and Afro-American Art and Philosophy* (New York: Random House, 1983), p. 191.

4. Maya Deren has drawn a powerful portrait of this aspect of Ezili Freda in *The Divine Horsemen: The Living Gods of Haiti* (New Paltz, N.Y.: Documentext, McPherson and Co., 1983), pp. 137–45.

Further Readings

Brown, Karen McCarthy. "The Center and the Edges; God and Person in Haitian Vodou." *The Journal of the Interdenominational Theological Center* 7, no. 1 (fall 1979), pp. 22–39.

———. "Olina and Erzulie: A Woman and a Goddess in Haitian Vodou." *Anima*, 5 (spring 1979).

———. "Alourdes: A Case Study of Moral Leadership in Haitian Vodou." *Saints and Virtues*, ed. by John S. Hawley. Berkeley: University of California Press, 1987, 144–67.

———. "The Power to Heal: Reflections on Women, Religion and Medicine." *Shaping New Vision: Gender and Values in American Culture.* Ann Arbor, Mich: VMI Press, 1987, 123–41.

———. "Systematic Forgetting, Systematic Remembering: Ogou in Haiti." *Africa's Ogun: Old World and New*, ed. by Sandra T. Barnes. Bloomington: University of Indiana Press, 1989, 65–89.

———. "Afro-Caribbean Spirituality." *Healing and Restoring: Health and Medicine in the Western Religious Traditions*, ed. by Lawrence Eugene Sullivan. New York: Macmillan Press, 1989.

———. *Mama Lola: A Vodou Priestess in Brooklyn.* Berkeley: University of California Press, 1991.

———. *Tracing the Spirit: Ethnographic Essays on Haitian Art.* Davenport, Iowa: Davenport Museum of Art, in association with the University of Washington Press, Seattle and London, 1995.

Dayan, Joan. *Haiti, History and the Gods.* Berkeley: University of California Press, 1998.

Deren, Maya. *Divine Horsemen: The Living Gods of Haiti.* New Paltz, N.Y.: Documentext, McPherson and Co., 1983.

Metraux, Alfred. *Voodoo in Haiti.* New York: Schocken Books, 1972.

Thompson, Robert Farris. *Flash of the Spirit: African and Afro-American Art and Philosophy* New York: Random House, 1983.

24

The Presence of Isanaklesh: The Apache Female Deity and The Path of Pollen

INÉS M. TALAMANTEZ

Facing an unknown yet profound transformation in their young lives, Mescalero Apache girls run vigorously at the first light of the rising sun during their female initiation ceremony. Isanaklesh, the Apache female deity, will meet the young initiate as she runs toward the eastern direction and then the young girl will bring her back once again to be present with the Mescalero people at yet another yearly ceremony celebrating the life of a young Apache girl who has reached puberty. Girls are prepared since their menarche and sometimes even earlier to enter into the sacred ceremonial tipi for four days of ritual in which they are transformed into Isanaklesh, given her name and healing powers, and instructed in Apache religious history, philosophy, and ethics. It is in these teachings that Apache culture bestows upon its women authority in leadership roles and

INÉS M. TALAMANTEZ is Associate Professor of Native American religious studies in the Department of Religious Studies at the University of California, Santa Barbara and managing editor of *New Scholar: An Americanist Review.* She is a frequent lecturer at conferences and universities nationally and internationally. Her major research interests are Native American female initiation ceremonies and Native American attitudes toward the natural environment. She has done extensive fieldwork in the Southwest and has directed the Society for the Study of Native American Religious Traditions. She has published a series of articles on Native American themes and two books of translations of ritual texts. Her awards include a Mary Ingraham Bunting Fellowship at Radcliffe College (1978), an Andrew W. Mellon Fellowship at Harvard University (1981), and a FIPSE grant to pursue her research on the relationship between Native American religious tradition, ecological concerns, and the documentation of sacred space. For the past twenty-five years, she has been working on a manuscript, *Isanaklesh Gotal: Introducing Apache Girls to the World of Spiritual and Cultural Values.*

religious ceremonial rules. Apache religious traditions consider women to be in a very special place within the culture as it seeks to establish balance and harmony in its historical continuity.

Women, especially those who are blessed and initiated into womanhood, are a powerful cultural influence. They inspire appropriate behavior by their own everyday examples as compassionate mothers, wise elders, grandmothers, wives, and political and religious leaders. From a woman's point of view, Apache ethnohistory provides an excellent paradigm that exemplifies and demonstrates the powerful ideals that are still practiced today in spite of Christian missionization and American assimilation campaigns. Concerns ranging from family to extended family to community, and from ecology to peace and justice are often expressed by Apache women. They are skilled at handling whatever comes their way, by living moral and unselfish lives. Isanaklesh, the Apache female deity, is the leading religious authority for most of the women. Even Apache Christian women often speak of her as the one that they pray to in times of need. Isanaklesh exemplifies compassion; she always understands us and the need for peace and justice in our lives. Oral tradition informs us that Isanaklesh brought knowledge and especially the healing arts to the people when, in the creation myth, she taught her son, *Tobasishine,* Child of Water, how to acquire and use medicines for the needs of the people.

It is Isanaklesh's power, her *diye,* ultimate spiritual strength, that makes her the perfect example of virtue and strength for the culture. It is clear that oral tradition throughout Apache history has provided the framework for female identity. Women in this culture have followed Isanaklesh's teachings and have worked toward a balanced sense of power whether as tribal chair, healer, teacher, council member, forestry worker, or in any other profession. Naturally, no culture is perfect, so here too there are those women who for many different reasons did not have a ceremony. Some of these women have expressed regret that they did not receive the guidance, support, ethics and philosophical teachings which the ceremony offers. Some have dreamed the ceremony, even though they themselves did not have it.

Dreams and power-visions can come from natural phenomena through the help of a supernatural being such as Isanaklesh or Child of the Water. Such dreams can be considered a vehicle of transmission of divine wisdom from Isanaklesh to a woman.

THE DREAM

I dreamed Isanaklesh about twenty years ago, during a ceremony held for the daughter of a friend on the Mescalero Apache reservation in New Mexico. I had worked during the day before my dream, helping the women in the cooking arbor to prepare food for the guests. For many hours, I listened silently as the women told of their own ceremonies and those of their daughters and granddaughters. That evening, my friend invited me to sleep with the initiate's female relatives in the family's tipi. Gazing up the smoke hole, I could see the night sky, clear and filled with glittering stars. Although we were all tired after a long day of work, we talked on, perhaps for several hours. Then I fell asleep. During that peaceful night, the dream began. The images are so sharply printed on my memory that it seems as though everything were happening today. . . .

I am walking near the river, towards the very center of Mescalero, following an old animal path. Slowly a female figure approaches, stirring the pollen dust on the path with every gracefully placed step. I sense that she wants something from me. I wonder who she is and why she is here. The air has become so quiet that only the rippling river can be heard. The green meadows disappearing behind me as I pass are covered thickly with grasses, fragrant with wild onions, and ferns. Fresh-smelling blue flowers are scattered here and there, and dropped evergreen needles make the ground soft underfoot. The entire landscape spread out before me is suffused with yellow pollen. Pollen falls like a soft rain from heavy boughs of nearby evergreen trees; the wet meadow grass shimmers, mirage-like with the yellow dust. The sunlight filtering under the pollinating trees, the forested mountains and misty passes under the slow-moving clouds all appear undisturbed, as they were at the world's beginning.

I know I am dreaming. Feelings and memories fuse together. I know why I am here; yet everything I see appears to be mysterious, veiled, hidden. As I approach, the mask pulls away, and I see what is actually there. Am I seeing the essence of the trees and grasses and wildflowers? Or am I remembering what I once knew—what I was always told?

I suddenly feel alone and anxious, disturbed without knowing why. The path ahead is clearly marked and the sunlight that filters through the trees has become quite bright; my shadow moves along beside me. The trees shimmer with yellow pollen that gently falls in the breeze. Suddenly I see Her again, walking toward me. All at once she is standing in front of me, tall and dark-skinned, with smooth black hair flowing to the ground. It too is covered with pollen. Her deerskin dress is carefully stained the same green as the evergreen pines. Hanging from her neck is an abalone shell that contains the pollen of the ocean floor. Her eyes are like shining obsidian, and her beads sparkle, catching the sun. I look down at her moccasins, beaded with crystals, and covered with small pieces of turquoise. At first I cannot speak; I take a a deep breath and raise my head slowly. She is still looking at me. I wonder what I should say. I hear my own words, coming as if from a distance.

"What are you doing here?"

"I've come to do a ceremony for you."

She turns and points with her lips in the Apache way, beckoning me to follow. As she walks away, I see pollen flowing from the fringes of her dress. Slowly she walks further and further away. I known that this is Isanaklesh, Mother Earth, the woman who never grows old because she is revitalized by the young initiate's life during our ceremony, she who witnessed creation and gives us what we need for life. I feel awed, yet balanced and peaceful, fearless, protected by a power that no outer source can penetrate. I have reached the place of meeting on the pollen path.

In Mescalero Apache culture, to dream the goddess Isanaklesh is to be ritually bound to her just as her myth is bound to the ceremeny that initiates young Mescalero girls into womanhood. Whomever she touches and enriches through a yellow cattail pollen vision or dream must always work for her, for she is asking for something; she wants something from the dreamer. Her power and beauty, utterly beyond that of earthly women, compel the dreamer to search always for the meaning of this wondrous vision.

I therefore told my dream to several spiritual advisors, for the Apaches feel that seeking such advice is proper when one has experienced such a powerful dream. One elder woman respected for her knowledge explained the general significance of dreams to me. She told me that understanding our dreams helps us to understand the world around us. Dreams, she said, reveal the many things that we do not apprehend during our waking lives. By reflecting on our dreams and their meaning, we learn to develop our senses and heed spiritual signs. Apache elders use this method of dream interpretation to see and study the world more carefully, and especially to locate the connections between the natural and supernatural realms.

Dreams full of color, like mine, are said to reveal nature and the spirit world. Others may lead one to understand a certain person or object, or they may yield sacred traditional knowledge about plants or animals.

In my dream, Isanaklesh showed herself amidst yellow pollen. Cattail pollen, *tadidine,* is the essence of *diye,* supernatural power. The quest for *diye* is at the very heart of the Apache religious system. Most traditional Apaches seek *diye* for protection, healing, and a spiritual knowledge. *Diye* assures one of a long and fruitful life. A second advisor and old friend interpreted my dream's imagery in the following way:

> All that pollen, the fir trees must be in their fourth year; that is when they drop their pollen. The bright light means summer is coming and you have to be alert and ready. If you look closely at everything, if you look inside, you can see what's going to happen ahead of you. For the next four years you must think about this dream. The more you pray about it the better it comes every time. It will stick with you because it is important. You were up about 10,000 feet in the forest; if you were walking on softness, you were among the clouds. These are the springtime clouds pushing under your feet. The breeze is behind you so you are going down canyon as the pollen falls from the trees and all around you. Walking towards the center means any place where you go it is with you. It is a good day when you see all of these things around you. That good strong feeling means you will be around for a long time. There is a lot of motion, a lot of feeling, as I have told you before; a good day is when you move around, when you accomplish something.

Still another spiritual adviser, a woman at Mescalero, told me about Isanaklesh.

> We must always remember Isanaklesh, her name means, "our mother," she is sacred Mother Earth. We depend on her for all of our needs. We ask her for our food both from the plant world and the animal world, as well as for shelter and healing. Because of her power, we have been given life, we are shaped and molded by her. All of our life we are protected by her; we experience her as we see with our eyes, hear with our ears, smell with our nose, as we touch, as we grow old, and become wise like her. If she appeared to you she wants you to work for her, you must do this or things could go wrong for you. Now you are tied to her. You must pray to her for *diye,* which will protect you and keep you to a healthy old age.

The Mescalero Apache preserve an extensive oral mythology about Isanaklesh. She is a living reality, as well as the creative Earth Mother. She *is* the earth; her name literally means "Woman (isana) of Earth or Clay (klesh)." She wears the earth's white clay on her face when she is seasonally painted with it during Isanaklesh Gotal, the girls' puberty ceremony. Because of our belief in her, and because the ceremony again and again renews her, Isanaklesh, the Woman of Earth, never grows old.

THE MYTH OF ISANAKLESH

In Mescalero Apache sacred stories about the beginning of the world, Isanaklesh is said to be one of the five great deities who were present when the world was made. The bottom half of her face was painted with white earth clay, and her body was completely covered with yellow cattail pollen. Wearing a necklace of abalone shell on her chest, she watched over all things growing on earth. She used her *diye* to ripen trees and fruits, flowers of the fields, all plants and herbs. Her compassion and creative wisdom as healer gave aid from the beginning of time to those who suffered from distress, injury, or disease.

An older woman friend told her clan's version of this myth to me (I recorded it in

Apache and then together we translated it into English). She took about five hours to explain the following portion of the myth to me. This segment depicts Isanaklesh as the mother of the culture hero, and as the one responsible for our knowledge of healing.

Isanaklesh hid her son, Child of the Water, and raised him with great care so Giant would not find him. When he was old enough, she made four sacred arrows for him and he went out to find Giant. Giant, as it is said, had a coat of hair that was four layers thick, and for that reason he was not afraid of anything. Child of the Water finally came upon Giant. He took aim and quickly shot the first sacred arrow, and the outer layer of Giant's thick coat first came off. Child of the Water then took aim again, and the second arrow took off his second coat. The third sacred arrow took off his third coat and left his heart still beating. Child of the Water then shot the fourth sacred arrow and pierced the Giant's heart. After this, the Earth became safe and Isanaklesh and Child of the Water taught Apaches how to live on this earth. This all happened on Sierra Blanca at the time of Creation.

Child of the Water spoke in sacred language while he was creating all of the things we need for life. But at one point in the story he stopped and asked his father Life Giver to look at all he had made for the people, and to tell him of anything that might still be needed. His father approved of what he saw around him, but said that the people would be exposed to disease; therefore, they must have something that they could prepare to cure it. Child of the Water said that he would ask his mother Isanaklesh for this. Isanaklesh then appeared and told him how to create the many herbs and minerals that would cure diseases. She gave him the names for sacred plants and taught him how to use them properly, explaining that:

> some they will have to gather and then boil them, some they will chew and swallow, some they will ceremonially paint on their bodies in very special ways, some they will burn and use for their healing smoke and ashes that will be used to heal the skin, some they will drink as medicine, and some they will breathe in for healing vapors.

Medicine from all the herbs that we know will be used to cure if it is breathed in four times in a ceremonial manner. Among Apaches, as among other Native American peoples, things of a sacred or ceremonial nature, for example blessings or healings, are usually repeated four times, facing in each of the four directions. One starts with the east, where the sun rises, then turns to the south, where the sun travels, then to the west, where the sun sets, and then to the north where it does not appear at all until it rises again in the east.

Isanaklesh then gave the ritual prescriptions for the use of cattail pollen, also known as the "pollen of the earth," which symbolizes the earth's life-giving powers as these powers go out to the four directions to bless all people. To live "in the pollen way" means to live in balance and harmony, like the balance and harmony that we see in nature. In this way, one will live to be old. If anything is even mixed with pollen, then Isanaklesh will give the added substance the power to heal.

Thus Isanaklesh spoke of all the herbs, trees, and minerals that are sacred to the Mescalero—everything needed to sustain life and heal humankind, so that people can live in a peaceful way, celebrating the goodness and beauty of life. In this version of the creation myth, she also gives the Isanaklesh ceremony to counteract diseases and imbalances that provoke disharmony and suffering for all women and all of humanity. This ceremonial gift, focused on the life of the Mescalero girl who is passing through puberty, is the ritual that Apaches still celebrate. By honoring each girl with these rites, Apaches honor Isanaklesh as well. They hence win for themselves a long full life by drawing upon Isanaklesh's healing power and wisdom.

THE CEREMONY

In southern New Mexico, east of the great White Sands, stands Dzil gais'ani, or Sierra Blanca. This 12,000 foot sacred mountain is the home of Isanaklesh, who has been revered as a powerful female deity since oldest Apache memory. At the time of creation, after the world was made safe for people, Apaches gathered together in small bands to receive *diye* and to learn the traditions. Isanaklesh then spoke and proclaimed her special ceremony:

> We will have a feast for the young girls when they have their first flow. Many songs will be sung for them, so that they will grow strong and live a long life.

This eight-day ceremony, called Isanaklesh Gotal, is celebrated in recognition of the significance of a young Apache girl's first menses. According to Apache myth, the ceremony was founded by Isanaklesh as a means through which the girl might temporarily experience herself as a manifestation of the goddess and be honored as such by the people. The first four days of ceremony are marked by elaborate ritual detail and festive social activities. The ceremony's songs, stories, and images combine to leave a powerful imprint of Isanaklesh both on the girl herself and on the relatives, friends, and family members who attend. Throughout the final four days the girl secludes herself to reflect on her ritual experiences.

The name given to this ceremony, Isanaklesh Gotal, literally means "Ceremonial Song for Isanaklesh." The Apache term *gotal*, "ceremonial sing," suggests not only a festive celebration, but also a raising of supernatural power to accomplish the many moments of transformation that the young girl experiences. Not only is the girl temporarily transformed into the goddess during this rite of passage; she is also permanently transformed into a mature Apache woman by the end of the ritual.

This transformation into womanhood is accomplished by ceremonially awakening the initiate to the world around her. For some girls, the ceremony is said to calm their adolescent imbalances. The Mescalero conceive of "fixing" the young initiate, ridding her of her baby ways and helping her through the door of adolescence, for at this young age the girls are said to be soft and moldable, capable of being conditioned and influenced by their female kin and others around them. Timid girls may need to be awakened to their powerful female identities, while others may need to be taught to settle down and be more sensible and feminine. This sense of awakening female potential is expressed in the words of a twelve-year-old, recalling her ceremony:

> While we were at my sponsor's house, she told us about how the feast would help me to be good, healthy, and keep the Apache tradition in its full swing. On Friday, she washed my hair in the soap suds of a yucca plant. Before she did it, she blessed it with pollen. She prayed in Indian while she washed. She said she would be here at 5:00 Saturday morning. Saturday morning, I woke up about 5:15 and washed up. She came and we began to build a small fire in the cooking arbor. She put four rocks in the four main directions around the fire. We waited until the fire got started. Then she put my hands in the flames and told me this was to keep me from being afraid of any kind of fire. That morning we waited until Willetto Antonio, my medicine man, had come so she could dress me. He came and we went into the white tent. She laid my buckskin dress and boots and jewelry down on the rug. She blessed it all, and just before she put it on, she pushed it towards me four times. Then she put the dress on me. After I was all dressed, people came into the tent to be blessed. . . . They went outside so I could do my run. She told me to turn to the east. Some more people came to be blessed. As Willetto Antonio started to sing, she told me to lie down so

> she could rub me (massage me for strength). After she did that, they laid a buckskin down and Willetto put four half-moons on it, two of yellow pollen and two of red ochre outlined with black galena. Just before I was to run, I had to step on these moons. Then they told me I was to run my hardest so that I could run my babyhood out of me. I ran around the basket four times. But each time they would move it farther. After the ceremony outside, we went into the tipi so I could bless people. My sponsor showed me how to bless little kids and babies.

This initiate was well aware that she had undergone special teachings during the ceremony and that she had emerged somehow different. Analysis of the ceremonial procedures and their religious implications helps us to understand the transformative aspects of the ceremony. There is no single moment at which the transformation of girl to goddess, or of goddess to woman, occurs. It is the fusion of all the ceremony's elements, over the eight-day period, that produces the desired goals. During the ceremony, great attention is paid to the ritual details, and the meanings of the symbols are carefully explained to the girls. As the Singer and sponsor explain these teachings to the initiate, the girl begins to understand important elements of Apache culture that from now on she will be charged to maintain. After her ceremony, she will be a keeper of Apache traditions and the pattern of everyday living in which they will continue to endure. Thus she is not only taught and protected by this ceremony; like Isanaklesh, who gave it, she will also teach and protect her tribe.

Sometimes it is not easy to convince young girls to participate in Isanaklesh Gotal. Many are intimidated by the prospect of becoming such a center of attention. Thus the mothers and grandmothers of the tribe's young girls try to prepare them psychologically for the ceremony long before the girls reach their menarche. The women try to convince the girls that they will change in a positive way if they participate fully—and that the ceremony will bring them a good and healthy life. Older women will often encourage pre-pubescent girls to observe the ceremonies of other initiates closely so they will know what to expect. I have heard mothers or other female kin say to a girl: "Go up toward the front of the Big Tipi where you can see and hear everything better."

The family begins preparations for the ceremony several years in advance of their daughter's menarche. They begin collecting the necessary ritual objects, including the sacred pollen which can only be gathered during the season when cattails are ripe. It is no less important to gather relatives' support, because the ceremony will be a tremendous burden on family resources. When the proud day of the girl's first menstruation arrives, her family celebrates with a small private dinner. Soon after, a male Singer and a woman sponsor are secured in the proper ritual manner: four gifts must be given, and the proper words must be exchanged.

Throughout the year following menarche, the girl's women kin and female sponsor then teach her the proper Apache ways. These include the use of medicinal herbs and healing skills. The women also prepare her deerskin dress, like Isanaklesh's dress, with elaborate symbolic beadwork; attached to the ends of the fringes are the tiny metal cones that now replace deer hoofs, which will gently jingle when she walks or dances. If the girl is to have a private ceremony, or "feast" as it is called today, her family and kin will usually host it at a carefully selected site well away from congested areas. The girl also has the option to join the several girls honored at the annual public Feast; in this case, her ritual will occur on the ceremonial grounds of the Mescalero tribal headquarters on whatever weekend falls closest to the Fourth of July. In either case, friends and family gather, supplies are stored, temporary tipis and cooking arbors are assembled, and preparations are made to feed all who come to the first four days of the ceremony.

Prior to dawn on the first day of the ceremony, the girl is placed in her own private tipi and carefully attended by female kin and her sponsor. The sponsor blesses the initiate with pollen, and ritually bathes and dresses her for the ceremony. She reminds the girl of how good it feels to be cared for, so that the girl will learn to care for others. The girl's hair is washed with *lzhee,* yucca suds; she is fitted with leggings and moccasins; she is ritually fed traditional Apache foods. She is given a special reed, or *uka,* through which she will sip water, since water is not allowed to touch her lips for fear that this will bring floods; she also receives a scratching stick, or *tsibeeichii,* for she is not to scratch with her fingernails.

Meanwhile, outside on the ceremonial grounds, the Singers and the girl's male kin begin to construct the sacred tipi. This will be the central structure where most of the rites take place. It is called the ceremonial home of Isanaklesh. According to Apache sacred songs, only when this tipi's four main poles are properly erected can the goddess reside there; then the power of the songs will go out from the tipi to carry the ceremony's benefit out to all of the people on earth. To raise these poles, four rocks are first used to mark the sacred place which was touched by the first rays of the sun. Then, at this spot, the four poles are sung into place. A song is sung for each pole as it is placed into the earth and tied to the others at the top of the structure. Thus the Apache sacred number four is established musically as well as visually. Ideally the first songs should be sung approximately at dawn, as the sun rises to the east, where the opening of the tipi must face. This way both song and sunrise mark the beginning of sacred time. Since the voice of the Singer can only carry so far in an outdoor setting, the songs also serve to mark off a sacred space for the circle of participants, who must move close enough to hear as well as to see.

The sacred tipi is now completed and readied for Isanaklesh, who has been approaching from the east with the early dawn light. The tipi's upper portion is wrapped with a clean white canvas cloth, and its lower portion is filled in with branches. The eastward opening is built out to the sides, in order to let the sun's light inside. After the tipi is in place, the initiate in her ritual garment appears with her sponsor and family. She is freshly bathed and dressed and carries a blanket and white deerskin to be unfolded and placed in front of the tipi. The initiate, now taking on the sacred role, then blesses with pollen members of the tribe who come forward, and the people in turn bless the initiate. An essential component of this rite is the *tadodine,* the cattail pollen, which is the pollen that Isanaklesh used in the creation myth. The girl motions in the Apache way to the four directions and then applies the yellow life-giving substance over the bridge of the person's nose, moving from the right to the left side; she may also apply it to other parts of the person's body. This blessing assures the people of a good long life; it also prefigures the healing powers of this young deity-to-be. Hence, to remind the girl of her role as healer, the sponsor now tells her:

> When you become Isanaklesh in the ceremony, you will have her power to heal because it is Isanaklesh who handed this knowledge to us. There is a sacred story about this. Since you will be Isanaklesh, you will be asked to heal and bless people who come to see you. You must always remember how you felt during your ceremony, when you were the living goddess; then later in life, you can call on her for help whenever you have problems; you will remember how you felt when you were her, when you became her.

The initiate's young soft body is next "molded," that is, massaged and aligned by her sponsor to insure the transformation of girl to Isanaklesh, as well as for continuing health and strength and a long, productive life. The Singer then draws four naturally paced footprints on the deerskin with pollen. While a sacred basket is put in place to the east of the tipi, the initiate steps on the pollen prints and is then gently "pushed off" to run around the basket and return to the tipi. This sequence symbolizes walking on the pollen path, again to bring the initiate a long, healthy life. The initiate runs around the basket four times, as four verses of the ritual song are sung. Before each run, the basket is moved a little closer to the tipi. Meanwhile, the girl's female sponsor makes the "ritual marker," a long high-pitched sound, to draw the attention of the supernaturals. For as she runs, the initiate meets the approaching Isanaklesh and escorts her back to the Apache people.

After the first morning's rituals, the initiate appears in public only during the next four nights. During the day, she may not have any ordinary social contact; only relatives, close friends, and those who wish to be blessed or healed may visit her in her private tipi.

When dusk arrives on the first night of the ceremony, male dancers appear to bless the young initiate and the central ceremonial fire. These dancers have been ritually transformed into *hastchin,* supernaturals who live inside the mountains near Mescalero. They wear buckskin kilts with long fringes finished with tin-cone jingles; above the waist, they are painted front and back with bold designs. Black cloth masks cover their faces and hide their human identities; yucca headdresses and ceremonial staffs complete their ritual dress. The *hastchin* dance in teams of four, each with its own drummer and group of singers. Trailed by one or more ritual clowns, or *libaye,* who are usually apprenticed *hastchin,* they also bless the ceremonial tipi. They bow toward it and back up four times from all four directions, making owl-like sounds. Then they return to the ceremonial grounds to dance around the central fire until the young initiate arrives.

At about 10 P.M., the initiate, her sponsor, and the Singer appear at the sacred tipi. The Singer leads the girl into the home of Isanaklesh by extending an eagle feather which he holds in his right hand. The girl takes hold of the other end of the feather and follows as he takes four steps into the tipi; each step is accompanied by the verse of a song that refers to the tipi as home of Isanaklesh. Inside, facing the fire at the center of the tipi, the initiate and her sponsor sit on deer hides and blankets. The Singer kneels in front of the girl with his back to the fire and prays and blesses the initiate, whom he now calls Isanaklesh.

As other songs are sung in groups of four, the initiate dances back and forth across a deer hide, looking always just above the fire or at the Singer's rattle, as the ritual rules prescribe. Accompanied by the light, regular pulse of the Singer's deer-hoof rattles, each song and dance lasts for about four to six minutes. Between songs, the girl rests for three to four minutes. Sometimes the Singer and sponsor will talk, but usually they are silent. As each group of four songs ends, a short formula is sung to mark its conclusion. Then the Singer lights hand-rolled cigarettes of ritual tobacco, and a longer break is taken, during which Isanaklesh is sometimes offered water through her drinking tube. During nights two and three, the same pattern occurs, with no morning or daytime activity. Only the content of the songs varies with each nightly performance.

A closer look shows that this seemingly endless repetition is a tightly structured and deliberate ritual form. The repetition establishes a stable place, quite literally when combined with the dancing, which is restricted to the area of a small deer hide. In the matrix of this stability, thoughts are free to wander. The young Isanaklesh appears to be in a trance-like state as she dances more vigorously each night. The Singer tells her to think in images about the tribe—to visualize troubles and illness and to send them over the mountain and away from the tribe. She is to set her mind and spirit in motion, even as her physical space is confined.

Similarly, the repetition also alters the sense of time. All necessary elements for a good life are said to be present in the ceremony; all the important symbols of Apache culture and of the world of women are contained in the songs that are sung each night. By calling on these symbols with the songs' powerful words, participants evoke images that are sometimes literally seen in the sacred space. The mind can travel between these images. When similar tunes are used, it is as if no time has elapsed between one set of songs and the next—or between the present ceremony and the first ceremony ever sung. Ishanaklesh is *there;* and her *diye,* her healing power, is present, as it was during the first moments of the world's creation.

The ceremony lasts almost until dawn on the fourth day. Songs are counted by wooden markers that are driven into the ground around the fire. Then, on the fifth and final morning of the ceremony's public segment, the ceremonial circle is completed by actions that reverse the pattern of the first morning. The sponsor and the Singer assemble in the tipi just as dawn is about to break. Isanaklesh has again been freshly bathed. The sacred basket is beside them, holding pollen, the eagle feather, tobacco, a gramma grass brush, several kinds of clay, and galena, a shiny black lead ore found in the mountains at Mescalero. Using the galena, the Singer paints an image of the sun on the palm of his hand. As he sings, he holds his hand up to the sun, so that the galena glitters as the early sun's rays hit it. When the song is finished, the Singer turns to Isanaklesh and touches his sunpainted hand to her shoulders and chest. Then he touches each side of her head and rubs the sun-image into her hair.

Singing another song, the Singer paints her with white earth clay, covering all the exposed skin on her arms and legs, as well as the lower half of her face. As this is happening, other participants remove the cloth and branches covering the sacred tipi, so that only the four main poles remain. Within this skeleton structure, the ritual blessing and healing of the tribe again take place. Taking red clay from a basket beside him, the Singer blesses every member of the community (and anyone else seeking blessing) by marking them with the clay, taking special care for young children, the elderly, and the sick. This period for blessing can last for over an hour.

The next and final ritual sequence occurs very quickly. Isanaklesh is led out of the tipi to the same tune that led her in; she walks on pollen footsteps, which are again painted on the deerskin. The sacred basket is once again placed to the east of the tipi, at the same distance from the tipi as it had been during the final run of the ceremony's first morning. Once again, she takes the four ceremonial pollen footsteps and runs off, accompanied by the four verses of her running song. This time, after each run, the basket is moved further to the east. On the last run, she runs to the basket—now very far to the east. She picks up her eagle feather and, while running back, begins to rub the white clay from her face as she returns to her private tipi, where she will stay during the next four days. During the past four days she has symbolically left behind her childlike youth and has been ritually transformed into Isanaklesh. After the next four days of quiet reflection, the initiate will emerge from her tipi as an adult Apache woman and Isanaklesh has departed.

As the girl performs her last run, the Singer chants as the rope that tied together the tipi poles is loosened and undone. Now the tipi's last four poles fall to the ground with a great crash. During all this excitement, the Singer has continued to sing, accompanied by his rattle. However, the crowd, which knows the traditions of this ceremony, has by now moved towards the cooking arbor. Here pickup trucks have driven in, loaded with candy, fruit, and household goods. These are thrown to the crowd as gifts from the family sponsoring the feast. The effect of the final run, the dismantling of the sacred tipi, and the giveaway with all of its accompanying excitement are meant to decisively break the sense of sacred space and time. The music also ends at this point, appropriately, after the Singer has sung over 100 songs during the total five-day period. Except for the girl, the participants now return to normal tribal life. In a traditional ceremony of incomparable beauty and coherence, another girl has reached womanhood, guided by the women of her culture and reassured of both her female and her Apache identity.

Isanaklesh is a potent symbol for Apache women. This deity whom the initiate has *been* for a while is also everything that a woman can hope to be. She is wise; she is powerful; she heals; she provides effective tools for living a life of harmony and balance. She is creative and fertile. As earth, she is the ultimate mother; but she also exemplifies ideal human motherhood by protecting and teaching her own child.

The ceremony of Isanaklesh Gotal constantly brings these female images to consciousness. All a woman has to do when she meets obstacles in her life is to remember how she felt during her ceremony when she was Isanaklesh. For the women who experience Isanaklesh, she becomes a deeply engrained model and source of empowerment. For men, knowing that women's lives are closely entwined with such a being implies that women must therefore be treated with respect and esteem. Moreover, the shared reverence for Isanaklesh that is focused in this ceremony forges a strong sense of Apache community. Thus Isanaklesh indeed brings power to the Apache; she helps us to find balance in our lives, and knowledge of our identity.

Further Readings

Basso, Keith H. *The Gift of Changing Woman.* Bulletin of American Ethnology Anthropological Papers, No. 196. Washington D.C.: U.S. Government Printing Office, 1966.

Hoijer, Harry. *Chiricahua and Mescalero Apache Texts.* Chicago: University of Chicago Press, 1938.

———. "The Apache Verb." *International Journal of American Linguistics,* Vols. XI: pp. 13–23, 193–203; XII: pp. 1–13; XIV: pp. 2147–259; XV: pp. 12–22 (1945–1949).

Mescalero Apache Tribe. *Mescalero Apache Dictionary,* complied by Evelyn Breuninger, Elbys Hugar, Ellen Ann Lathan, Scott Rushforth. Mescalero, New Mexico: 1982.

Nicholas, Dan. "Mescalero Apache Girl's Puberty Ceremony." *El Palacio* 46: pp. 193–204. Originally published 1939.

Opler, Morris E. *An Apache Life-Way: The Economic, Social and Religious Institutions of the Chiricahua Indians.* New York: Cooper Square Publishers, 1965. Originally published 1941.

———. "Adolescence Rite of the Jicarilla," *El Palacio* 49: pp. 25–38. Originally published 1942.

———. *Childhood and Youth in Jicarilla Apache Society.* Publications of the Frederick Webb Hodge Anniversary Publication Fund, Vol. 5. Los Angeles: Southwest Museum. Originally published 1946.

Talamanetz, Inés. *Ethnopoetics: Theory and Method: A Study of 'Isanaklesh Gotal with Analyses of Selected Songs, Prayers, and Ritual Structure, and Contemporary Performance.* Ph.D. Dissertation, University of California, San Diego, 1977.

———. "Dance and Ritual in the Study of Native American Religious Traditions," *New Scholar* 8 (1982): pp. 535–50. [Reprinted in *American Indian Quarterly* 6, no. 3–4 (fall–winter, 1983): pp. 337–57.

———. "The Mescalero Apache Girls' Puberty Ceremony: A Consideration of the Role of Music in Structuring Ritual Time and Transformation," with Ann Dhu McLucas, *Yearbook of the International Council for Traditional Music* 18 (1986).

———. "Images of the Feminine in Apache Religious Traditions," in *Feminist Transformations of the World's Religions,* Paula M. Cooey, William R. Eakin, and Jay B. McDaniel, eds. Maryknoll, NY: Orbis Press, 1991.

Turner, Victor W. *The Ritual Process: Structure and Anti-Structure.* Chicago: Aldine Publishing Co., 1969.

Van Gennep, Arnold. *Les Rites du Passage.* Translated by Monika B. Vizedom and Gabrielle L. Caffee as *The Rites of Passage* (Chicago: University of Chicago Press, 1960). Originally published 1908.

25

Menstruation and Childbirth as Ritual and Religious Experience among Native Australians

RITA M. GROSS

The subjects of this chapter are menstruation and childbirth, as they figure in both Australian aboriginal women's and men's religious lives. In the religious lives of women these biological experiences are the occasion of significant rituals. In the religious lives of men, who, of course, cannot experience them directly, they are often ritually imitated. The significance of menstruation and childbirth in both women's and men's religious lives has not been especially noted or studied by most scholars of aboriginal traditions. I believe that this oversight is a result of the fact that aboriginal religions have usually been studied by male anthropologists from a strictly male point of view.

A few comments on Australian aboriginal culture and on scholarship about it are crucial preliminaries to our discussion. The aborigines are a hunting and gathering society whose material culture is exceedingly simple. Yet their social organization and world view are so complex that they have long fascinated anthropologists and historians of religion. Two noticeable features of aboriginal religion have been the basis of all theories about the role of women in it. The first is the extreme

---

RITA M. GROSS, after completing her work on Aboriginal Australian religions for her Ph.D., went on to a distinguished career specializing in women's studies in religion and in feminist theology, especially in the Buddhist context. Her books include *Feminism and Religion: An Introduction* (Beacon, 1996), *Buddhism After Patriarchy: A Feminist History, Analysis, and Reconstruction of Buddhism* (SUNY, 1993), and *Soaring and Settling: Buddhists Perspectives on Contemporary Social and Religious Issues* (Continuum, 1998). Both of the books on Buddhism were awarded the "Outstanding Academic Book" Award by *Choice.*

Author's Note: This paper was first read at the national convention of the American Academy of Religion in St. Louis in November 1976. A more complete version of the paper was published in *The Journal of the American Academy of Religion* (December 1977). Portions of that article are used here by permission of *JAAR.*

sexual differentiation that characterizes religious life in aboriginal Australia. Women are almost completely excluded from the men's rituals; and—although this aspect has been much less noticed—men are completely excluded from women's rituals. Second, the most obvious, elaborate, and time-consuming dimension of aboriginal religion is represented by those men's rituals from which women are so rigidly excluded. These rituals alone are also the basis of most theories about aboriginal religion, because male anthropologists found them more interesting and easier to study than the women's rites. This situation led to the classic interpretation of sexual dichotomy in aboriginal religion:

> Masculinity is inextricably women with ritual cleanness and femininity is equally intertwined with the concept of uncleanness, the former being the sacred principle and the latter the profane. This sexual dichotomy and its correlation with the Murngin beliefs of what are the sacred and profane elements of the group, are again connected with a further principle of human relations, namely, that of superordination and subordination.[1]

This idea of women's "profaneness" also led many scholars to downplay the religious significance of women's rituals. It has been argued that women's religious life is so different from men's as to be unworthy of the label "religious" and that menstrual taboos and childbirth seclusions are imposed on women by men who abhor and fear these physiological events. Women's ceremonies are said to be uninteresting and insignificant in comparison to men's rituals:

> Aboriginal women have ceremonies of their own, some commemorating their "femaleness," some with highly erotic content, but little is known of these except that they seem to be a pale imitation of masculine ceremonies and they play little part in tribal life.[2]

In all these statements one theme predominates—the attempt to differentiate women's ceremonies from men's ceremonies and, in differentiating them, to indicate that women's ceremonies are inferior in scope, intensity, and religious significance. However, I would contend that, although women's ceremonies are indeed different from men's ceremonies, if we explore the differences rather than assume that the difference implies inferiority, other interpretations are possible. What is most significant about women's ceremonies is that, *by being different from men's ceremonies and by focusing on women's unique experience,* they perform the same function for women that the men's rituals perform for men. The women's unique experiences are ritual and religious experiences; they are symbols and metaphors through which women express and attain their adult status as sacred beings within the aboriginal community. Just as the men's ceremonies indicate the sacred status and potential of men, so the women's ceremonies indicate the sacred status and potential of women and not some opposite, "profane" condition.

The basic reason for my interpretation can be stated rather succinctly. The experiences and rituals of menstruation and childbirth are laden with clues and characteristics that, were they found in connection with anything else, would be automatically referred to as "sacred" or "religiously significant." *All* attitudes and behaviors that are correctly deemed clues to the sacredness of the male mode and of men's rituals are also found in connection with women's ceremonies; but, when observed in connection with women's ceremonies, their existence and significance have not been noted.

First, the exclusiveness and secrecy surrounding women's rituals are significant because, in aboriginal religion, both are indications of sacredness. Second, the ideological underpinnings of women's and men's ceremonies are identical. Both women's and men's ceremonies were instituted in mythic times by the totemic ancestors, and both confer great potency on those who perform them. The basic ritual patterns are identical, in general as well as in specific detail. Most important is the basic initiatory structure of withdrawal, seclusion, and return, thought of as death and rebirth, which is found in women's ceremonies to the same extent as it is found in men's ceremonies. Finally, neither men nor women achieve full initiation and sacred status until old age. All these parallel attitudes are important because they indicate a parallel (not identical) access to sacrality. The women's *different* religious life has the *same* outcome as the men's—membership in the sacred community, not exclusion from it.

Although girls undergo some prepuberty rituals, the first occurence of menstruation is the most significant event in a woman's ritual progression from the relatively insignificant status, religiously speaking, of being a child to the religiously significant status of being a woman. The reason for it lies in the significance of menstruation itself.

> Because menstruation was introduced by mythical characters—as, so to speak, a rite performed more or less automatically by women (although imitated artificially, in various regions, by men)—it has mythical sanction: it is . . . not a mundane or ordinary state of affairs. . . . Menstrual blood is "sacred," declared to be so by the mythical Sisters themselves.[3]

The details of first-menstruation rituals vary considerably, but the pattern is always the same. The girl is secluded by the other women of the group. During the seclusion men are avoided, and various ritual pratices are followed. After the seclusion the girl's return to the group involves a celebration and recognition of new status.

The parallels between these rituals and male initiations are obvious. Not only the general pattern, but also innumerable details of ritual behavior are identical. Also, before contact with missionaries, the attainment of womanhood probably involved much more elaborate rituals.[4] If this is true, the parallels would be even stronger, since the relative simplicity of girls' initiations often results in the interpretation that they have less religious significance than the more elaborate boys' ceremonies.

If the *one* existing early account[5] of girls' initiations is accurate, it is clear that, indeed, girls' menstruation ceremonies were quite lengthy and elaborate in earlier times. According to that account, an old woman took the girl out of the camp into the bush. They made a shade, and the old woman built a fire and performed the smoking ritual for the girl. She made the girl sit over a hole in the ground and told her that she was now a woman. In two months "you go and claim your husband," she said. After a two-month seclusion, they moved their camp closer to the main group. The girl was decorated and painted. "To show that the occasion was a sacred one, a spring of Dahl tree was placed through the hole in the septum of the nose," the account continues. Carrying smoking twigs, the girl walked toward the main camp, according to the old woman's instructions. When the women saw her coming, they sang to her. Her betrothed sat with his back to her. She walked up to him, shook him, and ran away, pelted with twigs and sticks by the women. For another month she camped with the old woman, moving even closer to the main camp. A few weeks later she camped just outside the main camp and then moved to the opposite side of her betrothed's fire. Finally, the couple slept on the same side of the fire.

Unfortunately, even this account cannot answer one of the most important questions that arise in connection with menstruation as an initiation into a woman's mode of sacred being. We know nothing of the spiritual teachings that may have been imparted during the seclusion, which, if this one early reporter was correct, was quite lengthy. It seems unimaginable that, during a three-month seclusion, secret instruction and initiation into women's modes of religious expression did not occur.

Nor can anyone claim that, if such teaching had occurred, we would know about it. So far as I can tell, none of the early fieldworkers in Australia who produced the standard descriptions of men's ceremonies actually saw a woman's menstruation ceremony. The instruction in mythic and cultural knowledge, if it occurred, would strengthen even further the interpretation that men's and women's ceremonies are different but parallel ways of achieving the same results. Many of those who focus only on the differences between women's and men's ceremonies and see men's ceremonies as having deeper religious significance than women's ceremonies also contend that men's rituals are somehow concerned with cultural and spiritual matters, while women's rituals are merely biologically oriented ceremonies.

Because menstruation is so significant, subsequent monthly periods are also ritualized to some degree. Three ritual practices usually include seclusion or avoidance of men as well as some dietary restrictions. Even today, when seclusion is impractical, some care is taken to ritualize menstrual periods. However, while menstrual blood is to be avoided by men, it is considered valuable to women so long as they observe the rituals correctly. For example,

> At each menstruation until she is fully developed a young girl receives some of her own menstrual blood, which is rubbed upon her shoulders by the older women. When she is mature, she may perform this duty for younger girls.[6]

Those who have tried to see women as "profane" vis-à-vis the "sacrality" of men have generally supposed that men have imposed menstrual taboos on women because they find this aspect of womanhood the most "profane" of all. However, this interpretation does not seem to point to the true reason why men avoid menstrual blood. Menstrual blood is powerful and magical, therefore, it must be handled carefully and circumspectly: but it is not shameful or unclean. A menstruating woman is taboo, but she is not impure. This realization is extremely important for an adequate interpretation of the role that menstruation plays in women's and men's religious lives.

Childbirth functions as a religious resource for women in much the same way. Pregnancy and childbirth are mythically grounded; female totemic ancestors underwent those experiences themselves, and provide the models for women today. In the relatively informal age-grading system that applies to native Australian women, pregnancy and childbirth mark another transition and another level of attainment. Childbirth ritual is secret. Children, younger women, and men are prohibited from the place where birth is occurring just as rigorously as the uninitiated are prohibited from the place where male sacred rituals are culminating. This prohibition is very widely reported. Even in those cases in which a medicine man attends some stages of labor, no man is permitted to see the actual birth.

Fortunately, the literature concerning child-birth rituals is richer than that dealing with menstruation. Phyllis Kaberry and Ursula McConnel have both provided extensive descriptions, based on their field experience, of aboriginal childbirth ceremonies.

Phyllis Kaberry's lengthy description is invaluable for its insights into the religious significance of these practices.

> The old women and those who had children went apart with a pregnant woman and danced around her . . . songs were sung. The old women examined her and then would sing. The women said it would make birth easier and charm the pelvis and the genital organs. . . .
>
> As the moment of birth approached the pregnant woman left the camp with her mother and an old female relative, one of

whom would act as midwife. During labor, songs were sung to facilitate delivery and prevent haemorrhage, the umbilical cord was cut and the placenta was buried secretly. . . . Mother and child were secluded from the men for about five days.

This ritual is characterized by features which would seem to be typical of that associated with most of the physiological crises of the individual:

(1) The observance of food taboos—this time by the mother on behalf of the child; (2) the spells and rites to safeguard them both during parturition; (3) the remedial use of smoked conkaberry bushes; (4) the belief that the blood from the female genitals is dangerous to the men; hence the secret burial of the placenta and the refusal of the women to discuss it in the presence of the men. (5) Finally, the segregation of the woman—a prohibition that is paralleled by the seclusion of a girl at her first menstruation and introcision, and by isolation of a boy after circumcision and subincision. These two factors are so closely interlocked that they can scarcely be considered apart. On the one hand, the child itself may sicken if the placenta is found by the men or if the cord is lost; on the other hand, both mother *and* child, whether the latter is a boy or a girl, may be harmed if they have contact with the men until four or five days afterwards.

> Now although the men know some of the details of childbirth, such as the severing of the umbilical cord by the female relative . . . still they are ignorant of those songs which are sacred . . . songs which for all their simplicity are fraught with the power that they possess by virtue of their supernatural origin . . . their efficacy is attributed to the fact that they are *narungani;* that they were first uttered by the female totemic ancestors. They have the same sanctions as the increase ceremo-nies, . . . subincision and circumcision. . . .
>
> The whole of the ritual surrounding pregnancy, parturition, and lactation . . . has its sacred and esoteric aspects, which are the most vital aspects to the women, and which are associated specifically with female functions. They are believed to be a spiritual or supernatural guarantee from the Totemic Ancestors that a woman will be able to surmount the dangers of childbirth.[7]

Ursula McConnel's materials are quite similar to Kaberry's. There are myths, known only to women, about the first birth. The myth that prescribes seclusion for the mother serves as a model that women still follow today. The women also have myths that establish the ritual method for extracting the placenta and naming the child. The two events occur simultaneously. The midwife tugs gently at the cord while reciting possible names for the baby. When she says the correct name, the placenta is expelled. It is then buried, and men are forbidden to go near that spot. The myths prescribe a seclusion of two weeks to a month following the birth, during which time no man, including the father, can see the mother or the baby. When the mother's afterbirth blood ceases, both mother and baby are painted for the presentation ritual, which also follows a mythic model. The painting takes place inside a shelter that is taboo to men. Then, followed by very old female relatives, the mother walks toward the father, who is seated on the ground waiting for her, and circles him twice. Then she kneels in front of him and hands him the baby.[8]

Finally, mythology also dictates certain ritual practices for the father. Among the Munkan he must observe dietary restrictions. In other groups he and other male relatives must remain silent from the time a woman enters her childbirth seclusion until the baby is born. Such rituals of support by men parallel some of the things women do for men during men's rituals. Women may observe dietary restrictions, silence, or other limitations for their male relatives while they are being initiated. Such parallel support rituals further strengthen the interpretation the native Australian men's and women's ceremonies are different but parallel ways of achieving the same "sacred" status and are not indications of men's "sacredness" and women's "profaneness."

Having demonstrated the religious significance of menstruation and childbirth for women, let us now discuss these events as symbols in the religious lives of men, for, as I said earlier, these events also play a central role in the men's ceremonies. Such a role indicates that not only do women have their parallel access to "sacred" status but men themselves see women as "sacred," in another complementary, although ambiguous, mode of sacrality.

The best-known fact about the role of women in aboriginal religion is their exclusion from the men's ceremonies. Many subtleties of that exclusion are not so well known. It is true that sexually mature women—those who menstruate and give birth—are rigorously excluded; however, in some rare cases *older* women past menopause are initiated into the men's rituals.[9] Furthermore, outside the men's ritual context, women are not generally avoided unless they are going through menstruation or childbirth. When these subtle aspects of women's exclusion have been noted at all, they have been interpreted as evidence that menstruation and childbirth are considered as negative symbols and as part of the justification for excluding women from men's ceremonies. However, the avoidance of women's blood in both menstruation and childbirth is part of a very complex ritual and mythical pattern in which these same events also serve as potent and important metaphors in the religious lives of men.

Let us consider the men's myths first. The northern Australian epic of the Djanggawul brother and his two sisters illustrates one kind of response to women's physiological events.[10] The sisters are perpetually pregnant and giving birth. During these childbearing activities the women are not kept separate from the man. Instead, the brother often helps his two sisters as they deliver their children. Although this myth dwells extensively on childbirth, there is no implication of danger and no ambiguity. It is also interesting that menstruation is not mentioned at all. Equally important is the fact that at this mythical time the sisters still carry the sacred emblems and perform the tribal ceremonies. Later, things change. The brother steals the religious paraphernalia and rituals from the women as part of a series of events that mark the transition from mythic to post-mythic conditions. Only when the women perform the tribal rituals do the men participate in childbirth. Thus it seems that what was mythically an undifferentiated complementarity became in post-mythic times two mutually exclusive, but still complementary, spheres.

The mythology of the Wawalik sisters, also from the north, contains others themes that can help us understand the men's attitude toward women. Few statements illustrate more clearly the ambivalent fascination with childbirth, menstruation, and women's blood than the central parts of this narrative. The two sisters are traveling. The elder is pregnant, and, after she has her baby, they take to the road again while the afterbirth blood is still flowing. They camp near a sacred well, and the python dwelling in the well is attracted by the smell of the blood. The snake causes a great storm as it emerges from the well, intent on swallowing the sisters. The younger one dances and is able to keep the python away, but she tires and asks the older sister to dance. She, however, cannot keep the snake away because the odor of her blood attracts it. Finally the intense dancing causes the younger sister to begin menstruating. At this point she, too, cannot fight the snake, and they are all swallowed by it. The sisters later revealed these events to the men in dreams and such events represent the mythic basis of the men's ritual cycle.[11] Clearly the women and their blood are quite potent. Although the older sister's "mistake" of traveling too soon after delivery had "negative" results, since that "mistake" is a mythic model often ritually repeated by the men, one cannot say that the menstruation, childbirth, and the attendant blood are evil, profane, or unclean but only that they are potent, fascinating, and ambiguous in their potential.

The men's rituals are even more interesting than their myths. It seems that, in addition to the avoidance of women coupled with a sort of fascination with women and women's biological functions, the complex of men's religion also involves ritual duplication of childbirth and menstruation. The women serve as models for men and their rituals, a point that has been made by prominent anthropologists and students of aboriginal culture: "Many of the rites which men carry out themselves, away from women, imitate, symbolically, physiological functions peculiar to women. The idea is that these are natural to women, but where men are concerned, they must be reproduced in ritual form."[12]

It is difficult to imagine an initiation that does not involve rebirth symbolism. Therefore, in an abstract way, any initiation is a kind of duplication of birth. It should also be noted that duplication of birth occurs in almost every religiocultural context, and not just among the Australian aborigines. The ways in which birth is duplicated in ritual are quite varied; overall, however, the duplication of the birth process on the part of the Australian men is self-conscious and graphic.

A man's initiation, marked by circumcision, signifies death to the world of women and children and rebirth into the male world. But the circumcisers behave like male mothers, and the novices are thought of as their infants. Before the circumcision, but after the boys have been taken from their mothers, they are sometimes carried about by their fathers in the same way women carry babies. After the operation, the pattern continues. The initiators imitate women in childbirth to the extent that sometimes "the old men build a stone fire and the men inhale the smoke and squat over the fire to allow the smoke to enter their anuses." The explanation given is that "'this is like the Wawalik women did when that baby was born.' "[13] (Women who have just given birth go through this same healing and purification rite today.)

Novices and initiators are both secluded from women—a practice that parallels women's seclusion from men at childbirth or menstruation. The newly circumcised boys learn from men how to behave in their new role, just as babies learn from women. The novices learn a totemic language unknown to women, which parallels their learning to talk when they were babies. Finally the boys are ceremonially exhibited as new beings by the men who have transformed them and seen them through rebirth, just as a baby is shown after its mother comes out of seclusion, or just as a girl is exhibited after her first menstrual seclusion. No wonder circumcision "is said to symbolize the severing of the novice's . . . umbilical cord."[14]

Although usually not so graphic and explicit as in aboriginal religion, the equation of birth and initiation is relatively common in religions around the world. However, male duplication of menstruation is much less common. In aboriginal Australia men's menstruation is less widespread than men's childbirth but still occurs over a wide enough area to be germane to this analysis. Two methods are used to produce male menstruation. Subincision is an operation in which the underside of the penis is repeatedly cut until it is grooved from root to tip. The initial operation is far less significant than the subsequent reopenings of the wound, which can be done periodically, yielding large quantities of blood. The large amounts of blood are used as body decoration and glue for attaching down and feathers to the body, thereby transforming the man into a totemic dream-time ancestor.

M. F. Ashley-Montague contends that subincision is considered valuable also because it allows men to menstruate, thereby getting rid of a collection of "bad blood" that results from sexual activity or dangerous tasks. Women lose this "bad blood" naturally, but men must take direct action to obtain the same result.[15]

Several authors who have written on the subject have made a further interesting observation concerning subincision. Not only does the male organ now produce blood periodically; the operation transforms the penis so that it looks much more like the vulva.[16] Thus the man can be said to possess symbolically the female, as well as the male, sex organs.

Other groups, which do not practice subincision, also imitate menstruation. Among some groups blood obtained from piercing the upper arm is used for the same purposes and interpreted in the same manner as subincision blood.

> The blood that runs from an incision and with which the dancers paint themselves and their emblems is something more than a man's blood—it is the menses of the old Wawilak women. I was told during a ceremony: "that blood we put all over those men is all the same as the blood that came from that old woman's vagina. It isn't blood any more because it has been sung over and made strong. The hole in the man's arm isn't that hole any more. It is all the same as the vagina of that old woman that had blood coming out of it. . . . When a man has got blood on him, he is all the same as those two old women when they had blood."[17]

Thus, the men's secret ritual life has a kind of double-edged quality. Men are introduced to a world that is closed to women, but myth and ritual proclaim that, nevertheless, this world is the province of women in important ways. Achieving the sacred status of maleness occurs through mythic and ritual appropriation and imitation of the female mode of being—even though women themselves are avoided. Then, once men are inside the realm of male sacrality—having made the transition by ritual imitation of childbirth and menstruation—the secrets that are now revealed to them can include myths about female totemic ancestors, rituals reenacting their adventures, and designs and emblems representing them. At a certain point, in some groups the male initiate learns of mythic times when men knew nothing about the sacred. One day, he is told, the man reversed that situation and stole religion from the women. The men's myth states that, when the Djanggawul sisters discovered what had happened, they said, "We know everything. We have really lost nothing, for we remember it all, and we can let them have that small part. For aren't we still sacred, even if we have lost the bags? Haven't we still out uteri?"[18] Contemporary aborigines seem to agree with that mythic statement.

> But we really have been stealing what belongs to them (the women), for it is mostly all women's business; and since it concerns them, it belongs to them. Men have nothing to do really, except copulate, it belongs to the women. All that belonging to those Wauwalek, the baby, the blood, the yelling, their dancing, all that concerns the women; but everytime we have to trick them. Women can't see what men are doing, although it really is their own business, but we can see their side. This is because all the Dreaming business came out of women—everything; only men take "picture" for that Julunggul. In the beginning we had nothing because men had nothing because men had been doing nothing; we took these things from the women.[19]

One could hardly find a more decisive statement that women's unique experiences